THINK
THEATRE

TH**I**NK
THEATRE

• MIRA FELNER •
Hunter College of The City
University of New York

Based on *The World of Theatre:*
Tradition and Innovation by
Mira Felner and Claudia Orenstein

PEARSON

Boston   Columbus   Indianapolis   New York   San Francisco   Upper Saddle River
Amsterdam   Cape Town   Dubai   London   Madrid   Milan   Munich   Paris   Montréal   Toronto
Delhi   Mexico City   São Paulo   Sydney   Hong Kong   Seoul   Singapore   Taipei   Tokyo

Editor-in-Chief, Communication, Film, & Theatre:
   Karon Bowers
Editor: Ziki Dekel
Development Editor: Erin Mulligan
Editorial Assistant: Megan Hermida
Marketing Manager: Blair Zoe Tuckman
Project Manager: Anne Ricigliano
Project Coordination, Text Design, and Electronic Page
   Makeup: Element-Thomson North America
Cover Design Manager: John Callahan

Cover Photo: *GEISHA* Conceived and Directed by ONG
   Keng Sen. A TheatreWorks Production. Performed at
   Lincoln Center Festival 2006, Spoleto Festival USA, 2006,
   Singapore Arts Festival, 2006, New Visions Festival, Hong
   Kong, 2006. Photography by William Strubs. By courtesy of
   TheatreWorks (Singapore)
Photo Researcher: Carly Bergey/PreMediaGlobal
Text Permissions: Katie Kosinski/Creative Compliance
Procurement Specialist: Mary Ann Gloriande
Printer/Binder: R.R. Donnelley/Harrisonburg
Cover Printer: R.R. Donnelley/Harrisonburg

Credits and acknowledgments borrowed from other sources and reproduced, with permission, in this textbook appear
on the appropriate page within text and on pages 361–364.

About the Cover Photo: Perceptions of gender collide when a Japanese *onnagata*—a man performing a woman—meets an American actress in *Geisha*, conceived and directed by Ong Keng Sen, for the Lincoln Center Festival in 2006.

Library of Congress Cataloging-in-Publication Data
Felner, Mira
   THINK theatre / Mira Felner.
      p.   cm.
   Includes bibliographical references and index.
   ISBN-10: 0-205-86959-9
   ISBN-13: 978-0-205-86959-6
1. Theater.   2. Drama.   I. Title.
   PN1655.F43 2011
   792—dc23
                           2011037046

6 2019

 www.pearsonhighered.com

ISBN 10:   0-205-86959-9
ISBN 13: 978-0-205-86959-6

For the men in my life—Richard and Joshua

Brief Contents

p. 195 High-Concept Directing
Breaking the Rules

▶ on the cover:

p. 164 Acting Conventions and Culture
Reading an Actor's Emotions Across Cultures

p. 302 Technological Advances and Design Innovations
Can Live Theatre Survive?

p. 117 Preserving Endangered Species of Theatre:
Saving Performance Traditions

p. 41 Everyone's a Critic!
The Internet and the Democratization of Criticism

Detailed Contents

Acknowledgments

No book of this scale and scope can be brought to completion without the help of friends and colleagues whose contributions of time and wisdom made this work possible. A debt is owed to all the artists and critics who gave generously of their time for interviews: Jane Alexander, Linda Cho, Judith Dolan, Tina Howe, Stanley Kauffmann, Robert Kaplowitz, Elizabeth LeCompte, Matsui Akira, Ong Keng Sen, Stanley Sherman, Alisa Solomon, Ruth Sternberg, Jennifer Tipton, and Louisa Thompson.

Special assistance was provided by Richard Emmert for his labor conducting and translating from the Japanese the interview with Matsui Akira. Thanks to Samuel Leiter for his consultations on Japanese theatre; James P. Taylor for his assistance with materials for the lighting section; Maggie Morgan for her material on costuming; Phillip Zarilli for his aid with photographic material; and Mark Ringer for his writing on opera. Thanks to David Howe at the Hudson Scenic Studios for his informational tour, and to Mei-Chen Lu and the Dance Notation Bureau.

I am fortunate to work in an exceptional Theatre Department with extraordinary colleagues to whom one can always turn for encouragement, advice, and knowledge. Several theatre faculty members at Hunter College and The Graduate Center of the City University of New York made particular contributions to this book. I would like to thank Claudia Orenstein for her collaboration on *The World of Theatre: Tradition and Innovation* from which this book is adapted, in particular her writing on Asian Theatre and Puppetry; Jonathan Kalb for insights into theatre criticism; Dongshin Chang for information on Chinese opera; Louisa Thompson for providing a glimpse into the mind of a designer; Jean Graham-Jones for her help with South American and Spanish Golden Age Theatre; Joel Bassin for information on production management; Ian Calderon for offering the resources of his design library; Brian Hurley for his explanations of sound design; and Barbara Bosch for her directing acumen and her moral support. Our department Administrative Assistant Bettie Haigler always gets me through those computer crises and listens to my frustrations with patience.

This book was inspired by my students. Hunter College, the most diverse campus in the United States, has offered me cultural encounters without leaving the lecture hall. A single semester might find a professional *kyōgen* actor, a kabuki dancer, a *kathakali* expert, a Chinese opera performer, and a student of Korean *Pansori* all enrolled in our department. In some places theatre faculty show films of performance traditions; at Hunter we can have live demonstrations in class by members of our student body. Watching these performances has enhanced my understanding and appreciation of global traditions. I would particularly like to thank the following graduate students: Boris Daussà-Pastor, Ibuki Kaori, Nara Lee, Ana Martinez, and Tatsuo Yasuda. I would also like to extend my gratitude to Gabriela Geselowitz for sharing suggestions about the manuscript from the undergraduate perspective.

I am grateful to all who made thoughtful suggestions about reorganizing, updating, and condensing *The World of Theatre*:

Eero Laine, City University of New York, College of Staten Island
Constance Frank, West Kentucky Community and Technical College
George Sanchez, City University of New York, College of Staten Island
Jessica Hester, State University of New York, Oswego.

My thanks to Erin Mulligan who made me say more with less; to Ziki Dekel, Anne Ricigliano, and Heidi Allgair for their coordination of this project; to Carly Bergey for chasing around the globe for photos; and to the terrific copyeditor, Kitty Wilson. Thanks also go to Jessica Del Vecchio for preparing the Instructor's Manual.

At Ido restaurant in Greenwich Village, on any given night of the week one can hear Spanish flamenco, American jazz, grand opera, Korean traditional music, or American musical theatre performed by an international group of New York-based artists. My appreciation to Tora and Jane Yi for this true mecca of interculturalism, multiculturalism, and performance traditions that provided sustenance and inspiration.

We need the people we love when we pursue our passions. My deepest gratitude to my husband Richard Cutler, who has supported me in this as in all endeavors, and to my son Joshua, who has taught me the true meaning of courage.

Mira Felner
Hunter College

MIRA FELNER is Professor of Theatre at Hunter College and the Graduate Center of The City University of New York. She received a Ph.D. from New York University and Diplome d'Etudes Théâtrales from the Sorbonne. She has acted and directed in the United States and France and headed a French language theatre in New York for several years. She is a specialist in mime and studied in Paris with Jacques Lecoq, and has written extensively on movement in actor training. Her first book, *Apostles of Silence: The Modern French Mimes*, was nominated for the Barnard Hewitt Award for Outstanding Research in Theatre History. Her book *Free to Act : An Integrated Approach to Acting* explores the physical base for acting technique. She was the American consultant editor of the *Bloomsbury Theatre Guide*. Her interest in performance traditions around the world led her to write *The World of Theatre: Tradition and Innovation*, the first introduction to theatre text to truly focus on diversity and globalism, integrating multicultural, international, traditional and experimental theatre.

THINK
THEATRE

▼ In this production of *The Good Person of Sezuan,* Singaporean director Ong Keng Sen worked with a German cast on this European production of a play set in imaginary China. The costumes were inspired by Japanese *manga* (comics), and using new technology, the gods were portrayed as video gamers playing with the lives of the characters. This integration of diverse elements is one of the hallmarks of postmodernism.

Theatre *A Global Experience*

Navigating the World of the Theatre

In tribal villages and temples, schools and opera houses, parks and playhouses, people come together all over the world to witness a singular event we call *theatre*. The impulse that draws people to these places of performance is universal and fundamental to the human spirit, but what they see is as varied as the human social experience.

Traveling the global world of theatre today, you might attend the Chinese opera and witness a tradition performed, staged and sung much the way it was 200 years ago. In Africa you could participate in a communal performance celebration paying homage to the king and his ancestors. You might find an abandoned factory in Paris converted into a theatre, where actors rehearse ancient Asian dance movements for their roles in a new production of a 2,500-year-old Greek tragedy. The great diversity of theatrical forms that coexist today is a reflection of the complex global world in which we live. They challenge us to reach beyond the traditions of our own society to embrace the artistic forms of other cultures. Although we hold deep inside us the values and prejudices of our own social experience, we can learn to appreciate the way people in other times and places have told and continue to tell their stories on the stage.

As we study performances around the world, we encounter two basic kinds of theatrical traditions. The first is based on a **performance tradition**, whose staging, music, dance, characterization, masks, and acting are passed from generation to generation as a totality of expression. Performance traditions are usually rooted in the values and beliefs of the community, are often linked to religious ritual, and sometimes involve total community participation. The second tradition is based on a written **play text** to be interpreted in performance. Although a play is born out of the values of its community, it is not tied to its original concept, time, or place, and it can be passed down for reinterpretation by future generations of performers.

Theatre is a living, vital art in which live actors engage the audience through the energy of their physical presence. Traditions evolve and are renewed through the work of innovative theatre artists who seek new ways to express changing social concerns. No form can be permanent in theatre, the most evanescent of art forms. Each performance lives on only in memory, leaving us free to create again.

1. Why does almost every society have some form of theatrical performance?

2. How do play traditions and performance traditions differ? How are they similar?

3. Why is theatre referred to as "the most evanescent of art forms"?

CHAPTER ・OI・

Theatre as a Reflection of Culture

The need to make sense of our world is the driving force behind all theatrical forms, and every culture has developed some form of theatrical presentation through which to examine the mysteries of life and the most pressing concerns of its society. Because the actor on the stage is a live human being, the theatre mirrors our lives more directly than any other art form. It is a glimpse into the meaning of our existence, with its aspirations and disappointments and crises and triumphs. It is also a reflection of our social values.

The mirror is an apt metaphor for the stage. When we look in the mirror, we stand outside ourselves, looking at ourselves, searching for an objective understanding of who and what we are. This is what we do in the theatre. In the theatre we are watching real people play fictions that have a greater reality than our own lives for the duration of the performance. So the image we see on the stage stimulates us to consider our lives more deeply. Theatre can be a spur to social consciousness and political action, and sometimes performance itself can be an act of protest or conscience.

To say that the theatre is a mirror of life does not mean that all theatre is always realistic or must create a replica of the real world on stage. Sometimes the theatre is more like a fun-house mirror, distorting, refocusing, and exaggerating to make us see ourselves in a different light. Although theatrical expression is a universal human activity, each society, culture, and time has its own lens through which it looks at and creates the mirror of the stage. For this reason, theatres in different places and times present different images to their audiences.

> Would **art** exist at all if men did not **desire** to **live** twice?

—Eric Bentley, *The Life of the Drama*

How can we understand how other people portray themselves and tell their stories in performance? How do we balance time-honored theatrical traditions with the need for innovations that reflect who we are at any given

moment? The journey through this book is an examination of what is universal to all theatre and what is specific to a given time, place, and culture. No book can look at every form of theatre that has ever existed, but in this book we hope to begin to develop a way to approach the unfamiliar. We can develop an understanding of difference that can lead to respect for, and admiration of, other traditions. We achieve this by examining the changing conventions of the theatre as a reflection of our values and beliefs.

Theatrical Conventions and Culture

Every society develops rules of behavior that define the ways individuals conduct themselves. Members of each society tacitly accept and internalize these rules. We learn how to read the significance of a touch, a kiss, a handshake, or a stare. In exchange, we receive tools for communication and conduct that help us interact with others without conscious thought. These behavioral norms are ever-evolving reflections of social values. They vary from era to era and from place to place, even within a specific culture. Theatre, as the most social of all the arts—human beings coming together in the same space to share an event—also has its rules of conduct and understood communication codes. We call these codes **theatrical conventions**, and just as we use social conventions to navigate the larger world, we navigate the world of the theatre according to the conventions of the stage.

Accustomed to the theatre of our own society, we may not realize how odd our own practices might appear in other cultures or eras. Imagine that you are from another planet, sent to observe people on earth. You watch many people approach a building. Each one hands a person standing at the door a small piece of paper that is torn in half. These people are then directed to seats in a large hall and are given larger papers to read. The people talk with one another naturally, but when the lights begin to dim, they all grow silent at once and sit expectantly in the dark. Then some new people enter a lit portion of the room and explain their most intimate feelings in loud voices; these new people live in rooms where all the furniture faces one direction, and they don't seem aware that a thousand eyes are watching them, even if they stand stark naked. The people in the seats, after remaining silent for two hours, bang their hands together, while the people who were talking in loud voices bend at the waist. How could you possibly explain

▲ Director Yukio Ninagawa uses a composite of theatrical traditions and conventions to question the traditions and conventions of samurai warriors and their cult of violence in *Musashi*, 2010.

this behavior? Of course, these are some of our accepted theatrical conventions that allow us to share a common theatre experience. Contemplating the strangeness of our own conventions allows us to understand and accept those of other eras and cultures.

> For a **theatrical style** to be successful, the audience must find it **authentic** and **meaningful** so they can engage in what British poet Samuel Taylor **Coleridge** (1772–1834) called the "willing suspension of disbelief."

Conventions affect every aspect of a performance; they dictate how actors will move, speak, and be clothed, as well as the form and content of the event, how and where it is staged and designed, and how the audience should respond. Some of these conventions reflect centuries of cultural tradition, and others are recent innovations; some transcend cultural borders, others are culturally specific, and some change according to circumstances within the same culture. The combined effect of these conventions working together is **style**—the manner in which a performance depicts the world. Theatrical styles vary widely in different eras and from one culture to another, so what is considered theatrically true embraces many forms.

Just as knowing your own society's theatrical conventions enables you to feel comfortable in the theatre and to better understand the embedded values in the performance, learning about theatrical conventions in other cultures and eras enables you to feel at home in the global world of the theatre. Go to the Concert Party Theatre in West Africa, and you will find audience members talking back to the actors, encouraging them to take action, warning them of danger. In contrast, American audiences typically sit silently at the theatre, watching the events unfold and becoming annoyed if other audience members speak out loud. At the Chinese opera, the audience is in constant chatter, while in Bali spectators may sometimes enter a performance-induced trance, absorbing the events through a semiconscious state. In India actors sometimes employ stylized hand movements and positions as an encoded language; throughout Africa, drama tends to incorporate drumming and dance, and a *t'alch'um* performance in Korea uses masks that may be burned in a postperformance ritual fire.

THINK

Why is it important for audience members to understand the conventions of a theatrical event they attend?

The Iranian Ta'ziyeh and Its Conventions

The *Ta'ziyeh*, or tragic play, performed in Shi'a communities in Iran, Iraq, Lebanon, Pakistan, and other places around the world, enacts the 680 C.E. martyrdom of Imam Hoseyn, the grandson of the Prophet Mohammad. Hoseyn, his male children, and his male followers were massacred, and the women were captured at Karbala by the followers of Yazid, who sought to head the Islamic community. These events mark the start of the historic division between Sunni and Shiite Muslims. *Ta'ziyeh* audiences regard the performance as a religious event and view it as a form of communal, ritual mourning for Shiite martyrs.

Ta'ziyeh performances take place in both indoor and outdoor venues. A performance may occur at a single location, or episodes may be enacted throughout the town. These community events involve dozens of actors, musicians, and live animals. They may be performed by professional actors, but most commonly they are performed by local amateurs. The performance indulges in emotion, arouses pity, stimulates religious fervor, and is heightened by dramatic singing. The director is called *mo'in-al-boka*, "the one who helps bring tears."

Ta'ziyeh is governed by a set of specific conventions that reflect the ritual nature of the performance and make the action clear to people familiar with the tradition. For those unfamiliar with the performance, its many theatrical conventions need explanation. Hoseyn and those who support him wear green and sing their lines, while those who are against him wear red and recite their text. Women are played by men who veil their faces. When an actor dons a white shirt, it signifies that the character will soon be martyred. Circling the playing area on foot or horseback indicates that a character has traveled a long distance to another location, while a diagonal walk across the stage represents a shorter journey. Turning around in place indicates a change of character or locale. Straw is used to place the action in the desert; a tub of water represents the Euphrates River, and a single tree branch indicates a palm grove. The performers, called "readers," carry strips of paper with their lines to which they may refer rather than relying on memorization. The director is visible throughout the performance, handing lines to actors, giving them entrance cues, and placing and removing stage props. *Ta'ziyeh's* traditional audiences also act according to a unique set of conventions. Caught up in the emotion of the event, they wail, weep, and beat their breasts in sorrow.

◀ In accordance with centuries old theatrical conventions, in this 2009 *Ta'ziyeh* performance in Iran the followers of Hoseyn wear green and members of the opposing camp wear red as they re-enact the 7th century battle of Karbala. Women are played by men in veils. The act of circling the space on horseback signifies travel to another location.

The Evolution of Conventions

Because theatre is a reflection of society, it follows that in other historical periods and in other places, we would find theatrical forms and conventions different from those we experience today. In fact, the history of the theatre is really a history of evolving conventions. A good example of this is the exclusion of women from the theatre. In the so-called "golden age" of Greek theatre, during the fifth century B.C.E., women were not considered worthy of participation in theatrical performance. Scholars even debate whether women were allowed in the audience. Women were also excluded from performing in Shakespeare's time; imagine Juliet played by a boy. Today, in certain societies, women continue to be locked out. The Japanese *noh* and the Indian *kathakali* are examples of centuries-old theatre forms that have continued to exclude women. Envision excluding women from theatrical activity in the United States today. Can you imagine the protests? This could not happen in the American theatre today because it would not reflect our value system and the role of women in our culture. In the United States, there was a long period during which actors of different races did not perform together, reflecting the segregated nature of American society at the time.

HIDDEN HISTORY

African Americans on the American Stage

The history of African Americans on the American stage mirrors the troubled history of race relations in the United States. The exact date when the first black actor appeared on the American stage has not been determined, but it is assumed that black servant parts were played by white actors in blackface during the colonial period and after. In 1816 The African Company became the first-known black theatre troupe. Later renamed The African Grove Theatre in 1821, it provided Ira Aldridge (1807–1867) the internationally acclaimed black tragedian, a start to his theatrical career. In search of opportunities not afforded black actors in the United States, he emigrated to England, where he debuted in 1825 and played leading Shakespearean roles including Othello, Shylock, Macbeth, and Richard II. Even positive reviews of Aldridge in the British press noted his "thick lipped" Othello but reassured the audience that his "labial peculiarity" did not interfere with his pronunciation and elocution.

Back in the United States, prospects for black actors continued to be bleak. The theatre remained a segregated place, with separate black and white theatre troupes, and it was not until 1878 that an integrated production of **Uncle Tom's Cabin** saw white and black actors performing on the same stage. This remained an anomaly, however, and the American theatre did not integrate until well into the twentieth century. Early integrated dramas cast blacks in roles that reflected the racial stereotypes of the times. It was not until after World War I that the black actor Charles Gilpin (1878–1930) played important roles

> "Through my singing and acting and speaking, I want to make freedom ring. Maybe I can touch people's hearts better than I can their minds, with the common struggle of the common man."
>
> —Paul Robeson

in integrated companies, earning praise for his performance in Eugene O'Neill's **The Emperor Jones**. More opportunities for black actors followed in the 1930s, but most plays were written by white playwrights, and the roles presented an outsider's view of black character. The Federal Theatre Project, which provided employment to theatre professionals during the Great Depression, integrated some productions, but for the most part, the races were separate. The Project had Negro units, the most famous set up in Harlem in 1935, under white directors Orson Welles (1915–1985) and John Houseman (1902–1988).

In 1943, Paul Robeson (1898–1976) became the first black actor to play Othello on Broadway, a role traditionally played by a white actor in blackface. The production with Uta Hagen as Othello's wife Desdemona occurred at a time when interracial marriage was still illegal in most states. It was not until 1953, when Ruby Dee (b. 1924) was cast as an angel in **The World of Sholom Aleichem**, that a black actor was cast in a part without any reference to color, paving the way for colorblind casting. As late as the 1980s, critic John Simon and producer Joseph Papp engaged in a public debate about colorblind casting that now seems impossible to imagine. Theatre can be colorblind only when society is colorblind, as theatrical conventions always reflect the cultural values. Some would argue that we have a long way to go before we see true equality on the stage.

In societies that have sustained and maintained performance traditions, theatrical conventions evolve more slowly, and ancient forms continue to exist. The *noh* theatre of Japan that began in the fourteenth century continues today, with many of its original conventions unchanged. But even these long-lived traditions evolve and experience some changes over the centuries, despite the remarkable stability of the form. For example, many traditional Asian forms, such as the Indian *kathakali*, had performances that long ago may have lasted from sundown to sunrise; today, although these performance traditions continue, most have abbreviated the performance time to three or four hours to accommodate contemporary lifestyles and new audiences.

Universals of the Theatre

WHAT are the four universals that apply to theatre everywhere?

Although theatrical conventions are specific to time, place, and culture, certain universals apply to all theatre everywhere. These qualities define our experience in the theatre and define the very nature of what theatre is.

Universal Properties of Theatre

- Theatre is *live in the present moment* and requires the presence of a *live actor* and an *audience*.
- Theatre is *ephemeral* in that no performance can ever be totally duplicated or captured.
- Theatre is *collaborative*: It requires the efforts of many people working together.
- Theatre is a *synthesis* of many arts.

Theatre Is Live

A quickening of the heart, a surge of anticipatory excitement—these are our feelings at the start of a performance. Even experienced theatre-goers feel this awakening each time they are in the audience for live theatre. In the movies, we merely reach for more popcorn, sit back, and relax. What is it about the theatre that continues to thrill?

A performer on the stage is alive and vital. We sense the inherent daring and danger as we watch a human being take emotional and physical risks before our eyes. A missed line, a fall, a malfunctioning prop, any unexpected event can strip away the mask and reveal the man or woman beneath the role. Suddenly we are aware of the person we have forgotten under the character. We know that each performance is a triumph over the odds. To go to the theatre is to believe in miracles. We watch in awe as the actor physically transforms and flexes the emotions. Virtuoso performances take our breath away. Every performance is a journey with infinite opportunity for mishap, and yet, each evening and matinee, all over the world, actors walk the tightrope without a safety net.

The audience is a part of the event. We can alter it by our presence, our actions, and reactions, and we may even be invited to actively participate. We must be vigilant and be ready to play our part.

Without these two elements—the live actor risking all and the live audience responding and creating invisible lines of communication—theatre cannot exist. Today, as we spend more and more time alone, confined to rooms with televisions and computers, the theatre has become one of the few places where we must come together, form a community, and become live witnesses to acts of daring.

As television and the Internet are increasingly called upon to bring us events "live," the definition of *liveness* itself must be reexamined.

Theatre Is Ephemeral

Theatre is live, in the moment, and no element can be exactly replicated because it depends on the interaction of live actors and audience and what they bring to uncapturable moments in time and space. The word *ephemeral* means *fleeting*. Theatre's time is the present. If you record it or film it, the reproduction is not a theatrical event; it is film or video. It is not what the audience experienced. A theatrical event is specific to a set time, place, audience, and performers. Move a production to a larger theatre, and the entire dynamic changes. See the same production on a different night, and the actors will have made infinite small adjustments to the new audience. Have the understudy step in, and the entire cast must accommodate the change. Actors also deal with

Think TECHNOLOGY

Live in a Wired World

The idea of theatre as live performance is challenged in today's wired world. Increasingly, theatrical performances incorporate film and video, taped sound, amplified voices, and recorded music to replace the live orchestra. Computerized characters can inhabit the same space as live actors. In the early 1990s, avant-garde artists began exploring *telematic performances*, which bring together actors and audience members at different locations through the use of high-speed Internet, allowing for long-distance collaboration. The Gertrude Stein Repertory experimented with "distance puppetry" through video conferencing. Using simultaneous performance venues in Iowa and New York, the company projected the faces and bodies of actors at one location as masks and costumes on actors at the other venue, creating characters who were amalgamations of live actors and virtual images.

physical and emotional stresses in their daily lives, and these affect each performance. Although the basic outlines of a production remain the same, you never see exactly the same event twice.

THINK

Why is it impossible to completely capture a theatrical performance on film?

Theatre Is **Collaborative**

How is it that lines are so seldom flubbed, props are rarely out of place, scenery almost never falls, the light and sound cues go off on time, costumes fit flawlessly, and actors appear on cue? The success of the theatrical event is the result of a community of people working toward a common goal, creating a seamless imaginary reality. Everyone in this collaborative effort is a valued contributor. Some are part of the creative team; others are support staff—stage managers, crew, and technicians. But all are equally necessary if the production is to be successful. A bonding occurs among members of a theatre company. This sense of family is what draws many people to the theatre. Shared creation is a joyous activity.

One often-overlooked part of the collaborative process of theatre is the one that occurs between the audience and the performers; the spectators' responses help shape the rhythm of a theatrical event. In communities all over the world, wherever people can come together, they make theatre. This book examines the roles of all the various contributors to explain exactly how theatre happens.

Theatre Is a **Synthesis of Many Arts**

Many people are involved in theatrical creation because theatre involves many artistic materials. Actors give life to a text or an idea through movement, dance, speech, and song, with the aid of directors, playwrights, musicians, and choreographers. They do this in a space that must be determined

" Theatre **art** has several voices no one of which is necessarily **more important** than the rest. . . . The importance or **expressiveness** of . . . the word, the music, the visual will vary according to what is to be expressed. "

—Stark Young, *The Theatre*

and designed, so theatre also relies on the spatial arts. The stage set is designed, painted, or sculpted. The set is lit to enhance the environment for the performance; the lighting designer sculpts and paints with light. The actor wears something or not; even the decision for nudity reflects an artistic choice of the costumer and director. Masks are made. Faces are painted. The audience hears music and sound effects, and each element must be composed or designed and executed by artists and technicians. All these elements unite to form a single vision of another world that is organized by the director or someone serving in that function. The theatrical form is a synthesis of many art forms and the work of many artists. Theatrical performances employ language, painting, sculpture, costume, music, dance, mime, movement, light, and sound to create effects.

Tradition and Innovation

Theatre is not a static art. Forms change over time, and even long-revered performance traditions can accommodate innovation. Theatre practitioners reach out to their public, inventing new forms, borrowing techniques from other cultures, reinterpreting plays, and integrating new technologies. With the ease of global exchange today, tradition and innovation transform each other and coexist around the world. In the United States, where innovation and reinvention are a way of life, theatrical forms transform and evolve rapidly, reflecting changing demographics, economics, and politics. To understand today's theatre, we must consider the forces that shape contemporary performance, including movements such as postmodernism and performance studies, as well as realities such as globalization, multiculturalism, and postcolonialism.

Postmodernism

Postmodernism, which evolved during the worldwide political and social changes of the late twentieth century, is a complicated concept that does not have a single definition. It encompasses a variety of ideas and trends in different disciplines and has had an enormous impact on the theatre. In contrast to the view of a world with fundamental truths, postmodernism poses a world of contradiction and instability, with no grand scheme of meaning or universal understanding. The "truths" of the past are seen as constructions of those in power, typically the Eurocentric, white, male, heterosexual establishment that excluded and invalidated the perspective of groups outside the power structure.

Postmodernism recognizes that what seems true to a master might not seem true to a slave; what seems true to a man might not seem true to a woman; what seems true to a heterosexual might not seem true to a homosexual.

Today we realize that the cultural dominance of some groups can lead to the exploitation and even obliteration of others. Postmodernism has invited those whose views were not included in the old world order to construct their own histories, philosophies, and art forms, and it considers all constructions of equal validity. This has called into question divisions between what used to be labeled "high art"—for which there were established formal aesthetic standards—and "low art"—the vernacular culture that surrounds us. By defying these divisions, postmodernism has helped the artistic expressions and voices of previously marginalized or disenfranchised groups to garner more general attention.

THINK

How would you define what constitutes a work of art?

Postmodernism has cast the long-standing question of what constitutes "art" in a new light. It has also engendered debate about what happens to aesthetic criticism in a world without absolute values: Can anyone say that a work of art is "good" or "bad" without being accused of cultural bias? Once there was an acknowledged canon, a list of unquestioned great works; today we question whether any such canon exists, and if it does, what it should include. What should be the place of the old traditional canon, and what time-honored works should be replaced by new ones? If postmodernism is to truly embrace a multiplicity of viewpoints, it must allow the great works of the old traditions to stand as important objects of study, even as we make room for new voices to be heard.

Although much of theatre today continues older traditions, postmodernism has changed the way we look at the world by creating an openness to other cultures as well as an awareness of how older structures impeded the development of particular ideas and forms. Aided by globalization, we live in an era that prizes the cultural contributions of all people.

Globalization

The expression "the global village" captures the reality of contemporary life. It is impossible to live in cultural isolation in a world where time and space are compressed through modern transportation and communication. People travel from place to place, bringing their cultural traditions with them, so we are all exposed to diverse theatrical forms in a way unheard of in past generations. Yet despite this constant contact, we still encounter forms that seem strange to us, that perplex us and defy comprehension.

Postmodern Eclecticism

Relinquishing fixed forms or traditional styles, postmodernists feel free to mix styles and genres to create new forms. This can be seen clearly in many recent theatre productions. It is not unusual today to see film and video combined with live action in a work by Canadian director Robert Lepage (b. 1957); acting, text, and dance together in a performance by Belgian Sidi Larbi Cherkaoui (b. 1976); or puppets on the Broadway stage with live actors, as in *Avenue Q*. There is also a free borrowing of styles from other cultures that were once seen as inferior but are now valued for their difference, as seen in the *Kathakali King Lear* at London's Globe Theatre, which incorporated stylized Indian theatrical movement, costumes, makeup, and songs with Shakespearean text. Along with these new styles have come new organizational systems and new ways of creating and collaborating to make theatre.

▶ The Comédie Française, the bastion of French theatrical tradition, did its first production of an American play in 2011. Lee Breuer's production of *Un Tramway Nommé Désir* (*A Streetcar Named Desire*) by Tennessee Williams used Japan as a metaphor for the American South and featured an eclectic mixture of styles.

Globalization has often had a negative impact on less modernized societies. Those societies have traditionally been held together by an ancient cultural glue of community values and ritual performance, which are threatened by new socioeconomic structures and exposure to "modern" lifestyles. Much traditional theatre, born in the premodern era, was part of the fabric of community life on which it depended for its sustenance. Today in these societies, a new generation questions the significance of traditional values and the ancient theatre forms that embody them. As a result, traditional performance may lose its place as an integral part of daily existence and an expression of communal values. These forms are often relegated to museum status in state-run or university theatres, used as cultural symbols and assertions of identity, or presented to attract tourists. Unlike other art forms that can be preserved in museums and libraries or on CDs, theatre lives only in the moment of active exchange with a live audience. Once a performance form fails to engage its public, its survival is threatened, and many ancient forms have been forced to adapt to changing times in order to continue.

The theatre as a direct reflection of cultural values is often the most enigmatic of the arts, and today, more than ever, we need to understand and appreciate difference.

Ironically, while some societies are abandoning their traditional forms, globalization has awakened others to the beauty and interest of these forms. One culture may be borrowing or appropriating what another culture is rejecting or forsaking. Sometimes this brings increased communication, but many fear it will dilute or destroy many traditional theatrical forms whose very survival may now depend on their ability to adapt to the contemporary world. When today's theatre moves away from its intimate communal roots, much of the community-based audience for traditional theatre may be excluded.

In a world without boundaries, where we watch each other's films, eat each other's food, and use each other's

Once all politics was local; today politics is global. We are united by shared problems, tensions, dilemmas, and fears. As the contemporary theatre seeks to address our common concerns, it is engaging similar themes and bringing similar forms to urban audiences the world over. In Tokyo, New York, Paris, Seoul, or Sydney, an educated, largely middle-class audience sees much of the same commercial theatre—big, corporate-sponsored productions that tour worldwide, American musicals, or performances of the established avant-garde that travel a circuit of international theatre festivals and centers. Pictured here is a scene from the musical *The Fantasticks* performed at the Setagaya Public Theatre in Tokyo.

goods, we also see an increasing homogenization of culture. Those who value cultural difference fear the eradication of many performance forms in favor of globally disseminated mass popular entertainment. Theatre itself may be an endangered art in the global electronic era.

THINK

What do you think are the benefits and disadvantages of globally disseminated mass entertainment?

EVE ENSLER—
The Personal is Political

ARTISTS IN PERSPECTIVE

Eve Ensler's (b. 1953) 1996 solo performance piece *The Vagina Monologues* was assembled from more than 200 interviews with women around the world who discussed their relationship to the most intimate part of their bodies. In so doing, she revealed thoughts about gender, love, marriage, and sexuality, as well as experiences of rape, incest, abuse, and mutilation. By simply breaking the social taboo against uttering any word for the female genitalia in a public forum, Ensler unveiled some of the most pressing issues of our time. The work is ultimately a poignant reminder that women suffer the consequences of world events, social repression, and domestic dysfunction in the most private places of their being. Women, long taught to think of their bodies as obscene and even not as their

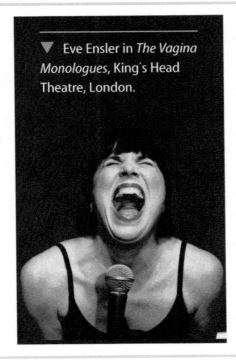

▼ Eve Ensler in *The Vagina Monologues*, King's Head Theatre, London.

own, were empowered by the performance to take back this forbidden identity with pride.

Ensler has used the piece as the inspiration for a crusade to stop violence against women and girls around the world. On V-Day, February 14, benefit performances by local groups and college students raise funds that have helped start organizations to protect women in 76 countries. In 2010, more than 5,400 V-Day benefit events took place. This amazing story of the work of an avant-garde solo performer spawning a global movement is testimony to the continuing power of theatre to transform our lives. In the era of globalization, the most private story can reverberate around the world.

Multiculturalism

Groups not fully represented in the majority culture have a long tradition of forming theatre companies to produce works that speak to the particular needs of their communities. These productions are often a source of pride in identity and can reshape public perceptions.

▼ A man and his two sons confront identity and duty in Julia Cho's *Durango* at East West Players. This important Asian American Theatre in Los Angeles has given voice to the Asian Pacific American experience since 1965.

2011 Stewart Goldstein

▲ The Saint Louis Black Repertory Company provides theatre from the African American perspective. In Sherry Shephard-Massat's *Waiting to Be Invited*, middle-aged black women attempt to integrate a department store lunch counter during the civil rights movement.

▶ *Canta y no llores* (*Sing and Don't Cry*) a bilingual celebration of the Day of the Dead was created by Martín Milagro and directed by Olga Sanchez at the Miracle Theatre Group, an Oasis of Latino culture in Portland, Oregon.

Multiculturalism

Multiculturalism calls for a respect for neighboring cultures living under the same political system. Multiculturalism grew out of the social and political awakening of the 1960s and 1970s, when the civil rights movement, the women's movement, and the protests against the war in Vietnam raised the consciousness of marginalized groups. The past few decades have been an era of identity politics, and minority populations in North America have felt increasingly empowered. Parallel political trends spread across Europe, Asia, South America, and Australia.

Pride in identity found expression in the theatre because the theatre enabled particular communities to represent and "re-present" themselves. Multiculturalism is linked to postmodernism because those whose viewpoints were overlooked or marginalized by mainstream theatre—women, the elderly, the disabled, African Americans, Native Americans, Asian Americans, Latinos, and gays and lesbians, for example—can create theatre pieces that speak to their concerns. In turn, as you will see, theatrical forms have been reconfigured to best give voice to the needs of particular communities. Detractors of multiculturalism claim that it has often led to a separation of various communities rather than fostering a deeper cultural exchange. At the same time, multicultural theatre has undeniably provided a valuable forum to affirm, explore, or challenge group identities, beliefs, and practices and has allowed new voices to be heard in the theatre.

Ethnic Theatres: What's New Is Old

In the early twentieth century, ethnic theatres in the United States and Canada provided entertainment to immigrant groups in their native languages. These theatres served as cultural hubs and meeting places and presented the aspirations and idealism of new Americans at a time when assimilation and abandoning of old traditions was demanded. Some early ethnic theatres used the theatrical forms of the dominant American and Canadian theatre culture; other groups used theatrical forms that they brought with them from their homelands. Few of these original ethnic theatres continue today because the subsequent generation of actors was assimilated into mainstream culture and lured by Broadway and Hollywood. Today new immigrant groups bring with them the theatre traditions of their native countries, but they come to an America that is more open to difference. These groups have developed new kinds of multicultural performance, in which they can celebrate their own traditions within an American context and still attract audiences outside the immigrant community.

Theatre is a place to explore who we are. What does it mean to be American? Female? Gay? Disabled? Latino? Of color? Don't we all possess multiple identities and belong to several defining groups? Is identity something we carry inside or something projected onto us by others? These questions have been the subject matter of many contemporary theatre works. New theatrical forms and texts explore these and other multicultural issues. Danny Hoch and Sarah Jones's performance pieces explore the perception of identity as they seamlessly slip into and out of Middle Eastern, Chinese, Black, Jewish, Latino, Caribbean, and gay characters, among a host of others, challenging audiences to question what constitutes a racial or ethnic identity if it can be taken on as a role. Other artists have explored the identity inherent in their own groups, as playwright Hanay Geiogamah does for Native Americans and Cherrie Moraga does for Chicanos.

▼ As other countries grow more heterogeneous, with increasing immigrant populations, multicultural theatre has spread the world over. Here Shabana Rehman presents what it is like to be of Pakistani origin living in Norway.

Postcolonialism

Postcolonialism explores identity within the geographic boundaries of formerly colonized states in Latin America, Asia, and Africa. Former colonies that lived under the oppression of colonialism are still reacting to that legacy. Where once an imposed imperial power sought to eradicate or exploit indigenous cultural forms, formerly subjugated populations now seek to understand their own cultural heritage and the impact of colonial rule on their traditions and self-image.

As Europeans colonized the world, they brought their dramatic literary tradition with them. Indigenous performance traditions were often suppressed and feared, or exploited for political purposes. Generations of theatre artists were taught that their homegrown forms were inferior and that they should emulate European models. Shakespeare was mandatory for high school plays in the British colonies, just as Corneille and Molière played in the parts of the world dominated by the French. Latin American colonies adopted the genres of the Spanish Golden Age that flourished at the time of conquest. Often, indigenous playwrights inserted local color, costume, or dialects, as in the *costumbristas* of South America, but the forms of plays remained fundamentally European and were written in the language of conquest.

The theatre work of Nigerian playwright, poet, novelist, essayist, and Nobel Laureate Wole Soyinka (b. 1934) marries African and Western European influences as it addresses Nigeria's evolving political conditions, its legacy of colonialism, and the power of its rituals and Yoruba belief in the flow between past, present, and future. Soyinka's life and works embody the conflicts and dilemmas faced by many postcolonial artists.

Born in Western Nigeria, Soyinka received a college education in Nigeria and then completed a degree in drama at Leeds, in England, in 1957. In 1960, when Nigeria won its struggle for independence from British rule, Soyinka returned to Nigeria, where he founded a theatre company that produced his first major play, *A Dance*

▶ European and African belief systems clash as Sergeant Amusa, a uniformed officer, confronts the Yoruba women in their traditional dress in Wole Soyinka's *Death and the King's Horseman* at the National Theatre, London, 2009.

of the Forests, as part of the country's celebration of independence. The play warned of coming political corruption if Nigerians did not develop the wisdom necessary to exercise self-rule. His use of European forms, which some called an elitist aesthetic, and his rebuke of Nigerian politics garnered criticism on many fronts.

Soyinka was arrested for his political activism in 1965 and again in 1967, during Nigeria's civil war, On his release, Soyinka left Nigeria and went into voluntary exile in England, where he completed his doctoral degree. He wrote important plays during this period, as well as critical essays on literature, politics, and ritual. In 1986 Soyinka was awarded the Nobel Prize for Literature. He now splits his time between his homes in Nigeria and the United States. He continues to write plays that are performed throughout the world and to speak out on political issues through his works.

Costumbrista **theatre, which began in nineteenth-century Spain, portrayed local customs and folklore.** Latin and South American **theatre celebrated local** culture **through this European genre in the period following** colonial rule**.**

Today artists in postcolonial states find themselves in a position of contradiction. While they are now free to celebrate native culture, many choose by habit or education to use the very European forms they once rejected to expose the hypocrisy and moral bankruptcy of imperialist rule. The result has been a tension between the imposed culture and native traditions. Many artists find that both forms live within them and that they are actually hybrid cultural beings. Try as they may to throw off the influence of the European theatrical tradition in favor of local performance styles, the imposed colonial forms have a hold on their consciousness that is reinforced by the idea of progress in today's global world. For this reason, when we look at the theatre in former colonies, especially in Africa, we often see the two traditions either mingling or standing side by side. Some view African theater pieces that mix indigenous performance with the written word as a way of taking control of the instruments of oppression to construct one's own narrative, writing in the stories of the people who were written out, or written off, by European history.

Most African performance **was not** text based**, and many dialects had no written** language**.**

Interculturalism

The blending of traditions from various cultures is called **interculturalism**. It goes beyond multiculturalism in that it promotes an exchange and interaction among various cultures in order to ignite interest or friction. Vibrant indigenous performance traditions somehow survived the colonial era, and in a peculiar reversal of history, they are now prized in Europe and America for their inherent theatricality and the communal values they embody. Theatre artists through the twentieth century to the present have been haunted by the belief that in ancient performance traditions based in ritual lies a theatre that connects to our deeper spiritual nature and can provide a universal human language. In a bit of historical irony, traditions that were once each other's scourge now stand side by side as a source of inspiration to today's theatre artists, who now blend, borrow, insert, and interweave each other's theatrical conventions in mutual appreciation.

Fascination with other cultures is not a new phenomenon. Travelers to other lands from as far back as we have documentation marveled at the traditions they discovered, and many artists have acknowledged the influence of foreign forms and ideas on their work. Globalization has intensified our exposure. What was once haphazard and crude cultural tourism has become a conscious borrowing, blending, absorption, and appropriating of other cultures'

art forms into new hybrid forms. Interculturalism is not without dangers. There is the risk of stereotyping, of misusing and denigrating cultural symbols, and of engaging in a kind of cultural imperialism.

THINK

Can traditional forms be used simply for their artistic expression, with artists borrowing freely from other cultures, or should the political and historical context always be taken into account?

Early explorations in intercultural theatre began at the start of the twentieth century, by European avant-garde artists who were intrigued by Asian performance that had begun touring the continent. During the 1920s in France, director-critic Jacques Copeau (1879–1949) used Asian movement techniques to train French actors. While these borrowings often occurred without understanding, even the misinterpretation of other cultures' forms can sometimes be a vital source of artistic renewal. Bertolt Brecht's inadequate knowledge of Chinese opera helped him shape his concept

GLOBAL TRADITIONS AND INNOVATIONS

Peter Brook's *Mahabharata* and Intercultural Theatre Practice

The controversy that erupted over English director Peter Brook's 1985 production of *The Mahabharata*, the foundational Hindu epic, crystallizes many issues surrounding intercultural performance. Already well known, Brook began a new period of theatrical exploration in 1970, when he founded the Centre International de Recherche Théâtrale in Paris. With an international company of actors, Brook sought a universal form of theatrical expression and communication.

The nine-hour *Mahabharata* premiered at the Avignon Festival in France in 1985. The production whittled down the enormous epic to events leading up to and including the monumental battle between the Pandavas and Kauravas and focused on the theme of war and destruction. The piece toured Europe, the United States, Australia, and Japan.

In Avignon and Australia, the performance took place in stone quarries, where the resonating sounds and the natural, open-air environment lent the production a primal intensity. The natural elements of fire, earth, and water were used to astonishing effect, with a real river on stage and, in one scene, a wall of flames. The Indian-inspired costuming was generally simple, and stage properties were few: mats and banners were used to help set the scene and actors' gestures replaced elaborate stage devices. Japanese composer Tsuchitori Toshi united international musical effects using eastern horns, Aboriginal didjeridus, conches, Japanese kodo drums, Indian tabla drums, gongs, and other instruments, for a score that was partly improvised in performance. Brook again created an exceptional theatrical experience.

Many Indian critics and South Asian scholars, familiar with performances and oral tellings of this epic in its home

country, although affected by Brook's theatricality, found his presentation a superficial "orientalist" view of the profound Hindu epic. Stories about Brook's disrespect for the indigenous tradition while doing research in India—his slighting of Indian village performers and his demands for performances at times and in ways out of sync with ritual and artistic considerations—compounded the feeling that Brook had stolen a central piece of Indian cultural heritage for his own purposes—oblivious to the culture, religion, or people who gave it birth and for whom it remained an important and living tradition. The British colonization of India served as backdrop to this cultural exchange, which seemed to replay that earlier exploitation and domination. The production did, however, provoke interest in Hindu philosophy and the *Mahabharata* text and raised consciousness of this ancient tradition. The production inspired much debate about intercultural practices.

▲ Intercultural borrowings go in all directions as seen in this production of *Richard III: An Arab Tragedy*. In this adaption by Kuwaiti director Sulayman Al Bassam, Shakespeare's play about a dictator's bloody rise to power is set in an oil-rich kingdom and becomes an allegory for our own times.

own lives at first seems contrary to our sense of having a stable, fixed identity. But when we consider how we "act" in different situations, it becomes clear that we don different masks for different occasions and interactions. The idea that we construct our identities—even things as basic as our gender and sexuality—has, in turn, influenced the contemporary theatre. Constructing and deconstructing identity has become a recurrent theme in contemporary theater, dissolving traditional notions of character. However, while theatre is an interesting metaphor for life, life is not theatre. Theatre is heightened, objectified, aestheticized, framed, delimited, and controlled.

THINK

What differentiates "real" life from performance?

of epic theatre, which we will discuss in the next chapter. Richard Rogers and Oscar Hammerstein used ritual Asian dance forms in *The King and I*. The term orientalism refers to this kind of exoticizing of Asian arts and now implies an imposition of a Western perspective on Asian forms.

Performance Studies

The scope of theatre studies has been widened by the new field of performance studies, which views theatre as only one of a continuum of events that possess "performative" elements. Other activities—such as religious rituals, storytelling, sports events, games, striptease, parades, lectures, and political conventions—also have a set space, a set duration, actors, audience, and the awareness that something outside the ordinary is occurring. The field of performance studies has given us a vocabulary with which to discuss these forms.

Performance studies has enabled us to move beyond a narrow view of what constitutes a theatrical event to examine performance in cultures using forms outside the typical European and American experience, as well as unusual forms within the Western tradition. An example of this might be the study of an African festival or a Balinese clown ritual in a theatre class. Or we might look at how a World Wrestling Entertainment match uses elements of theatre: It is live; it has actors playing roles before an audience; it is scripted, of set duration, and in a particular space; there is an interaction between the actors and the audience; and it cannot be exactly repeated.

Performance studies can provide a basis for understanding human behavior and social interaction. We are actually "performing," acting with a conscious awareness that we are in a role, a good deal of the time. In fact, we prepare ourselves for various roles every day, as we choose appropriate clothes, hairstyles, and demeanors for particular activities. To think we are "performing" our

▲ The growing use of theatrical elements—processional puppets, costumes, and music—in political protest reinforces the connection between theatre and other performative acts. In this London demonstration, Iranians voice opposition to President Mahmoud Ahmadinejad.

The human exchange between an actor and an audience is so central to the theatrical experience that we often think of science and machines as antagonistic to live performance. Yet in every period of theatre history, the stage has made use of available technology to heighten its expressive power. Technology is a force in our lives, and theatrical forms use, reflect, and comment on its power. Today theatre has unprecedented technical means at its disposal that expand creative possibilities and force theatre practitioners to rethink the limits of theatrical performance.

Technology is also competing with theatre through easily accessible media such as film, television, video, and the Internet. These forms of media employ storytelling techniques and thrilling special effects that in the past were the sole possession of live theatre. Early film often imitated theatre. Early television producers called television dramas "theatre in your living room." Once a good play might have served as the basis for a movie or television series; today movies are being turned into Broadway shows, such as *The Lion King*, *Sister Act!*, and *Catch Me If You Can*. The types of stories and scenarios produced in other media now guide the creation and appreciation of much theatrical fare. The Disney corporation produces its own shows based on its hit movies, such as *Beauty and the Beast*. There is concern that the commercial theatre increasingly resembles the corporate mass entertainment forms that permeate our culture.

Why Theatre **Today**?

WHAT is the role of the theatre in today's world?

Despite the easy accessibility of electronic media, people continue to be drawn to this ancient art form. Nothing can replace the vitality and thrill of live performance. The existence of MTV does not stop the lines of people buying tickets to hear Madonna live. When Lady Gaga appeared on *Saturday Night Live*, fans camped out on New York City streets for a week in order to get a place in the studio audience, rather than watch on TV. In fact, electronic media feed our desire to be present in the same space with the performer we long to touch. When film stars perform on Broadway, they attract crowds of theatre-goers who could more easily rent a video to see them. Theatre is about the immediacy and presence found in the reciprocal communication between the actor and the audience, and all electronic forms of entertainment are one-way streets. Here our fundamental yearning to respond and be felt is fulfilled. Rather than supplant theatre, electronic entertainment serves as a potent reminder of the living and immediate human essence of theatre and what it can and must provide in an increasingly depersonalized world.

There is great joy in working with others toward a shared goal. Facing the danger of opening night together is a bonding experience. This sense of belonging that comes from working on a production is especially pleasurable in a world in which our sense of community is increasingly eroded. For the individual, theatre provides a form of self-expression, use of every part of one's being. It tests our limits and our courage. It is a place to explore our inspirations, ideas, and values. It is a place to find appreciation, emotional reinforcement, and applause.

As you begin your study of theatre, you will see the history of civilization reflected in theatrical forms and find social concerns illuminated. You will learn how theatre is created, the potential of the art form, and what kind of theatre appeals to you most. You may even decide to participate. But, assuredly, you will become what every theatre artist desires most—an informed and passionate audience member.

Summary

HOW can we understand how other people portray themselves and tell their stories in performance? p. 4

▶ The theatre is a mirror of life because it allows us to look at ourselves with an objective understanding of who and what we are, but it is not necessarily a replica of the real world.

▶ Theatrical conventions govern every aspect of the art form and establish its boundaries.

▶ Theatrical conventions vary from one culture and historical period to another and evolve along with social values.

WHAT are the four universals that apply to all theatre everywhere? p. 8

▶ Throughout the world, all theatre is live; it requires the presence of an actor and an audience; it is ephemeral, collaborative, and a synthesis of many arts.

HOW do forces such as postmodernism, globalization, multiculturalism, interculturalism, postcolonialism, and performance studies shape contemporary performances? p. 10

▶ Tradition and innovation exist in a dynamic tension in the theatre, as artists adapt to changing times and audiences.

▶ The diversity of today's theatre is the product of many forces, including postmodernism, globalization, multiculturalism, interculturalism, and postcolonialism.

▶ Performance studies is an academic field that looks at theatre as one kind of performance on a continuum with other kinds of performance, such as ritual and sports events. It helps us understand and discuss today's varied theatrical forms.

WHAT is the role of the theatre in today's world? p. 18

▶ Despite the ready availability of easily consumable popular culture and electronic entertainment, theatre continues to draw audiences because of its immediacy and liveness, as well as the thrill of direct contact with the performers.

▶ Theatre remains an art that binds a community of people in a collaborative effort in an increasingly depersonalized world.

MySearchLab®

▼ More intimate than many modern theatres, Heisei Nakamura-za's reconstructed Edo period *kabuki* theatre brings audience members seated near the rampway close enough to reach out and touch the actor making his way to the stage. From his vantage point, the actor can take in the entire audience.

The Audience Response

Partners in Performance

All theatre artists toil in anticipation of that magic moment when the audience arrives. As you take your seat and wait for the event to begin, in all likelihood it has not entered your head that the actors have also been waiting for you. The performers *need* you to be there for their work to be complete; if you and everyone else in the audience suddenly vanished, leaving an empty theatre, there would be no performance. Your presence is vital to the theatre experience itself, for the most essential component of the theatre is the live actor–audience interaction.

Theatre is created to provoke a response. Whether attempting to give pleasure, to entertain, to touch, to anger, or to move to action, theatre practitioners always aim to engage the audience. It is almost impossible to imagine a member of the audience leaving the theatre without something to say, either positive or negative. Although most of us are satisfied with expressing our emotional reactions, there are also special audience members who are knowledgeable about the theatre. They step back from their emotional experience and analyze it more objectively. These are the critics, whose reactions can make or break a theatrical production.

Our reception of a performance—what impact it has on us, how we understand it, what we think about it, and how we talk about it after it is over—keeps the theatr e experience alive. When we connect a performance to the world around us and share our ideas with others, it becomes more meaningful. Although for that brief moment in the theatre, we are all part of a temporary community for a shared experience, our reactions are filtered through our personal experiences and knowledge to shape unique responses. One of the goals of this book is to make you aware of the factors that shape your reactions to provide the basis for an informed evaluation and a critical response that will enhance the pleasure and meaning you will take from theatre-going.

1. What are the responsibilities of the theatre audience?

2. What factors influence your reaction to a performance?

3. How are critics both members of the audience and set apart from the audience?

CHAPTER ·02·

The **Audience** and the **Actor:** The Invisible Bond

WHY is the actor–audience interaction the most essential component of the theatre?

To go to the theatre is to experience the special excitement of live performance and to enter into a new set of relationships with actors, a performance, and the spectators around you. Unlike a television or movie audience, a live theatre audience always participates in a performance in some way. The level of audience participation can range from community creation

> **Notoriously, there is what is called a chemistry in the theatre, a fusion of play, performance, and audience temper, which, if it does not take place, leaves the elements of an explosion cold.**

—Arthur Miller, playwright

and participation to quiet observation, but the audience is always a partner in performance.

Scholars believe that many forms of theatre evolved from religious ritual in which everyone present was a participant. According to this model, theatre is deeply tied to its communal roots, with the actor and the audience emerging from the same tightly knit group. When one member of the group first steps out to perform for the others, the performer also creates the audience. Even today, when the roles of actor and audience feel so distinct, they are still held together by an invisible bond. Actors on stage feel the audience's reactions, and consciously or unconsciously they adjust the performance accordingly. If the audience is laughing, an actor will wait until the laughter has died down to speak the next line. If the audience is unresponsive, an actor might work harder to get the audience to react. An unexpected noise such as the ring of a cellphone or a sneeze might cause an actor to lose focus for a moment. Performers are always playing in relation to the audience, as its members laugh, cry, sigh, and breathe together. The live actor–audience interaction is one of the special thrills of the theatre for both performers and spectators, and it pulls actors back to the theatre despite lucrative film careers.

The **Audience** Is a **Community**

HOW does an audience form a community?

In some places around the world, the audience comes from a tightly knit community linked by shared values and history outside the theatre. In other places, when you take a seat in a theatre auditorium, or gather around street performers, or join a dancing crowd, you become part of a temporary

community tied together only for the duration of the performance. Either way, this assimilation into a group empowers you. You can influence the actions of others around you, and they can influence yours. It is much easier to be openly responsive when we are part of a crowd than when we are

The Origins of Theatre

Because music, dance, costumes, props, and masks are commonly used in both rituals and theatrical performances, theorists have speculated that many forms of theatre evolved from rituals. The earliest rituals were performed to please or appease the gods who were the intended audience, and some extant traditions today remind us that ritual and theatre can coexist in the same form. Consider performance traditions such as the *kutiyattam* from the Kerala region in India, which uses special sacred places for performance. Actors face the shrine and the temple deity. Attendance at a performance is also an act of worship. In Japan at the Ise Shrine, the most sacred spot in Japan, priestesses of the indigenous Shinto religion perform special dance ceremonies. Here too, audiences may come to watch, but the performers face away from spectators because the dances are meant primarily for the pleasure of the divine spectators, the Shinto gods.

We have evidence that ancient Greek tragedy evolved from dithyrambs, hymns sung and danced in praise of the god Dionysus, the god of wine and fertility. From the ancient Egyptian Abydos ritual performance to the Christian passion plays of medieval Europe, many of the rituals associated with performance tell tales of resurrection and renewal often connected to fertility and rites of spring, linking theatre to beliefs that ensure the continuation of a community.

In some cultures shamans, priests or priestesses, are charged with communicating with the spirit world on behalf of the community to bring peace and prosperity to the populace or heal the sick. Donning a mask or costume, shamans in a state of possession may move, speak, and act like the spirit that possesses them, an image that parallels the work of the actor. The Buryat people of Siberia and Mongolia have incorporated shamanistic elements into contemporary theatre forms.

In many cultures religious events offer an opportunity to enact stories from a group's mytho-historical past. Such presentations may be necessary to pass on oral heritage, to ensure the health of the community and its members, or to effect a particular transition—such as an individual's passage from childhood to adulthood, as in the Apache puberty drama, or a seasonal shift from winter to spring.

Some scholars believe that the roots of theatre lie in storytelling, a universal activity that passes on shared experiences and knowledge. Entertaining narrators naturally embellish their tales by taking on the voices, facial expressions, and mannerisms of different characters, and they may even add props, costume pieces, and physical movement. Through these additions, storytelling blossoms into theatrical presentation. Others suggest that the origins of theatre lie in dance, where physical movement and mimed action gave expression to ideas before developed language.

It is unlikely that any single practice gave birth to the theatre, which embraces all of these elements and is influenced by so many traditions. It is more constructive to understand the development of theatrical activity as a movement along a continuum in response to the needs of communities to express their deepest concerns, to teach their members, and to ensure survival.

▶ In Metlakatla, Alaska, audience members join in the dancing of this Tsimshian dance troupe at a potlatch, a ceremony that includes feasting, music, speeches, singing, dancing, and gifts for the guests. Such events are held to bear witness to and celebrate a wide variety of occasions including the payment of a debt, a wedding, a funeral, or the building of a house.

alone. There is a special freedom that comes from being an audience member, just as there are special constraints.

Many factors can affect the degree of interaction among audience members. The theatre configuration and lighting can contribute to a heightened awareness of other people's responses. Performances outdoors in daylight tend to make us feel part of a crowd. But even in darkened theatres with the audience all facing the stage, we can sense an atmosphere in "the house"—the term theatre people use for the collective audience. Actors can sense the audience as a group from the stage immediately. The audience is the one thing that changes completely every night, and because of the interplay between actor and audience, no two performances are ever exactly alike.

Stage managers may report backstage before curtain that it feels like "a good house" tonight, commenting on the invisible currents of energy circulating among the audience members.

Audience Members Construct Meaning as Individuals

HOW do our personal histories influence how we react as audience members?

Although theatre artists usually address the audience as a group, an audience, like any other community, is made up of individuals with varying backgrounds and points of view. In close-knit societies, with shared values and histories, the differences among audience members may not be great, but no two people bring the same set of life experiences to a performance, and each audience member perceives a theatrical event through a personal lens.

Our personal histories influence how we react as audience members in many ways. If you are watching a performance from a culture outside your own, you may not understand its nuances, or point of view, or performance style. If you have recently gone through a traumatic event such as the death of a parent, you might have a particularly strong or empathetic reaction to a play addressing this subject. If you are seeing a play or a performance tradition you have studied, you will measure this production against how you imagined it. If you are an experienced theatre-goer, you might not be as impressed by a lavish set or spectacular scenic change as a novice would. If you are attending a play that you have already seen, you may find yourself comparing the interpretations, directing, acting, and design. All of these individual experiences and others will affect your response, just as taking this class will probably make you a very different audience member in the future.

Factors such as our age, culture, race, religion, ethnicity, gender, sexuality, education, and economic or social class, play a part in our response to a performance. Usually theatre attempts to bridge the space between audience members'

experiences and the content of a performance through the creation of empathy, the capacity to identify emotionally with the characters on stage. Sometimes theatre artists choose to exploit these differences for social or political reasons.

THINK

How should we approach performances presented from a cultural viewpoint different from our own?

The Free Southern Theater's 1968 production of *Slave Ship* by Amiri Baraka (b. 1934; also known as LeRoi Jones), enacted a history of African Americans in the United States and deliberately divided its audience along racial lines. A symbolic slave ship was constructed in the middle of the large playing area, with close seating on all sides. The hold of the ship, where slave bodies were piled in cramped quarters, was eye level with the audience, magnifying the inhuman conditions on board. During an enacted slave auction, female slaves were stripped topless and thrust at white men in the audience, who were asked what they thought the women were worth. Many white audience members left at this point. At the end of the piece, cast members, invoking black power movements, invited black audience members to join them in shouting for violent revolution while encircling the white audience. At many performances, black audience members, feeling empowered by the performance, did join the cast. Many white audience members felt threatened and angry or felt helpless to express their sympathy with the blacks in an atmosphere of hostility. This play was meant to provoke different responses from different audience members to teach the lessons of history. Racial background could not help but influence the audience's experience of the play.

Chicana playwright Cherríe Moraga (b. 1952) focuses on the problems of the community of Mexican Americans in California. In her play *Heroes and Saints*, the bodiless central character Cerezita represents Chicano children with birth defects due to pesticides used in the fields. In *The Hungry Woman*, Moraga loosely draws upon the Medea myth to portray the alienation of the Chicano lesbian from her culture. Her treatment of homosexuality interweaves sexuality with religious symbolism and seeks to expose the oppressive aspects of Catholicism. Moraga liberally mixes English and Spanish dialogue, reflecting the actual speech patterns of the Chicano community. Her plays draw heavily on Chicano cultural images, and audience members unfamiliar with Spanish or with the social world Moraga depicts might feel unable to appreciate her reworking of cultural symbols. Her charged themes provoke different responses based on sexual preference and religiosity.

▲ Cherríe Moraga's *The Hungry Woman: A Mexican Medea* depicts conflicting cultures and identities and holds special meaning for the Chicano community.

Audience Members Choose Focus

At a theatrical event, individual audience members can choose their focus and control their personal experience of a performance. A theatre spectator sees the entire playing space and can choose to look anywhere. Lighting effects and other staging techniques may draw the audience's attention to one area or another, but spectators decide whether they want to watch the actor who is speaking or see the reaction of the actor who is listening. Where spectators choose to focus will affect their interpretation of a performance. This puts a burden on stage actors and directors to create a center of compelling dramatic action. Compare this to film or television, in which the director, through the camera lens, and the editor, with a cut, preselect what they want the audience to see and from what perspective.

> **Theatre, the most public**
> **of all the arts,**
> **is also a private act**
> **with personal meaning.**

Theatre experiences that address race, ethnicity, religion, sexual preference, and gender seek to create awareness of the life conditions of people both like and unlike ourselves. What we take away from such provocative performances and what meaning we construct depends on how we filter the staged events through our personal histories.

▶ In this production of Jean Genet's *The Blacks: A Clown Show* by the Classical Theatre of Harlem, direct confrontation of white audience members by black actors reverses the traditional power structure to illuminate the play's themes.

▶ The British avant-garde group Punchdrunk stages *Sleep No More (2011)* based on the events in Shakespeare's *Macbeth*. Audience members wear white masks (the actors are unmasked) as they wander freely through abandoned buildings with minimally illuminated, furniture-cluttered rooms and corridors. In each room a different scene from the play is performed. While clues to the plot are in each scene, what the audience experiences depended on where each individual decides to roam and in what order he or she witnesses the scenes.

Some stage directors create productions with many stages and many events occurring at the same time and ask the audience to choose its own focus time and again. In Richard Schechner's (b. 1934) environmental theatre work during the 1960s and 1970s, there was no demarcation between the audience space and the performance space, and simultaneous action occurred in many places (see Chapter 9). Actors engaged individual audience members, sometimes whispering dialogue in their ears. This required each member of the audience to actually construct the drama based on a completely individual experience.

Conventions of
Audience Response

HOW does the actor–audience relationship vary in different places, societies, eras, events, and venues?

When you attend the theatre, most likely you are not aware that you have entered into a silent contract determining how you will behave during the performance and what your relationship will be with the theatrical event and the performers. In general, audiences conduct themselves according to time-honored traditions that are observed by spectators and actors alike. When these rules are broken, on purpose or by accident, as when an actor planted in the audience interrupts the stage action or an audience member leaps uninvited onto the stage, it can be exciting or disturbing, but it is always provocative, because it is a violation of

the prevalent theatrical conventions and audience expectations. A performance constructs its conventions of audience response through cues given by the actors, the spatial arrangement, directorial concept, lighting, and set design. In the chapters ahead, we will look at how each of these elements determines the role of the audience.

Although the audience's presence is a vital part of theatrical performance, the nature of the audience's participation may vary from place to place, society to society, era to era, and even at different kinds of events or in different venues within the same culture. At evening performances

Audience Conventions Around the World

Many theatrical traditions expect vocal audience response of one kind or another during the show. In the Japanese *kabuki* theatre, at the climactic moments of a play, the fans yell out phrases such as "I've been waiting for this my whole life!" or "Do it the way your father did it!" Through this yelling they support their favorite actors, cheering them on the way a baseball fan in America might yell to a pitcher during a game. At performances of Chinese opera, whenever a performer does something praiseworthy, members of the audience will applaud and shout "*Hao, hao*" ("Good, good"). They do not feel compelled to hold their applause until the end. In African concert party theatre, audience participation is expected, and spectators are invited, even drawn, into the performance by the actors, who encourage them to hiss at the villains and warn characters of danger. When these kinds of performances are played to spectators who do not respond as expected, the performances can seem lifeless, and actors who have come to rely on the vocal support of their admirers can feel let down. One of the most important things to learn about the theatre is how to be an appropriate audience member.

of the opera in the Roman arena in Verona, Italy, the locals in the upper tiers picnic during the performance, passing around bread, salami, and wine. Those in the high-priced seats behave more like opera house audiences in New York or Paris, where people come to be seen in their designer best and await intermission to sip champagne. Although eating is taboo during most performances inside opera houses and can disturb the performers and other audience members, when the New York Metropolitan Opera performs in Central Park, audience members picnic on the grass and drink wine. Expected audience behavior can be different for the same kind of performance in different settings.

In theatres in the Western tradition around the world, we expect to be silent during a performance and to hold our applause until the end. Sometime after we take our seats, the lights dim and a hush settles over the crowd as we become quiet and attentive listeners. Although this is the prevalent convention in Western theatre today, it was not always the case.

The **Once-Active** Audience

The outdoor daylight performances in ancient Greece took place in a festive atmosphere in which social interaction, eating, and drinking were all part of a daylong theatre event. In ancient Rome, theatre was performed at religious festivals that offered an enormous array of entertainments. Both sacred and secular, performances were meant to please the gods as much as the human spectators. The theatre competed with chariot races and wild animal fights for its audience's attention, and it was common for spectators to walk out in the middle of a play if they thought that something more interesting might be happening at another venue.

Throughout the Middle Ages, theatre was very much a community affair. Audiences would gather around wandering players in town squares and interact with each other and the performers. The Christian cycle plays that began in the fourteenth century and depicted stories from the Old and New Testaments were projects that engaged entire towns in preparation. The audience who had shared in the creation of the piece, providing sets, costumes, props, and other needs, attended in a spirit of camaraderie to watch their fellow townspeople perform.

An open exchange between actors and the public continued even as performances became more formal events

► At the Roman Arena in Verona, Italy, audience members play their part in the operatic spectacle by lighting small candles during the overture. The entire arena is aglow in an audience-created lighting effect.

The Astor Place Riots

During the nineteenth century in Europe and the United States, passionate audiences protested vociferously over issues of concern, from ticket prices to theatrical forms and the treatment of stars.

Lingering American antagonism against the British may have been at the root of the violent riots that erupted on May 10, 1849, at the Astor Place Opera House in New York City. The riots were ostensibly a result of a professional rivalry between the American actor Edwin Forrest (1806–1872) and the English actor William Charles Macready (1793–1873). Macready's subtle and intellectual style contrasted with Forrest's vigorous acting and muscular bearing that many felt embodied American democratic ideals. Their simultaneous performances in New York translated into a call to arms for home-grown American culture.

Forrest's admirers assailed Macready with critical newspaper articles, and after a disastrous opening night in New York, when audience members threw chairs at the stage, along with the usual vegetables and fruit, Macready was ready to return home. When they heard that Macready was persuaded by a group of powerful New Yorkers to continue his run, Forrest's supporters drummed up a nationalist fury against the production. At the next performance, the house was full to capacity, and police officers and crowds of thousands gathered outside the theatre in protest. When Macready walked on stage, the gathering erupted beyond the control of the police, and Macready barely escaped with his life. The National Guard was called in from a nearby armory, and soldiers shot at the crowd. According to various accounts, the Astor Place riots left between 20 and 31 people dead, more than 100 wounded, and the theatre in ruins.

◄ National Guardsmen at Astor Place shoot at rioters.

performed by professional actors in theatre buildings during the sixteenth century. In his own time, Shakespeare's plays were performed before a rowdy audience who booed, hissed, cheered, conversed, ate, drank, and even threw food at the performers. Many believe that the open roof of the Elizabethan playhouse was a means to let the stench of food, drink, and unwashed bodies escape.

If we remember that Shakespeare wrote for a popular audience, we can appreciate the earthy humor, double entendres, and theatrical devices that made him a crowd pleaser.

In late seventeenth-century Europe, as theatre moved increasingly indoors, the behavior of the audience was somewhat more subdued, but spectators were still actively engaged in the event. Indoor theatre in this period was a social event for an elite audience. Candelabra lit up the audience as well as the stage, and the horseshoe-shaped auditorium made it as easy to be seen by others as to see the show. Those seated on the long sides of the horseshoe actually had to turn their heads to the side to see the stage; when they looked straight ahead or down, they looked at each other and could easily observe who else was in the audience, what they were wearing, and who their escorts were, feeding the social gossip of the time.

In eighteenth-century London, spectators often arrived early and entertained each other before the show began. The plays of the Restoration and early eighteenth century, with their depiction of an artificial social world with pretentious manners and behavior, can be seen as mirrors of the audience in the theatre.

In one of his many journals, diarist James Boswell (1740–1795) recounts how on one occasion, while attending the theatre, he imitated a cow to the delight of other audience members who cried, "Encore the Cow!"

European plays of the sixteenth through the nineteenth centuries were punctuated with dramatic devices addressed directly to the audience, such as asides—short comments that revealed a character's inner thoughts often to comic effect; soliloquies—lengthy speeches through which a character revealed state of mind; and dazzling poetic monologues, or speeches. The audience might erupt in appreciative applause after a monologue or soliloquy, much the way they do today at the opera after an aria.

The eighteenth- and nineteenth-century theatre, reflecting the democratic revolutions occurring in the outside world, increasingly included popular entertainments and easily accessible drama. American audiences were some of the rowdiest of all. They exercised their democratic freedom at theatre events and brought tomatoes, cabbages, and rotten eggs with them to throw at the actors if they didn't like the performance. At a good performance they cheered ecstatically and cried out for encores; an actor would have to repeat a speech as many times as the crowd demanded.

With this long history of involved audiences, how did it come to pass that today, in Western Europe and the Americas, the audience is generally more passive?

The Rise of the Passive Audience

The quiet, passive spectator is a relatively recent historical phenomenon and dates only from the late nineteenth century, as a result of the advent of a theatrical style known as realism. In realistic theatre, the audience is asked to accept the stage world as a believable alternate reality where things happen, much as they would in life, and people behave in seemingly natural ways. In realism, actors conduct the lives of characters as though the audience were not watching, in spaces designed to look like their counterparts in the real world. In turn, the audience, representing a different reality,

agrees not to intrude on the imaginary world on the stage. This preserves the illusion and creates the convention of an invisible fourth wall, which separates the stage from the audience.

Realism is a Style

It is important to remember that realism is not any more *real* than any other style of theatre. In fact, actors are not talking in their everyday voices or volumes; they are not any more like their characters than actors in nonrealistic plays; the sets and costumes are just as artificial as those that present an abstract or poeticized style. What realism provides is the *illusion of the real*, and that is as much an illusion as every other stage world. Because realism came to dominate the American theatre, we refer to the nonrealistic theatre as *stylized*; but realism is as much a style—a manner of presenting the world through accepted conventions—as any other approach to the theatre.

Realism as a style resulted from a confluence of forces: the ideas of naturalist Charles Darwin (1809–1882) that presented human beings as objects of scientific study; the birth of sociology and psychology, which sought to objectively observe human behavior; and a surge of playwrights interested in applying these ideas to the theatre. It also became possible because of advances in stage lighting—first gas and later electric—that permitted the darkening of an auditorium to separate the audience while simultaneously shining a focused light on the stage to illuminate human behavior as though it were under the lens of a microscope. The advances in lighting enabled the actors to move away from the front of the stage, into the realistic stage environment.

As more and more playwrights chose to write in this realistic style, it came to dominate the Western theatre, and its impact on acting, directing, and design can be seen to this day. Theatre architecture altered to reflect social change and to facilitate this new approach. The horseshoe-shaped theatre was abandoned in favor of a theatre in which all the seats faced forward, focusing the audience on the stage and altering its relationship to the performance. Economic motives pushed theatre managers to place upholstered armchair seating in front of the stage in the pit, in what we now call the orchestra section. Where rowdy lower-class spectators once stood or sat on backless benches, wealthier audiences now sat in expensive reserved seating, changing the atmosphere in the theatre.

Aesthetic Distance

Peculiarly, the more the conventions of realism separated the audience from the actors, and the more passively the audience watched, the more they lost their aesthetic distance. Aesthetic distance refers to the ability to observe a work of art with a degree of detachment and objectivity. Realism drew audiences into the performance. The presentation of a world so like their own, inhabited by characters whose concerns and problems so closely paralleled their own experience, heightened the level of audience identification and emotional involvement with the characters on the stage.

Styles other than realism still provide a constant reminder of the fiction before us, and this awareness enables us to separate psychologically from the work.

Every theatrical experience sets up an emotional relationship with the audience that is regulated by theatrical convention. This can range from icy dispassion to overwhelming emotional involvement. Some amount of distance is always necessary; without it, we would be unable to discern that the events unfolding on the stage are a fiction and that the actors are really playing characters who live only for the duration of the performance.

Distance maintains the audience's sanity, or else we would all be leaping onto the stage to stop Romeo from killing himself.

THINK

Are violent and disturbing images and language on stage so provocative that they require government regulation and censorship?

Theatre critics from Plato (circa 427–347 B.C.E.) to the present have debated the importance of aesthetic distance and its moral implications. Many have feared that exposing the audience to violent or sexually explicit acts and offensive language can foster such behavior. Others have argued that aesthetic distance permits a purging of our aggressive desires through art and enactment. Aristotle (384–322 B.C.E.) referred to this emotional release as catharsis. These concerns are echoed in today's discussions of violence in the media.

Reach Out and Touch Someone— Theatre One on One

In an era when an audience of thousands—or even millions—can be readily accessed via the Internet or Twitter, theatre, the most communal of arts, has become a private event in some avant-garde circles. "Performances for one" have been catching on all over the world. In 2010, the Battersea Arts Centre (BAC) in London hosted a festival of one-on-one performances. In this festival, 35 artists awaited individual audience members in 35 different spaces, in which theatre one-on-one attendees might be bathed, cradled, embraced, or nourished by naked actors. In each case, the expected barriers between actor and audience are shattered, and part of the event is simply having an unpredictable experience, in an age where consumers are collecting experiences the way they once collected designer shoes or handbags.

Also in 2010, Christine Jones set up a 4- by 9-foot box in Times Square, in which she staged six new plays for an audience of one on a first-come, first-served basis. These were fully staged events with sound, light, and costume designers. The peep show feeling fit in well with the history of the neighborhood, which was once overrun with crime and home to numerous sex shops and peep shows. Similarly, *Appointment*, directed by Aaron Landsman, invited audience members to be "performed for, negotiated with, read to and led one-by-one on a treasure hunt" and has been staged in cities from Austin to Berlin. Dozens of other such performances are happening around the world. Performers see this new personal theatre as a response to the lack of intimacy in relationships lived out on social networks such as Facebook. These performances answer the audience's need to look the actor in the eye and be truly touched.

▲ Christine Jones performs in an intimate encounter with an audience of one.

Rebelling Against **Realism's** Passive Audience

As soon as realism became an accepted convention, the continuing cycle of tradition giving way to innovation produced experimental artists on a divergent course. Since the turn of the twentieth century, theatre practitioners have been seeking ways to tear down realism's fourth wall and reengage the audience in performance, creating new sets of conventions in the process. Some have simply sought ways to reinvigorate the stage, as in Thornton Wilder's use of a character called the Stage Manager who speaks directly to the audience as he sets the scene, narrates events, and introduces the characters of *Our Town* (1938). Other theatre practitioners manipulate aesthetic distance for their own political or aesthetic ends. Avant-garde theatre artists have even toyed with the audience's aesthetic distance, confusing them about what is *real* and what is *pretend*, which is an unsettling experience. In *The Last Supper* (2002), Ed Schmidt invited the audience into his home, promising them a wonderful dinner as part of the event (see Chapter 9). Bantering with the audience in seemingly unscripted remarks as he cooks in his kitchen, he realizes he's forgotten to defrost the fish and has run out of ingredients. Sitting in the intimacy of the actor's home with real rumbling stomachs, the audience could not distinguish where the real person left off and the role began and were baffled about what was true and what was false, raising questions about perceptions of reality.

Political Theatre: Moving the Audience to Action

WHAT is the history of political theatre, and what is its role today?

Playwrights have used the theatre for political commentary since as far back as the ancient Greek comic playwright Aristophanes (448–c. 380 B.C.E.), who satirized the people and institutions of ancient Athens. However, in the early twentieth century, a different kind of political theatre— aimed at activating audiences for real social change—took root. Such theatre places special demands on its audience, and its goal is to spur them to take action. In political theatre strategies for audience activation are adapted to specific circumstances and political goals.

Agitprop: **Activating** the Audience

Agitprop (from *agitation and propaganda*) was an early form of political theatre developed during the 1920s in Russia and later adopted abroad. Born in the Marxist fervor of the Russian Revolution, it supported the workers' struggle for political, social, and economic justice. In the spirit of the ancient town criers, agitprop brought the day's news to illiterate peasants and factory workers. It was employed to enlist their support for the massive economic and social changes in the aftermath of the revolution. As songs and skits on relevant issues were added, these presentations grew into "living newspapers."

Agitprop became a model for political theatre in many countries. German troupes such as the Red Megaphone incorporated group declamatory speeches and cabaret-style skits into their performances. During the Spanish Civil War (1936–1939), players used agitprop to inspire the people to fight against fascism. The Federal Theatre Project, organized to provide jobs for unemployed theatre artists during the Great Depression in the United States, performed *Living Newspapers* from 1935 to 1939. *Living Newspapers* used documentary material to inform the American public of pressing social concerns. In the 1960s, groups such as the San Francisco Mime Troupe mixed agitprop with popular American and European theatrical forms such as vaudeville, *commedia dell'arte,* and circus clowning to create extended outdoor plays that brought home a political message and urged the audience to adopt a position.

Agitprop reached out to its audiences, playing where ordinary people gathered, in workers' cafes and community halls, expressing important information in a short, simple, explicit, and entertaining way.

Challenging the Audience: Bertolt Brecht

Throughout the world, theatre artists look to the work of the German playwright and director Bertolt Brecht (1898–1956)

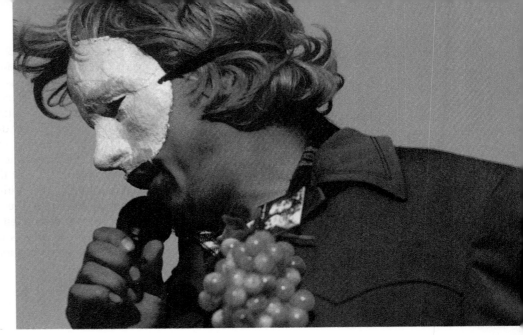

▶ The Teatro Campesino was founded in 1965 by Luis Valdez to dramatize the conditions of migrant farm workers. The troupe, performing on flatbed trucks, brought its performances to workers in the fields and in union halls. It championed California grape pickers' demand for higher wages and better working conditions and stirred the workers to action.

for a model of how to engage the audience. Brecht built on, and extended, the work of German director Erwin Piscator (1893–1966), an early pioneer in political theatre who developed a series of anti-realistic stage devices—projections, placards, film clips, and treadmills—that increased the audience's aesthetic distance and prevented emotional absorption in the play, so they could see the political issues more clearly. Mood lighting was replaced by utilitarian illumination to provide visibility. Brecht revealed the means of creating theatrical illusion, such as light fixtures, ropes, and pulleys, to keep the audience fully aware that they were watching a theatrical event. Brecht wrote plays (which which we will discuss in the next chapter) that could utilize these staging techniques. The action is interrupted by narratives, projections, and songs that comment on the situation and whose music and content are frequently jarringly dissonant. The finales of his plays often leave the situation unresolved or directly ask the audience to come up with a resolution. Brecht worked with a troupe to develop a style of acting that could enable the actor to comment on the character, not become the character.

Through these and other techniques, Brecht hoped to achieve what he called the *verfremdungseffekt*, translated as **distancing**, or **alienation effect**, a separation of the audience emotionally from the dramatic action. The audience is thus in the role of observer, able to decide the best course of action to resolve social ills. As politically motivated theatre practitioners around the world adopted Brecht's methods, these devices became a part of our theatrical vocabulary and no longer have the same startling effect on audiences; artists therefore continue to look for new techniques and strategies.

Involving the Audience: Augusto Boal

Brazilian theatre theorist and practitioner Augusto Boal (1930–2009) extended Brecht's ideas in a theatrical form in which all barriers between actors and audience are destroyed, returning theatre to its communal roots, in which we can all become participants in social drama. He turns passive spectators into active "spect-actors" who don't just think about alternative solutions but try them out on stage, as rehearsals for social revolution.

Under the umbrella of the **Theatre of the Oppressed**, Boal developed different theatrical strategies for different situations and audiences. In *forum theatre*, members of a community create a short piece about shared problems that they perform for other spect-actors who are invited to stop the show at any time, take over roles, and try out new solutions. In his *invisible theatre*, provocative dramas about burning issues are enacted in normal everyday settings such as subway cars or restaurants, as if they were happening in real life. The unsuspecting public, unaware that the action is rehearsed and planned, unwittingly join the debate or action and become actors themselves. During a term spent as a city councilman in Brazil, Boal worked on *legislative theatre*, a form of *forum theatre* designed to reveal issues of primary concern to the community to guide political policy. Boal's Theatre of the Oppressed was originally designed to reach the poor of Brazil, but now there are centers for the dissemination of his methods all over the world.

In one **Theatre of the Oppressed** piece **performed** on a boat in Sweden, a young woman pretended to be **pregnant** and in labor to catalyze a **discussion** about the shortcomings of the **health** care system.

The Living Theatre: Confronting the Audience

During the 1960s many theatrical groups in the United States and abroad spoke out against the Vietnam War and

Fiona Shaw plays the title character in Bertolt Brecht's *Mother Courage and Her Children* at the National Theatre in London. This scathing anti-war play depicts the dehumanizing effects of conflict.

sought new ways to galvanize their audiences against the war and the political–industrial complex that supported it. One of the most innovative and influential groups was The Living Theatre, founded by Judith Malina (b. 1926) and Julian Beck (1925–1985). The company has a long history of important productions, beginning with a staging of Jack Gelber's drama about drug addiction, *The Connection*, in 1959, and Kenneth Brown's *The Brig* in 1963, which placed a mesh fence between the audience and the dehumanizing action of military prisons depicted on stage. The group lived out their anarchist politics by moving to Europe and living as a nomadic collective. They created *Paradise Now* in 1968 to make audiences aware of the restraints social and political institutions imposed on individual freedom. Goading audience members, the group used inflammatory political statements that brought spectators to their feet, and sometimes to the top of their seats, screaming back in anger. Company members then invited spectators to join them on stage and in their nomadic, tribal lifestyle.

THINK

Must audience members accept the conventions of a performance, or can they refuse to participate as the show prescribes?

The work of The Living Theatre became famous and inspired many theatre artists of the 1960s and after to adapt the group's techniques for their own purposes. The Living Theatre continues to perform today, with pieces such as *Resist Now!*, a play involving anti-globalization demonstrations, and *Not in My Name*, an action against the death penalty. *Not in My Name* is enacted in Times Square in New York City on the eve of every state execution. In this piece, performers confront passers-by individually, avowing that they themselves will never kill and asking spectators for the same commitment, continuing their use of direct encounter to motivate an end to violence.

Engaging the Audience Today

Today a new breed of activist-artists is expanding on the methods of the pioneers to engage spectators in political activism that is responsive to contemporary issues. The Internet and Twitter have provided rapid means of contacting large groups of participants and calling them to theatrical political action with information about when and where to show up. Reclaim the Streets, a group boasting participants in New York, London, and elsewhere around the globe, turns street corners and subway cars into spontaneous parties to reclaim overregulated open spaces for general public use. Some performer-participants get messages via the Internet, while others simply become part of the show by walking down the street. The Surveillance Camera Players raise awareness of the loss of privacy in our daily lives by performing short, silent pieces in public for surveillance cameras. Their performances point out the unobtrusive cameras that watch our every move.

The Evolution of a Convention

Although experimental and political theatre artists in the twentieth century first used audience participation as a form of rebellion against the passive bourgeois audience and other theatrical conventions of realism, tamer forms followed. The idea of the active spectator eventually left the realm of the avant-garde and became a firmly established convention.

Theatre for Social Change

Theatre companies that speak to local audiences about local issues have been a force for education and consciousness raising and an inspiration for political action. Much of the work of theatre groups with social agendas calls on the techniques of Brecht and Boal, but many groups also employ innovative theatrical forms and strategies. They may reach out to their audiences by incorporating traditional songs and folk or local performance conventions. For more than 30 years, the Peruvian troupe Yuyachkani has produced popular theatre that incorporates traditional celebrations, masks, songs, dances, and costumes to raise awareness of Peru's social and political problems. During the 20 years of violent civil war that left 36,000 dead or missing and 80,000 displaced, Yuyachkani created pieces that explored the effect of political terrorism on the individual psyche. Yuyachkani has developed new theatrical strategies to keep alive the memory of the dead and disappeared while continuing to address current social concerns. The Sistren theatre in Jamaica focuses on improving the socioeconomic condition of women. Performances are in Creole and draw on oral history, traditional games, and folk tales to call attention to issues such as violence against women.

In times of political repression and censorship, a special bond can form between theatres and their audiences, as artists seek to act as a community's mouthpiece. Under President Suharto's oppressive dictatorship in Indonesia, Teater Koma was founded in 1977 to critique contemporary society and politics. Blending Western-style structured scripts and musical theatre with influences from Indonesia's indigenous folk forms, Teater Koma calls attention to societal ills. Suharto may be gone, but Teater Koma continues to keep its sights on the abuses of the present government. In today's global world, theatre groups have also taken on international issues. Australia's ActNow was founded in response to the 2001 imprisonment of the Australian David Hicks by the United States in Guantanamo Bay.

While theatre for social change is often a theatre of protest, under the leadership of Joanna Sherman, New York's Bond Street Theatre has taken on the role of ambassador for peace, visiting countries ravaged by war. The troupe created and trained Jerusalem's first street theatre company, involving 60 Israeli and Palestinian performers, and held workshops for Catholic and Protestant children in Northern Ireland. Refugee camps in Kosovo, Albania, Macedonia, and Pakistan have been magnets for the troupe's work. The troupe went first to use art to heal, creating performances with and for children, and then to empower local artists to resurrect their own theatres destroyed by war. Bond Street Theatre has made several visits to Afghanistan, the most recent funded by the U.S. Institute of Peace in 2010. There the group performed theatre sketches aimed at educating the population on health issues meant to empower women. Teaching theatre techniques for conflict resolution and peace building, the troupe has helped Afghan artists who fled the Taliban to rebuild theatres. It encourages these returned local performers to put on stage dramas that help audiences recover from the trauma of war and the terror of Taliban rule.

▶ *Beyond the Mirror*, a collaboration between Exile Theatre based in Afghanistan and New York's Bond Street Theatre, depicts the horrors of war and is based on the accounts of Afghans who have survived three decades of war and cruelty.

Bill Talen is an author and actor who performs as the televangelist Reverend Billy. He began as a sidewalk preacher in Times Square in the late 1990s, fighting against the "Disneyfication" of the neighborhood and preaching against the invasion of transnational chain stores that eradicate small local businesses. His focus is now on the relationship between consumerism and the destruction of the environment. He and his partner Savitri D lead the "Church of Earthalujah," where the Earth itself is the object of veneration. They perform in the lobbies of Earth-damaging corporations and big banks. Reverend Billy was recently arrested for protesting mountaintop removal and tar sands extraction. Reverend Billy ran for mayor of New York in 2009.

▲ Reverend Billy preaching against the evils of trans-national capitalism.

How do you get reluctant audiences to participate?

The audiences break through their hesitation and get up on stage to sing with us for the Earthalujah altar call. They are rising to the "Sacred State of Embarrassment" because they want to save the Earth, and themselves. And the hilarity and music of the whole thing—it's infectious. The reluctance to shout "Change-a-lujah!" is difficult to maintain when people all around you are laughing and the air is vibrating with good gospel.

Do your performances spawn other grassroots activism efforts?

We hope so. The emergency of the Earth's crisis, the floods, fires, tsunamis, tornados, extinction waves. . . . We are so consumerized that we can't seem to go down to the commons and shout "Emer-

gency." That would be the beginning of community and a re-starting of the theatrical tradition—to be able to express yourself when you are endangered. We have partnered with Yes Men, Brave New Theatre, Climate Ground Zero, Rainforest Action Network, the UK Tar Sands Coalition. We stream sermons and songs through Youtube, and our Facebook site "Reverend Billy Talen." There is always an Internet welcome, a way for anyone to witness and comment. On the other hand—point is the activism: Get out into public space and shout about the Earth down at your own Tahrir Square or your own Madison rotunda. Exercise your 1st Amendment freedoms and Earth-friendly theatrics will follow.

What long-term impact do you think your performances have on audience members?

The long-term impact that really matters is survival. In theatre we always want high stakes. Well the stakes are life and death. We literally hope to save our audience's life, and our own lives too! Look, climate change is not eventual. The heat-waves and freak storms and rising seas are not theoretical. Our behavior after the curtain comes down is dramatic. What do we do when we leave the theatre? Our uncontrolled consumption is causing this crisis—so the drama doesn't end when the theatre lights go out—it begins. The Earth itself is giving us the drama we need—so let's answer the call! Earthalujah!

Source: Used with permission of Bill Talen, aka "Rev. Billy."

THINK

In what ways do some recent audience participation performances resemble reality TV?

Productions such as Off-Off-Broadway's *Tony and Tina's Wedding* (1988) treat audience members as guests at a wedding. They attend the church ceremony and walk as a group to the reception, where they sit at tables and eat a full dinner, complete with champagne, as they watch Tony and Tina's family relationships explode around them. A far cry from agitprop theatre, the event is now a national franchise

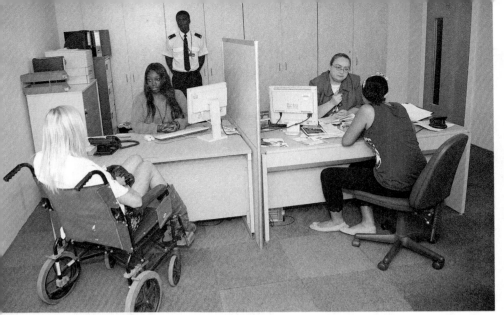

In *You Me Bum Bum Train* (2010), the audience is whirled through a participatory adventure. Thrust into wheelchairs, audience members are taken through a maze of scenes from real life, where they are forced to become actors. Here, at the job centre, the audience member must pass the interview and land the job.

with a website, gift certificates, and commercial performances in cities around the United States. Such mainstream performances demonstrate that what was once a defiant radical strategy to overturn prevailing conventions can evolve into a popular and accepted theatrical form. Countless websites for customized interactive murder mystery or comedy performances can be found on the Internet.

Theatre directors are now seeking new and exciting forms of audience participation to push the boundaries of the permissible. In Flemish director Ontroerend Goed's *Internal* (2008), the actors cruelly lure the audience members into making private revelations and then reveal them to the rest of the audience, raising questions of what should be permissible in the actor–audience interaction. In the past two years, British theatre artists have also made bold experiments in audience participation. In *A Small Town Anywhere* (2009) by the Coney Company, every audience member becomes a character in an imaginary town. They then go on to collectively develop a story that leads to the ultimate banishment of one of their fellow audience members. The audience is performing for themselves; the audience and the actors are indistinguishable. As a recent lawsuit filed against Blue Man Group by an audience member forced to participate against his will demonstrates, the boundary between coercion and empowerment is not always clear.

THINK

Should there be limits on how performers may treat unsuspecting audience members?

Meeting Theatre's **Challenges**

WHAT kinds of challenges does theatre pose to its audience?

We often think of the theatre as a place of entertainment, but in addition to entertaining us, the theatre poses special challenges to its audience and critics alike. In the theatre, you must be attentive as you decide where to focus, or you will miss significant information. Theatre often depends on language more than does a visual medium such as film and therefore demands good listening skills. As an audience member, sometimes you are confronted by an unexpected theatrical style—difficult language, stylized movement, strange sets, and costumes that might seem jarring—and you must do your best to remain open and adjust to the new form and how it communicates. Theatre, unlike television, is often imagistic, evocative, suggestive, and metaphorical, so it is important to bring your imagination to the theatre.

"Getting There is Half the Fun"

Sometimes the journey to a production becomes a challenge but also part of the magic of the event. *The Demons* (2010) by Peter Stein (b. 1937) requires more than just sitting through 12 hours of theatre. When it was presented in New York, the performance took place on an island in the middle of the harbor, requiring the audience to travel by bus or subway to the Maritime Building to pick up a ferry to Governors Island. The voyage became part of the event. The Théâtre du Soleil's location in the woods of Vincennes, France, requires a trip to the last stop on the Paris metro and transportation from there to the theatre on a special theatre shuttle bus. Arriving at night, through the woods, to the theatre's courtyard, where tiny lights bedeck the trees, is a magical experience in itself that prepares the spectator for the rest. As more and more urban theatre groups are priced out of downtown space, performances may occur in out-of-the-way places and seedy areas. Making the trip to such places can become a test of faith. People will travel far to experience that special feeling of being part of a theatre audience.

Some productions ask spectators to make a special commitment by challenging them physically, emotionally, or intellectually. "Marathon performances" may last as long as 12 hours. The 6-hour *Rwanda 94* (1999), produced by the Belgian company Groupov with artists from Rwanda, challenged its audience with more than length. It presented the horrors of the Tutsi genocide and Hutu massacre in Rwanda in 1994 through video images of dead bodies hacked by machetes and first-person accounts of victims whose children and spouses were slaughtered before their eyes. Audiences had to deal with these emotional presentations as they learned the causes of the violence and faced the culpability of European and American powers.

◀ Many who live in remote regions consider a theatrical event worthy of a pilgrimage. Members of the Montana Shakespeare in the Parks company bring their performances to remote areas around the state and are housed by local families. Featured here is a performance of *Tartuffe* in Poker Jim Butte, Montana. The audience travels a long distance to partake of this cultural event.

The **Critical** Response

Many have argued that criticism is unnecessary, that a creative work speaks to its audience on its own terms, without the need for further reflection or discussion. This is true up to a point. The theatre does take place between actor and audience in the moment of performance, but as an ephemeral art it lives on only in memory, and how we shape our memory is part of the event's life. The audience's and critic's reception determines how we will think about a particular theatrical experience. As a public act, the theatre has always invited and received critical response, so wherever we find vibrant theatrical traditions, we also find critical engagement.

How we analyze a production and what perspective we take in our scrutiny says a lot about what our culture finds interesting or valuable. Perhaps you have already experienced this while watching an old movie. The values and mores expressed in the film might seem comical today. You will also notice that acting styles have changed. Because theatre has a much longer history than film, these changes in critical perspective over time are even greater. For example, the psychoanalyst Sigmund Freud (1856-1939) found the subject matter of neurosis in ancient Greek tragedy, but no playwright in the fifth century B.C.E. could have understood such an interpretation almost 2,500 years before psychology was a science.

> **Only 50 years ago, on film and in the theatre, we would not have been shocked to see all the African Americans in servant roles. Today this would feel reactionary, if not racist, and would affect our critical response.**

Can we impose new cultural assumptions on a work of art? Shouldn't we try to approach a Greek tragedy as if we were ancient Greeks in order to truly understand it? No matter how hard we try, we cannot completely reconstruct the ancient Greek worldview, or become a member of a 2,500-year-old society, or imagine that we are at the theatre

◀ In *The Real Inspector Hound*, playwright Tom Stoppard makes mock of critical distance by creating two characters who are critics and placing them in the audience at the start of the play. Over the course of the play, he allows the audience members to hear their running commentary and critical jargon.

in Athens in the fifth century B.C.E. If you are a woman, you might not have even been permitted to attend. If you are not Greek, you might have been a slave. Once we confront the insurmountable cultural gaps between our era and eras past, we are left with the realization that the best we can do is to find the interpretations that are valid for our own times, constructing meaning through contemporary values and tastes and using the methods of analysis we esteem. We use our knowledge of history to help formulate a contemporary interpretation.

Professional Criticism and Cultural Theory

Every society develops its own theatrical theories. These theories reflect the biases and interests of its culture and become the tools of criticism. For centuries, Aristotle's ideas framed most European and American theatrical analysis; he minimized the importance of certain genres, such as comedy, and reflected the sexual and cultural biases of his time. Today, in our pluralistic society, we find a multitude of critical lenses through which to analyze a performance. Marxist theory, feminist theory, psychoanalytic theory, gender theory, race theory, and structuralism are just a few of the many methods applied to critical analysis in the past 50 years. Some fall out of favor, while others gain credence, reflecting our society's changing values. Today, the lens through which the critic chooses to view the theatre offers us a gauge of the critic's interests and viewpoint as well as a means of understanding a work of art. It follows that critics are never completely objective. They hold their biases like other members of the audience.

Cultural Insiders

Theatre that emerges from a particular ethnic or social community often benefits from critical discussion that grows out of the community itself. In the United States, theatre produced by members of minority groups has often been the subject of critics who share the artists' experiences of marginalization. Such critics can both introduce such work to outsiders and broaden critical perspectives within the community itself. These writers are not outside observers; they form critiques from a position of alliance and understanding and are partners in formulating new theatrical models that respond directly to their community's unique social and artistic needs. Gay and lesbian critics such as David Savran and Jill Dolan have provided techniques for understanding the presentation of gender and sexuality on stage. Jorge Huerta has explained the myths and values embedded in Latino drama, and Errol G. Hill, James V. Hatch, and Harry Elam have placed African American theatre in historical context. Today, more and more critics are emerging from the cultures that are the subject of their examination.

The Many Faces of the Critic

WHAT different forms does criticism take, and how does criticism affect the theatre?

Like light flooding into a dark room, good criticism defines and clarifies. Although some critics explain new and innovative theatre work and help the audience appreciate it, not all criticism comes after the creative act. Some artists are themselves critics, and others find artistic inspiration in critical writing. Criticism has even been presented in artistic form, and some theatre pieces could themselves be considered acts of criticism. While some criticism is descriptive, some is prescriptive, or even visionary, pointing the way toward new theatrical invention. Partnerships in which critics and artists enrich each other's work are common. If a Broadway-bound play has an "out of town" run, the local critics may influence the rewriting process. Criticism need not be just a final judgment; it can also bring thoughtful engagement with an artistic work throughout the creative process.

The Critic as Interpreter

Critics serve as interpreters of theatrical events by providing a framework for comprehension. This may simply consist of explaining the historical context of a play or, for an experimental or particularly difficult piece of theatre, a critic may need to discover what new point of view or style is being expressed and explain it to audiences.

Martin Esslin (1918–2002) presents a good example of this kind of criticism. During the 1950s, Samuel Beckett, Jean Genet, and Eugène Ionesco wrote plays that were unlike anything people had come to expect in the theatre. They lacked clear story lines, recognizable plots, or psychologically rich characters, and dialogue often broke down into nonsense. Audiences were confused and even angry at these plays. Esslin understood that these plays reflected the sense of alienation and meaninglessness of a generation that had lived through the horrific events of World War II, and he coined the term **theatre of the absurd** in his book by that name. His analysis of these new plays made them comprehensible to a large audience, and today, plays of the theatre of the absurd are classics in the theatrical repertoire. Esslin, the critic, clarified a new world of theatrical experience for generations to come.

The **Critic** as Artistic Muse

Criticism is often the inspiration for artistic creation and directly influences new theatrical styles or the rediscovery of old texts or dramatic forms. The critic Jan Kott (1914–2001) had this effect on some of the most innovative directors of his time. His 1961 book *Shakespeare Our Contemporary* demonstrated how Shakespeare's plays can be reinterpreted to speak to modern sensibilities. Having lived through both the Nazi and Stalinist occupations of his native Poland, Kott discovered in Shakespeare's dark Elizabethan world direct parallels to his own experiences that illuminated hidden meaning in the play texts. Peter Brook's staging of King Lear as the modern alienated man rather than an archetypal Elizabethan was directly inspired by a Kott essay that linked Samuel Beckett's play *Endgame* and its alienated characters to a way of thinking about Shakespeare. Many of the thousands of reimagined Shakespeare productions since the 1960s can be traced back to Kott's inspirational book.

Boston theatre critic Elliott Norton (1903–2003) was known for writing reviews that gave playwrights new ideas. Neil Simon rewrote the ending to *The Odd Couple* (1965) based on a suggestion of Norton's during the play's out-of-town run.

The **Critic** as Visionary

Some critics can be as passionate about transforming the theatrical world and propelling it in new, unexplored directions as those who make theatre. Antonin Artaud's (1896–1948) collection of essays *The Theatre and Its Double* became the theatre bible for the avant-garde 20 years after his death. He outlined a new kind of theatre, which, like a plague or a similar moment of crisis, pushed people to an extreme confrontation with their own existence. Artaud called for a **theatre of cruelty**—a dynamic and poetic world of images, sounds, and movement—and sought a universal language that could assault the senses of the audience, opening up new levels of awareness. He advocated a shared performance space for audience and actors. Artaud inspired many great artists of the 1960s. Jean-Louis Barrault in

▼ In this modern dress version of Shakespeare's *Pericles, Prince of Tyre* at the Globe Theatre in London in 2005, the influence of Jan Kott's pioneering 1961 critical writing can still be felt.

The Internet has offered the opportunity for the average audience member to express opinions about theatre productions in a public outlet where they can reach a vast readership once available only to professional critics in newspapers, magazines, and journals. This democratization of criticism has both broadened the dialogue about theatre performances and lowered the level of discourse. When the well informed and the uninformed may use the same outlets to express their points of view, how can an audience member judge the value of what is being said?

The Web does provide information in a timely manner, while events are still happening, and the nominal cost of posting and reading reviews permits more information to be quickly disseminated to a wide audience. Unfortunately, the easy access also invites people with personal agendas and no knowledge of theatre to post reviews on blogs. The site StageGrade.com, which offers both professional reviews from New York theatre critics as well as posts from the general community, also has direct links to Telecharge.com, an online ticket purchasing site. This raises the possibility that online criticism could eventually be tainted by commercial interests.

Once a bad review in the New York Times could make or break a theatre production, but internet publicity and "word of mouth" is providing a formidable challenge. We now see shows that received pans from the mainstream press continuing to play to full houses. Playwright A.R. Gurney wonders whether the wide range of opinions available on the Web may lead to a time "when a few reviewers in print no longer determine the future of a play or musical."

With the demise of more and more print outlets for reviews and criticism, it is clear that increasingly the Web is the source to which theatre-goers turn for evaluation of theatre productions and to guide them in their ticket purchases. How much of what they read will be serious and thoughtful criticism remains to be seen.

> "The Web teems with on-line journals, blogs and other sites that claim to serve a true critical function, providing objective, expert opinion about new theater productions, films, art shows, and more, but upon close inspection most turn out to be ill-informed, sloppily edited or compromised by a veil of anonymity."
>
> —Jonathan Kalb, Professor of Theatre at Hunter College and editor of HotReview.org

France, Jerzy Grotowski in Poland, Peter Brook in England, and a host of American theatre companies, such as The Living Theatre, created impressive performances drawing on Artaud's critical writings.

The **Artist** as Critic

Artists sometimes take on the role of critic as they try to explain their artistic intentions or gain a following. In the early twentieth century, practitioners in the movements of realism, symbolism, expressionism, and futurism wrote manifestos describing their hopes for new directions in the theatre, while their productions tried to realize the goals they set in their writings. Bertolt Brecht—prolific playwright, poet, and director—also wrote volumes of criticism and theory about his epic theatre, which he contrasted to Aristotle's model of tragedy. While many people believe that Brecht's critical writings do not accurately portray what he achieved in his remarkable productions, his essays connect his novel methods of playwriting, directing, acting, and design to the political philosophy behind them and provide us with insight into his artistic process. Playwright Arthur Miller (1915–2005) wrote essays about the theatre and defended his concept of the "common man" as the subject of tragedy. In fact, many playwrights have attempted to frame their work through critical writing.

Actors and directors have also ventured into the domain of criticism, especially when their work is innovative and needs explication. French director André Antoine explained the idea of the fourth wall in realism. Constantin Stanislavski, who transformed actor training and about whom you will read in Chapter 7, wrote three volumes on his theories of acting.

THINK

Do theatre artists need to read criticism?

The practice of artists writing criticism can be found in other periods and cultures as well. Zeami Motokiyo

 THE REGARD EVENING offered actor Bill Irwin a chance to poke fun at theatrical conventions and postmodernism as a clown critic on stage.

> "An actor demonstrates what an **excellent** actress she is when she plays a character **different** from her own type. So strive to grasp the **nature** of the roles you play, and to transform **yourself** so you are what you **pretend** to be."
>
> —Molière, *The Versailles Impromptu*

(c. 1363–c. 1443) wrote treatises on the Japanese *noh* theatre to pass on the secrets of performance to future generations. He spoke from the points of view of both an actor and a playwright and captured the importance of crafting characters through the text.

> **THINK**
>
> Is it important for creative artists to understand their own work within the larger cultural and historical context that critical and scholarly writing can give?

Criticism from the **Stage**

Playwrights have often used the stage to speak critically about the theatre of their times. Seventeenth-century French playwright Molière (1622–1673) used his short play *The Critique of the School for Wives* to answer the critics of one his earlier works, *The School for Wives*, and then he wrote *The Versailles Impromptu* to stage a mock rehearsal with commentary on acting by the character Molière. Many have pointed to Hamlet's speech to the players, telling them how to act, as Shakespeare's criticism of the flamboyant acting style of his day. In 1966 German playwright Peter Handke wrote *Offending the Audience*, which makes a mockery of the conventions of audience behavior. These and many other theatrical works reveal the power of the artist, using the performance medium for critical commentary. It can be argued that many revolutionary stagings by avant-garde directors are implicit criticism of the old styles they are rejecting.

The **Audience** as Critic

Every theatrical production—whether it be in the smallest community theatre, an ancient traditional performance, a Broadway mega-production, or a college show—begins with a daring leap of faith that an empty space can be transformed into a place of magic and illusion in the enactment of an artistic vision. Like every act of faith, theatre has risks; it is a public event and subject to public reaction from the general audience and from the critics who help shape the public's perception of a theatrical production.

You will probably be asked at some point in your introductory theatre class to transform from an audience member to a critic—to go to the theatre and write about your experience. Knowing that you will have to be very precise in your description of the show will probably force you to watch it with greater attention than usual. This assignment can heighten your awareness of the many disparate elements that come together to create a theatrical piece and give you insight into how they work together successfully or unsuccessfully. This may intensify the experience, and it will also make you more aware of the critic's process.

Attendance at the theatre is demanding, and it is also rewarding. As an audience member, you have the power to express your response and have your presence felt and acknowledged by the artists. This is the special thrill of being in a theatre audience. Some theatre pieces may affect you deeply and cause you to undergo a transformation that may affect your life. Opening yourself to new theatrical experiences and what they proffer is the true challenge and pleasure of being a member of a theatre audience.

The Reviewer

Most of us are familiar with **reviews**—brief immediate responses to theatrical events that appear in print in a newspaper, magazine, or blog or in a television or radio segment. A review is different from the criticism that is published in scholarly journals or books, which may take a more sophisticated or intellectual approach. Some distinguish between the two types of authors, calling one a *reviewer* and the second a *critic*, but others use the terms interchangeably. The essential differences between these two types of criticism are the amount of time the authors have to digest what they've seen, how much depth of analysis they apply, how much space they have to express themselves, and the intended audience for their ideas.

Because reviewers serve as guides to the theatre marketplace, they can influence the financial success of a production. Reviewers who write for influential newspapers such as the *New York Times* can make or break a show. A single bad review can seriously damage ticket sales, whereas a good one can bring crowds in from across the country. The reviewer can give valuable publicity that keeps a show going for years, or can destroy the months of efforts of a creative team with a few strokes of the pen. This results in an inevitable tension between reviewers and artists. Because the number of important newspapers has so greatly diminished, a few well-placed reviewers can determine the public's theatre-going practices and choices and inhibit a new or unusual production from finding its own audience.

A review reflects the reviewer's subjective experience and knowledge. Often, different reviews of the same play will express very different perspectives on the work. Frequent theatre-goers learn which reviewers have similar tastes to their own and whose opinions they can trust. Even when reviewers agree about a piece, their reviews may not reflect an audience's opinion. Most reviewers panned the Broadway musical hit *Cats!*, but audiences all over the world loved it and kept it running for years.

Reviewers need to be extremely observant audience members, noting all the details of a performance. Professional reviewers get press packets when they come to a show. These may include previous reviews of the show, background information on the artists, notes from the director or dramaturg, and other relevant material to inform their judgments. Almost all professional reviewers make notes about the elements of production during the course of the show. Theatre reviewers need to be educated about the theatre to write with accuracy and understanding. Not only do they need a thorough knowledge of theatre history, dramatic literature, and theatre criticism, they must also know about acting, directing, and design elements in order to discuss these contributions intelligently. Unfortunately, many reviewers have little theatre training or knowledge, and even prominent newspapers hire theatre reviewers who are untrained in the field.

Newspaper reviewers generally get free tickets and may go to the theatre three or four times a week, sometimes more, especially if they attend a theatre festival where they might see several shows in a single day. Professional critics might see more than 200 productions a year. This familiarity with the theatrical world allows them to make informed judgments and comparisons between different productions. By knowing what the theatre can do, they are more conscious of where it may have failed to hit its mark.

STANLEY KAUFFMANN

ARTISTS IN THEIR OWN WORDS

Stanley Kauffmann's critical writings have earned him international recognition. During the 1960s, he was a theatre critic for Public Broadcasting in New York, and in 1966, he was a theatre critic for the New York Times. *From 1969 to 1979, Kauffmann was the theatre and film critic for the* New Republic, *and he was the theatre critic for the* Saturday Review *from 1979 to 1985.*

Does the theatre need critics?
Yes, but the theatre doesn't want them—not serious critics, anyway. Theatre people usually think of criticism as a gauntlet that a new production must run, and of course they dislike any response that threatens the various sorts of investment that a production entails. But to a critic, the theatre needs perceptive and empathic comment for its own sake, as well as an audience service. I have heard theatre people complain, in New York and in cities with resident companies, that the lack of respectable criticism makes them feel that they are working in the middle of the Sahara. In any case, the theatre needs good criticism in ways that every art needs it: as informed response, as esthetic-intellectual ambience, and, in the long run, as history.

What do you feel is your most important contribution to the theatre in your career as a critic?
Practically, I think my only contribution was the pioneering I did against the silly pattern of opening-night reviews—rushing from the theatre, banging out a review. Thematically, my chief contribution,

(continued from page 43)

I'd say, was in the matter of homosexual playwrights. In 1966 I wrote two Sunday articles in the *Times* attacking social pressures that at that time prevented gay playwrights from writing frankly about homosexuality. Proscriptions then were still so stiff in this matter that I couldn't even mention the names of the three playwrights who had prompted the piece—Williams, Albee, and Inge. The two articles caused an uproar. (Echoes of it still persist.) Within five years or so, the atmosphere around this subject changed drastically, on the way to present-day liberalism, and I take some pride in believing that I contributed a bit to the change.

Source: Copyright 2006 by Stanley Kauffmann.

THINK

Does theatre need criticism?

THINK

Is an uninformed critical evaluation by a novice theatre-goer of value?

ALISA SOLOMON

ARTISTS IN THEIR OWN WORDS

Alisa Solomon (b. 1956) has combined careers in journalism, criticism, and scholarship. For more than 20 years, she has written dramatic criticism for New York's Village Voice. *Among her many writings, her book* Re-Dressing the Canon: Essays on Theater and Gender *won the George Jean Nathan Award for Dramatic Criticism. Professor Solomon also directs the Arts & Culture concentration in the master's program at the Journalism School at Columbia University.*

What do you think is the primary role of a theatre critic who writes for a newspaper?

Newspaper critics serve several simultaneous functions. Certainly there are some readers who look at reviews merely as consumer reports. They want to know: What's this play like? Would it interest me? How long is it? Is it worth my $25 (or $125)? Meanwhile, reviews often come to constitute the historical record of a production—the materials scholars pore over even only a few years after the fact to piece together a theatrical experience and its public reception. A newspaper review ought to provide a vivid description of the experience (not just of the plot) and provide information and interpretation that allow readers to decide whether the work sounds worth their while and their cash. However, to my mind, a review that seeks to address only such questions is not only incomplete but destructive (even when it is favorable toward the work in question), for it encourages a simple-minded, thumbs-up/thumbs-down way of engaging the theatre, and, by extension, the world.

> "The theatre needs critics because the world needs critics. Reviews (good ones, anyway) participate in and foster public discussion that values analysis, context, nuance, and reasoned argument. Public discourse on every level needs these qualities."
>
> —Alisa Solomon

A critic has a larger responsibility: to contribute to and cultivate intelligent analytical discourse about theatre specifically, and, more generally, about our culture and our world. . . . I believe the theatre is a place where the public practices and sharpens their critical attitude; reviews ought to participate in that process. Critics can go a long way toward doing so not by setting out to pronounce whether a work is any good but by seeking to discuss what a work means, how it means what it means, where and when it is conveying that meaning (its context), and why.

Your scholarly work addresses feminist concerns. What is the effect of that interest on your work as a theatre critic, and how do you feel it affects your readers?

Feminism is itself a critical attitude that enables one to see how meanings are constructed and to what ends: This is a useful practice for a theatre critic. Women aren't the only ones who can bring a corrective view into the conversation—and not all women would do so. I'm more comfortable saying that *feminists*, rather than *women*, have a special responsibility to unpack the tacit assumptions about gender that are expressed in plays (and in criticism) as part of their overall meaning. At the same time, I think we need to be careful not to fall into the trap of simply becoming cheerleaders for playwrights or directors who are women. I agree with George Bernard Shaw, who said that loyalty in a critic is corruption.

Source: Used with permission from Alisa Solomon.

Summary

WHY is the actor–audience interaction the most essential component of the theatre? p. 22

▶ The immediate interaction between actor and audience is one of the special thrills of live performance.

HOW does an audience form a community? p. 22

▶ The presence and participation of an audience reflects the theatre's communal roots in ritual. When you join an audience, you become part of a unique temporary community.

HOW do our personal histories influence how we react as audience members? p. 24

▶ Audience members respond to the theatre as individuals influenced by their own personal histories.

▶ Ethnicity, religion, race, class, or gender can divide or unite an audience.

▶ Unlike film audiences, theatre audiences choose their focus. Where they choose to focus will affect their interpretation of a performance.

HOW does the actor–audience relationship vary in different places, societies, eras, events, and venues? p. 26

▶ Conventions of audience response may be inherited through tradition or set up by a director and can vary from place to place, throughout history, and even from one production to another.

▶ Aesthetic distance is the ability to observe a work of art with a degree of detachment and objectivity. Artists manipulate aesthetic distance by changing theatrical conventions.

WHAT is the history of political theatre, and what is its role today? p. 31

▶ Political theatre places special demands on its audience, challenging and confronting beliefs to spur audience members to real action. Strategies for audience activation are adapted to specific circumstances and political goals.

▶ Playwrights in ancient Greece first used the theatre for political commentary.

▶ In the early twentieth century, political theatre aimed at activating audiences for social change in the real world took root.

WHAT kinds of challenges does theatre pose to its audience? p. 36

▶ Theatre challenges the imagination, intellect, emotions, and sometimes stamina of audience members.

HOW does understanding a critic's or a culture's values inform critical analysis of theatre? p. 38

▶ All theatre provokes both emotional and critical responses.

▶ Theatre criticism reflects its time and culture. Critics are not objective but have their own biases and interests.

▶ Today criticism offers a multitude of critical lenses through which to analyze performance.

WHAT are the different forms that criticism can take, and how does criticism affect the theatre? p. 39

▶ Good criticism can help interpret a theatrical event by aiding comprehension, or it can inspire artistic creation and influence new theatrical styles

▶ Artists may become critics, and theatrical works can themselves critique the theatre.

MySearchLab®

Understanding Plays

Storytelling and Cultural Tradition

We define our culture and ourselves by the stories we tell about ourselves. Others define us by the stories they tell about us. Through stories we create our histories and transmit to others the lessons we have learned. There are many ways of telling stories in the theatre, and these are determined by culture and convention. Even the language we speak may shape how we view the world and our relationship to others, as well as how we narrate our lives. Western tradition usually thinks of a play as telling a story through a progression of related events across linear time. Other cultures build stories out of a sense of cosmic time and sacred space in which all events evoke the past and the future, as in the Australian aboriginal tradition, which traces the interrelatedness of the sacred, physical, and human worlds to *dreamtime* when the world took shape. Some cultures focus on the role of an individual in triggering events; others focus on the role of the community or the ancestral spirits in forwarding the dramatic action. Today many of us experience the world as a barrage of simultaneously occurring sensory events and seek a form that can capture the multiplicity of experience. Many recent plays present the sounds and images of this fragmented reality.

Whatever the nature of the story, the challenge for the playwright is to find a form through which the events of the story can materialize in the theatre and speak to the audience. The playwright must always keep in mind the performability of the text. The artistic value of a play lies in its capacity to be imagined and reimagined on stage; the true test of a play is performance. No writer for the theatre ever intends the reading of the dramatic text as an end goal. A play's ability to inspire new performance concepts is key to its longevity on the stage. All playwrights create in the hope of seeing their work realized in a performance before an audience. Because of this, reading a play is not like reading a novel or short story, where reading completes the intended communication.

As a reader of a play, you are challenged to create the performance in your mind's eye by playing the roles of designer, director, and actor in your imagination. You must envision the setting, the theatre space, the kind of stage, the mood created by the colors of the lights, and the style of the performance. You must imagine what the characters will look like—their costumes and movement. Each choice you make defines what the play will mean to you. Everything you learn about the theatre will contribute to the power of your dramatic imagination.

1. What is the predominant feature of Western storytelling? How does it differ from storytelling in other cultures?

2. What do we mean when we say performance is the true test of a play?

3. How does the experience of reading a play differ from seeing it performed?

CHAPTER 03

The **Western Play** Tradition

HOW do cultural values influence the dramatic form a playwright chooses?

Europe has the longest theatrical tradition based on the written play. We possess a body of dramatic literature in the European tradition that dates back to the fifth century B.C.E. While non-literary performance has always existed in the West, it has traditionally been valued as secondary to the written text. Plays also exist in performance traditions, but they use different forms and structures and are accompanied by elaborate systems of gestures, mime, music, and dance that are seen as equally important as—and often more important than—the written word.

We may decry the way the European tradition was imposed on former colonies, but important plays inspired by European genres and structures can now be found the world over. In this chapter, we focus on the written play text and discuss the most common conventions of playwriting in the Western tradition. How the playwright constructs dramatic action, character, and language to tell a story is as much an expression of culture and convention as the story itself.

THINK

If telling stories is a way of expressing culture and identity, do only some people have the right to tell certain stories by virtue of their cultural heritage or gender?

Story and **Plot**

HOW do playwrights use the plot to create dramatic tension in a play?

The **story** of a play includes all the events that happen or are mentioned in the text. A play's story may include many incidents that have taken place before the play begins. In Sophocles' play *Oedipus Tyrannus* (c. 430–425 B.C.E.) in which King Oedipus discovers that he murdered his own father and married his mother, the crimes of patricide and incest that lead to his downfall have taken place many years before the events of the play itself. A play's story may include many things that do not actually occur on stage that are only spoken about. In ancient Greek tragedy, for instance, it is a theatrical convention that violent events always take place off stage. Spectators never see these graphic scenes but only see their aftermath or hear about them through the reports of a messenger. Although they don't happen on stage, these events are essential to the story.

The **plot** of a play is the ordering or structuring of the events that actually take place on stage. The plot defines *how* the events unfold for the reader or viewer. Playwrights use the plot to create dramatic tension, usually through developing **conflict** and creating struggles and obstacles for the characters to overcome. Characters define themselves through the choices they make to win this central conflict. In the modern era, many plays refocused the struggle on forces inside the character, creating dramatic tension through a progression of increasingly intense emotional states. Plots are constructed to have the **maximum** emotional impact on the audience.

Authors can tell the same story through different plots to focus on particular ideas or themes. Where an author chooses to begin a story, from whose perspective it is told, what events occur on stage, or which characters

Different Cultures and Different Ways of Using Language

Different cultures sometimes use language in very different ways. Guy Deutscher is an honorary research fellow at the School of Languages, Linguistics and Cultures at the University of Manchester in the United Kingdom. A *New York Times* article adapted from his book *Through the Language Glass: Why the World Looks Different in Other Languages* (2010) informs us that " . . . a remote Australian aboriginal tongue, Guugu Yimithirr, turned up, and with it came the astounding realization that not all languages conform to what we have always taken as simply 'natural.' . . . Guugu Yimithirr does not use words like "left' or 'right,' 'in front of' or 'behind,' to describe the position of objects. . . . The Guugu Yimithirr rely on cardinal directions. If they want you to move over on the car seat to make room, they'll say 'move a bit to the east.' To tell you where exactly they left something in your house, they'll say, 'I left it on the southern edge of the western table.' Or they would warn you to 'look out for that big ant just north of your foot.'"

or facts a playwright includes or highlights all make one telling different from another. You may have listened to someone telling a story of a shared experience and noticed that the person didn't tell it the way you would. You may even have interrupted to add information you considered vital that the other person left out. How a story is told reflects what the storyteller values. The "how" of storytelling is as important as the tale itself and reflects the identity and perspective of the storyteller. A good storyteller will capture our attention even if we already know what is to come. The ancient Greek tragic poets drew from legend and history that were well known to their audiences, so they were judged by how well they told familiar tales.

HIDDEN HISTORY

An Ancient Art Forms the Foundation for a Cultural Bridge

This production of *Samritechak*, a Cambodian classical dance-drama based on Shakespeare's *Othello*, was choreographed by Sophiline Cheam Shapiro, who was among the first to train in classical Cambodian Dance at the School of Fine Arts (now the Royal University of Fine Arts) after Pol Pot's brutal regime left only one in ten dancers alive to carry on this tradition. Shapiro now lives in California, and her position between cultures enabled her to retell Othello using the classical dance vocabulary, expanding the reach of the ancient art. The play's theme of taking responsibility for one's actions has deep meaning in her homeland.

▲ The dancers shown here wear the traditional ornate costumes and masks of the *lakhon khol* masked dance-drama. The upward curve of the fingertips is typical of this form's elegant gestures.

Kayte Deioma

A New Twist on an Old Plot

It is not unusual today to see playwrights from disempowered groups reclaiming their own stories. Playwrights may take classical texts and explore them from some unusual perspective that can reveal the point of view of a character who was disenfranchised in the original version. David Henry Hwang's (b. 1957) *M Butterfly* (1986) twisted the plot of Puccini's opera *Madame Butterfly* (1904). In Puccini's original opera, Butterfly (Cio-cio San), is betrayed in love by an American naval officer for whom she has sacrificed all. In the Hwang play, an Asian "actress" who is really a man, hides his gender and victimizes a French diplomat, Gallimard, upsetting our stereotypes of the "submissive Oriental." The two stories are conflated through the use of famous music from the opera and Gallimard's donning of Butterfly's traditional costume at the end of the play. Hwang's play not only reflects on the racist values embedded in cultural myths, his replotting of *Madame Butterfly* also asserts an Asian American understanding of Asian identity.

▶ John Lithgow, as the French diplomat Rene Gallimard, admires the Chinese opera star, Song Liling, whom he believes to be the ideal Asian woman.

Playwrights in different eras may pick up the same subject matter and turn it on end by changing the plot. Both Euripides' fifth-century-B.C.E. play *Hippolytus* and Jean Racine's (1639–1699) seventeenth-century play *Phèdre* tell the story of Phaedra's incestuous love for her stepson Hippolytus. The two playwrights chose to focus on different characters, as evidenced in their titles, which alters the audience's perspective on the events. Euripides' Hippolytus is a haughty, prudish young man who rejects love, marriage, and passion and is the favorite of the virgin goddess Artemis. Aphrodite, the goddess of love, punishes him for his allegiance to the chaste Artemis by afflicting Phaedra with the passion that will drive them both to their doom. Racine's version has no gods and focuses instead on the destructive force of Phaedra's unbridled passion, putting her at the

Aeschylus (c. 523–456 B.C.E.), *Sophocles* (c. 496–406 B.C.E.), and *Euripides* (c. 480–406 B.C.E.) **each wrote about the murder of the Greek queen** *Clytemnestra* **by her children, yet each tells the story in a completely different way, focusing on different characters and offering different accounts of their** *motivations* **and moral** *responsibility*.

Tina Howe (b. 1937) is the author of plays such as Museum, The Art of Dining, *and* Pride's Crossing *that put center stage the primary personal concerns of women— motherhood, marriage, and menopause— celebrating the courage with which women confront the crises of their daily lives. Howe's style moves the family drama beyond real- ism, where the dark hidden side of everyday relationships can be explored.*

"We're ladies after all! Look at the restrooms theaters give us. The line stretches for miles because there are only three stalls! Backstage and on stage we deserve more room to take care of our business."

—Tina Howe, playwright

Are there special concerns for women playwrights?

Sure, we're praised for our plays about women as victims—plays that show us at the mercy of disease, abuse, and self-doubt. But how much of our work is produced that celebrates strong women? Sexy and canny women? Daugh- ters, sisters, wives, and mothers who

move mountains, not just dust rags? . . . there's nothing I enjoy more than show- ing a household under siege and watch- ing the women transform—grow antlers, fins, and wings as they seek, and ulti- mately gain, salvation. These plays . . . deal with panic, not nostalgia—how a mother reacts to her four-year-old child who's

played by a large, hairy man, the stages of delirium a wife goes through as her house sinks further and further into the ground, or a woman struggling to avoid eviction due to her husband's obsessive hoarding . . . if we shimmy out of our traces, we're labeled "sentimental," "undisciplined," or worse.

center of the drama. In 1924 Eugene O'Neill (1888–1953) wrote an updated version of the tale in *Desire Under the Elms*, in which he explored repression and desire through the lens of Freudian psychology.

Today we are aware that in past eras, some people were excluded from the storytelling process in the theatre, while others told their tales. Women's voices were rarely heard until the modern era. For example, the ancient Phaedra plays are about a woman's passion, but all were written by men. Indigenous people and racial and ethnic minorities

had few opportunities to express their own narratives on the Western stage. Through multiculturalism and intercultural- ism we have begun to appreciate the diverse stories told by people of different genders, races, ethnicities, classes, cultures, and sexual orientations and the many ways they shape their tales in the theatre. Today we are sensitive to the many perspectives people bring to the telling of a story. Understanding how the playwright uses the plot to empha- size particular themes provides audiences and readers with a tool for analyzing a play.

Dramatic Structure

HOW do different types of dramatic structure help to convey a play's meaning?

Dramatic structure is the scaffolding on which a playwright plots a tale to frame or shape the action. Different dramatic structures become conventions of playwriting in differ- ent times and places. When playwrights have new ideas to convey, they may create new dramatic frames to help

express them. If enough artists follow this new structure, it too becomes a convention. The choice of dramatic struc- ture strongly influences the impact of a play and can help convey a play's meaning as expressively as its characters or its dialogue.

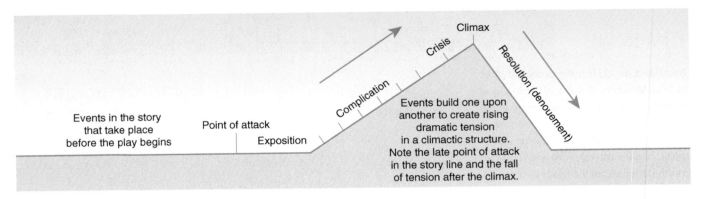

Dramatic structure describes the scope and progression of the action. Some plays cover a wide scope of time and a large number of characters and events, while others are more tightly circumscribed. Some plays evolve in a linear fashion so that one action leads inevitably to the next, whereas others may move back and forth between different locations, plots, characters, time periods, and levels of reality, such as dreams and fantasies. Each play has its own structure, but the few basic structural models outlined in the following sections reflect traditions that have prevailed over time. It is important to remember that how a play does *not* fit into one of these models is often as significant as the ways it does.

Climactic Structure

A play with a **climactic structure** has a tight-knit form that limits the scope of events, the time in which they transpire, and the number of characters. Because the Greek philosopher Aristotle was the first to describe this structure in his famous essay on dramatic criticism, the *Poetics*, climactic structure is sometimes referred to as an **Aristotelian plot**. Aristotle's ideas have been so influential in Western theatre

that plays that deviate from his descriptions of plot are often called "non-Aristotelian."

In climactic structure, the **point of attack**, the place in the story where the action begins, is usually late in the story. **Exposition** is the part of the play where events that occurred before the start of the play are revealed, sometimes through devices such as a confidant **soliloquy** or **monologue** that enable a character to voice all the necessary information to set up the plot. Circumstances build on each other through cause and effect, causing **complication** of the dramatic situation leading toward a **climax**—the point of highest emotional intensity—followed by a final resolution. We usually use the French word **denouement**, which translates as "unknotting," to refer to the resolution.

When the plot cannot easily resolve itself, playwrights often use a convention called a ***deus ex machina***—literally, "a god from the machine"—to resolve the drama. In ancient Greece, plays literally had god figures lowered from a crane who put an ending on a play. Today the term *deus ex machina* refers to any dramatic device, outside the main action, used to bring the play to a final resolution.

Aristotle

The ancient Greek philosopher Aristotle (384–322 B.C.E.) was the first person to devise a method of dramatic analysis. In his essay on literary criticism, the *Poetics* (350 B.C.E.), Aristotle lays out a system for critiquing Greek tragedy, which he considered a branch of poetry, along with comedy, epic poetry, and lyric poetry. Aristotle broke tragedy into six elements: plot, character, language or diction, ideas, music, and spectacle. For Aristotle, plot was the most important element, followed by character, which he saw as being defined by the dramatic action.

Language addressed the quality of the words chosen by the poet. Music referred both to the sounds of the words and the accompanying music of Greek tragedy. Spectacle, the element he associated with the emotional effect of a play achieved through its staging, was the least important, lying outside the realm of poetry. Aristotle spends most of the *Poetics* on the elements of plot, character, and language, saying relatively little about elements of performance.

Aristotle's writings became the foundation of European theatrical

criticism, and his prioritizing of elements was the dominant mode of writing and thinking about the theatre for two millennia. The twentieth century saw a revision of these assumptions. Theatre critics now consider performance elements as integral to the total theatrical experience as the written play. Free from Aristotle's prejudices, Western scholars can study performance traditions not rooted in a written text without bias. Explorations of new forms of plays that challenge Aristotle's precepts are common today.

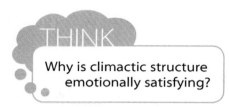

THINK

Why is climactic structure emotionally satisfying?

THINK

Can you think of a time when your emotions were manipulated by a play, movie, or TV show that employed a well-made play structure?

HIDDEN HISTORY

The Well-made Play or "Tune in Next Week"

In the nineteenth century, Frenchmen Augustin-Eugène Scribe (1791–1861) and Victorien Sardou (1831–1908) wrote for the popular Boulevard Theatre. To keep their audiences coming back, they created a variation of Aristotelian structure known today as the **well-made play**, which became a formula for producing one successful script after another. This dramatic structure is in reality no more "well made" than any other, and the plays of Scribe and Sardou have not withstood the test of time. The formula they created, however, is still the basis for many popular entertainment forms. You will probably recognize it in the plots of familiar movies and television shows.

The well-made play keeps spectators on the edge of their seats by continually introducing new obstacles and complications. The opening scenes often include **foreshadowing**—hints about events to come that set the audience up. Once the stage is set, the play introduces an **inciting incident**, an event that sets the action into motion. An inciting incident is like a bomb with a lit fuse that keeps the audience watching to see if and when it will explode. The characters work vigorously to keep the real or metaphorical explosion from taking place, driving the action forward. Just when a character believes she has prevailed, another bomb goes off, and this pattern is repeated throughout the course of the play to keep the action moving and building. A serious incident usually occurs at the end of an act so that the audience is impatient during intermission to find out how this last twist of fate will

be resolved. In nineteenth-century melodrama, audiences anticipated the resolution of what was literally a **cliffhanger**. An act might end with someone hanging off a cliff in actual physical peril. Today we use this term to refer to anything that keeps the audience guessing about the outcome during a break. Television borrows these theatre conventions by placing cliffhangers before commercials or at the end of an episode or season to entice viewers to tune in to the following installment.

The action comes to a head in a **crisis**, after which all elements must be resolved once and for all. The resolution comes in what is called the "obligatory scene." In this scene, all questions are answered, all mysteries solved, and all outcomes revealed.

We can recognize this type of scene in the common conclusion of many murder mysteries, when at the end all the characters gather together to hear the detective reveal who the murderer is and how the crime was committed. The well-made play has been a formula for an endless stream of popular and entertaining plays since the nineteenth century.

▼ Television drama borrowed the cliffhanger from the conventions of the well-made play to sustain audience interest and ensure that they "tune in next week." Seen here is a cliffhanger from the popular television show *Lost*.

In the hands of Norwegian playwright Henrik Ibsen (1828–1906), the well-made play became a form capable of addressing the most pressing social issues of the era. Ibsen helped to establish theatrical realism through a series of controversial plays exposing social ills. Ibsen's dramas focused on venereal disease, infidelity, failed marriages, corrupt business practices, and other topics not thought to be appropriate subject matter for the public stage. Ibsen was among the first playwrights to employ **naturalism**. He created a "realistic" stage by doing away with devices such as direct address to the audience and poetic soliloquies and by creating fully developed characters whose actions are motivated by heredity, environment, and internal psychology.

In *A Doll's House* (1879), Ibsen introduces the audience to the plight of Nora, a conventional bourgeois woman who discovers that the measures she took long ago to secure her husband's health could destroy her and her family. Ibsen uses the visit of Nora's old friend, Kristina Linde, as an opportunity to present exposition about the past. Another visitor, Mr. Krogstaad, threatens to reveal that Nora once committed the crime of forging her dead father's signature, unless she persuades her husband to give him a job. This provides the *inciting incident*; Nora works vigorously throughout the play

▲ This photo captures the growing tension between Torvald and his wife Nora in Ibsen's *A Doll's House*.

to keep these facts from her husband, Torvald. A letter reveals the whole situation to Torvald, bringing about the play's *crisis*. Initially Torvald is furious with his wife, but when Krogstaad vows to keep the crime a secret, Torvald is appeased and forgives her.

In a well-made play, Torvald's forgiveness would move the action toward resolution. In this play, however, just when the action should end in a *denouement*, Nora undergoes a transformation. Torvald's behavior toward her has opened her eyes to the real nature of their relationship and her subordinate position in the house. She walks out on her husband, leaving her children behind and her fate unresolved, in a scene that indicts society and its treatment of women. Ibsen led his audience through a familiar well-made play plot structure but thwarted their expectations as a means of presenting his social message. The original audience was so appalled at this ending, which violated both social custom and theatrical convention, that Ibsen was forced to write a new one for the German production.

Episodic Structure

A play with an **episodic structure** is characterized by an early point of attack in the story and a proliferation of characters and events. The events are not necessarily related through cause and effect, and the dramatic action builds through cumulative tension. Episodic structure is less restricted than climactic structure and tends to take place over a longer time span and involves multiple locations. An episodic play may also follow many different stories at once. When there is one main plot, the less central action is called the **subplot**. **Parallel plots**, in which the action of the main plot is echoed in a minor plot, often drive home the central meaning or comment on it through common subjects and themes.

Dramatists of the Elizabethan era (1558–1603) were influenced by the English medieval tradition in which plays could jump from Jerusalem to Europe, from biblical times to the present, from scene to scene. Shakespeare (1564–1616), for example, almost always used an episodic structure; his plays take place across a wide range of locations, moving from palaces, to battlefields, to private chambers, or even from one country or city to another over extended periods of time. The large number of characters, some of whom may appear only once or twice, give an opportunity to present various perspectives on the events of the play and their ramifications. His play *Hamlet* portrays the contrasting behavior of three sons, Hamlet, Laertes, and Fortinbras, each avenging his father's death.

In Shakespeare's *A Midsummer Night's Dream* the audience follows numerous characters and love plots including a tangle of alliances between Helena, Demetrius, Lysander, and Hermia. The confusion is evident in this 2008 production at the Globe Theatre in London.

Tony Kushner's (b. 1956) *Angels in America* (1991) is a more recent example of a play with episodic structure. It presents the landscape of American political conservatism as a backdrop for individual struggles and the AIDS epidemic and links the consequences of public actions to private lives. The play's portrait of the moral crisis in America is personified by the character Roy Cohn, who made his reputation in the 1950s as Senator Joseph McCarthy's chief aide, hounding Communists out of hiding while he himself was hiding his homosexuality. Cohn died of AIDS in 1986, never having revealed his secret and remaining faithful to the tenets of the conservative right. The play creates several parallel plots, each of which reinforces the central ideas. The audience encounters staunch Mormons who struggle with mental illness; a gay couple, dealing with the scourge of AIDS; and an unrepentant Roy Cohn, as he confronts illness and the ghosts of his past. Characters interact with real and fantasized people in their lives in interweaving plots that frame a portrait of America at the millennium. Its epic structure allows the play to move from location to location, from fantasy to reality, and from character to character to present a sweeping panoramic vision of national hypocrisy in historical context.

THINK

What difficulties do you think episodic structure might present for an audience?

Circular Structure

Both episodic and climactic structures move forward to a conclusion. Some plays, however, seem to end where they began. Plays with this sort of **circular structure** reflect the ideas of French writer-philosopher Albert Camus (1913–1960), who used the myth of Sisyphus as a metaphor for our existence. Sisyphus was condemned by the gods to endlessly roll a heavy

This powerful visual image from George C. Wolfe's direction of Tony Kushner's *Angels in America* captures the sprawling scope of this drama that paints a panorama of American politics and religion and the intimate effects of the collision of these historical forces on individuals' lives.

BERTOLT BRECHT

The German director and playwright Bertolt Brecht (1898–1956) used episodic structure for political ends, providing a model that politically committed playwrights around the world could use to engage their audiences. As a young medical student during World War I, Brecht was called up to work as an orderly in a military hospital, where he saw up close the dehumanizing effect of military conflict. His early poems and antiwar plays reflect his horror.

Brecht viewed the world from a Marxist perspective and thought that the inequitable distribution of wealth and power under the capitalist system were the foundations of social and moral problems. Believing that the theatre should be used to expose social and economic problems, Brecht rejected climactic structure because of the close emotional involvement with the characters it elicits from the audience and its *denouements* that leave the audience feeling that all has been resolved in the world. Episodic structure, on the other hand, with its constant shifting of time, place, and characters, keeps the audience at an emotional distance from the action, so spectators can rationally determine the social conditions that caused the characters' problems and better contemplate necessary social change.

Brecht believed that the climactic structure of the Aristotelian theatre showed characters whose actions are determined by who they are, unlike his epic theatre, in which actions are determined by social and economic circumstances. A person who is rich and powerful will act to safeguard his position, adopting ideas sympathetic to his own concerns, whereas a person who is poor will likewise work for his own advantage. Each may be driven to despicable acts in the name of self-interest, a fact often displayed in Brecht's plays.

The Good Person of Szechuan (1938–1940) describes the plight of the kind young woman Shen Te, scraping by in hard times. She is so exploited by scoundrels who take advantage of her good

▼ In this unique blend of traditions, Jaram Lee uses the Korean *Pansori* sung storytelling tradition to enact an adaptation of Bertolt Brecht's *The Good Woman of Setzuan.*

nature that she must transform herself into the evil man Shui Ta to survive. The mask she dons to transform into her fictitious uncle is a theatrical device that both distances the audience and provides a metaphor for the social masks we are obliged to wear to survive. As Shui Ta, she ruthlessly abuses others as they had abused her, demonstrating the impossibility of virtue in an unjust world where behavior is determined by economics. The play's episodic structure allows us to see the many situations that lead to Shen Te's plight and the way all the characters change according to the situation in which they find themselves. Unlike the *deus ex machina* of the Greeks, the gods abandon Shen Te and the rest of the world at the end of the play and leave us to find our own solution to social ills.

▶ Mrs. Smith (Jan Maxwell) recites a string of banalities to her husband, who ignores her behind his newspaper. The repetition of the flower pattern on the walls, carpets, and furnishings captures the way this play transforms the ordinary into the absurd in the Atlantic Theatre Company's New York production of Eugène Ionesco's *The Bald Soprano.*

boulder up a hill, only for it to roll back to the bottom each time he got to the top, at which point he would restart the tedious journey up again. For Camus, all human activity was like Sisyphus' burden—the exertion of energy toward the ultimate accomplishment of nothing. Camus saw the absurdity of existence in our collective delusion that we are actually getting somewhere when in fact our lives are filled with meaningless routines and pointless daily activities. The events of World War II contributed to this dark view of life.

Circular structure is an expression of the **futility** and **meaninglessness** of **human** efforts.

One of the best examples of a play with a circular plot is *The Bald Soprano* (1950), subtitled "an anti-play" by Romanian-born playwright Eugène Ionesco (1909–1994). The play presents characters engaged in empty conversation and activities and routines of daily life. The play begins with Mr. and Mrs. Smith, an English couple, sitting in their comfortable middle-class home after supper. Mr. Smith is smoking his "English pipe" and reading an "English newspaper," while Mrs. Smith, darning some "English socks," recounts a series of inane details related to the evening meal. The scenes do not move in any kind of logical progression, and the play culminates with the four main characters exchanging nonsensical and familiar phrases, suggesting that language and the ability to communicate have broken down. At the end of the play, the opening lines are repeated by the Smiths' friends, Mr. and Mrs. Martin, who have taken the couple's place, implying that the characters, their words, and their lives are interchangeable, and the whole series of events just witnessed could proceed again, and is proceeding again and again everywhere.

Serial Structure

A play with a **serial structure** is composed of a series of scenes that don't follow a continuous story or even include the same characters. Each scene may be an independent vignette that could, under other circumstances, stand on its own. The scenes in such plays are often thematically related and give a varied perspective on a subject through the juxtaposition of characters and events rather than through the progression of a single story. In some plays, scenes may be unrelated, like a series of skits in a variety show.

Serial structure has been a format for popular entertainments in many times and places. American vaudeville used a serial format, presenting jugglers, singers, dancers, magicians, and actors one after another on the same bill. In the late twentieth century, many postmodern playwrights wrote texts that incorporate the variety show sensibility and yet provide the experience of a single play; an example of such a show is David Ives's *All in the Timing* (1993). We will look at performances that incorporate this structure in Chapter 6.

THINK

In what ways do you think the unrelated scenes in serial structure might contribute to a play's theme?

Feminist playwright Megan Terry (b. 1932) created a serial structure for her feminist plays. In *Calm Down Mother* (1965), each scene ends with the actor in a physical position that takes on an entirely new meaning within the context of the next story. Actors create instantaneous character switches through physical and vocal technique. Each sketch focuses on some aspect of female identity and explores various

When Samuel Beckett's (1906–1989) *Waiting for Godot* premiered in Paris in January 1953, audiences were confronted with a play that defied the theatrical conventions of the time. Instead of developing to a climax and *denouement*, the plot seemed to go in circles; the second act repeated the events of the first act with only slight differences. Two tramps wait on a nearly barren stretch of road, waiting for an elusive character named Godot, who never arrives. Unlike psychological characters, these characters have no pasts, nor is the audience told how they came to their present circumstances. They speak in succinct, almost mundane sentences, and the only long speech in the play is a collection of nonsensical phrases. The stagnant action unsettled its audience to such a degree that one critic famously stormed out, proclaiming, "I will not wait for Godot!" Since this first disturbing encounter, scholars and audiences have come to understand Beckett's work, recognizing him as one of the foremost dramatists of the twentieth century.

Beckett's work has often been characterized by its minimalism—the reduction of theatrical elements to their barest essentials. Language, character, and action are distilled, but each phrase and movement is carefully chosen and full of implications. Beckett was deeply critical of directors' attempts to add to his plays through production choices not specified in the text. His later works, among them *Not I* (1972), *Ohio Impromptu* (1981), and *Rockaby* (1981), so condensed dramatic elements that they led some to question whether they were plays at all.

In Beckett's plays, characters are often cut off from their physical beings. In *Endgame* (1957), an elderly couple live in garbage cans; only their upper bodies are exposed when they emerge from their bins. In *Happy Days* (1958), Winnie is half buried in a mound of sand in act one and buried up to her neck in act two. As she disappears, she speaks an endless chatter about herself to her nearly mute husband. In *Not I*, the only character is a woman's mouth speaking a long stream-of-consciousness monologue about her life. In her rambling, she tells of hearing a buzzing, which she later realizes is her own voice. In the absence of physical presence, language takes on a greater role in the construction of self.

Many characters in Beckett's plays form duos dependent on each other for the validation of their own existence. The two tramps and the master–servant duo of Lucky and Pozzo in *Waiting for Godot* are examples. Characters often require others as listeners to the stories they tell about themselves. Being heard helps affirm that you are there.

Beckett demonstrates that constructing the self through storytelling and memory is unreliable because both language and memory can deceive. In *Krapp's Last Tape* (1958), a 69-year-old man has celebrated each birthday making and listening to tapes that document his life. The striking dissonance between the man on the tape and his present condition records an ever-changing self and makes us question the nature of identity. For Beckett, life itself is a kind of dying, a series of repetitions and dimmings, a winding down of memory, language, and consciousness.

▲ Nathan Lane, John Goodman, and Bill Irwin perform in the Roundabout Theater Company's production of *Waiting for Godot* in 2009.

---

societally prescribed women's roles. Written in a time of social upheaval and change for women, the play's use of serial structure through transformation actually serves as a metaphor for the thematic material in *Calm Down Mother*.

Serial structure appears more often today, which may be attributed to postmodernism's acceptance of *pastiche*, a mixture of styles and forms generally executed in a playful manner that comments ironically on the forms themselves. George C. Wolfe's (b. 1955) *The Colored Museum* (1986) uses a serial structure as a way of providing a postmodern perspective. The 11 scenes, sometimes comic, sometimes serious—and unrelated to any single story—explore issues of identity and the struggle of African Americans to define themselves as individuals. Each scene explores a different cultural myth, using a completely different set of characters and a new situation. For example, the scene "Symbiosis" shows a middle-aged black businessman struggling with his younger self over the objects of black power, such as an Afro comb and *dashiki*, that he accumulated in his youth. The older self wants to assimilate into the mainstream middle class, while the younger self still tries to express a revolutionary image of black power. In "The Hairpiece," a woman's two wigs—one an Afro and the other with straightened hair—argue over which one of them she should wear to break up with her boyfriend. The Afro wig claims the advantage of projecting "attitude" and accuses the other of being a "Barbie doll dipped in chocolate," while the straight-haired wig denounces the Afro's black authenticity by revealing that the afro was made in Taiwan. The woman herself, torn between the two images she desires, is bald. In "The Last

◀ The Mama in this scene from "The Last Mama-on-the-Couch Play" in George C. Wolfe's *The Colored Museum* satirizes a popular character type. She is so much a cliché of black middle-class aspiration that she literally blends into the surrounding set.

▶ Tom Stoppard plays with notions of time, as characters living two hundred years apart occupy the same house in *Arcadia*, a play that delves into chaos theory.

Mama-on-the-Couch Play," characters drawn from various Black Theatre forms share the stage. With its serial structure and pastiche of different dramatic styles, *The Colored Museum* offers a variety of perspectives on how to express racial identity in a world saturated with imposed cultural definitions.

Structural Variation: Playing with Time

For thematic purposes, playwrights may play with notions of time, breaking with the idea of moving in normal chronological order through a story line. Several classic American plays use flashbacks to transport us back and forth through time, creating a variation on traditional structure. In *The Glass Menagerie* (1945) by Tennessee Williams (1911–1983), Tom, who is both the narrator and a character in the play, tells us he is going to take us back in time, and we travel back cinematically to an earlier period. Arthur Miller's

(1915–2005) *Death of a Salesman* (1949) constructs the character Willy Loman through flashbacks that reveal the formative relationships and moments in his life.

> **Arthur Miller's use of structural variation enables us to see Willy Loman's past reflected in his present view of reality.**

David Henry Hwang's *Golden Child* (1998) is a more modern intercultural memory play. By traveling back and forth through time, the characters explain the legacy of traditional Chinese culture and beliefs in the lives of present-day Chinese Americans. Actors double as both modern American and traditional Chinese characters, which enhances the sense of cultural continuity through time, despite the geographic relocation of the action. Caryl Churchill (b. 1938) jumps through time in her play *Cloud Nine* (1979). Act one takes place in 1880 in British colonial Africa, and act two takes place 100 years later in London. For the characters, however, only 25 years have elapsed. Churchill compresses history to comment on the status of women and sexual relationships in the present.

Playing with time, playwrights can present events in the opposite order of how they would occur in life, starting with the end and moving back in time toward the beginning. As we move backward through events, we discover the origin of situations we've already seen and the motivations for actions already revealed. English playwright Harold Pinter (1930–2008) made use of this type of regressive storytelling in his 1978 play *Betrayal*, about a love triangle in which Emma has a seven-year affair with her husband Robert's best friend, Jerry. The play begins two years after the liaison has ended and moves back in time to the lovers' breakup, and then further back to the moment the relationship began. The characters are attempting to reconstruct how they arrived at the present as the audience tries to construct the story. The regressive structure presents the architecture of betrayal, allowing seemingly insignificant gestures and dialogue to convey their true import because the audience has already witnessed the hidden truths.

Dramatic Characters

WHAT makes a dramatic character memorable and moving?

Every play expresses its ideas through the actions and words of characters, so it is impossible to completely separate plot from language and character. Meaning comes not just from what happens—*story*, or *how* it happens (*plot*), but from *who* makes it happen and to *whom* (*character*).

Some have argued that characters drive the dramatic action and are the most important element in a play. Others believe that plot is the most significant because it sets up the situation out of which the characters will emerge. This is a bit like the "nature or nurture" argument in human psychology. Just as we are creatures of both our genetic makeup and our environment, dramatic characters are created with certain traits, but they are also caught in the web of circumstance, and are shaped by it, and act on it. Characters create action, and action creates character. Our role as an audience or reader is to interpret these actions and to give them significance.

You already know how to analyze dramatic characters. You do this all the time when you try to figure out people in your life. *You listen to what they say* and you ask yourself *what they really mean.* Are they honest, or do they have a hidden agenda? *You observe what they do.* You sense when words and actions don't quite align. *You listen to what others say about them* and make judgments based on what you hear. *You observe their interactions with others.* In everyday life, you do much of this unconsciously. In the theatre, we tend to be more conscious of our observations and conclusions, but the process of analysis is the same.

Playwrights strive to create characters who are compelling and magnetic, who stimulate our interest, provoke our compassion, and sometimes incite our rage and frustration. With the exception of recent experimental plays, it is almost impossible to think of a truly great play that does not have a memorable character. The character who leaves us passive and unmoved fails to generate dramatic action and provide a presence that fills the stage. We may forget the exact order of events in *Hamlet,* or *Tartuffe,* or *A Doll's House,* or *A Streetcar Named Desire,* after we see the play, but we remember Hamlet, Tartuffe, Nora, Blanche, and Stanley in all their pulsating humanity.

Why are these characters so indelibly imprinted on our memory? What makes their brief two-hour lives of interest to us? All characters are presented at moments of difficulty, often at times of great crisis, always confronting obstacles to their desires. This is as true of comedy as it is of serious drama. It is a universal struggle we can all identify with as we grapple with the difficulties of our own lives. For this reason, we call the lead role the **protagonist**, from the Greek word *agonistes*, which means both "actor" and "combatant." Sometimes, another character directly thwarts the desires of the protagonist; this character is the **antagonist**. To some extent, every drama is a kind of combat, and it draws us the way we would stop to watch a fight on the street or attend an athletic contest. In the magnetism of battle there are winners and losers, and the fight defines character, just as it helps us define ourselves.

Character and Culture

Every era and culture develops its own view of the human psyche and how we understand people and their motivations. Playwrights of every era reflect the way human action is valued by their culture. Ancient Greece saw human action in a struggle with the gods. The medieval period viewed life on earth as insignificant in relation to eternal life. In the twentieth century, under the influence of Freud, human behavior was viewed as the result of the dark inner forces of repressed desire. Marxist theory describes actions as resulting from economic circumstance. It follows that characters are drawn differently in different periods and that not all characters are equally compelling to us today. Consider the way painters of different periods have created portraits that reflect values and styles. Leonardo da Vinci in the Renaissance and Pablo Picasso in the twentieth century present the human face in very different ways, yet each tells us something important about the character's humanity. Just as the visual artist brings these different approaches to character portraits, so does the playwright.

THINK

What should a playwright consider when creating characters outside his or her own culture? Can such characters ever be "authentic"?

Archetypal Characters

Archetypal characters embody significant human traits that enable them to speak across cultures and centuries. They are extraordinary people placed in extraordinary conditions, and their actions loom larger than their circumstances.

Archetypes help to shape the way we think about the world and ourselves. Because of the extreme circumstances presented in most Greek tragedies, they are filled with such characters. Oedipus, the king in *Oedipus Tyrannus* by Sophocles, is the archetype of a man blind to his own flaws who is only able to see within when he is blinded. Medea, as envisioned by Euripides, is the archetype of the wronged woman who seeks revenge at all costs. Modern plays can also present archetypes who have a peculiar hold on our imagination and whose names stand in for all of us in similar straits. Willy Loman in *Death of a Salesman* became the archetype for the little man with big dreams and delusions. These archetypal characters embody the quintessence (the concentrated essence) of particular virtues, vices, and emotions and seem to transcend the specific context of their stories. They become universal symbols of what we all can become. Archetypal characters should not be confused with the allegorical characters found in late medieval drama who embody clear-cut virtues and vices, often with names such as Good Deeds, Beauty, Death, and Mischief. Unlike archetypes, allegorical characters do not have the psychological complexity to haunt us.

THINK

What qualities must a character possess to speak to audiences across millennia?

Psychological Characters

Some playwrights paint portraits so rich in detail and interest that we feel it is possible to understand their characters in depth, to comprehend their motivations and desires, even to create a life for them that preexists their appearance in the play. We call these characters **psychological characters.**

Psychology as a modern science dates only from the 1870s. Before that time, metaphysical or physiological explanations were given for human behavior. Characters written with more psychological complexity became common during the twentieth century, but in fact, complex characters have been with us for a long time. In his book *Hamlet and Oedipus* (1949), the Freudian analyst Ernest Jones placed the imaginary character Hamlet on the psychoanalyst's couch to

The Influence of Freud

Sigmund Freud (1856–1939) was an Austrian neurologist and the founder of psychoanalysis. His theories of the unconscious and the interpretation of dreams as sources of insight into personal psychology were revolutionary.

Freud's view that sexual desire is a primary motivation of human behavior influenced many disciplines but had particular impact among American theatre practitioners and playwrights such as Eugene O'Neill and Tennessee

Williams. Although today many of his ideas are questioned, discussions of identity, memory, childhood, and sexuality have been shaped by Freud's pioneering work.

◀ We are made aware of the inner thoughts and feelings of the complex psychological characters in this production of Tennessee Williams' *A Streetcar Named Desire*, performed by the Artists Repertory Theatre in 2008.

plumb the depths of his psyche. Hamlet is an example of a psychological character predating the notion of psychology. His complicated psyche also explains the continuing fascination with Hamlet's character.

Many American plays feature portraits of psychological characters that reflect a deep interest in Freud and psychoanalysis. Eugene O'Neill (1888–1953) was the first important American playwright to directly explore Freudian theories through his characterization. Tennessee Williams and Arthur Miller gave us deep psychological portraits. Blanche DuBois, the fading Southern belle in Williams's *A Streetcar Named Desire* (1947) is such a character. Watching her putting on superior airs, cavorting in fancy clothes, and fantasizing about millionaire lovers, we imagine her childhood and even see the child hiding in her present persona. We begin to get a picture of her life in her former estate, Belle Reve; the behavior in which she engaged; and the depths to which she sank before losing everything and turning up in the play. We feel this character had a past worthy of psychoanalysis and that to know about it would help us understand her needs and actions as they unfold before us. Miller's use of flashbacks in *Death of a Salesman* to construct the psychological past of Willy gives us the impression of a life lived fully and helps us flesh out relationships between Willy and his brother, his sons, and his wife. We see the false values he passed on to his sons, his lost opportunities, and the lies he tells himself and others. Again, these characters seem able to take on an imaginary life beyond the play itself.

Stock Characters

In many ways, stock characters are the opposite of psychological characters. They are representative of a type and are defined by externals—class, occupation, marital status—rather than by their individual characteristics. In Roman comedy, wily slaves or servants, miserly merchants, shrewish wives, braggart soldiers, and innocent lovers were recycled into various comedies. They differed little from play to play and were delineated by their function in the plot more than by anything particular to the individual roles. The villains, damsels in distress, and heroes of melodrama worked in much the same way. Imagine a mask that defines a character. Now imagine an actor wearing this same mask moving from play to play to fulfill a designated role whose function is to advance the plot, and you have a sense of the stock character. In fact, stock characters were referred to as "masks."

Today, we most often see this kind of character in television sitcoms that return season after season, with the same characters playing their predetermined roles within new stories. Think of the wily housekeeper Berta, the manipulative mother, and the shrewish ex-wife in the television situation comedy *Two and a Half Men*. These kinds of characters are the soul of accessible popular entertainment, and before electronic media, they were most often found in the theatrical forms that entertained mass audiences. They are immediately accessible and comprehensible.

From Roman times through the nineteenth century, acting companies were organized around an assortment of stock characters who could carry any play. Some actors played one "type" of character for their entire mature careers.

Characters with a Dominant Trait

In ancient times, the human body was thought to be composed of four kinds of fluids—blood, phlegm, yellow bile, and black bile—*humors* that regulated body function and emotional life. An imbalance in one of these fluids could cause extreme physical and mental disorder. Out of this view of biology came the idea of an obsessed personality with a dominant trait. Shakespeare's contemporary, Ben Jonson (1572–1637), created many characters based on the concept of humors, even giving the title *Every Man in His Humour* (1598) to one play in which he exposes the follies of his fellow Londoners. The idea of humors was also reflected in the late-seventeenth-century Restoration era's use of character names indicating particular personality types. The plays of Etherege, Congreve, and Wycherley treat us to Sir Fopling Flutter, Mrs. Loveit, Fainall, Petulant, and Old Lady Squeamish. In the hands of the French comic genius Molière (1622–1673), the obsessive personality took on psychological depth. In *The Misanthrope* (1666), originally subtitled *The Black-Biled Lover*, we see Alceste, a character so obsessed with unmasking the truth at all costs that he hurts those he loves, drives away friends, and destroys his own hopes for happiness. Alceste, despite his extreme behavior, is not a two-dimensional cartoon but a complex human being unable to cope with the dominant traits of his personality and consequently driven to self-destruction.

THINK

Can you think of "characters" from current popular reality television that could be described as obsessed personalities with dominant traits?

Depersonalized Characters

In many modern plays, we encounter characters who fill their lives with games and rituals that substitute for deeper connections. These characters may be searching for meaning, purpose, or relationships in an inhospitable world. Creatures of their current circumstances, their hold on their identities feels tenuous at best. Although they appear to have no psychological past, they are not stock characters. They possess individuality without complexity. We associate most of these characters with the modernism and postmodernism of the twentieth century, although precursors of this kind of persona appear in earlier periods. They represent the individual caught in an increasingly impersonal and dehumanizing world, isolated, lonely, and alienated from the community.

As the twentieth century unfolded and the horrors of two world wars forced playwrights to question the very possibility of finding meaning and purpose, characters were caught in futile quests for these goals. Characters in the plays of Beckett and Ionesco struggle to find significance and relationships. In *Endgame, Waiting for Godot*, and other Beckett plays, the characters find themselves in mutual dependency that substitutes for deeper relationships. Although we learn nothing of their lives before the moment of the play, we are engaged by their struggle to fill their existence. The generic married couples in Ionesco's *The Bald Soprano* can define their relationship only from the coincidence of living in the same apartment and sharing what they think is the same

child. We sense that depersonalized characters are replaceable with the next set of characters who happen along a lonely road or into a living room. Their relationships are of convenience and circumstance, and they remain essentially unknown to each other and themselves. Although these characters are not fully realized psychological beings, we identify with their struggles and their isolation.

Most American playwrights of the post–World War II period continued to create psychological characters in search of personal fulfillment, whereas most European writers painted a bleaker, more pessimistic view of the world through their depersonalized characters. Perhaps the devastation and mass annihilation on their home soil pushed European writers to question the value of an individual life.

Deconstructed Characters

During the later twentieth century, playwrights sought ways to reveal that all character is a performance of socially prescribed roles and that identity is often a creation of those in control of the social order. In *Cloud Nine* Caryl Churchill exposes how prevailing notions of class, sexuality, and politics determine character. The obedient wife who does all to please her husband is played by a man, demonstrating that such a character is a construction of the male ego. The daughter who has no identity until it is conferred on her by a man is played by a dummy. The gay son is played by a woman, and the black servant, who does everything to please his master, is played by a white man, reflecting the servant's self-loathing and desire to be white. In *True West* (1980), Sam Shepard (b. 1943) explores the American myth that you can be anyone through self-invention by having the two brothers who are the central characters in the play trade identities. In the 2000 New York revival of Shepard's play, actors Philip Seymour Hoffman and John C. Reilly traded roles each night, underscoring the flexibility of identity. In *Day of Absence*, playwright Douglas Turner Ward (b. 1930) reverses the historic stereotypes of white minstrelsy in which blacks were played by whites in blackface. In his play, black actors play whites in whiteface, and white identity is constructed from the African American point of view, reversing and revealing the roles created by the white power structure in American society.

A person plays many roles in life, and we behave differently as a function of which role we are in and how others relate to us.

Under the influence of psychology, we have come to think of character as something formed from within, so at first encounter deconstructed characters are difficult to understand and interpret. As the Freudian view of human behavior and identity is losing favor, deconstructed characters offer another concept of how we form ideas of self. They demonstrate how much of our identity results from our external situation and social roles. The self is shown as a performance.

Dramatic Language

The playwright's basic tool of expression is language, but the language of the theatre cannot be judged by its literary value alone. Most writers write for readers, but playwrights write for actors, so language in the theatre must be actable and speakable and inspire physical expression so it can be used by an actor to create a vibrant stage character. No matter how beautiful the writing, if the language of a play is not a good vehicle for acting, it fails as dramatic language. This does not mean that dialogue must be written exactly the way we speak in everyday life. Everyday speech would seem uninteresting in the theatre. Language on the stage by its very nature is heightened, intensified, and stylized.

The primary form of language in the theatre is dialogue. Unlike a novelist, who can use long descriptive passages to convey information and explain events, emotion, and setting, a playwright must find a way to reveal all the necessary exposition and story through what the characters say on stage. Magnificent language can fail as theatre if it does not possess the basic requirements of the spoken word on stage.

Advancing the Plot

On the simplest level, dramatic language must help to tell the story and advance the dramatic action. Each line a character utters should give the audience information and move the plot forward. The opening lines of Aeschylus' *Agamemnon* (458 B.C.E.), one of the earliest Western plays available to us, begins:

> O Gods! Grant me relief from this long weary watch.
> Release, O Gods! Twelve full months now, night after night
> Dog-like I lie here, keeping guard from this high roof
> On Atreus' palace.[1]

Look how much information Aeschylus gives us in three short lines: We know who the character is, his situation, and his state of mind. The speech is addressed to the gods as a plea, making it active and theatrical instead of a passive description.

Sometimes language can help tell a story by establishing location and character through dialect and usage, as in this passage from Hwang's *Golden Child* (1998):

> **Ahn:** Remember? When you are little boy? You lie on my stomach, and I tell you story of our family. My father, Tieng-Bin, he make this family chosen by God. My father work in Philippine, make money. But like all oversea Chinese, he leave behind most important part of life—his three wife,

his children—(Ahn begins to speak in the voice of a ten-year-old girl)—all your future, Papa, you left behind in China.[2]

In this passage, Hwang establishes two locations, the United States and China, and the passage of time by changing the voice in which the character speaks, transforming an 85-year-old woman into a 10-year-old girl. Dialogue must be shaped rhythmically to build intensifying action or set up a climactic moment or a comedic punch line.

> Language **patterns**
> **can alter in rhythm**
> **and intensity** at
> **heightened moments** in the **plot**
> **to indicate a change in**
> **a character's emotional** state.

Expressing Character

Every character possesses a singular voice—a way of using language to express thoughts and emotions. This voice has rhythm, vocabulary, inflection, dialect, and grammatical structure that reflect education, class, values, personality, age, and emotional outlook.

Note the revelation of character and basic attitude toward life expressed in this short piece of dialogue from Oscar Wilde's (1854–1900) *The Importance of Being Ernest* (1895). The character's upper-class speech and smugness are present in these lines:

> **Gwendolen:** Do you allude to me, Miss Cardew, as an entanglement? You are presumptuous. On an occasion of this kind it becomes more than a moral duty to speak one's mind. It becomes a pleasure.[3]

The playwright's first burden is to capture these idiosyncratic patterns of speech that define the character. Actors use these language patterns as clues about how to portray a role.

Language must chart the character's inner emotional journey through the play as well as the character's physical

---

[1] Aeschylus, The Agamemnon, trans. By Phillip Vellacott, (London: Penguin Books, 1959), 42.
[2] Henry David Hwang, *Golden Child*. Used with permission of author in *Understanding Plays* (Boston: Allyn & Bacon), 680.
[3] Oscar Wilde, *The Importance of Being Ernest*, in *The Genius of the Later English Theater*, ed. Sylvan Barnet, Morton Berman, and William Burfo (New York: Mentor Books, 1962), 289.

A Call to Action

journey through the plot. It is therefore a bridge between a character's inner and outer worlds. In realistic plays, language is always linked to a character's psychological intent. Sometimes it reveals what a character is thinking and feeling so the audience can make sense of the character's actions. When characters are withholding information, language must be used to disguise intent. The language of the stage can be read on two levels: what is actually said and what is actually meant. This level of internal meaning is the subtext—literally, what lies under the text. It is the job of the playwright to craft dialogue that can play on two levels, and it is the job of the actor to reveal what the words mean to the character. Playwrights must therefore capture not only how characters say what they feel but also how they use language to hide what they feel.

Provoking and Embodying Action
The theatre is a place of action. Implicit in dialogue is the need to act—to give physical expression to the spoken word. For this reason, plays are rarely written in the past tense. Theatrical language is about what is happening now, not what has already occurred. Good playwrights see the play unfolding in their mind's eye and write dialogue that will support and trigger gesture and strong physical action. When the language leaves actors stationary and immobile, with no available choice of action, the text is static and difficult to play.

Compressing Emotion
Because on stage a lifetime of meaning is compressed into a two- to three-hour event, the language of theatre is heightened and emotionally charged. Conversations that might take place over hours in real life cover the same ground in five minutes on the stage. The playwright carefully selects words for maximum impact to enable emotions and relationships to build quickly. In this rapid exchange from Harold Pinter's *Homecoming* (1965), the characters progress from conversation to sexually charged language in six short lines:

Lenny: Just give me the glass.

Ruth: No.

Lenny: I'll take it then.

Ruth: If you take the glass . . . I'll take you.

Lenny: How about me taking the glass without you taking me?

Ruth: Why don't I just take you?[5]

THINK

How does the language we use in everyday life differ from the language we use on the stage?

Setting the Mood, Tone, and Style
The sound of language, its rhythm and structure, sets a mood and tone for a play. During certain eras, playwrights were, by convention, required to use particular kinds of language for certain theatrical forms, so some types of language are associated with specific theatrical styles and forms. Classical tragedy was almost always written in verse, the strict metrical patterns giving dignity to the style. Verse was filled with

[5]Harold Pinter, *Homecoming* (New York: Grove Press, 1965), 34.

Onomatopoeia, Assonance, and Alliteration

The line "Blow, blow, thou winter wind" from Shakespeare's *As You Like It* (circa 1600) combines onomatopoeia, assonance, and alliteration. Say this line, and you will feel the wind in the repeated *w* sound, the sound of the howling in the repeated *o* in *blow*, and a suggestion of explosive force in the repeated *b*s.

Shakespeare perfected the use of such poetic clues to meaning.

The Failure of Language

During the course of the twentieth century, the power of language to express truth and communicate was challenged. Freud's theories of the unconscious suggested that there were deeper meanings beyond the literal, and while some playwrights used this idea to create complex characters with hidden motives, others wondered whether we could ever truly understand each other's inner thoughts through language. Dictators such as Stalin and Hitler hid their vile intentions in rhetoric, and politicians, advertising, and the media exploited language for obscured ends or reduced messages to sound-bites. In Ionesco's *The Lesson* (1951), language disintegrates before our eyes. And English playwright Harold Pinter wrote plays in which silences were often as important as words. In some plays, language completely disappeared, as in Beckett's *Act Without Words* (1957) and Peter Handke's (b. 1942) *My Foot, My Tutor* (1967).

images and metaphors that enabled the drama to play on the literal and symbolic levels. Its **meter**—the patterns of stressed and unstressed syllables—could subtly draw attention to significant meanings in the text. In *Romeo and Juliet* (circa 1591) by Shakespeare, listen to Juliet's plea for time to pass quickly as she waits for news of her love Romeo: "Gallop apace, you fiery footed steeds." If you say this line out loud, you will feel the rhythm of galloping horses and the urgency of her desire. Devices such as **onomatopoeia** (the use of words that express the feeling of their meaning through sound), **assonance** (the repetition of vowel sounds), or **alliteration** (the repetition of consonant sounds) can directly provoke an emotional response in the audience through their aural sense.

The comedies of Molière, many of which were written in rhyming verse, were constructed to get the laugh on the rhyme. Enjoy these lines from *School for Wives* (1662), as Arnolphe rails against his betrayal by a young ignorant girl he tried to keep under his control:

> Women, as all men know, are fraily wrought:
> They're foolish and illogical in thought,
> Their souls are weak, their characters are bad,
> There's nothing quite so silly, quite so mad,
> So faithless; yet despite these sorry features,
> What won't we do to please the wretched creatures?[6]

Form and **Innovation**

HOW do playwrights employ different forms to tell different types of stories?

Playwrights are not always constrained by convention. Some playwrights invent new ways to express their ideas. Modernism and postmodernism rejected literal realism in the search for alternative forms. Many playwrights have found new ways of working within old structures, and others have broken with linear plot, causality, and conventional notions of story, creating meaning as a collage of effects rather than through literal narrative.

THINK

Does bringing new ideas to the stage necessarily require new dramatic forms?

August Wilson (1945–2005) and Suzan-Lori Parks (b. 1963) are African American playwrights whose plays document the history of the black experience in the United States. Their different perspectives on that experience are reflected in the forms they have chosen for their works. In a cycle of plays dramatizing African American life in each decade of the twentieth century—among them *Ma Rainey's Black Bottom* (1982) set in the 1920s, *Fences* (1985) set in the 1950s, and *The Piano Lesson* (1987) set in the 1930s—Wilson uses the traditional models of climactic plot and psychological characters to paint a detailed portrait of the longings and frustrations inherent in black life. His rich imagistic language captures the rhythms and spirit of African American speech and music.

[6]Molière, *The School for Wives and the Learned Ladies*, trans. Richard Wilbur (San Diego: Harcourt Brace Jovanovich, 1991), 71.

Works by German writer Heiner Müller (1929–1995), such as *Hamletmachine* (1978), became hallmarks of postmodernism. A political playwright and Marxist influenced by Brecht, Müller was caught in a web of historical events. His father was imprisoned by the Nazis; he was arrested by the Allies in 1945, and he lived a restricted life in East Germany until fame allowed him the freedom to travel. His plays express the dilemma of the individual trapped by the movement of history. He uses figures from the masterpieces of Western theatre and places them in a decaying European civilization that has lost its way, allowing one text to comment on other. Müller's "texts" (some would argue that they are not plays in the traditional sense) are jumping-off points for imaginative staging. A production of a 15-page play can take three hours to perform. The difficult-to-comprehend montage of images and rambling speeches of his plays are intended to disturb the audience and provoke a response to a world without values.

▶ The strange images brought together in this staging of Heiner Müller's *Hamletmachine*, at The Cutting Ball Theater reflect the fragmented postmodern style of the text.

◀ In the 2010 Tony Award winning revival of August Wilson's moving play *Fences*, Viola Davis, as Rose, and Denzel Washington, as Troy, struggle with the far reaching consequences of racial inequality and deferred dreams.

By contrast, Parks does not believe history can be captured in discrete snapshots of particular moments. She believes we are the product of the totality of our history, which resides in emotions, the unconscious, and the images, relationships, and stereotypes that continue to reincarnate themselves in each new generation. Parks creates a new dramatic form that compresses historical forces into a single moment. Parks's plays are in a new form that challenges us to look past a linear sequence of cause-and-effect events to an accumulation of images and incidents that have an impact through their collective weight. In plays such as *Imperceptible Mutabilities in the Third Kingdom* (1989) and *The America Play* (1994), scenes, characters, and lines appear a number of different times, and each time they are slightly altered, echoing the theme and variation of jazz music.

THINK

Should playwrights strive to make their works accessible to their audiences or seek to challenge them through new dramatic forms?

Suzan-Lori Parks (b. 1963) was born in Kansas and spent her childhood on the move in the United States and Germany as an army brat. She attended Mount Holyoke College and the Yale School of Drama. Her plays were first produced in experimental venues such as BACA Downtown in Brooklyn, New York; The Actors' Theatre of Louisville, and the Joseph Papp Public Theatre. Topdog/Underdog moved to Broadway in 2001 and garnered her a Pulitzer Prize in 2002, the same year she received a MacArthur "genius grant." On November 13, 2002, Parks decided to write a play each day for a year. The result of this effort was 365 Days/365 Plays. The staging of these plays was unique; during 2006 and 2007, a network of theatres and universities in different cities staged them a day at a time in seven different locations (sometimes linked through Internet connections). The plays were staged with complete artistic freedom. The event brought the American theatre community together. In 2008 Parks was named the first recipient of the master writer chair at the Joseph Papp Public Theater, where her play The Book of Grace premiered in 2010.

The following quotations from Parks's essay "Elements of Style" express her views on the relationship between form and content and demonstrate how a fresh personal vision brings a new sense of dramatic structure, character, and language.

On Form and Content

"A playwright, as any other artist, should accept the bald fact that content determines form and form determines content; that form and content are interdependent. Form should not be looked at askance and held suspect—form is not something that "gets in the way of the story" but is an integral part of the story. This understanding is important to me and my writing. This is to say that as I write along, the container dictates what sort of substance will fill it and, at the same time, the substance is dictating the size and shape of the container."

On Repetition and Revision

"'Repetition and Revision' is a concept integral to the Jazz esthetic in which the composer or performer will write a play or a musical phrase once and again and again; etc.—with each revisit the phrase is slightly revised. "Rep&Rev" as I call it is a central element in my work; through its use I'm working to create a dramatic text that departs from the traditional linear

▲ A family drama becomes an allegory for racial tensions in America in The Book of Grace.

narrative style to look and sound more like a musical score. . . . Characters refigure their words and through a refiguring of language show us that they are experiencing their situation anew. . . ."

Parks shuns the term *characters*, preferring to talk of her personages as figures, figments, ghosts, or shadows through which we construct the present. In *The Death of the Last Black Man in the Whole Entire World* (1990), characters have names like "Black Man with Watermelon," "Black Woman with Fried Drumstick," "Lots of Grease and Lots of Pork," and "Before Columbus," reflecting the cultural stereotypes that can become inherited identities. The play, which has no easily discernable story, serves as a kind of ritual whereby the forgotten struggles of all **black people** are remembered and written into history in an attempt to bring emotional resolution to a past marked by oppression and violence.

Understanding how language, character, and structure shape meaning unlocks the door to the world of the play.

> **"**They are not **characters.** To call them so could be an injustice. They are **figures, figments, ghosts, roles, lovers** maybe, speakers maybe, shadows, slips, **players** maybe, maybe **someone else's pulse.""**
>
> —Suzan-Lori Parks

Summary

HOW do cultural values influence the dramatic form a playwright chooses?   p. 48

▶ The kinds of stories we tell and the way we tell them reflect our culture and our values. Story telling in the theatre is determined by culture and convention.

▶ Plays are meant to be performed not read. Plays challenge readers to imagine the elements of performance as they read.

HOW do playwrights use the plot to create dramatic tension in a play?   p. 48

▶ The story of a play includes all the events in or mentioned in the play. The plot is the ordering or structuring of events for the stage. The interaction between story and plot shapes a play's meaning.

▶ Playwrights use plot to create dramatic tension, usually through developing conflict and creating struggles and obstacles for the characters to overcome.

HOW do different types of dramatic structure help to convey a play's meaning?   p. 51

▶ The choice of dramatic structure creates the emotional arc of a play and strongly influences the impact of a play on the audience. Dramatic structure determines the scope and progression of the action and can help convey a play's meaning as expressively as its characters or its dialogue.

▶ Climactic, or Aristotelian, structure begins late in the story; past events are revealed through exposition, and complications lead to a climax followed by a *denouement*. The action usually covers a relatively short time span and is developed in a linear manner, with events linked through cause and effect. The well made play formula introduced the elements of foreshadowing, inciting incidents, cliffhangers, and the obligatory scene in a climactic model that kept audiences on the edge of their seats. The action in episodic

structure usually spans an extended time and several locations and includes many subplots, characters, and short scenes. In circular structure, events seem to end where they began, creating a feeling of futility. In serial structure, the action of each scene is independent of the action in the others.

▶ Playwrights often create unique structures to fit their content. They may play with time, using flashbacks, regressive storytelling, and other devices for thematic purposes.

WHAT makes a dramatic character memorable and moving?   p. 60

▶ Every era and culture develops its own view of the human psyche and how we understand people and their motivations. This in turn shapes how dramatists envision characters for the stage.

▶ The dramatic character must be a compelling figure who can stimulate our interest, provoke our compassion, and sometimes incite our rage and frustration.

WHAT is the role of dramatic language in a play?   p. 64

▶ The primary form of language in the theatre is dialogue, which must be actable and speakable; advance the plot; express character; provoke or embody action; compress emotions; chart a character's journey; and set the mood, style, and tone.

▶ Since the twentieth century, many plays have used dramatic language that expresses the failure of language to communicate.

HOW do playwrights employ different forms to tell different types of stories?   p. 66

▶ New ideas often call for new dramatic forms, resulting in unconventional and challenging dramas.

▶ The dramatic elements of structure, language, and character must work together to reveal the world of the play.

MySearchLab®

▼ Driven to kill her own children, Medea (Fiona Shaw) is both murderer and mourner in this updated staging of an ancient Greek tragedy.

The European Written Tradition *and Its Genres*

Genre and Cultural Context

All human beings feel joy and sorrow, love and hate, despair and hope. We perceive and express these feelings in ways that are dictated by the traditions and beliefs of our cultures. The theatre presents a public portrayal of these private emotions. Genre—the way we categorize types of drama— therefore reflects both universal human emotions and their social and cultural contexts. It follows that genre categories evolve over time and vary from place to place, as they always reflect prevailing social values.

A cultural bias is inherent in any system of categorization. To illustrate this, Argentine writer Jorge Luis Borges (1899–1986) imagined "a certain Chinese encyclopaedia" in whose pages animals are divided into categories such as "those that belong to the emperor," "embalmed ones," "suckling pigs," "those that tremble as if they were mad," "those drawn with a very fine camelhair brush," and "stray dogs."[1] We laugh at this list because none of us can imagine grouping animals in this way. The humor reveals something important about categorization: We divide things up according to how we look at the world, our habits, our traditions, and our cultural values. Because genre is a way to categorize theatrical works, it reflects our worldview, customs, and values, so applying dramatic categories cross-culturally becomes problematic instantly.

The European theatrical tradition has been shaped by ideas of comedy and tragedy defined in plays and practice. These ideas have evolved in the legacy of criticism begun by Aristotle's strict distinction between tragic and comic forms. All subsequent discussions of plays have been haunted by this sense of opposing genres. In other societies, theatrical categories may evolve from the perspective of the artist, the historical development of the form, or other cultural or religious influences. A tradition may divide works by the nature of the main character, such as God, Warrior, or Demon plays. We see this in the *noh* theatre of Japan. In some cultures, works may be categorized according to the dominant feeling or mood of a piece, such as the erotic, the marvelous, or disgust, as we see in Indian Sanskrit theatre. In the Congo and in Native American performance, we find performances categorized by ritual function, such as war, healing, or wisdom. We may encounter types of plays and performance that are unfamiliar when we step outside our own culture or era, just as our own divisions might seem puzzling to those outside our tradition.

1. What is genre?

2. How do the categorizations we make reflect our worldview, customs, and values?

3. How do European genres differ from other cultures' ways of categorizing performances?

[1] Jorge Luis Borges, "The Analytical Language of John Wilkins," in *Other Inquisitions 1937–1952*, trans. Ruth L. C. Simms (Austin: University of Texas Press, 1984), 103.

CHAPTER 04

Genre and Theatrical Convention

HOW do European genres help us to make sense of a play's emotional impact and point of view?

European genres, such as comedy and tragedy, are useful for making sense of a written play's emotional impact and point of view. These categories imply the kind of attitude the playwright brought to the subject as well as the attitude spectators should bring to the experience. Plays fall into particular categories because they express particular shared views or elicit similar emotional responses—not because of their form. The kinds of stories that are appropriate to tell, the structure of the plot, whether characters should be noble or lowborn, and the use of poetic or prosaic language are all theatrical conventions that reflect the values and concerns of a given society. They do not define a genre; they only explain a particular period's conventions of genre. For this reason, we can find two tragedies or comedies that, although they are considered to be of the same genre, use different kinds of plot, language, or character.

European theatre history reveals that traditional categories were more illusion than fact. The Greek and Roman classical eras and the French and Italian neoclassical periods are notable because their genre designations were so rigid. We often find mixed forms: An Elizabethan tragedy may have a comic subplot. A serious drama can conclude with a happy ending, as in Shakespeare's (1564–1616) *The Tempest* (1611–1612). Or a comedy may be unresolved, as is the case with Molière's (1622–1673) *The Misanthrope* (1666). Playwrights create works because they have something to express, and they will not be held back by arbitrary categories if they impede their message.

> **Shakespeare poked fun at genre conventions in Hamlet,** when he has a character introduce a troupe of actors with these words: "The best actors in the world, either for tragedy, comedy, history, pastoral, pastoral-comical, historical-pastoral, tragical-historical, tragical-comical-historical-pastoral, scene individable, or poem unlimited."

Artists play with categories, push the boundaries of delineated forms and conventions, and possibly develop something new. Consider postcolonial playwrights such as Soyinka (b. 1934, see Chapter 1), who fused indigenous African forms with European genres to create hybrid forms that held an internal discourse between cultures within a play. Nonetheless, studying the European written tradition and its genres helps us understand plays in the Western tradition.

Tragedy

HOW has tragedy evolved throughout Western theatre history?

How we struggle and confront our limitations is the subject of tragedy. Our fate may be preordained, but we meet it in individual ways through acts of will and, ultimately, as the instruments of our own destruction. The choices the tragic hero makes are the trigger of the drama, so the tragic character is of primary interest. The tragic hero refuses to accept

Ancient Greek Theatre and the Community

Theatre played an important role in ancient Athens. The government sponsored an annual theatre competition during the City Dionysia, a festival honoring the god Dionysus. Three tragic playwrights competed for a prize, with each assigned a day of performance. They each submitted three tragedies and a satyr play—a burlesque of mythic legends—that provided comic relief after a day of tragedies. The entire citizenry of Athens was expected to attend. The central role accorded the theatre reflects the perceived significance of tragedy's moral vision in maintaining the order of the state.

fate, protests against the limits of human power, and is determined to achieve self-fulfillment. Implicit in the tragic view is the inevitable failure of human efforts to overcome our destiny. We are all doomed to death and defeat in a world ruled by forces beyond our control, yet we live our lives struggling to affirm our essential individual humanity.

Tragedy documents the struggle between our desires and the necessities of conscience. The tragic universe encompasses an accepted value system that imposes constraints on our behavior. When the hero's choices lead to failure or disaster, the hero assumes responsibility for the drama's chain of events. The lessons of tragedy are always learned too late, so tragedy is a drama of character and belated self-realization. Tragic heroes become archetypes who claim a place in our imaginations and become symbols of conscience. Tragedy embodies a moral lesson.

Tragedy in Ancient Greece and Rome

Although the people of fifth- and fourth-century B.C.E. Athens took enormous pride in their cultural accomplishments—they created the first democracy, investigated science and philosophy, and developed new styles in art and architecture—they were also acutely aware of the limitations imposed on human affairs by divine action. For the ancient Greeks, tragic suffering grew primarily from the conflict between duty to society and duty to the family and self in a world governed by a pantheon of often capricious, wrathful, or unfathomable gods who held enormous power over human destiny. The gods set the tragic action in motion, and then individuals did their part to bring on their inevitable end, often by challenging the gods themselves.

Hubris is the term used to describe the overwhelming pride that leads a character to believe a triumph over the gods could be possible. The conflict between human pride and divine power is at the heart of Greek tragedy, and it couples with a clash between public obligation and personal feelings. Should Antigone, in Sophocles' tragedy by that name, bury her brother in violation of the law against funeral rites for traitors? If she buries her brother, she loses her future husband and sentences herself to death; if she chooses love and survival, she dishonors her family and the gods. Aeschylus (c. 523–456 B.C.E.), Sophocles (c. 496–406 B.C.E.), and Euripides (c. 480–406 B.C.E.) all wrote plays about the responsibility of Orestes, the son of Agamemnon. Must

Orestes murder his mother, Clytemnestra, because she killed his father? Honoring his duty to his father will require him to commit an egregious act and continue an endless cycle of revenge killings; unavenged, his father's death will have no justice. Such are the dilemmas confronting tragic heroes.

Ancient Greek tragedies featured a particular dramatic form with distinct text and staging conventions. Some of these formal features became intrinsically linked to the very idea of tragedy. Most Ancient Greek tragedies began with a *prologue* that provided exposition, followed by the *parodos*, or entrance of the chanting and dancing chorus; five episodes punctuated by choral odes; and the *exodus*, or exit of the chorus.

> The chorus provided exposition, commented on the action, engaged with the characters, and represented the citizenry. Most importantly, it provided spectacle and movement.

Aristotle's *Poetics*, written in the fourth century B.C.E., outlined what Aristotle considered the essential qualities of a tragic text. The *Poetics* describes tragedies from the fifth century B.C.E., but others have used it as a prescriptive model of the tragic genre. Most important of all to Aristotle was a unified climactic plot.

Tragic characters in Greek plays were always highborn; this reflects both the rigidity of the Greek social order and the Greek view that the actions of the ruler could bring ills to the land and its people, just as the crimes of Oedipus bring a plague to the land of Thebes and all its citizens. The actions of the tragic character are of consequence to all. Only the highborn could inspire both pity and fear. When Aristotle wrote that comic characters are inferior to tragic characters, he meant that comic characters allow us to laugh without fear. Later scholars labeled comedy an inferior genre as a result of their misinterpretation of Aristotle's words.

In contrast to the Greeks, the Romans had little interest in serious drama, and by the first century C.E., tragedies ceased to be performed in the public theatre. It is believed

According to Aristotle, the best plots contained the following elements:

- **Tragic character**—Highborn and prosperous, an essentially good person with whom we can identify, who does not deserve his misfortune.
- **Tragic miscalculation**—Sometimes translated as character flaw, a miscalculation that causes the hero's downfall.
- **Recognition**—Seeing the error of one's ways at the moment of downfall.
- **Reversal of fortune**—The hero falls from a high position and loses everything.
- **Pathos**—Suffering of the tragic hero.
- **Pity and fear**—Emotions evoked in spectators as we watch the travails of the tragic hero.
- **Catharsis**—The purging of the audience's emotions that allows the lessons to be learned through feeling.

that the tragedies of the Spanish-born Roman playwright Seneca (4 B.C.E.–65 C.E.) were intended to be read, not performed. Seneca took his stories from Greek myths, but his plays in no other way resembled Greek tragedy. From the myths he extracted pretexts for violence and bombastic speeches. His plays often include ghosts demanding vengeance for their deaths with murder and mayhem the result. These bloody dramas became known as **revenge plays**. Classical tragedy and other theatrical activity gradually came to an end with the fall of the Roman Empire, as the Catholic Church, always hostile to the theatre and its pagan roots, assumed increasing political control of Europe between the fourth and sixth centuries.

THINK

Can plays written in an outmoded genre, such as Greek tragedy, still have relevance to us today?

Aristotle's *Poetics* and Sophocles' *Oedipus Tyrannus*

Aristotle based his analysis in the *Poetics* on *Oedipus Tyrannus* (c. 430 B.C.E.) by Sophocles which he believed to be the perfect tragedy. This play is the story of the brilliant, proud, and arrogant King Oedipus, who despite all his best efforts to avoid his decreed fate to kill his father and marry his mother, unknowingly makes every choice that will lead him to this destiny. Oedipus is an essentially virtuous man, who, blinded by a stubborn nature and overwhelming pride, commits *the tragic miscalculation* of believing he can run from his fate and defy the gods. The misjudgment of Oedipus enables the audience to identify with its own frailties and failures. At the moment of his *recognition* of what he has done, Oedipus moves from ignorance to self-knowledge. Taking responsibility for his actions, he pierces his eyes, ironically blinding himself at the moment he sees most clearly. He suffers a *reversal of fortune* as he falls from his once lofty position as king. His

prosperity at the outset accentuates his fall, rendering his inevitable suffering, or *pathos*, all the greater, causing *pity and fear* in the public that underscores the moral lesson. The tragic events take

the audience on a spiritual and moral journey. *Catharsis*, an emotional release, purges pity and fear and allows the audience to take in the lesson.

◀ Oedipus tears out his own eyes after recognizing the acts he has committed in spite of his attempts to outwit the gods and avoid his fate.

Neoclassical Tragedy

Starting in the fourteenth century, as a result of political and economic changes in Europe, there was a renewed interest in classical forms that grew over the next two centuries. This period of rediscovery is called the Renaissance—literally "rebirth." Scholars called for the collection and preservation of the Latin manuscripts that had been kept in monasteries. The fall of Constantinople to the Ottoman Turks in 1453 brought fleeing scholars carrying manuscripts of ancient Greek tragedies to Italy. These texts were widely disseminated by the sixteenth century due to the invention of the printing press. The rediscovered *Poetics* was interpreted by Italian scholars as a rule book for tragedy, and this and other misinterpretations resurrected tragedy in an altered form.

This new neoclassical form required the three unities of time, place, and action that limited tragedies to a single day, in one location, and a single climactic plot, although such restrictions were not required in ancient Greece. Neoclassical tragedy introduced the idea of **verisimilitude**, the appearance of truth—not realism but an idealized truth. This led to the elimination of soliloquies and the Greek chorus. In an attempt to be more faithful to reality, the chorus was replaced with a confidant to whom central characters would speak their inner thoughts. To reconcile Christianity with classicism, playwrights were also expected to use their tragedies to teach moral lessons. During the seventeenth century, the French took these Italian models to extremes, enforcing strict notions of decorum or proper behavior, strict genre categories, and the three unities. Playwrights often performed plot contortions to conform to these rules.

Elizabethan and Jacobean Tragedy

Although neoclassicism was studied in universities, its influence was not immediately felt in England's professional theatres. Instead, a dramatic form emerged that combined the Renaissance questioning of the role of human responsibility with medieval ideas and expansive theatrical forms. A large theatre audience demanded new entertainments, and playwriting burgeoned in England during the reign of Elizabeth I (1558–1603) and continued through the Jacobean period under James I (1603–1625). The works of the many great playwrights of the period are still performed today. Among them are Christopher Marlowe (1564–1593), Ben Jonson (1572–1637), John Webster (1580–1634), and, of course, the undisputed great of the era, William Shakespeare (1564–1616).

The medieval world believed in a chain of being with God presiding over a hierarchy from the angels down to the lowest inanimate objects. The more secular Elizabethan world extended this idea and saw the universe as having parallel systems of order: the cosmic order involving the sun, the planets, and natural phenomena ruled by God; a political order ruled by the monarch functioning metaphorically as a god figure, meting out justice and keeping order over a social order from nobility to commoner; a family order ruled by the household patriarch; and a personal order with our physical and emotional well-being ruled by the mind.

▲ Helen Mirren as Phèdre reveals the unbridled passion for her stepson Hippolytus (Dominic Cooper) that will bring about her downfall in Nicholas Hytner's 2009 London production.

"...high and excellent Tragedie...that maketh Kings feare to be Tyrants...."

—Sir Philip Sidney, *Defence of Poesie*, 1595

Elizabethan tragedy often traced the effects of disruption in the political and familial order. In *King Lear* and *Hamlet*, we see family relationships gone awry paralleled by corruption in the political order. As the guardians of a divine order on earth, human beings must purge the kingdom of its debasing forces, and almost all Elizabethan tragedies end with the political order reestablished and the corruptive force removed from the land. Elizabethan tragedy served as a warning to would-be tyrants of what might await them should they abuse their power.

The Elizabethans saw morality from a Christian perspective, and human struggle was directed against vice in all its various forms. The conflict between an ideal of Christian virtue and the corruption of the everyday world are common subjects. Characters who embody greed, ambition, jealousy, vengeance, and unbridled passion, among the range of destructive human motivations, head for disaster. In a break with medieval thinking, deep questioning of God's will on earth and the place of humankind in the grand scheme haunt the plays of this period. Hamlet, Lear, and Macbeth are among the Elizabethan legacy of complex tragic figures who seek this understanding. Hamlet's monologues are excellent examples of a character's search for answers to these imponderable questions.

> **"What a piece of work is a man! How noble in reason, how infinite in faculties, in form and moving how express and admirable, in action how like an angel, in apprehension how like a god! The beauty of the world, the paragon of animals! And yet, to me, what is this quintessence of dust?"**
>
> —*Hamlet* II, ii

Like the Greek tragedies before them, Elizabethan and Jacobean tragedies focus on characters of high status, who speak in elevated poetic language. These later plays, however, follow an episodic structure, usually five acts long, with many scenes and subplots. Elizabethan plays do not have a chorus in the Greek sense; characters reveal their thoughts in soliloquies, and subplots and clowns provide commentary on the central action.

During the Elizabethan and Jacobean periods, neoclassical rules for decorum were largely ignored by professional playwrights, who catered to a public that loved a share of action and gore.

▲ Driven to horrible acts by blind ambition, Macbeth, played by Patrick Stewart, suffers pangs of conscience in Rupert Goold's production.

Schools of this period also studied Seneca's tragedies, so revenge motifs and bloody duels and battles are a part of many tragedies. The open panoramic feel of medieval drama remains present, and a resistance to formal rules is in evidence. Examine the plays of just one playwright, William Shakespeare, and you will find him bending the form to fit the particular needs of each play. Neoclassicism did eventually come to England after 1660, when King Charles II was restored to the throne after his exile in France. He brought with him a taste for continental drama, and the strict new neoclassical tragic form took hold for a brief while on British soil.

Bourgeois and Romantic **Drama**

A rising middle class and democratic revolutions brought on social, political, and economic changes during the eighteenth century. As a result, serious drama began to concern itself with the lives of the new bourgeoisie, and so we see vicars and merchants—people from the ordinary walks of life—becoming the subjects of serious drama. Eventually members of the middle and lower rungs of society take the place of kings and queens as the people of central

► In Schiller's *Mary Stuart* (1800), the action moves freely between the palace of British Queen Elizabeth I (Harriet Walter) and the prison of Mary, Queen of Scots (Janet McTeer) and includes a meeting between the two queens in an open field. The play is a study in contrasts, with Elizabeth nominally free but weighed down by the obligations of her office, and Mary, imprisoned and destined to be beheaded, but free in spirit even as she goes defiantly toward her death.

concern to the theatre. It has been argued that tragedy in the strict sense no longer exists when drama concerns itself with people whose actions are of little social or political consequence.

George Lillo's (1693–1739) *The London Merchant* (1731) was the first true bourgeois domestic drama. The play centers on a young merchant's apprentice who kills his own uncle and betrays his employer, under the sway of an evil seductress. He reflects on his evil deed and its consequences in lofty prose, and he accepts his death at the gallows, hoping it will serve as a warning to others. Lillo claimed that a tragedy about an ordinary individual could teach lessons of virtue to a greater number of people than classical tragedies about noble heroes. Indeed, young apprentices were sent to see *The London Merchant* during their holidays for years.

Romanticism, which began in the late eighteenth century, revolted against the constraints of neoclassicism and celebrated heroes who pursue their natural impulses and ideals in love or politics. Shakespeare was the inspiration for romantic tragedy with his expansive style and brooding heroes.

Johann Wolfgang von Goethe's (1749–1832) early plays of the *Sturm und Drang* ("Storm and Stress") movement in Germany contributed to the development of German Romanticism. In *Goetz von Berlichingen* (1773) the main character, based on a historical figure, is a knight who follows his own mind and whose defiance lands him in jail. The play is almost unstageable, as is much of the other drama of the period, with 54 scenes and numerous characters. Important events in the life of the main character, rather than a neatly developed plot, shape the drama. Between 1797 and 1805, Goethe and Friedrich Schiller (1759–1805), who had also been active in the *Sturm und Drang* movement,

took German drama in a new direction. Working together at the court theatre in Weimar, they forged a middle path between the rigidity of French neoclassic tragedy and the freer English form of tragedy, using characters modeled on the romantic individualist. This style is now called *Weimar classicism*.

Modern Tragedy

It has been argued that the tragic worldview cannot be expressed today because we have no fixed value systems against which to measure human action. Playwright Arthur Miller (1915–2005) and others proposed a new view of tragedy, which saw the tragic experience as independent of universal moral concerns. In this view, tragedy could be expressed as an attitude toward personal experience in plays about the lives of everyday human beings speaking in ordinary language.

> **In his article
> "Tragedy and the Common Man,"
> Miller argued
> that what evokes a tragic feeling in us
> is "the presence of a character
> who is ready
> to lay down his life, if need be,
> to secure one thing—his sense of
> personal dignity."[2]**

[2] "Tragedy and the Common Man," copyright 1949, renewed ©1977 by Arthur Miller, from *The Theater Essays of Arthur Miller* by Arthur Miller, ed. Robert A. Martin. Used by permission of Viking Penguin, a division of Penguin Group (USA) Inc.

In his play *Death of a Salesman* (1949), Miller stages the drama of Willy Loman, an ordinary salesman, who struggles to make ends meet and achieve self-validation in spite of the economic and social forces acting against him. Measuring himself against the promise of the elusive American dream, he chooses death as his only possible and honorable option. Many have argued against Miller's view, believing that tragedy is impossible in a world of moral relativity. Willy Loman, having lost his moral compass, is either incapable of tragic or heroic status or is the embodiment of a new kind of tragic hero. Whether or not you believe that tragedy is possible today, there is no doubt that all people, including once-voiceless populations, can now be the subjects of serious dramatic exploration.

▲ Willy Loman is an ordinary salesman who becomes a tragic figure in Arthur Miller's *Death of a Salesman*. Here he gives flawed advice to his son Biff on how to get ahead.

THINK
Do you believe tragedy is possible today?

Other European Genres

HOW did the genres of the medieval period and the Spanish Golden Age reflect the values of their times?

There have been times and places in the course of Western theatre history when tragedy has not expressed the prevalent worldview. New genres have developed to express the dominant cultural viewpoint. The Middle Ages and the Spanish Golden Age present two interesting examples of periods in which other genres developed to address religious and social concerns or tastes.

European Medieval **Theatre** and Its **Genres**

The Middle Ages saw the emergence of theatrical genres unrelated to the traditions of tragedy and comedy. In the fifth century C.E., the Christian church denounced theatrical activity long associated with pagan religious worship. The tragic and comic plays of ancient Greece and Rome were almost completely erased from the memory of Western Europe. Some texts remained in monasteries, where they might be used for learning Latin or rhetoric, and many were

preserved in the Eastern Byzantine Empire, but they were not performed.

We know that Hrosvitha of Gandersheim (c. 935–973), a nun from Germany and the first known female playwright, had access to the works of the Roman comic playwright Terence (185 or 195–159 B.C.E.), which she used as models for the six plays she wrote on Christian themes. We do not know if they were performed in her lifetime.

Ironically, the church, which had banned theatre, ultimately ended up using the elements of theatre—costume, music, and visual spectacle—to speak to the people. By the tenth century, there were processions and enactments associated with biblical events. The beginnings of **liturgical drama** are usually traced to the addition of *tropes*—words sung to music responsively by the chorus. The Easter trope known as the *Quem Queritas* representing the voices of the angels and the three Marys at Christ's tomb is thought to be the origin of liturgical drama circa 925 C.E. Sung mostly in Latin, with clergy and choirboys serving as actors, these dramas were performed at important holidays such as Easter. Eventually they grew to include multiple scenes and small scenic structures called *mansions* set along the side of the knave. Complex plays might require flying machinery for angels or the star of Bethlehem to descend from on high.

These performances were successful in teaching religion and grew in complexity. The laity were called on to help, and between the thirteenth and fifteenth centuries, performances of a cycle of stories from the Creation to the Last Judgment moved outside the church onto the public square. Latin was replaced by the vernacular, and the plays became common throughout Europe. Each scene was sponsored by a guild, a union of workers, merchants, or craftsmen who protected each other and the secrets or mysteries of their trade. For this reason these **cycle plays** are often called **mystery plays**.

After 1264, when Pope Urban IV created the festival of Corpus Christi, it became customary to perform the cycles on this day. This practice was adopted throughout the Christian world by 1350, and Spanish conquerors brought the tradition to the Americas, where indigenous performance traditions incorporated Corpus Christi plays, many of which are performed to this day in Latin America.

The sets for the mystery plays were pulled to their performance locations in village squares on **pageant wagons**. Guild members performed, and the sets and performances also served to promote the guilds. For example, the shipwrights were often given the episode of Noah's Ark, for which they could build a moving ship onstage. Cycle

Think TECHNOLOGY

The Machinery for Paradise

A device to create a Paradise effect for the Feast of the Annunciation was developed by architect Filippo Brunelleschi (1377–1446) in Florence, c. 1426. A wood structure holding rings of lanterns representing stars and 12 choirboys dressed as angels was hoisted through a pulley system high up into the rafters of a cathedral and suspended from the church roof. Below this device, eight more angels and the angel of the Annunciation hung with star lanterns, which could be lowered toward the actor playing the Virgin in the church.

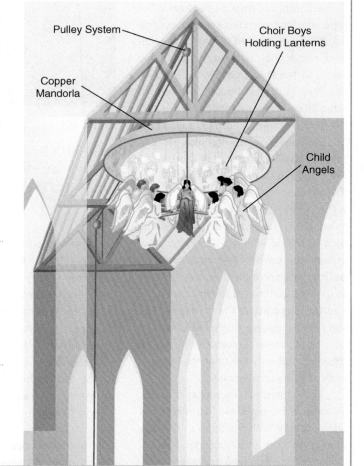

"The thing was truly **marvelous,** and displayed the ability and industry of the **inventor.**"

—Giorgio Vasari (1511-1574)

plays could take up to 40 days to perform in their entirety, depending on the performance practices of the region. They expressed religious doctrine and also included local comic references.

The popularity of the cycle plays waned in Europe during the sixteenth century, and these plays were forbidden in England by a royal edict in 1558. Variations on the cycle play include **passion plays**, episodic plays depicting events from the passion of Christ, and **saint plays**, or **miracle plays**, which depict events from the lives of saints. **Morality plays** use allegorical characters to depict moral lessons. These genres continue in new incarnations today.

LOPE DE VEGA
and Pedro Calderón de la Barca

Lope de Vega (1562–1635) was the first Spanish playwright to make a living writing plays, which might account for the sheer number of works he created. His output is estimated at around 800 plays, although some have attributed as many as 1,800 titles to him. The quality of his writing varies widely, but he dominated the theatre of his time and set a model for future playwrights in his attitude toward ancient classics, the scope of his subject matter, and his skill in crafting plots.

In contrast to writers elsewhere in Europe, who looked to classical models, Lope was firmly wedded to pleasing his audience rather than adhering to academic ideals. In *The New Art of Writing Plays for Our Time* (1609), a theoretical work, he listed 28 points for the drama. He allowed the mixing of comic and serious elements but prescribed one central plot. He said that the time limits should be dictated by the story, and language should be suited to the characters. Lope's best-known work is *The Sheep's Well* (*Fuente Ovejuna*, c. 1614), in which a villager, driven to the brink by a tyrannical lord, kills the lord. Under torture, the townspeople stick together, declaring that no individual, but the town as a whole, committed the murder. In the end, the king pardons them. The work has surprisingly modern overtones of revolution, but in the end, authority rests with the king, and only the tyrannical actions of the lord are condemned.

Lope's personal life was as dramatic as some of his plays. He had many love affairs, fought with the Spanish Armada, and in his later years became a priest, while continuing to lead a cavalier life.

▲ The villagers of Fuente Ovejuna band together to defend their honor by killing their tyrannical lord in this Spanish Golden Age drama. Lope de Vega's *The Sheep's Well* (*Fuente Ovejuna*) at the Yale School of Drama.

Lope was succeeded by Pedro Calderón de la Barca (1600–1681), who wrote 200 plays. Eighty of his surviving works are *autos sacramentales*, a form that he perfected and that took up much of the latter part of his career because, like Lope, he turned to the priesthood in his declining years. Many of his plays were intended for the court rather than the public audiences Lope favored.

Calderón's most famous work, *Life Is a Dream* (c. 1636), concerns Prince Segismund, who is imprisoned from infancy by his father to avoid prophecies that the prince would become a cruel tyrant. When Segismund comes of age, the king brings his son to court to put the prophecies to the test. Segismund's cruel acts lead the king to send him back to prison, where he awakens wondering whether prison life or palace life is the true dream. He eventually learns the truth about his situation and, after battling his own father for the kingdom, becomes a judicious ruler. The play is full of action, places honor over love, and is a philosophical meditation on the nature of reality and illusion.

The Genres of Spanish Golden Age Drama

As Spain became an international political power during the sixteenth and seventeenth centuries, Spanish literature, art, and drama flourished as well. Although religious dramas never fell from popularity, a vibrant secular theatre developed out of *entremeses*, the short pieces used as interludes in church plays. The *género chico* included one-act plays of various types, from farces to dramatic sketches. These eventually developed into full-length *comedias*, a word that sounds like "comedy" in English but refers to any secular dramatic work.

Golden Age plays did not keep to the classical distinctions of tragedy and comedy; *comedias* mixed serious and comic subject matter. The many types of *comedias* included swashbuckling cloak-and-dagger plays (*comedia de capa y espada*) that included intrigue, adventure, and love affairs; comedies of manners (*comedia de costumbres*); honor plays (*comedia pundoñor*); and romantic comedies (*comedias fantasía*). Subjects were history, legend, the lives of saints, and current social issues. These plays were generally kept to three acts and catered to the interests and taste of the popular audience. The importance of honor (*pundoñor*) was a central theme, although *comedias* dealt with love, religion, and patriotism as well. In response to popular demand, Golden Age playwrights were prolific.

Around the sixteenth century, just as religious plays were on the wane in other parts of Europe, Spain developed its own version of Christian religious drama called *autos sacramentales*. These productions, typically staged as part of the Corpus Christi celebrations, combined elements from both the cycle and morality plays, using biblical and allegorical characters and telling biblical tales and other stories that expressed religious doctrine. They were performed inside churches and in public plazas. These religious dramas held a place of importance, and all playwrights, including the premier dramatists Lope de Vega (1562–1635) and Pedro Calderón de la Barca (1600–1681), wrote *autos* as well as *comedias*.

Spanish *comedias* were presented to a popular audience in outdoor *corrales*, named after the courtyards where plays originally took place. Most of the audience stood in a yard area in front of the stage. Structures surrounding the square yard housed several stories of galleries and boxes for wealthy families, including the *cazuela*, or "stewpot," a gallery reserved for women, who were not permitted in the yard. The separation of men and women was a bow to moral authorities who worried about the overall rowdiness of the theatre and the honor of women who attended and performed on stage. The theatres were unruly, with spectators rattling noisemakers, yelling their approval at the players, and calling for refreshments. The *cazuela* could be particularly noisy, with as many women as could squeeze onto the benches banging their beads and keys on the guardrails to attract the attention of handsome men down below. Men dressed as women would steal into the *cazuela* and cause a ruckus.

Comedy

Comedy encourages laughter and the merry gloating that comes from a stolen and momentary triumph over fate. In tragedy, we learn life's lessons too late; in comedy, we learn in the nick of time. When luck leads us past life's obstacles, comedy celebrates our having prevailed over the odds. This optimistic celebration of our capacity to endure is revealed in the happy ending usually provided by comedies.

It is believed that ancient comedy evolved from rituals that rejoiced in the regeneration of the earth at springtime and the ensuing renewal of hope. These rustic celebrations of fertility explain the sexual humor found in many early comedies. Greek Old Comedy of the fifth century B.C.E., notably the plays of Aristophanes (448–380 B.C.E.), are filled with bawdy jokes and choruses of men singing lewd songs and wearing giant padded phalluses. Rebirth and renewal are often the culmination of comic action, and many comedies end with a marriage, or sometimes several, celebrating the rites that eventually bring a community together and guarantee its future.

Comedy generally works toward a reknitting of the social fabric by first showing us its unraveling. It exists in a topsy-turvy world where discord and disturbance have upended the social order. Lost children, lovers, fortunes, and identities must be recovered in a world manipulated by charlatans, petty tyrants, and knaves. But the realm of comedy is also a protected one. We know that no matter how much danger looms, there will be no painful consequences, and all will be put right in the end. The trickster will hold the day for just so long before order is restored. In the meantime, we watch at a safe distance. We observe the parade of human foibles before us, see the truth about ourselves, and laugh in relief that we pay no price.

Comedy, unlike tragedy, serves a universal social function. Clowns, fools, and tricksters are free to ridicule even those in power and to question values to reestablish their legitimacy.

THINK

Are some subjects taboo for comic treatment?

Comedy is often considered an inferior genre to tragedy, or tragedy's polar opposite. In fact, neither is true. While tragedy presents ideals and focuses on the philosophical, comedy is pragmatic and tells it "like it is." But in fact, they both deal with how we survive and get by. Tragedy helps define our place in the grand scheme of things, and comedy shows us the way in the here and now. Because comedies deal with the familiar world, they are often topical and remain deeply tied to the particular social concerns from which they emerge.

Ancient Greek comedy was social and political, confronting the issues of its time. Today's comedy is often personal, dealing with the neurotic concerns of individuals. Comedy presupposes a world where norms exist, where social expectations prevail, and where divergence from custom can be immediately recognized. By demonstrating the consequences of deviant behavior, comedy can teach us how to lead our lives.

**Public or personal,
comedy
is always good for what ails us.**

The Tools of Comedy

Human beings need to laugh. Doctors tell us it is good for us and even helps the immune system. We seem to be born with a comic sensibility; even babies will laugh at a funny face, a silly noise, or a pratfall. Simultaneously, some forms of comedy require sophistication and a mature understanding of the world.

Because a baby can respond to a ridiculous face and an adult to ridiculous manners or language, the tools of comic expression must range from the broadly physical to the subtle or intellectual. The magic formula for making something funny has challenged theatre artists and theorists. The more we try to dissect its components, the further removed we are from the comic realm and its impulsive spontaneity. Nonetheless, writers call on certain devices to launch comic action on the stage.

**The term *malapropism*
was coined in
Richard Sheridan's (1751–1816)
play *The Rivals* (1775).
Mrs. Malaprop's misuse of terms,
such as asking for the "perpendiculars"
when she wanted the particulars,
was made all the funnier by
her exaggerated pretentious behavior.**

Comic Forms

Many forms of comedy draw on the various comic devices in different combinations and degrees. When a device becomes

---

What Makes Us Laugh

Surprise, contrast, and incongruity.
Although the unexpected is often a central dramatic element in all kinds of plays, when the element of surprise opposes all expectations, contrasts with what we anticipate, or seems out of place or out of character, a serious situation can turn comic.

Exaggeration. The comic lens exaggerates characters, actions, language, voices, emotions, and situations like a fun house mirror and, ironically, often pulls them into sharper focus. Parody is the exaggerated imitation of individuals or artistic styles to make them appear ludicrous.

Obsession. Obsession sends characters out of control in pursuit of a single desire and sets off the comic situation. The miser obsessing over his money, the husband or wife obsessing over a spouse's possible infidelities, and the moralist consumed with thoughts of sin are characters we see woven into endless comic plots.

Slapstick. Slapstick humor is named for the fool's slapstick, two long flat pieces of wood fastened together that created a loud slapping noise when used. Today we include knockabout humor—chases, pratfalls, collisions, comic beatings, or semi-acrobatic feats and practical jokes—under this label.

Transgression. Scatological (bathroom humor) and sexual jokes violate social taboos and offer comic release. Comedy can even violate the moral and religious values of society and court outrage and censorship.

Language. Humorous language includes puns (plays on words), jokes, understatement, sarcasm, witty repartee, and sometimes nonsensical exchanges. Often comedy is found in the misuse of language. Mistakes in pronunciation or grammar, peculiar accents, and malapropisms—the ludicrous misuse of words, often by confusing them with similar sounding ones—can all be employed for comic effect.

an end in and of itself, it may actually become a form of comedy, as in the cases of slapstick and parody. Although comic plays can achieve their effect through a number of tactics, certain comic theatrical forms are fairly distinct and represent major divisions in the approach to comic material.

Satire

Sometimes comedy is used as a form of attack on the follies or institutionalized vices of a particular society. Marked by irony and wit, satire can explore pressing social issues and provoke debate. Successful satire is always topical, and its subjects are immediately recognizable to its audience. It usually has a moral or critical position.

> **Successful** satirists can often **provoke** the wrath of individuals and **institutions.**

Aristophanes, the first great comic writer in the Western tradition, turned his comic lens on the artists, philosophers, politicians, and even the gods of his time. Each of his plays begins with a prologue addressed to the audience to get them in the comic mood, followed by a debate over some current issue of interest that sets out the comic premise for the play. Many of the comedies of Aristophanes satirize the social and political concerns of an Athenian society stressed by the seemingly endless Peloponnesian War. Satirists target figures or ideas that offend a particular group or themselves, and often satire is a way of releasing personal and public emotion. The central character is often shown to be foolish or morally corrupt. Satire is often disrespectful and lacks sympathy for its subjects.

Because satire is always topical, in today's 24-hour news cycle, television has been the site of much of today's satire. Shows such as *The Colbert Report* and *Saturday Night Live* lampoon public figures and events with an immediacy that sharpens their impact. We need only think of Tina Fey's depiction of vice presidential candidate Sarah Palin to understand satire's force. When television satirists seek further engagement from their public, they turn to the power of live performance to move people to action, as in Jon Stewart and Stephen Colbert's *Rally to Restore Sanity and/or Fear*, the 2010 political event of the season. The rock musical *Bloody Bloody Andrew Jackson* uses a satirical portrait of the populist President Andrew Jackson to poke fun at today's Tea Party activists.

THINK

Is laughter always at someone else's expense?

Situation Comedy

Unlike satire, situation comedies do not rely on topical humor. Instead, they often are concerned with eternal social problems, such as business and financial disputes or family conflicts—husband versus wife or mother-in-law, father and son with conflicting goals, rivals in love. As such, they are plays for all eras. Such comedies often turn on a ridiculous premise, and chance or accident leads to plot complications. Mistaken identity, hidden lovers, eavesdropping, and misunderstood conversations make characters behave in absurd ways that create a snowball effect of confusion. The chaos is happily resolved in a comic *denouement*, where errors of perception are corrected, true love prevails, and all is forgiven.

This comic form originated with the Greek Middle and New Comedy during the fourth and third centuries B.C.E., when the public demand for new plays forced writers to rely on these plot formulas. Later, Plautus (c. 254–184 B.C.E.), a popular Roman writer, recycled these Greek plots with Roman stock characters. Situation comedies have played in every era, with writers adding and subtracting elements to appeal to the popular audiences of their times. Today this form is the basis for weekly television sitcoms.

Farce

Despite its high entertainment value, farce is often denigrated as a low form of comedy because of its reliance on broad slapstick humor, extreme situations, and superficial characterization. Intricate, carefully planned plots are woven out of misunderstandings and coincidences. Characters encounter obstacles that become so enormous and compound at such a rate that they are sent into ridiculous social and physical contortions to overcome them. The audience suspends its disbelief and accepts the far-fetched premise that sets the plot in motion. Farce is usually set in some familiar social setting, be it living room, bedroom, or boardroom. Each farce develops an internal logic of its own that keeps the action moving. In fact, the breakneck speed sustains the illogical logic of the plot and prevents characters from untangling the confused web in which they are caught. Characters are trapped in extreme situations, and character is shaped as a response to the situation, not by an in-depth psychological portrait. The joy of farce is derived from the characters' ability to meet the overwhelming challenges they face and survive.

> **Reading a farce reveals little of its theatrical energy** because farce is an actor's medium, relying on physical virtuosity and exquisite **timing.** It is perhaps the most difficult form of **comedy** to stage.

Although elements of farce can be seen in Greek comedy, the form developed during the Roman era. In the medieval period, the foolishness of human nature on display in farce provided a respite from religious drama. Although early farces focused on buffoonery, as the form evolved, it developed plot complexities.

Today farce usually centers around the suspected violation of fundamental social taboos. Endless threats to the sanctity of marriage are key to *bedroom farce*. Several French

◀ The *Rally to Restore Sanity and/or Fear* (2010) was political satire meant to move the public to take back control of the political narrative. As in the course of history, the clown/jester figures of Jon Stewart and Stephen Colbert spoke truth to power.

▼ Comic mix-ups and sexual escapades lead to embarrassing situations in farce as in this scene from Michael Frayn's *Noises Off*, in which the backstage relationships in a theatrical company intrude on onstage performances.

playwrights—Victorien Sardou (1831–1908), Eugène Labiche (1815–1888), and Georges Feydeau (1862–1921)—were masters of this form. Upright bourgeois families lose their decorum when they are caught in compromising situations. They struggle through manic scenes in which characters are hidden under beds or in closets, in order to hold their marriages intact. Because farce releases repressed energy as we chafe under society's rules and obligations, it is harder to write farce when social rules relax. Many successful farces, such as Michael Frayn's *Noises Off* (1985) and Alan Ayckbourn's *Comic Potential* (1998), are British and reflect the need to escape the tighter structure of that society; however, American farce, such as Ken Ludwig's *Lend Me a Tenor* (1986) also continues to hold its appeal for American audiences.

Romantic Comedy

Romantic comedies center around the relationships between sympathetic young lovers whose destiny in marriage meets with obstacles to fulfillment. The obstacles can be overbearing parents, jealous former lovers, or life's adversities. The young couple is always appealing, and we root for the fulfillment of their relationship. These plays inevitably end in consummation of the promised love in marriage. Many of Shakespeare's comedies—*As You Like It, Twelfth Night, Much Ado About Nothing,* and *Love's Labour's Lost*—fall into this category. The form derives from the tradition of the Greek New Comedy and Roman comedy, whose plots often turned on thwarted love. Elizabethan comedy also reflected the conventions of medieval courtly love, in which wooing was a ritualized art. These plays are not a laugh a minute like farce but offer lighthearted fun, usually spoofing courtship rituals. The audience's involvement comes from romantic and fantasied identification with the promise of love fulfilled.

Comedy of Manners

Comedy of manners makes fun of ridiculous social mores or practices and the people who engage in them. It holds a magnifying glass to the comportment of the privileged (as concern with manners is a luxury not afforded the poor) and derives its humor from pointed portraits of contemporary trendy society. Comedy of manners relies on the audience's familiarity with expected social custom among the elite or would-be elite. It uses exaggeration and caricature, clever language, wit, and social repartee to present self-satisfied people in a social environment with distorted values. Yasmina Reza's (b. 1959) *God of Carnage* (2009) is a recent example of the form.

The French playwright Molière is usually credited as the inventor of this genre. In his work, he depicted the pretentious individuals he encountered in the court of Louis XIV (1638–1717) and the world of the Parisian bourgeoisie who aspired to be like them. The great comic playwrights of the English Restoration, such as William Congreve (1670–1729) and George Wycherly (1640–1715), and later writers such as Richard Brinsley Sheridan, wrote in this vein. Oscar Wilde (1854–1900) may be the undisputed master of the form. The British upper class and those who aspired to it provided endless fodder for his searing wit. *The Importance of Being Ernest* (1895) draws on all the comic devices and is a masterpiece of the form.

▼ In this production of *The Importance of Being Earnest*, Brian Bedford's portrayal in drag of Lady Bracknell emphasizes the pretentious behavior, attitudes, fashions, and deportment of the upper classes satirized in Oscar Wilde's plays. The characters' elite status is expressed on stage through Wilde's witty dialogue, the characters' stiff physical bearing, and the overly elegant costumes.

Molière (1622–1673), born Jean-Baptiste Poquelin, is the undisputed comic genius of the Western theatre. It is no coincidence that Molière was a great actor before he was a great playwright. He knew what could get a laugh and how to work an audience, and he mastered and employed every comic device, from the broadest slapstick to the subtlest wit, writing himself some great roles along the way. His plays pushed comedy past the light entertainment of his day into probing studies of human excess. Molière's comedy of character is the hallmark of most comedy today.

Molière's early plays borrowed the plots from the improvised Italian *commedia dell'arte* (see Chapter 5) and the medieval French farce, but his search for the essential human element added another dimension. The comic buffoon in his hands became the poignant fool at whose foibles we could laugh while simultaneously feeling the pain of his humiliation or defeat. Many of the plays of Molière's later years are driven by character, reversing the plot-driven comic formula that had dominated since ancient Greece.

Blind to the ridiculousness of their own behavior, Molière's characters send the world into a spin to fulfill their needs. There are usually moments of comeuppance when characters are forced to confront themselves and the disorder their behavior has caused. Their social masks slip, and we see their suffering. The world is set right in the end, but unlike other forms of comedy, the characters do not find happiness unless self-understanding is gained, adding the recognition moment of tragedy to the comic form.

Molière was a satirist of his times. In Molière's comedy of manners, efforts toward conformity with false social values are exposed and ridiculed. Pretentious bourgeoisie, religious hypocrites, manipulative patriarchs, and arrogant nobles populate his plays, and scandal often followed when portraits were too closely drawn. Molière revealed his audiences to themselves, and often he paid the price of public outrage. *Tartuffe*, his play about religious hypocrisy, was banned and set off a five-year public dispute from 1664 to 1669 that embroiled the archbishop of Paris, the Senate, the papal emissary, and Molière's faithful champion, King Louis XIV, with Molière prevailing in the end, at the expense of his finances and his health.

His *School for Wives* (1662), despite its box office success, was deemed a mockery of family, marriage, and religion. This popular play is constructed around the character Arnolphe, who is so fearful that he will be a cuckold that he raises a girl from infancy to be his ideal wife. Despite Arnolphe's best efforts at complete control, the girl discovers true love elsewhere and turns on him. The play ends as a romantic comedy in marriage between the two young lovers, but the broken Arnolphe is left to face his own foolish quest for domination of another's will. In *The Misanthrope* (1666), the central character, Alceste, turns virtue into a vice, driven by obsessive belief in the rightness of his values. We laugh at his excess until his bitter end, when Alceste's character drives the play past the easy comic *denouement* into emotional ambiguity, pushing the limits of the comic form itself.

◄ In this modern staging of *The Misanthrope* at the Tarragon Theatre in Toronto, Alceste expresses his disapproval of the social hypocrisy others find amusing.

The difficulty of fitting all plays into neat categories is apparent as we try to place the work of George Bernard Shaw (1856–1950). Shaw went beyond just presenting a portrait of the social excesses he witnessed; he questioned the cultural institutions that permitted such behavior. Shaw's plays stand apart from other comedies of manners because of his desire to provide a corrective for social ills and a vision for change. His plays are often referred to as *comedies of ideas*.

Tragicomedy

WHAT makes tragicomedy a modern genre?

The term *tragicomedy* first appeared circa 195 B.C.E., in *Amphitryo*, a comedy by Plautus (254–184 B.C.E.) in which the god Mercury appears in the prologue and addresses the audience:

> Are you **disappointed** to find it's a **tragedy?** Well, I can easily change it. I'm a **god**, after all. I can **easily** make it a **comedy** and never **alter** a line. Is that what you'd like?... I'll **meet** you half way and **make** it a **tragicomedy**. It can't be outright **comedy**, I'm afraid, with all these kings and **gods** in the **cast**.[3]

Although Plautus is mocking the rigidity of the imposed forms and the absurdity of tragicomedy, he has captured something significant: He can change a tragedy to a comedy "and never alter a line" because the difference between the genres is not so much what happens as our perspective on the events.

Tragicomedy has sometimes been wrongly viewed as a cocktail of elements of tragedy and comedy; however, a tragedy with scenes of comic relief, a comedy with melodrama, a serious drama with a happy ending, and a comedy with sentimentality are not automatically tragicomedies. This genre is not a little of this and a little of that. It has its

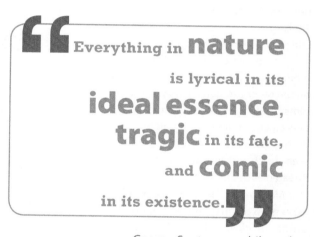

> **Everything in nature** is lyrical in its **ideal essence**, **tragic** in its fate, and **comic** in its existence.
>
> —George Santayana, philosopher

own particular ironic perspective on life that perceives the opposing elements of comedy and tragedy as coexisting in dramatic tension at all times.

For centuries, theatrical conventions demanded purity of form. Tragedies and comedies had their proper endings and characters. Yet playwrights always broke the rules. They sensed the fundamental irony of the human condition and from the time of ancient Greece, the great dramatists expressed it. Several of Euripides' (480–406 B.C.E.) plays do not fit neatly into the tragic form. Molière pushed the comic genre in plays like *Tartuffe*, in which villainy threatens family love and order, and the play takes us to the brink of tragedy and then rights itself back into comedy. Many of Shakespeare's later works mixed genres and placed happy endings on plays that in every other way seemed like tragedies. *The Tempest*, which begins as a revenge play, presents a portrait of the evil that people can do. Yet in *The Tempest*, Miranda, marooned on a desert island and knowing no man other than her father, proclaims upon first sight of men, "How beauteous mankind is. O brave new world that has such people in't." Her father, Prospero, replies, "'Tis new to thee."[4]—a line filled with ironic commentary on her innocent mistaken perception. We laugh at the line, although we know it holds a bitter truth. This perception of dual truths makes plays like these feel contemporary to us today. Others of Shakespeare's plays, such as *Measure for Measure* and *All's Well That Ends Well*, are disturbing tales

with happy endings and were labeled "the problem plays." Serious drama that mixes in comic elements always has some explaining to do.

THINK

Can you think of a moment in your life when you simultaneously felt joy and sadness?

[4] William Shakespeare, *The Tempest*, V, 1, 183–184.

WILLIAM SHAKESPEARE
Crossing Genres

ARTISTS IN PERSPECTIVE

William Shakespeare's (1564–1616) plays, translated into every major language, continue to move audiences around the world and challenge actors and directors with poetic language, compelling portraits, and deep understanding of human behavior. Yet despite these achievements, Shakespeare has been assailed by some critics for his violation of genre categories.

Shakespeare's plays all combine humor and darkness using one to comment on the other through characters and subplots. And many of his later plays truly defy categorization. The comic and tragic do not just inhabit the same plays; they seem to coexist in each moment and to threaten each other's worlds.

Measure for Measure (c. 1604) is an expression of this uncertain universe. Unlike medieval allegorical figures of Good and Evil and the Elizabethan characters that embodied these ideas, no character in this play can be labeled good or evil. The Duke, a basically good man, does not have the strength of his convictions because of his desire for public adulation. Angelo, the leader of impeccable moral standards, demonstrates that excess of good can lead to bad decisions and that even he can be overcome by his passion. Isabella, the self-righteous religious figure, is cold and unfeeling and willing to sacrifice another woman in her place. Claudio is a coward and will sacrifice honor rather than his life. The violation of genre distinctions enabled Shakespeare to explore new dimensions of character.

▲ In this scene from Shakespeare's *Measure for Measure* at the Joseph Papp Public Theater in New York, the novitiate Isabella bemoans her predicament.

The Elizabethans, accustomed to genre violations, still found these plays perplexing. Many decried the mixing of tragic and comic elements. Philip Sidney (1554–1586), a contemporary of Shakespeare, referred to these mixed genres as "mongrel-tragi-comedy."[1] Continental European critics believed Shakespeare was catering to the vulgar tastes of his audience. The French writer Voltaire (1694–1778) spoke of "the barbarous irregularities"[2] in *Julius Caesar* and called Shakespeare "a full-fledged prolific genius without a shred

of good taste or the smallest understanding of the rules [of dramatic genre]."[3]

The late-eighteenth-century and early-nineteenth-century romantics embraced Shakespeare's rejection of the rules. In his plays they saw a true picture of nature, which does not follow categorization. By the end of the nineteenth century, as the romantic impulse faded, scholars were again questioning these perplexing mixtures of forms, but the attitude toward mixed genres was changing. Shakespeare's combined comic and tragic vision was seen as reflecting the modern temperament. Critics have attempted to understand the impact of comic resolutions on the content of serious dramas. Was Shakespeare intentionally mixing genres to shape a play's meaning? Was he questioning the Elizabethan world and its hierarchies? Was he deliberately showing us a world with unclear boundaries and moral ambiguity, where the good do evil and the evil can do good? When we look at the complexity of these later plays, it is hard to believe that Shakespeare was simply writing to popular tastes or was undisciplined. He saw that life and people do not fit into neat categories and neither should the theatre, if it is to present true portraits.

[1] Sir Philip Sidney, *Defense of Poesy*, ed. Lincoln Soens (Lincoln: University of Nebraska Press, 1970), 49.
[2] Voltaire, *Oeuvres Complètes*, Volume 1 (Paris: Garnier Frères, 1877), 316. Trans. Mira Felner.
[3] Voltaire, *Oeuvres Complètes*, Volume 22 (Paris: Garnier Frères, 1877), Letter XVIII, "Sur la Tragédie," trans. Mira Felner, 146.

From the seventeenth century on, increasing numbers of plays broke with neoclassical rules for genre, and labels were sought to describe these forms. *Tearful comedy, sentimental comedy,* and the French *drame* (serious drama) were all considered. Most of these plays were hybrid forms and not tragicomedies in the modern sense. However, their growing numbers indicated that values in the larger society were evolving and that dramatists were seeking forms other than the comic and tragic to better express the uncertainty of a world without a fixed moral vision, where human beings found no certain place in the social hierarchy.

Modern **Tragicomedy**

Human existence is marked by loss—loss of youth, loss of health, loss of love and fortune, and eventually, loss of life itself. Despite our awareness of this sober fact, we continue on in the hope that we can overcome the inevitable outcome. We celebrate each victory and savor the memory of each triumph, but in the end, every significant moment of our existence, when viewed from a larger perspective, is bittersweet. Tragicomedy is the genre that captures our simultaneous anguish and joy.

To the many generations before us that lived in structured societies with rigid social orders and the human position in the cosmos clearly defined, this simultaneous experience of anguish and joy did not seem so obvious. When an entire society believed that gods controlled fate, or that a better life awaited us in the hereafter, the futility of our optimism and our struggle was not apparent. So tragedy could celebrate our heroism, and comedy could rejoice in our ability to overcome. As societies have grown more diverse and complex, the idea of a single worldview and

Anton Chekhov and Tragicomedy

Anton Chekhov (1860–1904), the great Russian dramatist of the turn of the twentieth century, was the first great writer of modern tragicomedy. Chekhov's plays puzzled the public of his time. They do not possess the kind of central action seen in climactic structure, nor are they episodic. They are dramas of inaction; they dramatize the human condition as Chekhov saw it—lonely, uncomprehending, locked in self-ignorance, and doomed to failure. Chekhov's work portrays a self-indulgent Russian aristocracy living unaware of the pending changes that would eventually transform their lives and Russia. These are dramas of disappointment and frustration; there can be no facile *denouement*. No one can find love and artistic fulfillment in *The Seagull* (1896), although all the characters are searching for it. Everyone in *Uncle Vanya* (1899) ends in despair or resignation, and the orchard, the central symbol of the characters' lives in *The Cherry Orchard* (1904), is lost. The audience members see the gap between the characters' aspirations and dreams and the futility of their attempts at self-realization. The tragicomic truth of the self-deception that underlies our existence as we strive to find meaning in empty lives is summed up in Masha's sad and comic line from *The Seagull*: "I'm in mourning for my life."

"Life is an insoluble problem."[5]

—Anton Chekhov

Chekhov's first productions led to misunderstandings between him and the great director Constantin Stanislavski (1863–1938), whom the playwright believed did not fully understand the ironic comedy of his plays but instead staged them as serious drama.

▲ Masha (Joe Kazan), in mourning for her life, seeks comfort from Dr. Dorn (Art Malik) in *The Seagull* (2008).

[5] Robert Corrigan, *The Theatre in Search of a Fix* (Delacorte Press, 1973), 125–126.

Luigi Pirandello and Tragicomedy

The great Italian playwright Luigi Pirandello (1867–1936) saw life as a struggle for permanence and meaningful identity in a world governed by time and change. He questioned the very nature of reality as we know it. In his plays, characters are trapped in the social masks they wear to maintain a sense of stable identity. In the end, they are mocked by time and appear comic in their attempt to change their fate. In his famous essay "Umorismo," Pirandello describes the old woman who dyes her hair red and cakes on makeup to hold onto a lover or a philandering husband. Her battle against the ravages of time appear both tragic in her desperation and comic in her execution. While we pity her, she is a clown.

value structure that could give meaning to life has become a remnant of a past when gods and kings ruled our lives. In the modern era God, religion, and government are questioned, and the secure value systems of the past are repudiated. The elusive quest for meaning we find in tragicomedy began in earnest.

After World War II, the Holocaust and the atom bomb seemed to confirm that dark irrational forces were in control of a godless world. Tragicomedy grew correspondingly more dark and pessimistic. Plays were set in a senseless world where human beings could no longer communicate because they were surrounded by a void of meaninglessness. This worldview was reflected in **existentialism**, a philosophy developed in mid-twentieth-century Europe. The plays of this period were logical extensions of the tragicomic vision put forth by Chekhov and Pirandello, shorn of the trappings of realistic stagecraft. In *Waiting for Godot* (1953), discussed in Chapter 3, the playwright Beckett (1906–1989) took Chekhov's drama of inaction a step further. Characters wait for Godot all throughout the play, and they simultaneously wonder how they will recognize him if he comes. This is the tragicomic setup of the play. Gone are the trappings of introspection. These characters are acknowledged clowns caught in the impasse of life. There is no way out, save death, and there is no way to self-realization in life. We watch and wonder in terror at our own lives, our own illusions. This dramatizes the tragicomic paradox: Our laughter at others who share in our plight only heightens our tragic sense of our own existence.

THINK

Can any subject be treated through any genre? Do some subjects inherently appeal to a particular treatment?

Melodrama

HOW does melodrama create its broad popular appeal?

Melodrama is characterized primarily by three crowd-pleasing qualities:

simplicity, sensationalism, and sentimentality.

When we watch a melodrama, we root for the hero, we boo the villain, we fear for helpless victims in distress, and in the end we weep for joy at the happy resolution to horrific events. Melodrama speaks directly to our emotions. It stages our deepest, if sometimes unrealistic, anxieties and appeases them with endings in which vice is always punished and virtue duly rewarded. Melodrama is an easily accessible, popular genre, with roots in the eighteenth century. It is still available to us today in the form of soap operas, westerns, and horror movies.

▲ August Daly's play *Under the Gaslight*, which opened in 1867, was perhaps the first American play to use the train-tracks rescue scene pictured in this publicity poster. This sensational effect would become a staple of nineteenth century melodrama and silent films.

Melodrama describes an emotionally satisfying and simplistic moral world. Characters are not complex or conflicted. They are simply good or bad. The disasters that visit good people result from outside forces beyond their control—usually the evil machinations of a villain; suffering does not stem from any flaws within the good characters themselves. The heroes of melodrama do not bear moral responsibility for the woes that beset them; they are instead victims of circumstance or foul play. Their innately good characteristics, and the generous or noble actions they take in the face of distress, result in eventual good fortune, leaving them blessed with riches, admiration, and other rewards. The villains of melodrama are rarely drawn to elicit sympathy. Motivated by greed, anger, or other vices, they perpetrate wrongdoings on innocent folks. There are few mitigating circumstances here, few insights into character that would serve to justify or pardon their actions.

The struggle of good against evil is cast in extremes of nightmarish horrors and worst-case scenarios. Villains go to unimaginable lengths to terrorize and antagonize their victims. Natural and economic disasters compound to put characters in the direst circumstances.

Melodrama allows us to experience our worst fears in all their excess, with the knowledge that somehow things will be put to rights in the end.

On the nineteenth-century stage, melodrama tapped into the audience's emotions by allowing them to experience disaster in overwhelming and immediate theatrical forms. Masterful special effects made possible horrific events—floods, avalanches, and collapsing bridges—that took place right before the audience's eyes. Theatres competed for crowds by developing new technology, just as we see in the movie industry today. Sometimes the ingenious perfection of a new special effect would require the writing of a new play to display it.

In the face of these disasters, simple and heartfelt emotions toward loved ones—family, friends, innocent children—are signs of grace and human connections that in the end outweigh strife. Melodrama elicits tears, both on stage and in the audience. Typical scenarios include a mother separated from and then reunited with her children and lovers forced to part only to find each other again. In a morally simple world, tears and deep sentiment help distinguish the virtuous from the duplicitous.

Melodrama traveled to England and America and became the most popular theatrical form of the nineteenth century. It played to the working-class populations drawn to the cities to meet the needs of the Industrial Revolution. The simple ideals of melodrama responded to the public's nostalgic longing for the past in the face of widespread social and economic distress caused by displacement and the effects of unregulated capitalism. Melodrama's focus on evil as an external force also helped people feel free from responsibility for the growing social problems around them. The happy endings provided hope to the underclass

THINK

Must all successful theatre combine emotional appeal with intellectual content, or can good theatre play to either the emotions or the intellect?

that flocked to the theatre for these plays. Early silent films presented melodramas to the masses, usurping theatre's audience for this genre.

Easily one of the most popular American melodramas of all time was *Uncle Tom's Cabin, or Life Among the Lowly*, based on the novel by Harriet Beecher Stowe (1811–1896). The book and its many theatrical incarnations gripped the minds of Americans on the eve of the Civil War because of the dramatic plot and critical look at the institution of slavery. The slave Eliza's forced separation from her husband and son, her dangerous escape north to freedom with a babe in her arms, the violence of the villainous slave master Simon Legree, and the simple sincerity of Uncle Tom and Little Eva provided the excitement, emotion, and sentiment audiences demanded. At this play, white Americans confronted the most pressing issue of their day in a way that was vivid and personal. Its success continued long after the war, and in the 1890s, 400 companies performed some version of the story of Uncle Tom.

Now the word *melodrama* is often used in a derogatory manner to conjure images of contrived sentimental and emotional stories. Nonetheless, this genre's ability to contact our anxieties and fears, to show us an ideal world where good and bad are easily discerned and in which each is given its due still absorbs us today and appeals to our deepest urge to feel that the world, even at its worst, is under the control of benevolent forces.

Think TECHNOLOGY

Technology and Melodrama

The nineteenth century saw increased interest in the application of science to all aspects of life, including the arts. Even popular journals ran articles on the application of new technologies to the theatre. One of the editors of *Scientific American*, Albert A. Hopkins, wrote "Magic: Stage Illusions and Scientific Diversions" (1897) to describe scientific applications in performance.

Nineteenth-century melodrama, with its emphasis on sensationalism as mass entertainment, was quick to draw on the new technologies. Producers kept devising ever-more-startling stage effects to compete for audiences. Explosions, earthquakes, and avalanches,

kept the audience on the edge of their seats. The stage of the Sadler's Wells Theatre in London was once equipped with a 40 by 100 foot water tank in order to stage a naval battle with fully rigged ships. Pulling off special effects required dangerous stunt work that intensified melodrama's visceral effect with characters swinging by ropes from ledge to ledge, tightrope walking across telegraph wires, diving off cliffs into the sea, or remaining suspended inches away from real buzz saws. American producer and playwright Steele MacKaye (1842–1894) contributed to the development of stage technology using the new invention of electricity. Revolving

stages, elevator stages stacked one on top of the other, and flying scenery all facilitated rapid set changes.

Moving panoramas were created by painting scenery on long spools of cloth that when unwound behind characters, ships, and carriages could give the illusion of change of place, travel, and chase. Within two years of the invention of the motion picture (before it was a narrative form), film was being used to project scenery on the stage. In 1898 a film projection took the audience on a frightening high-speed train ride past perspective scenery, integrating film and stage special effects in early multimedia performance.

Melodrama's Origins

Jean-Jacques Rousseau (1712–1778) used music to express the character's emotions for a monologue he wrote around 1762, called *Pygmalion*. Unlike in opera, the music in the monologue was not sung. Instead, it was used to underscore silence and reflect the dramatic content and the character's mood at the moment. We can still find this use of music on stage, screen, and television. Most movies today use musical scores to heighten the emotional

impact of dramatic action. In Germany the term *melodrama* was originally used to designate a passage in opera in which words were spoken and accompanied by music rather than sung. Rousseau's device influenced other writers. The use of music as background to the dramatic action also provided a way around licensing laws in France and England that permitted only a few theatres to perform regular drama.

It was French author René Charles Guilbert de Pixérécourt (1773–1844) who popularized a new kind of performance that combined lurid tales from the newspapers with music between the dialogue that came to be called, in French, *mélodie drame*, or melodrama. Pixérécourt's first success was in 1797, with *Les Petits*. He addressed a popular, uneducated audience, catering to their desire for special effects, emotional extravagance, and moralism.

▲ The slave Eliza and her baby son's daring and dangerous escape to freedom across a frozen river, as captured in a lithograph engraved by Charles Bour (1814–1881) from the book *Uncle Tom's Cabin* by Harriet Beecher Stowe (1811–1896). Tense, dramatic, and emotional scenes such as this made Beecher Stowe's book an excellent source of melodrama for the nineteenth-century stage.

Urban Poverty on Stage

The urban poverty that resulted from rapid industrialization was an international phenomenon. One of the early popular melodramas, a hit both in America and abroad, was *The Poor of New York*, performed at New York's Wallack's Theatre in 1857. The play depicted the sad plight of urban families living in poverty. Different accounts of the journey of this play exist, but it was probably first performed in Paris in 1856 and then was retitled and adapted to fit each city in which it was performed. In 1864 Dion Boucicault (1822–1890) adapted it as *The Poor of Liverpool* and *The Streets of London*, incorporating local issues in each version. Melodramas clearly expressed the problems of the poor everywhere.

Genre Today

HOW do genres serve today's audiences?

Today traditional genre categories no longer dictate what playwrights create; they may even inspire rebellion or innovation. Nevertheless, genres still give us a convenient framework through which we can approach dramatic material as readers and as theatre-goers. Our local movie store arranges films by genres taken from the theatre, such as drama, romantic comedy, and today's melodramas—horror, sci-fi, and western—to give us some general indication of what kind of emotional experience we will have: whether we will be moved or frightened, whether we will laugh or cry. We still ask before we buy a ticket to the theatre whether we are off to a comedy or a serious drama, a romantic story, or an existential examination of life, and then we prepare ourselves for the experience to come.

Summary

HOW do European genres help us to make sense of a play's emotional impact and point of view? p. 72

▶ Theatrical genres or categories of drama reflect a society's traditions and cultural values; therefore, the types of plays and performances we encounter outside our own culture may be puzzling to us.

▶ In the European tradition, *genre* refers to the emotional response a play engenders rather than to its dramatic form.

▶ Artists have always pushed the boundaries of genre categories if they impede their message.

HOW has tragedy evolved throughout Western theatre history? p. 72

▶ Tragedy dramatizes our struggle against the limits of human power. Because the tragic hero assumes responsibility for the drama's chain of events, tragedy embodies a moral lesson.

▶ Tragedy in ancient Greece played an important part in uniting Greek society. The Renaissance reinterpreted ancient tragedy in a Christian world. Elizabethan tragedy was an expansive form that did not seek to follow classical rules.

▶ Many question whether tragedy can exist today in a world without fixed values and norms against which to measure human action.

HOW did the genres of the medieval period and the Spanish Golden Age reflect the values of their times? p. 78

▶ During the medieval period, when the Catholic church dominated European life, religious drama of various genres was the dominant form.

▶ In sixteenth- and seventeenth-century Spain, a variety of theatrical genres developed that reflected the values and tastes of the populace.

WHAT social function does comedy serve? p. 81

▶ Comedy celebrates our ability to overcome life's setbacks. It rejoices in regeneration, with fools and clowns representing the forces of renewal. Comedy is a corrective for society and personal behavior.

WHAT makes tragicomedy a modern genre? p. 87

▶ Tragicomedy captures the simultaneity of anguish and joy in the human condition in a world without certain values. It gives an ironic perspective on life, perceiving the comic and tragic in a constant dramatic tension.

HOW does melodrama create its broad popular appeal? p. 90

▶ The world of melodrama is emotionally satisfying and sentimental. It presents simplistic divisions between good and evil. Vice is always punished, and virtue always triumphs.

HOW do genres serve today's audiences? p. 94

▶ Traditional genre categories no longer dictate what playwrights create, but they still provide a framework to help us categorize dramatic material.

MySearchLab®

Performance Traditions
Legacy and Renewal

Performance Traditions: Living Cultural Heritage

Performance traditions can be found in almost every culture. Some performances become attached to written texts; others leave little tangible evidence of their form and live through memory and inherited practice. All performance forms are impermanent and change over time. Great performers leave their personal mark, and forms adapt to social change and audience demands as well. A tradition is a living thing, and like everything vital in this world, it must evolve to survive.

Performance traditions often present a heightened theatricality. The integration of music, dance, movement, masks, elaborate makeup, and costumes creates a total sensory experience for the audience. Today's theatre artists increasingly turn to ancient forms as a source of inspiration and training. Of course, the practice of mining another age or another place for material does not belong to our age alone. As we saw in the last chapter, the Renaissance looked to the golden age of Greece and Rome for theatrical models. In the same way, early twentieth-century artists seeking to revitalize Western performance looked to Asia and the *commedia dell'arte*, which is presented in this chapter, for acting techniques. In our postmodern era of global cultural homogenization, this time of technology and unknown possibilities, we celebrate diversity through traditions rooted in community and ritual, forms that can tie us to each other and to our spiritual selves. The course of cultural history is marked by tradition and renewal, and the path to innovation is often through the past.

Every performance tradition has its own sets of conventions that influence acting, training, writing, design, and directing. Each also has its own history, but often there is no clear point of origin. There are so many performance traditions around the world that it is difficult to select only a few representative models. The ones presented in this chapter are of particular interest because of their longevity, ubiquity, influence, or the strange journey they have traveled.

1. How does the integration of elements in performance traditions present a heightened theatricality?

2. In what way do traditions rooted in community and ritual tie us to each other and to our spiritual selves?

3. Why does every performance tradition have its own set of conventions?

Indian **Sanskrit** Theatre

The poetic Indian Sanskrit theatre flourished sometime between the first centuries before and after the common era. Specific dates and historical background are difficult to pin down. The tradition traces a mythic origin to the god Brahma, who, at a time when the world was full of vice, took important parts of the four Hindu *Vedas*, or sacred texts, and combined them to create a fifth *Veda*. The fifth text, or *Veda*, is called *natya*, or "theatre."

According to legend, *natya*, unlike the other *Vedas*, was to be available to people of every class and contain every kind of knowledge and art.

Sanskrit theatre developed elaborate codes of performance, but the plays survived divorced from a continuous performance tradition, leaving us only dramatic texts and the **Natyasastra**, which means "authoritative text on the theatre." Written sometime between 200 B.C.E. and 200 C.E., it is a veritable encyclopedia of information about theatre from the classical Sanskrit tradition. Although it is credited to the mythic sage Bharata, whose 100 sons were said to be the first performers of *natya*, it is thought to be an accumulation of knowledge and performance rules based on well-established theatre practices.

The Natyasastra
influences Indian theatre to this day.

Just as Aristotle's *Poetics* provides a lens through which to understand Western tragedy, the *Natyasastra*, the earliest critical writing in India, functions as a guide to understanding Sanskrit theatre and many subsequent Indian performance traditions. In contrast to the *Poetics*, the *Natyasastra* does not focus on the written play text but addresses all aspects of production equally. It describes how actors should train for and perform a variety of role types, what kinds of makeup and costumes they should wear, what types of theatre spaces are appropriate for performances, and even what makes an ideal spectator. Influenced by the *Natyasastra*, India has not emphasized the centrality of the dramatic text as Western countries do. In India, as in many other Asian countries, the line between theatre and dance

remains fluid, and most traditional theatre forms are performed to musical accompaniment. Indian classical dance forms have their roots in temple dances that blended the sacred and the sensual. Under British rule (1858–1947), these temple dances fell into disrepute. After independence, artists looked to the *Natyasastra* to help with their revival and reconstruction.

The Theory of **Rasa**

The *Natyasastra* introduces the idea of **rasa**, tastes or flavors that contrast and complement each other. Although they do not exactly correlate to Western genres, each *rasa* presents a different mood or feeling. A play should offer a mixture of *rasa*, and a good Sanskrit drama is expected to offer all eight of the *rasa*—love, mirth, sadness, anger, heroism, fear, disgust, and wonder—although one *rasa*, or mood, should dominate. Theatre practitioners prepare a piece for their spectators as a master chef would make a sumptuous meal for a gourmet, mixing the flavors, or *rasa*. They take care that the venue and atmosphere of the performance contribute to the overall effect. The theatre event unites the theatre artists and the connoisseur. This aesthetic model underlies many Indian performance traditions and highlights the important connection between performer and spectator.

According to the *Natyasastra*, the best theatrical events are those in which text, acting, music, and dance all combine to create multiple emotional experiences meant to satisfy the most discriminating theatrical palate. This view contrasts with Aristotle's clear distinction between comedy and tragedy as separate genres as well as the view of Renaissance

love mirth sadness anger heroism fear disgust wonder

▲ **RASA OF SANSKRIT DRAMA**

neoclassicists that these genres should never be mixed. The final goal of a Sanskrit theatre performance is not a purging of emotions, as in Aristotle's tragic catharsis, but a sensual banquet that brings its audience a sense of peace and fulfillment. In fact, later Indian scholars described "peace" as a ninth *rasa*.

Sanskrit Performance **Conventions**

Sanskrit performances began with a number of preliminaries, including a benediction to a god, for whom the play acted as an offering, and a prologue in which the head of the company not only told the audience about the play and players they were about to see but also eased the audience into the fictional world of the performance.

The *Natyasastra* devotes numerous chapters to the actor's art, especially to movement. It breaks down the body into parts—eyes, head, hand, limbs—and describes a number of different positions for each. These positions are combined to represent different emotional states. Dance was part of performance, and songs accompanied by drums, cymbals, and flutes were used for a number of different purposes, such as introducing characters or underlining the mood of the action.

Since the *Natyasastra* has no illustrations, figuring out exactly what costumes, sets, props, acting, dance, and music were like in performance still entails a good deal of guesswork and interpretation. The *Natyasastra* notes three kinds of stages—square, rectangular, and triangular—and recommends the rectangular stage because of its superior sight lines. Scene location may have been designated by simple set pieces representing a house, temple, or mountain on a mostly bare stage, and an actor could indicate a new location simply by moving from one part of the stage to another. Costumes were highly ornamented, with characters dressed according to character type. Makeup was used on the actor's face and body. The color of makeup also indicated a character's type.

Sanskrit Plays

The Sanskrit plays that have survived are polished dramatic works written in poetic verse. The main action of a Sanskrit play is the hero's struggle to attain an object of desire. The ultimate objective of the performance is to leave the audience with a sense of well-being, so the hero is always successful in the end.

In *Sanskrit drama,*
**the hero achieves
one or more of the three ends
of Hindu life:**
dharma, **or duty;**
kama, **or controlled
sensual pleasure;
or** *artha,* **the wealth
that allows one to provide
for others.**

In *The Little Clay Cart*, the hero Charudatta's poverty at the beginning of the play derives from his generosity. His honorable nature leads a wealthy and virtuous courtesan, Vasantasena, to fall in love with him. A king's villainous brother pursues her and, in the process, accuses Charudatta of her murder. In the end truth is revealed, the king is deposed, and the lovers are united. The cart of the title is Charudatta's son's simple toy. Vasantasena put her jewels in it, showing that even a humble vessel can carry great wealth inside. The play's dominant *rasa* is love or the erotic, but the story's scope and its myriad characters express many other *rasa* as well. The villain creates a situation of trepidation for the lovers, and characters such as Charudatta's comic friend bring in humor.

Like many other plays of the tradition, *The Little Clay Cart* reflects the Hindu idea of *maya*—a force that allows one to become attached to worldly desires instead of realizing that the sensory world is an illusion. The play reveals that things are not as they appear at first glance. The ending brings clarity and a happy resolution to events.

Kutiyattam and Kathakali

Although Sanskrit drama as a performance tradition is lost to us, *kutiyattam*, one of the oldest continuous performance traditions in India, in existence since before the tenth

▼ *Nangiar kuttu* is a form of solo performance that is an offshoot of *kutiyattam*.

century, may be its direct descendent. Temple servants perform *kutiyattam* in temples (see Chapter 9). Performers, in fabulous costumes and makeup, use elaborate facial and hand gestures in presentations that can extend over a period of several days.

Kathakali, a vigorous seventeenth-century form, originally performed by members of the warrior class, has its own language of hand gestures and vibrant stage makeup and costuming. In Chapter 7 we will take a closer look at *kathakali* and see how it uses the theory of *rasa* as a basis for acting techniques, giving us some idea of what Sanskrit acting may have been like. Through *kathakali* and other forms that have been influenced by *Natyasastra* and Sanskrit drama, we are able to glimpse extinct performance traditions.

Mime and the *Commedia dell'Arte* Tradition

HOW have mime and the *commedia dell' arte* performance traditions evolved from antiquity to today?

What do circus clowns, acrobats, stand-up comics, silent film comedians, mimes, and sitcom actors have in common? They can all trace the origins of their performance style to the oldest European tradition. Although we often think of the European theatre as one that focuses on text, we know that perhaps as long ago as 200 years before the first written ancient tragedy, there existed a popular unscripted theatrical performance form—ancient Greek **mime**.

The **Mime Tradition** in Antiquity

Many scholars believe that tragedy evolved from the fertility rituals honoring the god Dionysus and that mime performances either spoofed these rites or provided comic relief from their intensity. These Greek comic players traveled the ancient Mediterranean world, spreading their performance tradition, which entailed stock characters, short improvised comic sketches, broad physical and acrobatic humor, juggling, music, and bawdy jokes. They were often masked and wore padded phalluses to aid in lewd innuendo.

No one knows to what degree Roman mime, comedy, farce, and popular entertainment were indebted to these Greek traveling players. The Atellan farce, named for the town of Atella in southern Italy in the third century B.C.E., resembled Greek mime, with its use of masks and stock characters. Roman mime and popular entertainment extended the variety entertainment form. Concurrently, a Roman **pantomime** form developed that resembled a silent storytelling dance and was a distinct performance genre from mime. As Christianity spread, the mimes turned their eye on the Catholic Church, just as they had spoofed the rituals and gods of antiquity. This provoked criticism and censorship, and the mimes were driven underground during the Middle Ages.

Commedia dell'Arte and Its Heirs

During the sixteenth century, with the freedom and humanism of the Renaissance, a form resembling ancient mime and early Atellan farce with masks, stock characters, and improvisation emerged—the ***commedia dell'arte***. This performance tradition dominated European theatre for the next 300 years, and its influence can be felt to the present day. Because of its many similarities with ancient forms, some historians believe the *commedia* is a direct descendent that emerged from hiding. Others believe that it is a fresh creation of the Renaissance. The form was first called ***commedia all'improviso***, or improvised drama. It came to be called *commedia dell'arte* out of respect for the great *arte*, or skill, shown by the professional actors of this tradition. The *commedia* was like any other fine art of the time, with masters, apprentices, and families transmitting skills from generation to generation.

Commedia dell'arte players used **scenarios**—general outlines of plots with short descriptions of each scene—as the basis for improvisation. These were always simple in outline—young lovers kept apart by a cruel parent must be united, or a rich man must be bilked of his money in some elaborate scheme, for example. Once on stage, there were certain set bits of comic stage business called **lazzi**—to which an actor could turn for comic effect. These ranged from pure slapstick to acrobatic stunts, poems, and speeches, all guaranteed to get a laugh. Actors inserted these comic turns as needed to warm up an audience, heighten humorous effect, or save a lackluster performance. Because actors played the same stock figures throughout their careers, they mastered speech patterns, movements, and reactions, which facilitated improvisations.

Harlequin.   Zany Cornetto.

Non, non, n'eftime pas en couranr en barbet, | Ie fay l'arbre fourchu, portant les piedsen l'ær, | Dy ce que tu voudras, ie feray des premiers
En clabaut ou maftin, me raur Frācifquine, | Pour (difpoft) triompher en fi haulte conquefte | Au cōbat amoureux, que fur tout ie pouchaffe,
Ie veux eftre pendu maintenant au gibet, | Et toy plus l ourd qu'vn Ours, ne fçaurois reculler, | Il n'eft chaffe ōn tout tēps ǯ de bōs vieux hmiers,
Si plus vifte que toyfur les mains ne chemine. | Ny aller en auant, tant tu és groffe befte. | Qursçauēr des cōnls le terroir & latrace iiij.

This eighteenth-century French engraving shows a scene of two commedia dell'arte *comic servants. On the left, Arlecchino, recognizable by his black mask and his patchwork patterned suit, performs one of his famous acrobatic stunts.*

commedia used grotesque leather half masks that
mouth, enabling characters to speak. Language,
ondary to physical expression, and like
es, the *commedia* demanded enlarged
character, except for the women
esented by a particular mask that
t patterns of movement belong-
e learned and passed from one
the next.

were the darlings of the Italian
h century. Their antics pleased
ike, and they played on street
t often, *commedia* acting compa-
town in wagons that could be
ny of the characters represented
ily recognizable to locals. When
1589) married King Henri II of
47 to 1559, she brought her love
cluding the *commedia dell'arte*.

the Italian players were the
they metamorphosed French
ch actors imitated the robust
ys were actually written *com-*
at first in Protestant England,
ry the *commedia* had found an
gh much of Europe from the
enth centuries, the *commedia*
r favorite television situation
asily accessible entertainment
edia.

The **Evolution** of the *Commedia*

As with all other traditions, in time the *commedia* responded to social change and metamorphosed into other forms. By 1760 there were almost no Italian-born *commedia* players in France, and the robust, earthy performance was falling victim to French refinement. *Commedia* characters and scenarios were integrated into written plays in Italy and France, but the incorporation of an actors' tradition into a written text diminished the vibrant physicality that marked the *commedia* at its high point.

Although the *commedia* was unwelcome in England in the late sixteenth century, its British descendants were embraced 100 years later. The English pantomime form, born in the early eighteenth century, traced two story lines—a traditional *commedia* scenario and a narrative dancing of a mythological tale. After a wild, acrobatic, knockabout chase scene, Harlequin whirled a magic wand and resolved the two stories. This was the most popular theatrical form in England for over a century, thanks in part to the Licensing Act of 1737, which restricted plays but did not apply to pantomime. Christmas pantomimes are still performed today.

The greatest performer of the English pantomime was Joseph Grimaldi (1778–1837), whose character, named Clown, usurped Harlequin's dominant position to become the hero of the new urban working class. Grimaldi created original makeup for Clown—whiteface, two bright red triangles on the cheeks, heavily colored enlarged lips and eyebrows, a comic wig, a brightly patterned shirt, and baggy pants with big hidden pockets for stolen goods. This became the origin of a tradition of circus clowns known

Commedia Stock Characters

Through time, a set repertory of *commedia* characters developed: Pantalone, the miserly, lecherous, sometimes impotent merchant, often cast as a father figure who thwarted young love; Dottore, the pedantic, pompous intellectual scholar or medical doctor who quoted in bad Latin and dispensed idiotic advice under the guise of elevated knowledge and prose; Capitano, the braggart soldier who is really a coward; the *inamorati*, young lovers with frustrated passions; a group of female maids who scolded or aided and abetted plotters; and most vital, a collection of male servants who schemed, manipulated, and challenged authority. Some were wily, some were fools, some were cruel, but all advanced the comic plot. The most famous of these servants were Arlecchino (or Harlequin), Brighella, Piero, and Pulcinella (also known in English as Punch). This cast was recycled into endless comic plot permutations.

today as "Joeys," named for Grimaldi. This name illustrates the link between character and actor in non-text-based performance traditions.

The French Revolution created a newly liberated class of citizens who wanted to see themselves reflected onstage. Fairs and variety shows continued the *commedia* tradition. Licensing laws limited the use of spoken words on stage, and a new form of mime captured the spirit of the *commedia* in silence, demonstrating how traditions will adapt to social conditions. This is the first time the terms *mime* and *pantomime* come to be used interchangeably. Again, a single actor transformed the *commedia* tradition. Jean-Gaspard Deburau (1796–1846), like Grimaldi, created a character, Pierrot, who was a hero of the working class. Pierrot, too, usurped the lead position of the Harlequin character. He played in simple *commedia* scenarios and always prevailed over the upper classes. Tall and thin, he chose as his costume a billowing white chemise with wide sleeves and large buttons, loose pants, no collar, and a tight-fitting black cap against his white-face makeup. The costume we associate with Pierrot today is the creation of the actor who brought the character to prominence.

In later generations, the pantomime form waned in popularity, and many performers moved to music hall and vaudeville variety entertainment, or to the circus, and later to silent films. Charlie Chaplin (1889–1977) and Buster Keaton (1895–1966) are heirs to the great *commedia* tradition. In the twentieth century in France, a modern mime form was created. Marcel Marceau's (1923–2007) Bip character was the embodiment of the *commedia*'s spirit more than 400 years after its first incarnation. The *commedia* is now a tool for actor training, and many performers have tried to revive the form. If we look around, we see the influence of the *commedia* everywhere—in the written drama, in television sitcom characters and plots (Berta on the television sitcom *Two and a Half Men* is a direct descendent of manipulative *commedia* servants), in the circus, and in the tradition of new vaudeville we will examine in the next chapter.

◀ The French actor Jean Louis Barrault portrays the famous nineteenth-century mime Jean-Gaspard Deburau in a still from the film *Les Enfants du Paradis* ("Children of Paradise"), shot in occupied France during World War II.

ount history? In Chap-
d at the many ways play-
eir stories. History is also
rytelling. When we set out
istory of theatre and its de-
ent, we decide what should be
and determine a structure to help
rrange our points and express our
perspective, just as playwrights do.

The events included in a history reflect what is valued by the historian or the culture. No history of any kind can be all inclusive, so judgments are made about what is of interest and worthy of study. Decisions about which histories to tell change over time. If you look at an American theatre history book written 50 years ago, you find little attention paid to non-European or nontext traditions. Africa and South America might not even be mentioned, and the contributions of women and minorities are marginalized.

The one important difference between the work of the playwright and the work of the historian is that history presumably tells a story based on facts. The very notion of a "fact" can be questioned, however, especially as we move back in time beyond living memory and written records. What some groups consider history, others might call myth. For example, some think of the events recorded in the Hebrew Bible and the New Testament as fact or miracles, while others see them as inspired literary invention.

No tradition is static.

The models we use to express history reveal how we think about the subject at hand. One of the most common models for expressing a view of history is a time line, in which events are located at specific dates or points in time in a singular, linear, continued progression. Important dates and events appear as a result of a sequence of causally related events, but many cultures do not view time in this way.

A standard time line is inadequate for representing many performance traditions that evolved over an extended period and had no specific moment of creation. This is especially true of traditions that reach back before written records. The word *tradition* itself evokes what has been continually handed down rather than a moment of birth or inception. It implies something that has seemingly always existed. When dates do exist for performance traditions, they are often approximate. In the case of the Sanskrit *Natyasastra*, dating of the text ranges over a period of 400 years.

Performance forms naturally change as new performers take up the mantle and adapt the form to their own times and cultural interests. How do we determine when enough changes add up to something new? When does one form end and a new one begin? Even traditions that have come and gone may continue to exert their influence on future generations in new and unpredictable ways. Traditions may also be disseminated throughout a wide geographic region, dying out in one area even as they achieve a new vitality in another. Today's global communication has increased this phenomenon.

A standard time line fails to capture the reality and nuances of the lives, deaths, and rebirths of many performance traditions that have left us no tangible record of their trajectory. We are challenged to find new models to represent their historical evolution.

Japanese **Traditions**

WHAT distinguishes the important theatrical traditions of Japan?

Like an apparition from another realm, an imposing figure holding a red and gold fan and wearing a small white mask, a golden headdress, and several layers of beautifully embroidered robes glides so slowly down the smooth wooden pathway leading to the stage that the movement is almost imperceptible. Though the mask displays the subtle, delicate features of a young woman, a middle-aged male actor's robust chin sticks out from underneath. Once on stage, his voice is low and guttural, and his movements are accompanied by the droning chants of a male chorus, the high-pitched sound of a flute, intermittent beats of two drums, and strange yelps from the onstage musicians. The main character of this *noh play, Hagoromo,* or *The Feather Mantle,* is an angel. In return for her feather cape, picked up by a fisherman while she bathed, the angel offers a dance of blessing. Her appearance marks a union of heaven and earth, and the angel serves as a personification of Buddhist wisdom.

The **Noh** Theatre

Japan's *noh* theatre is a highly stylized ritualistic form in which a few pages of text can take hours to perform. The plays of the *noh* have been passed down from generation to generation as performance texts that include dance, movement, music, vocal patterns, masks, and costuming. *Noh* theatre reflects Buddhist and Shinto religious practices and values of the fourteenth-century Japanese court world. *Noh* plays create an atmosphere or mood through poetry and distinct staging and do not focus on action and dialogue.

Many ritual and performance forms contributed to the creation of *noh*, which evolved into a highly refined

▲ This *noh* actor, wearing a delicate female mask and exquisite kimono, moves slowly along the *noh* theatre's bridge toward the main stage. The tension the performer creates in stillness is valued in the art as much as the beauty of the costumes and stage properties.

art in the court of Shogun Ashikaga Yosl 1408). There the performers Kanami Kiyotsu and his son Zeami Motokiyo (1363–1443), founders of *noh*, wrote poetic texts inspired their elite audience. These texts remain a sul the *noh* repertoire. From 1603 to 1867, *noh* exclusively before audiences of the ruling s medieval noble warrior class.

Buddhist and Shinto Influence on Performance Practices

Zen Buddhism, an esoteric religious practic Shogun's court, was an important influenc all aspects of the art blend a formal simpl mystery reflective of Buddhist ideas. In world is an illusion. Enlightenment, an ins sence of all things, can be achieved only th and by relinquishing attachments to the p his treatises on *noh*, performer and autho the two "pillars" of *noh* as *monomane,* or d and **yūgen**, which can be translated as " pillars constitute a balance between concr transcendent intangible truth. They para division between the illusory material v metaphysical essence. Today the feeling of dominates *noh*, which has become mor ritualistic than in Zeami's time.

Noh staging practices continue to sensibility, exemplified in *noh*'s emphasi fessional *noh* actors, who are all male, r to disguise their low voices for fema Buddhism's view that all reality is illusor properties also reject theatrical illusion. ways protrudes from beneath the mask, image on the mask are visible at once. Fa can represent a variety of objects, such a ladle. The stage itself is bare except for c that may indicate a special location asse These set pieces are always minimalist suggest a place. They are constructed l performance.

Many conventions of the *noh* the and space, reinforcing a sense of in dreams. Walking around the stage o one has traveled a long distance and a tion makes it so. The ghosts that app between realities: the domains of the the present and the past. Their memor earth and entice them to reenact ever also breaks down individual identity. themselves in the third person, as c the eight-member chorus often spea them, freeing the actors to act and da project through the masks.

Shinto is an ancient Japanes back to 500 B.C.E. Traditionally, Shin

shamans, and their handheld objects, such as fans or flowering branches, served as conduits for spirits to enter and possess them. *Noh* actors continue to use these simple objects in performance, harkening back to their ritual function. The plays present the visitation of gods, demons, or human spirits to the earthly realm, and the space itself is modeled on Shinto shrines (Figure 5.1). The *hashigakari*, or bridge, that leads to the stage from which actors make their entrances, is like a passage between the world of spirits and our own (see Chapter 9).

> " Those who truly **understand** the art watch it with the **spirit**, while those who do not merely watch it with their **eyes**. "

—Zeami, the creator of *noh*, from "The True Path to the Flower"[1]

Noh Plays

There are five different categories of *noh* plays: god plays, warrior plays, women plays, miscellaneous plays, and demon plays. Each has a different sensibility and dynamic, ranging from the slowest and most refined (the god and women plays) to the fastest and most vigorous (the demon

[1]*The Art of the Nō Drama*, trans. Thomas Rimer and Yamazaki Masakazu (Princeton, NJ: Princeton University Press, 1984), p. 71

plays). Ideally, a day of *noh* would include a play from each category in the preceding order, reflecting a rhythmic pattern known as *jo–ha–kyu*: introduction (*jo*), development (*ha*), and climax (*kyu*). This movement from slow to fast governs all aspects of a *noh* performance, from the structure of a play to an actor's every move.

The *noh* genres God, warrior, woman, and demon refer to the main character, or *shite*—literally, the "doer" of the action of the play. The main characters of *noh* are drawn from history, literature, and legend. In the first half of a play, they usually appear in humble form, and then in the second, they reveal their true natures as spirits. A change of mask or costume represents this transformation.

Many *noh* plays focus on the longing and sadness of characters who cling to the ephemeral world, even in death, thus highlighting the Buddhist belief that release from earthly attachments is necessary to put the soul to rest. In *Matsukaze*, a woman play, the spirits of two young fisherwomen return to Suma Bay, where in life they met and fell in love with Yukihira, a court poet. As they scoop brine into their cart, their poetic text speaks of the salt tears they shed over their lost love when Yukihira returned to court without them. In the end, lost in a kind of mad melancholy, the title character Matsukaze clings to her earthly love. She is blind to true Buddhist happiness. Her spirit continues to live in longing, never finding peace.

Words with more than one meaning, image patterns, and other forms of poetic language make *noh* plays richly symbolic and difficult to translate. They are replete with allusions to famous poems that courtiers of the period would have recognized. Word play deepens the thematic content and the feelings it evokes. The name Matsukaze, for instance, combines the word *matsu*, meaning both "pine" and "to wait," with *kaze*, meaning "wind." Matsukaze waits for her lost lover and describes their love as wind in the pines; they are two beings intertwined and inseparable. The play is also saturated with images of water—for example, the women's salt tears and the brine they collect.

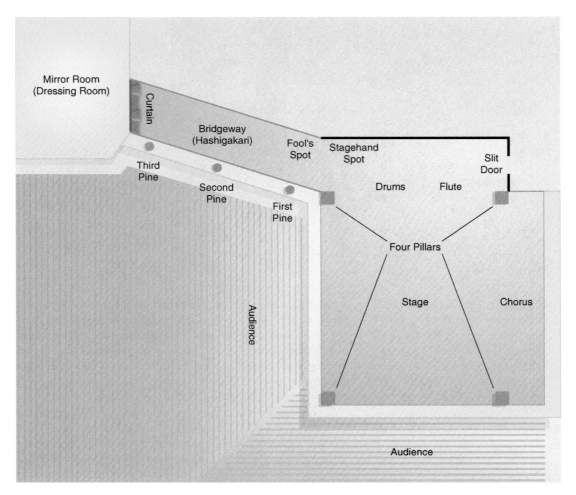

▲ **Figure 5-1: *NOH* THEATRE** Actors emerge from behind the curtained mirror room and are considered to be on stage as soon as they step onto the bridge. They share the stage with the chorus and musicians. With the exception of a few set pieces, the stage is basically bare, and the rear wall of the stage is covered by a painting of a pine tree. This stage is used for all *noh* performances and is not altered for specific plays.

The Art Behind The Noh

Noh actors and musicians devote a lifetime to honing their craft. Actors grow up in **noh** families or enter the profession as children through study with a master artist. Actors specialize in either primary (**shite**) or secondary (**waki**) roles. Like opera singers, **noh** actors learn a repertoire and only then perform with other actors and musicians, usually with only one group rehearsal beforehand. Performances are singular events that bring a particular cast together for only one presentation. **Noh** actors never retire, and elderly performers play some of the most challenging roles, which often call for evocations of deep emotion by means of little movement.

Noh masks are carved from specially treated wood and are delicately painted in such a way that the actors' subtle movements completely transform their apparent expressions. (See additional photos in Chapter 7.) The masks' facial features follow traditional models, yet each has a life of its own. They are cherished and passed down from one generation to another in performance families. The richly woven and embroidered kimonos of **noh** are also beautiful artistic creations treasured by performers.

Kyōgen

Noh's partner, *kyōgen*, which means "mad words," is a comic form that shares the *noh* stage but has its own acting, speaking, and costuming conventions. Whereas *noh* deals with the metaphysical realm, *kyōgen* engages with the concrete world and exposes everyday foibles, conflicts, and follies.

Kyōgen are generally performed between *noh* plays and often complement them, although today they are sometimes performed on their own program. In the past, a full presentation might have included a *noh* play from every category, each followed by a complementary *kyōgen*. *Kyōgen* performers come from different performance families than *noh* actors and appear in *noh* plays only in the roles of commoners or to perform the *ai-kyōgen*, or interlude, between the two main sections of a *noh* play. All *kyōgen* pieces use colloquial language rather than poetry, and the *ai-kyōgen* explains the events of the *noh* play in easily understood terms. These sections were not usually written out in *noh* texts; the *kyōgen* actor was expected to improvise.

Kyōgen acting, though not nearly as subtle as that of *noh*, is surprisingly formal and stylized for physical comedy. Whereas some *kyōgen* characters require masks, masks are less prevalent in *kyōgen* than in *noh* because the actors' facial expressions are essential to the comedy. The most common masks are of animals.

Kyōgen characters are ordinary people—masters and their servants, husbands and wives, fathers and sons. *Kyōgen* is often compared to the *commedia dell'arte* in its reliance on stock characters its master and servant types. Also like the *commedia*, there were no written *kyōgen* scripts until late in the tradition. Tarōkaja, like Harlequin, is a clever servant who outwits his master, and many plot lines revolving around this character parallel *commedia* scenarios. When gods appear in *kyōgen*, they are literally and metaphorically brought down to earth and forced to endure the indignities of daily life.

▼ In this *kyōgen*, the clever servant Tarōkaja has convinced his master that he can sing only when drunk and lying in his own wife's lap, so the master gets him drunk and provides him with his own comfortable lap to coax a song out of him.

Noh and *kyōgen*, both treasured national arts in Japan, continue with the support of the government and devoted fans. Professional performers are still exclusively men, but amateur performers, who are not members of professional families, include many women who study *noh* and enjoy developing their skills. Although there is some resistance to experimentation within these traditions, Japanese theatre artists have created *noh*-style adaptations of Shakespeare and Beckett, along with other experiments.

THINK

Why preserve a tradition whose appeal has waned?

Kabuki

Kabuki, Japan's other major theatrical tradition, is the complete aesthetic opposite of the *noh* theatre. Whereas *noh* is subtle and introverted, *kabuki* is explicit and extroverted. *Noh* is elite and refined; *kabuki*, popular and brash. *Noh* focuses on enlightenment; *kabuki*'s goal is entertainment.

The Japanese *kabuki* theatre is an actor-centered tradition with extraordinary costumes and makeup (see chapter opening photo), lavish sets and scenic devices, and moving domestic and historical plays, all developed to draw in popular audiences and spotlight the talents of celebrated performers. *Kabuki* originally catered to Japan's merchant class, at a time when their wealth and power were on the rise, offering them a place to spend their money and their leisure time. Stiff competition among *kabuki* theatres led to a constant search for novelties. Passed down from generation to generation, today's *kabuki* artists are concerned with preservation of the tradition and its current role as a Japanese national artistic treasure and cultural export. *Kabuki*'s unique performance style and imaginative theatrical devices still thrill audiences and inspire artists the world over.

The origin of *kabuki* goes back to Okuni (c. 1570–c. 1610), a woman calling herself a priestess, who, around 1603, performed radical dances in the dry bed of the Kamo River. According to screen and scroll paintings, she dressed in men's clothes, wore a Christian rosary, and performed scenes of assignations with prostitutes. These performances were called *kabuki*, whose original meaning is "tilted," or "off-kilter."

Today the word *kabuki* is written with three Japanese characters that mean music, dance, and craft or skill.

The form appealed to boisterous crowds who chafed under the Tokugawa shogunate's rigid government. Okuni's dances were copied by female prostitutes until 1629, when the shogunate banned women from performing in an attempt to control this erotic form and its rebellious and

▲ *Kabuki onnagata* actor Tamasaburo Bando V completely fulfills an ideal of female grace and beauty in his performance.

woman could compete. Most *onnagata* actors play women's roles exclusively throughout their careers, and every woman character on the professional *kabuki* stage is played by a man.

Two different styles of male performance forged by prominent actors developed in *kabuki*'s two centers, Kyoto-Osaka and Edo (today's Tokyo), eliciting different kinds of scripts. In the Kyoto-Osaka area, the actor Sakata Tōjuro (1647–1709) created the soft, or *wagoto*, style of acting, used for figures in domestic dramas, which usually depict middle-class merchants caught between their love of a courtesan and their duty to family and business. *Wagoto* characters are almost feminine in their movements and speak with soft, high-pitched voices. They wear simple white makeup and kimonos that are modest in color and style.

In Edo, actor Ichikawa Danjuro (1660–1704) developed the *aragoto*, or rough, style of performance used for superhuman figures from heroes to gods incarnate. Many of the more extravagant aspects of *kabuki* are associated with this style. These characters are found in history plays and wear the bold red and black makeup called *kumadori* and wild, colorful costumes. (See the chapter-opening photo.) In *Shibaraku*, or *Wait a Minute*, one *aragoto* character's costume is so large it requires steel supports for its enormous square sleeves. *Aragoto* movements are broad, taking up space in every direction to accompany the characters' booming voices. These characters display their superhuman strength in stylized fight scenes in which, with a simple push, they can send up to 20 attackers reeling in somersaults.

Kabuki began in dance, and physical movement still remains central to *kabuki* performance, allowing an actor to display his personal beauty, charisma, and talent. Mastering the physicality of the role types is of primary importance. *Kabuki* actors begin their training by learning Japanese classical dance, and some *kabuki* solo pieces are told entirely through dance. In all *kabuki* plays, the high points are captured in physical poses called *mie*. Underscored by the beats of wooden clappers, the actors wind into poses that serve as physical exclamation points for the scene. Aficionados wait for these climactic moments.

Catering to the Audience

The close association between actor and audience gives *kabuki* its dynamism. Audience members have always supported their favorite actors, both by yelling and applauding as well as with more substantial gifts of money or goods. At performances, fans can get close to their idols by sitting near the flower path, or *hanamichi* (Figure 5.2). A descendant of the bridge used in *noh*, this runway cuts through the audience. (See Chapter 2 opening photo.) The name *hanamichi* likely derives from the flowers that fans threw to their favorite actors as they came on stage. Actors use it for most exits and entrances and to make important speeches and perform famous *mie*.

A desire to cater to audiences fed *kabuki*'s search for novelty and theatrical marvels. Some pieces have actors fly over the heads of the audience, and one crowd-pleasing feat calls for one performer to play an entire cast of characters, changing into elaborate costumes and makeup on his way to the next entrance.

disruptive audience. Young male prostitutes, who had also borrowed Okuni's sensual dances to promote themselves, filled the gap until 1652, when the shogunate banned their performances as well. When only older men were left to perform in this style, *kabuki* evolved toward its present form, the domain of male actors, but it has retained its early emphasis on dance, its highlighting of the performer's physical beauty, and a close connection between performer and spectator.

Kabuki Acting Conventions

Kabuki acting openly expresses its theatricality, and the actor's identity is acknowledged. Costumes often display the actor's family crest, and a stage assistant might bring an actor a cup of tea or a glass of water during a particularly long or arduous scene, or arrange his costume to make sure he looks good. These assistants, usually dressed in black, make no attempt to hide themselves; the audience is meant to read them as invisible. (See chapter opening photo.)

Kabuki uses several basic character or role types that are depicted through movement, makeup, costume, and vocal pattern. When women were banned from the stage, *kabuki* developed the *onnagata*, or female role type: an idealized woman played by male actors in white makeup, black styled wigs, and women's kimonos. Their high-pitched, singsong voices and constrained, graceful movements make them paradigms of feminine beauty with which, some say, no real

Notice the lively activity in the audience and the proximity of the actors to the spectators in this woodblock print by Kiyotada, circa 1743, of an old-time *kabuki* theatre.

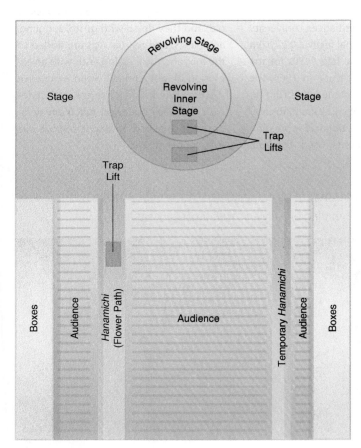

▲ Figure 5-2: *KABUKI* THEATRE Actors enter on the *hanamichi* through the audience. Note the technical devices of traps, elevators, and revolving stages developed to create dramatic effects.

Without the aid of electricity, the *kabuki* developed many mechanical stage devices, including an elevator trap, first used in 1736, an elevator stage in 1753, and a revolving stage platform in 1827. Each device allowed for astonishing transformations and fed the merchant class's desire for theatrical excitement.

The *kabuki* repertoire covers a wide range of themes, but plays were first and foremost vehicles for star actors and meant to highlight their talents. Under the guidance of a head author who put together the whole play, each member of a team of writers wrote the kinds of scenes at which he excelled. A play filled a whole day, but the most interesting scenes appeared at the time of day when most spectators were likely to attend. Today's *kabuki* performances are shorter than the original daylong offerings, and famous scenes are performed on their own, without the rest of the original play. The shogunate forbade the *kabuki* from making political commentary or speaking about current events, so theatre companies thinly disguised contemporary subject matter and altered

Korea's T'alch'um Tradition: Suppression, Resurrection, and Renewal

The history of Korean *t'alch'um* demonstrates the durability of ancient performance traditions. *T'alch'um* (*t'al* for "mask" and *ch'um* for "dance"), the ancient Korean masked dance theatre, finds its roots in shamanistic ritual, and according to some scholars, can be traced back as far as 5000 B.C.E. *T'alch'um*'s ritual origins are evident today in the *kosa*, the ritual ceremony honoring local spirits that precedes a performance, and in the grotesque masks once used to drive away evil spirits. *T'alch'um* grew increasingly secular as Korea moved from early shamanistic belief.

The *t'alch'um* stock characters—an old priest, monks, noblemen, servants, a lion, a prodigal, an old couple, a concubine, and coquettes—represent the types of an ancient era. They were recycled into several basic sketches that satirized the piety of monks, insulted the power of the nobles, rebelled against patriarchal rule, exposed the harsh life of the common peasant, and ridiculed marriage and the competition between wife and concubine. Music is played on traditional Korean instruments and evokes tunes and rhythms known to the audience. The outdoor performances usually begin at sunset and can last all night. The improvisational nature of the performance permitted the insertion of topical names and events that kept the satirical content current over hundreds of years. The audience is drawn into the action and encouraged to shout out *pullim*—well-known phrases.

T'alch'um, the most popular form of Korean theatre, came to a crashing halt when the Japanese invaded Korea in 1910 and banned any form of performance that embodied Korean cultural identity. The period from 1935 to 1945 saw the most brutal oppression. The Korean language was banned, Koreans were forced to take Japanese surnames, youths were conscripted into the Japanese army, and many women were shipped into war zones to provide "comfort" for Japanese soldiers. All theatres were closed except those performing pro-Japanese propaganda plays. When Japan was defeated in 1945, Korean traditional theatre, forbidden since 1910, had long been forgotten. The civil strife that ended in the division of Korea saw left-wing theatre in the north and imitations of Western theatre in the south.

As the situation stabilized in South Korea, there was a call to recover Korean cultural identity, and with it came the resurrection of *t'alch'um*. Through government preservation initiatives, university research, and a national festival, *t'alch'um* was seen again in the late 1950s for the first time in half a century. In 1964, the Korean government named *t'alch'um* an "Important Intangible Cultural Property of Korea." During the political repression of the 1970s, students used *t'alch'um* as a form of protest, updating the old peasant characters with factory workers and replacing the noblemen with political figures. Simultaneously, during the 1970s, the experimental theatre movement in Korea found ways of interweaving *t'alch'um* elements into productions of Western classical plays. New dramas were written, incorporating ritual elements from *t'alch'um*.

Today, Korean new wave theatre artists draw from various traditions. *Cookin'* (2004) has a loose story about a restaurant kitchen whose harmony is upset by the entrance of the owner's nephew. Slide projections direct the audience to participate in the performance as in days of old, and they do so with gusto. Juggling, acrobatics, and martial arts are added to the mix, and the evening ends with an explosion of indigenous Korean percussive rhythm. This fusion of forms and styles with the once-outlawed **t'alch'um** demonstrates that old traditions seldom die; they simply evolve.

▼ The enthusiastic drumming of the Korean cast of *Cookin'* harkens back to the rhythmic drumming of early *t'alch'um* ritual dance drama.

the settings to other historical periods or legends. This was just one way the *kabuki* evaded restrictions to please its audiences and participated in the counterculture of its day.

THINK

Should all-male performance traditions permit women to perform professionally today for the sake of equality, or should age-old traditions preserve their original conventions?

Today's *kabuki* is more a cultivated taste than the popular form of the past, but *kabuki* continues to grow. Ichikawa Ennosuke III has repopularized the form in Japan, with his energetic "super *kabuki*" that uses high-tech special effects like a real waterfall on stage and dynamic stage lighting; a faster pace achieved by cutting long, slow passages; and adding contemporary Japanese language. Nagoya Musume Kabuki, founded in 1983, is an all-woman *kabuki* company. *Kabuki*'s larger-than-life emotions and artistic displays are adopted for highly stylized productions in many places. Ariane Mnouchkine (b. 1939) borrowed from *kabuki* for the Théâtre du Soleil's 1982 *Richard II*, as did Ninagawa Yukio (b. 1935), for his 1985 production of *Macbeth*.

Chinese Opera

WHAT are the primary characteristics of Chinese opera?

Cymbals clang and gongs ring out as a battalion of acrobats in ornate red, green, blue, and gold flip across the stage in succession. Chinese opera is an explosion of excitement and physical virtuosity that brings together music, dance, song, acting, mime, spectacular makeup, martial arts, conventionalized characters, and dramatic storytelling.

The History of *Xiqu*

Xiqu (*xi* means "play" or "game," and *qu* means "melody" or "song") is a generic term that encompasses various theatrical forms developed in China from the thirteenth century to the early twentieth century. Central to these forms are two characteristics: musicality and the integration of the arts of acting, dancing, storytelling, gymnastics, and martial arts into an organic whole. Traditional Chinese theatre is structured around the selection and arrangement of melodies or songs. Most of the lines in plays are sung, and some are recited or spoken. The entire performance is accompanied by music, and percussion instruments are used to heighten dramatic tension. *Xiqu*, in other words, is a form of musical theatre.

Among the hundreds of existing forms of *xiqu*, *kunqu* and *jingju* have attained nationwide popularity, while many others are appreciated locally in different regions of China. *Kunqu*, born in the region of Kunshan, dates to the mid-sixteenth century and is a highly refined and poetic form of *xiqu*. Kunqu attained nationwide popularity in the seventeenth and eighteenth centuries; its repertoire and performance techniques were absorbed into many later forms. When performers of various regional forms from around the country were summoned to the capital

> " The term **Chinese opera** is a Western appellation used to describe traditional Chinese theatre. The **term** is somewhat **misapplied** as 'opera' suggests an emphasis on singing. While singing is very important in traditional Chinese theatre, it's the characteristics of **musicality** and **synthesis** of many arts that define traditional Chinese theatre. "

—Dongshin Chang, assistant professor of Theatre, Hunter College

◀ The young romantic female lead in *The Peony Pavilion* uses her entire body to express her longing for the man she fell in love with in a dream. The delicate, stylized gestures of her fingers are typical of acting in Chinese opera, as is the graceful lifting of the long water sleeve. Both convey feeling and add beauty to the performance.

Beijing to celebrate the Qianlong emperor's seventieth and eightieth birthdays in 1780 and 1790, a fusion of their styles developed into the form called *jingju*, or Beijing opera. Subsequently, *jingju* supplanted *kunqu* as the most popular traditional Chinese theatre form.

The plays of *xiqu* depict a range of subject matter, from comic to serious to fantastic. There are love stories such as *The Peony Pavilion* (1598), a *kunqu* classic of 55 scenes by Tang Xianzu (1550–1616). Du Liniang, a 16-year-old maiden, visits a deserted garden at spring's peak and enjoys a daydream in which a young man makes passionate love to her. Du Liniang dies pining for the ideal man of the dream, but the play traces her path to love's fulfillment as she returns to life and eventually marries the young man of the dream and reunites with her family. *The Legend of the White Snake*, a fantastic tale rendered in many forms of *xiqu*, depicts an ancient love story between a commoner and a beautiful woman who is actually a snake spirit. In *Silang Visits His Mother* and *Mu Guiying Commands the Army*, two popular *jingju* plays, the lead characters are based on historical figures who, in times of war, are torn between caring for family and responding to the urgent call to protect the country.

Role Types, Makeup, Costumes, and Set

The makeup and costumes of traditional Chinese theatre are arresting; their vibrant colors help define the characters. There are four basic role types: male (*sheng*), female (*dan*), painted face (*jing*), and clown (*chou*). Each of these role types breaks into subcategories that are distinguished by social status, age, temperament, and the practice of martial skills.

Makeup and costumes follow set conventions. Especially remarkable are the painted-face characters whose makeup is detailed with elaborate swirling lines and patterns. There are more than 1,000 different facial patterns, but spectators familiar with the conventions know that a painted-face character with makeup dominated by red indicates the character is loyal or courageous and facial makeup dominated by white suggests a cunning or wicked nature. The comic nature of the clown role type is marked by a patch of white around the nose and eyes.

The costumes of Chinese theatre are sumptuous, with lavish embroidery and brocades. Costume color, pattern, cut, and decoration are used to differentiate the role types and their subcategories. Members of the imperial family wear a specific hue of yellow; characters from the lower or poorer social ranks are dressed in blue; characters of the well-to-do class wear robes or vests with openings cut in the middle of the chest; and emperors have dragons embroidered on their robes. High platform shoes and padding worn by officials and generals enhance their physical stature and indicate social rank. The pennants on their backs symbolize the armies they lead. Long, flowing "water sleeves" made of light cloth add grace and beauty to the movements of actors playing the male and female roles. Jewels and headdresses add further adornment to stage dress.

In *xiqu*, a table, two chairs, and a red rug suffice as a stage set. The actors depict the setting, convey the occasion and portray the characters through conventionalized gestures and movements. Actors step over an imaginary threshold to indicate a doorway; they carry a whip if they are riding a horse and adhere to prescribed motions for mounting, riding, and dismounting; and they bend up and down at the knees to step into an imaginary boat swaying in the water. Entrances, exits, and startling moves are underscored by beating cymbals and gongs. Actors punctuate important moments by turning their heads in a single dramatic move and fixing their eyes on the audience.

Music and Actor **Training**

As its Western name implies, the soul of *xiqu*, or Chinese opera, is its music. Unlike Western operas, Chinese operas are not linked with particular musical compositions. Instead, each form of *xiqu* has its own collection of tunes from which musicians select songs to create the score for a production. Singers try to select musical pieces best suited to their own vocal strengths. The singing and musical dialogue may seem slightly shrill or jarring to Western ears unfamiliar with the form. To the trained ear, subtleties in musical delivery make the difference between a good performance and a great one.

Actors of *xiqu* begin training in childhood. After a few years of basic training in voice, footwork, gesturing, and movement, actors focus on a specific role type, determined by their physical features and talents, and then spend a lifetime mastering the portrayals of the characters from the role type and the repertoire associated with it. Cross-dressing, either women playing men or men playing women, is common.

The Twentieth Century and **Beyond**

In the twentieth century, traditional Chinese theatre underwent many changes. During the Cultural Revolution (1966–1976), various forms of *xiqu* were outlawed because of their perceived aristocratic and bourgeois content. To fill the gap, *yangban xi* ("model opera") was created, which combined some old conventions with new Western influences and was intended to exalt communist heroes and the proletariat. Until the end of the revolution in 1976, only plays of model opera and works based on them could be performed. Many *xiqu* actors were vilified for their association with the traditional forms and were sent to work camps or prison. When *xiqu* was later revived as an important part of the national heritage, a generation of actors and audiences had been lost. The Chinese Ministry of Culture now subsidizes the art, paying substantial salaries to performers and commissioning new works. In 2010 the state-run Chinese Central Television broadcast a national Beijing opera student competition. Today some forms of *xiqu* flourish in its homeland and in communities in the United States and elsewhere that have welcomed Chinese immigrants.

New experiments continue to challenge *xiqu* and reach out to new audiences. Three different productions of the *kunqu* classic *Peony Pavilion* in recent decades illustrate this point. In 1999, the New York–based Chinese director Chen Shizheng created a 19-hour version, including all 55 scenes of the original play. Scenes were performed in various styles and fusions of styles, not only *kunqu*. In the same year, American director Peter Sellars presented a pared-down 4-hour version, with Chinese performers alongside Western-trained actors, video sequences, and a musical mix of traditional instruments and synthesizers composed by Tan Dun. In 2004, well-known Chinese literary figure Kenneth Pai produced a nine-hour version of the

▼ Famed actor Lin Weilin performs the lead role in the Zhejiang Kunqu Opera theater production of *Gongshunzidu* at Jinsha theater in Chengdu, China.

The famous performer Mei Lanfang **(1894–1961)** introduced the world to Chinese opera through tours from 1919 to 1956 to Japan, the United States, and the Soviet Union, where he gave demonstrations witnessed by Charlie Chaplin, Constantin Stanislavski, and Bertolt Brecht, among other theatre luminaries. Mei Lanfang's demonstration influenced Brecht's views on acting for the epic theatre.

Trained from age 8, Mei attained stardom while still in his teens. Mei innovated within the form of Chinese opera. Developing an original style, he mastered song, dance, and martial arts in the female

"…Above all, the Chinese artist never acts as if there were a fourth wall. … He expresses his awareness of being watched."

—Bertolt Brecht, "Alienation Effects in Chinese Acting"

role. New pieces were created as vehicles for his enormous talents. Although artists usually master only a single role type, Mei perfected both the loyal wife or daughter role and the woman warrior role, eventually creating a new type called *huashan*, a female who is both vivacious and seductive. Although Mei was a female role performer himself, he supported bringing women back into these roles at a time when they did not perform, which ironically led to the end of the male performer in female roles, the art that had brought him fame.

play, starring younger *kunqu* performers, that was intended to preserve the play's essence and attract new and younger audiences. *Xiqu* performance traditions still offer opportunities for daring innovations, perhaps even the chance to give birth to something wholly new. Some people, however, still question a particular artist's right to experiment with this revered age-old form.

THINK

Who, if anyone, owns a theatrical tradition or has the right to innovate within it?

Carnival Tradition

WHAT are the roots of the Carnival tradition, and how has the tradition adapted and changed over time?

The tradition of Carnival across Latin America traces a peculiar lineage from ancient Rome through medieval Europe to the present. Its history demonstrates the need for cultural expression through the performing arts, even in the face of brutal oppression. What began as festive revelry evolved into a complex hybrid theatrical tradition, with role-play and dress-up used to subvert authority.

Almost all societies observe periods of approved exuberant merrymaking, through which people give vent to pent-up emotions in communal celebrations where they transcend normally acceptable behavior. New Year's Eve and Halloween often provide that release in our own culture. The ancient Romans had festivals throughout the year that

served this social function. The most extravagant display came at Saturnalia, the celebration of the winter solstice at which people exchanged gifts and engaged in elaborate role-play in which the world returned to a time when all were equal. Slaves exchanged roles and even clothing with their masters. They dined at the master's table and rejoiced in this brief period of freedom. With the spread of Christianity, the Church understood that it could not stop these celebrations and still win converts, so it adapted them and incorporated them into Christian ritual.

The Catholic Church transformed Saturnalia into a celebration of wild festivity before the period of Lent. Lent is traditionally observed by abstaining from the eating of meat; *Carnival* literally means "farewell meat" (*carne vale*). Throughout the Middle Ages, the time before Lent was observed with banquets and masked costume parties. The custom spread from Italy across Catholic Europe, although the exact nature of the festivities varied, depending on local customs. As the Spanish, Portuguese, and French colonized the world, they brought Carnival celebrations to Latin America, where the European tradition encountered the cultural influences of African slaves and indentured labor from China.

During the eighteenth century, European colonists continued their Carnival masquerade celebrations in the colonies, mainly as private masked costume parties. Just as the Romans released their slaves from work for Saturnalia, many colonial slave masters did not make their slaves work on Carnival; this was the only time of freedom from work during the year. African slaves were permitted to celebrate Carnival as long as no ritual worship occurred that would violate Christian religious belief. It was not long before slave celebrations reflecting African customs—such as the ancient African traditions of circular parading through villages at festival time—took hold. While the colonists celebrated at private banquets, slaves and their descendants turned Carnival into a lively outdoor street theatre. As in Africa, when skits were performed, the parading crowd would encircle the performers. African dance, music, and drumming accompanied the pre-Lent celebrations, as did sculptural masks and costumes made of feathers, beads, and grass, typical of African tribal festivals. Many of these elements can be seen in Carnival costumes to the present day.

Carnival as Political Street Theatre

In the Caribbean, after the end of slavery in 1838, metaphorical combat was often part of Carnival celebrations and was meant to challenge repressive authority structures. Stick fights, a combat sport amusement from the slave yards,

> "Since midnight on Sunday this **festival** has broken the slumbers of our peaceful citizens with its usual noisy **revelry** and **uproarious** hilarity. Bands of music including those 'elegant' instruments, the **tin kettle** and salt box, the bangee and schack-schack have **paraded** the town."

—From the *Port of Spain Gazette*, February 20, 1849

were choreographed into elaborate mime routines. Calypso, with its call-and-response format, was used to both engage the public and as fodder for competition among calypso singers who would vaunt their prowess in suggestive lyrics. The combative mode also harpooned colonial authorities and satirized public figures. Performers used masks and the

▼ The masked *Taimácaros* characters that appear in Carnival celebrations in the Dominican Republic parade through the streets of Santo Domingo. European colonizers brought Carnival to the island of Hispaniola by the mid sixteenth century.

▲ West Indian immigrant groups have brought the spirit of Carnival to their new homes. Seen here is New York's West Indian Day celebration on Eastern Parkway in front of the Brooklyn Museum.

anonymity they provided as protective cover for the behavior displayed in Carnival skits. In the British colonies, a *commedia*-like form developed that was the verbal counterpart of the stick combat routines. A Dottore-type character spoke in elevated language filled with lapses of logic about the rule of law. His foil was provided by the Pierrot Grenade, a low-born comic servant figure who improvised in the local patois and depended on his wits to survive. As the dialogue performances grew, a host of local stock characters were added.

The origin of the steel band lies in Carnival's creative response to oppressive authority.

By the late nineteenth century, slaves and their descendants had transformed this celebration of white European colonists into an element of black culture and a theatrical celebration of freedom from slavery. Eventually, whites stopped participating in Carnival festivities. The transgressive nature of the event often created a spirit of lawlessness in the streets. In 1883 the British colonial authorities banned the use of African drums. In keeping with the improvisational nature

of Carnival, musicians devised instruments out of bamboo sticks, shells, cookie tins, and dust pans and finally turned to discarded oil drums as devices for percussive expression.

Around Latin America, Carnival took slightly different forms and lasted from a single day to two weeks. Everywhere, the European celebration was co-opted by slaves and those on the lowest rungs of society. The Cuban Carnival, one of the oldest traditions in the region, was for some time celebrated on January 6, the day of Epiphany, also as a single day of rest. It is now celebrated in July as a festival of the revolution, reflecting the original spirit of Carnival. In Cuba, the music mixes a Chinese trumpet-like instrument with conga drums, revealing not only African roots but the influence of the many indentured Chinese laborers brought to the island. Chinese motifs also appear in the visual elements of Cuban Carnival, notably in the large lanterns carried aloft during the procession. The Carnival in Brazil is actually a later development of the mid-nineteenth century and was basically a European affair of polka and waltzes until the slaves were freed in 1888. The *samba*, a fusion of Angolan *semba* rhythms (*semba* is an erotic dance brought from Luanda by slaves) with polka, the slow Cuban *habanero*, and other Caribbean dance influences, was created in the early twentieth century in the slums of Rio. Its rhythms permit performers to dance, parade, and sing simultaneously, and it is now closely associated with Rio's Carnival festivities, where community groups called samba schools challenge each other with dance performances.

Carnival **Adapts** and **Evolves**

During colonial times, attempts to ban Carnival as unruly and lawless were repeated around Latin America to no avail. The form itself triumphed as an expression of freedom. Eventually Carnival's jubilations became a government-sanctioned social release valve for the poor. Caribbean peoples have taken their Carnival heritage with them wherever they go. Large celebrations can be found in London,

THINK

What is the difference between developing a form and transforming it into something new?

Brooklyn, and Toronto, and smaller festivities continue to spring up in many other cities. In keeping with old practices, festivities adapt to local surroundings, customs, and music, in an ever-evolving tradition.

GLOBAL TRADITIONS AND INNOVATIONS

Preserving Endangered Species of Theatre

Many performance traditions around the globe are endangered species of theatre. The legacy of colonial repression and today's economic, social, and political change have placed many forms at risk of extinction. They are losing their place in community life, their artists, and even the languages that sustained them. Attempts to save these cultural practices for future generations are under way. International organizations, national governments, universities, and local communities are experimenting with strategies for preserving traditions.

In the past decade the United Nations Educational, Scientific and Cultural Organization (UNESCO) has expanded its notion of cultural heritage from tangible artworks to include intangible heritage—"traditions or living expressions inherited from our ancestors and passed on to our descendants, such as oral traditions, performing arts, social practices, rituals, festive events, knowledge and practices concerning nature and the universe or the knowledge and skills to produce traditional crafts." Currently UNESCO has designated 212 "masterpieces of oral and intangible heritage," outlining a unique plan of action for preserving each.

UNESCO's efforts have a global scope. The *kutiyattam* Sanskrit theatre

from Kerala, India, the *kunqu* Opera tradition in China, and the *bunraku* puppet tradition of Japan are among the masterpieces cited by the organization, as are various Carnival traditions of South America and the Caribbean, as well as storytelling forms. In Benin, Nigeria, and Togo, the *Gelede*, a yearly Yoruba-Nago rite that includes singing, dancing, and the use of carved masks and costumes to retrace local history and myth is endangered because of a loss of skilled artists. Preservation efforts have led to the recording of the rites, the identification of master artists, and the creation of arts festivals.

Many communities have long been engaged in preserving their own traditions. On the island of Bali in Indonesia, the impact of tourism on performance traditions and village life inspired the community to devise innovative means to preserve a rich heritage of dance-drama, shadow puppetry, and masked performance forms. The Balinese cultivate two streams of performance, one for tourists and one with religious elements observed for the Balinese. An annual month-long Bali arts festival enables artists to perform traditional works to discerning audiences, maintaining a high technical standard.

Around the world, government-sponsored national theatres, training schools, and international festivals sustain traditional performance, and universities often harbor cultural centers

for the study and promotion of indigenous art. This institutional support is key to preserving traditional forms. Often theatrical traditions fall victim to political events. During the brutal communist dictatorship of Pol Pot (1975–1979), 80 to 90 percent of Cambodia's artists died or were killed, endangering all of the indigenous Cambodian arts. Various government and educational institutions have united to revive Cambodia's classical arts, including dance-dramas and shadow puppetry.

These solutions, whether undertaken locally or by international groups, inevitably create their own contradictions and may transform the forms in their attempts to revitalize them. The questions of who pays for these measures as well as how traditions are elected for salvation remain issues for debate. Visit the UNESCO Intangible Cultural Heritage site (www.unesco. org/culture/ich/) for videos and photographs of the traditions discussed in this chapter and many others.

THINK

Who should be responsible for preserving a tradition—the government, an international organization, the community of origin, or the people who perform it?

Rabinal Achí: Surviving Colonial Oppression

Rabinal Achí is a rare example of pre-Hispanic Mayan masked dance drama and may represent the oldest surviving theatrical text from the Americas uncontaminated by European influence. Elaborate costumes and masks accompany poetry, music, and symbolic choreography in a drama of Mayan mythology that depicts a conflict between warriors from Rabinal and the Quiché nations in what is now Guatemala.

The *Rabinal Achí* play text is part of a long oral tradition transmitted (sometimes clandestinely) to the next generation by elders who learned all of the 3,000 verses by heart. The participating elders view this as a duty to the preservation of the Mayan community and its history, and the play is still passed on through oral transmission from generation to generation. Actors learn their parts by having the play read to them and repeating the lines until they are memorized. According to Mayan belief, the performance bridges the past, present, and future, bringing the living participants into contact with dead ancestors (represented by masks), whom they will join in the future. Once European written dramas arrived and with them the idea of a written text, transcriptions of the performance were made from the Achí language to the Roman alphabet by Mayan writers, members of the clergy, and scholars over the course of four centuries to the present day.

Although there are other plays performed in Mayan communities, *Rabinal Achí* is the only one that dramatizes the events in Mayan history that culminated in the fifteenth century before the European colonization of the Americas. It is speculated that some of the story may have roots as far back as the fourth through tenth centuries. The drama telescopes these events through a montage of scenes.

In the play, violence and sacrifice are seen as legitimate recourse to protect land and people. Although the violence is narrated or expressed in suggestive movement, fear of this message led the Spanish authorities to issue repeated bans against native plays from 1593 to 1770. European missionaries, intent on destroying indigenous religious images and temples, believed they could adapt native performance to Christian goals as celebrations of saints. During the pre-colonial period, dialogue was sung or chanted by a chorus to ancient Mayan music performed on trumpets, drums, and cymbals, but after the arrival of the Spanish, dialogue was spoken, and Christian hymns were substituted for the indigenous music. Today, indigenous music has been restored in performance. The Spaniards also reorganized the traditional performances of *Rabinal Achí* around the Christian calendar and moved some performances to January 25, the day of the conversion of Saint Paul, the patron saint of Rabinal.

◄ An actor portraying a *Quiche* warrior speaks to his captors during a performance of the ancient play *Rabinal Achí* in the streets of Rabinal, Guatemala in 2006.

Carnival Art and Commerce

Today's Caribbean artists find themselves in a position of contradiction toward Carnival. With the tourist trade a staple of many Caribbean economies, Carnival has become an object of touristic voyeurism performed to entertain the very people it co-opted, satirized, and demonized. Simultaneously, it is the true voice of a culture and its fight for freedom and independence. Carnival has been a tremendous presence in Caribbean written drama, where the rhythms of calypso inhabit the language and movement is an inherent part of performance. The dueling songs of calypso can be felt in intense dialogue exchanges between various postcolonial authority figures and Pierrot Grenade, the poor fool outwitting his betters. The Nobel prize–winning Caribbean poet and playwright Derek Walcott (b. 1930) pits two such Carnival figures against each other in *Dream on Monkey Mountain* (1967), through the characters of the prison guard and his captive.

Puppet Traditions Around the Globe

WHAT roles do puppet traditions play in communities around the globe?

In the United States, puppetry is often considered a form primarily for children, but around the world, from Belgium to Brazil, from Thailand to Turkey, from Mali to Myanmar, we find sophisticated puppet traditions that entertain adults and children alike. Puppets pass on myths and legends, illustrate moral teachings and philosophical questions, and present stories of emotional complexity. They are used in political activism and rituals of magic and healing. Some

▶ *Wayang golek*, pictured here, is a wooden rod puppet tradition from West Java, Indonesia. The delicate features and white paint of the puppet on the left belong to a refined character, while the bulbous eyes and nose and the red color of the puppet on the right show this to be an unrefined character. The puppeteer, or *dalang*, operates all the puppets to the music of a gamelan orchestra, which he conducts by banging a small metal hammer held between his toes.

traditions go back hundreds of years and serve as the essential theatrical experience for a community.

Instead of a human performer claiming center stage, puppeteers, puppets, and sometimes a narrator join to take the actor's role. Puppetry uses all the elements of theatre, but the visual takes precedence over the oral in this form. Traditions identify themselves by the kinds of puppets they use, and the special capabilities of objects determine the nature of the performance.

Puppets can take many forms and can be manipulated with various methods: Hand puppets, string marionettes, rod puppets, and shadow puppets are the most common. The number of puppeteers required to operate a single puppet depends on its size and type. An operator can manipulate two small hand puppets at a time. String marionettes, generally more complicated, might require two hands for a single figure. Some Burmese marionettes with many strings can perform amazing feats; the Alchemist puppet, for example, performs flips and other acrobatics. In many shadow traditions, the puppeteer manipulates an entire world of characters by placing cutout figures, usually of leather, against a screen lit from behind by a lamp or another light source. There are various types of rod puppets. Some, like those found in Sicily, are quite large—4 to 5 feet tall and weighing up to 80 pounds each. The puppeteer works from above, holding a metal pole attached to the puppet's head and ropes attached to the arms. Other puppets, such as the West Javanese *wayang golek*, are small, and the puppeteer grasps the wooden sticks that support the bodies and hands from below.

There are as many kinds of puppets as there are ways of manipulating objects, and each is adapted to its performance context. Vietnamese water puppets perform on water stages in rice paddies and temple pools. The puppeteers stand behind a screen in water up to their waists to operate underwater poles attached to the floating figures.

Puppets and Ritual

Puppetry's origins may lie in rituals in which objects imbued with life revealed the presence of a god or became a god incarnate and were worshiped as totemic figures. According to Indian legend, puppetry began when the god Shiva and his wife Parvati, seeing some excellently carved wooden figures, possessed them and made them dance. India boasts numerous puppet traditions whose performances all begin with prayers, and puppet figures have been found in some of the oldest archeological sites. Indian puppets are still treated reverently, and many continue to serve ritual functions.

Native peoples in the Americas used puppetry for both ritual and enjoyment long before colonists brought European puppet theatre to their land.

The Egyptians had a processional figure whose phallus was lifted by a string as part of a celebration, in what was probably a fertility rite. In ancient Rome the statue of the oracle of Jupiter-Ammon appeared to move on its own and spoke with voices that emerged from tubes in the wall. (An *oracle* is a priest or priestess who acts as a medium through whom advice or prophecy was sought from the gods.) During the Middle Ages, European churches housed statues of holy figures with moving eyes and nodding heads, and some even wept or bled. Medieval marionettes also performed plays with religious themes.

Many puppet traditions still serve various ritual functions. In Awaji, Japan, puppeteers go from house to house, conducting rituals of blessing for the new year. In Indonesia, puppeteers are people of power and perform with either shadow or rod puppets at weddings, births, and other ritual celebrations.

Africa has a rich heritage of masked performance but surprisingly few ritual puppet traditions. In Mali, masquerade performances combine masks and puppets, all of which are referred to as "masks." Puppet figures in the shape of mythical animals and symbolic characters pop out from the back of costumes and from the top of masks worn on the head. The performers dance about, moving both their own bodies and those of the puppets. Although not a sacred ritual, this community performance acknowledges a connection between the world of spirits and that of humans.

Puppets and the Popular Voice

In Europe the tradition of popular puppetry extends back to ancient Greece and Rome. There is little evidence to reliably state what these puppets performed, but some may have done comic sketches. Later puppet theatres incorporated the characters and improvisational style of *commedia dell'arte*, relying on scenarios rather than play texts even for long and intricate stories.

The sixteenth century spawned a progeny of rabble-rousing *commedia dell'arte* puppet characters defiant of authority, including Italy's Pulcinella, England's Punch, and later versions of these characters in Belgium, France, Russia, Argentina, and elsewhere. First performed with hand puppets and small portable stages on street corners and in marketplaces, these shows provided popular entertainment and served as a voice for the common people. They relied on knockabout humor but also took up topical issues of the day. Guignol, a nineteenth-century French figure, reported on contemporary events for illiterate workers. The Turkish and Greek shadow traditions served a similar cultural role, centering on an anti-authoritarian rogue. In both Sicily and Belgium, rod puppets perform medieval tales. Battle scenes draw the main focus, with comic relief provided by popular *commedia*-style characters.

In the eighteenth century string marionettes rose in popularity in Europe, especially as entertainment for bourgeois audiences, and puppetry's role in catering to popular audiences declined.

A long-established tradition of Czech folk marionette theatre found its political voice in the late nineteenth century in the Czech nationalist movement against the Austro-Hungarian Empire. The puppet form, which predated the empire, kept local languages and legends alive and stood as a symbol of the indigenous cultures of early Czech history. Before World War I, Czech puppet plays protested Austrian domination, and during the Soviet period, they cleverly critiqued Communism. The Drak puppet company, founded in 1958, is still one of the Czech Republic's most important puppet theatres.

Joseph **Haydn (1732–1809)**
and
Wolfgang Amadeus Mozart
(1756–1791),
among other
great composers,
wrote operatic works
specifically for
marionettes.
The Salzburg
Marionette Theatre,
founded in 1923, tours the world
with its
renowned performances
of opera.

Today puppets also have a decidedly political role; large processional puppets are staples of political rallies. Peter Schuman's (b. 1934) Bread and Puppet Theater began this trend in the 1960s, when Schuman attended anti–Vietnam War protests with his papier-mâché masks and puppets of various sizes. His silent images of women in pain and mourning made a dramatic impact and proved an effective means of conveying the antiwar message. Large puppets carried down the street by a crowd made puppeteering a communal act of protest. The Bread and Puppet Theater derives its name from the belief that art is as necessary to health as bread, and the actors hand out their homemade bread to spectators when they perform. Bread and Puppet is still active, and it continues to inspire new generations of political puppeteers.

Puppets and Written Texts

In puppetry, the performing object is of more interest than a written text. As a result, many puppet traditions rely on the puppeteer's improvisations. Even when a written epic tale exists as the basis for a performance, puppeteers often improvise, model a performance on an earlier puppeteer's practices, or use language passed on through an oral tradition. Nonetheless, some great written literature has been developed for the puppet stage.

Japan's **bunraku**, a combination of puppet manipulation, ballad singing, and playing of the three-stringed *shamisen*, has engendered both exquisite puppets and

▼ An old couple express their affection in a scene from the silent puppet play *Em Concerto* (In Concert) (1994) from Paraty Brazil's Grupo Contadores des Estórias.

literary masterpieces. *Bunraku* puppets are 3 to 4 feet tall and operate through direct manipulation by three puppeteers who work together.

Bunraku **performers**
spend 10 years **learning**
to manipulate
the puppet's feet
and 10 years
learning to work
the puppet's left hand;
only then
can they take the place
of master puppeteers **who**
manipulate
the doll's head, face,
and right hand.

Puppetry in the Early Twentieth Century

In the early twentieth century the development of psychology and the explosion of technology made the puppet an important symbol for artists commenting on the modern human condition. Many famous European writers, such as Michel de Ghelderode (1898–1962), Paul Claudel (1868–1955), and Gerhart Hauptmann (1862–1946), either wrote plays for puppets or used the puppet as a figure or metaphor in other dramatic works. The Bauhaus movement in Germany, which focused on the union of art and technology, not only created puppets but also designed costumes that transformed actors into moving objects. The Swiss artist Paul Klee (1879–1940) brought his abstract style to 50 hand puppets he made for his son Felix that were used in a Bauhaus performance.

A chanter sits at the side of the stage, narrating the story and performing all the voices and dialogue to musical accompaniment. Narrating for *bunraku* is a demanding art of its own, and famous chanters are the primary attraction for many aficionados. Chikamatsu Monzaemon (1653–1725), often called the Shakespeare of Japan, wrote his most famous plays for *bunraku*. They are beautiful literary works with themes of love and honor that combine dialogue and prose description.

▲ In *War Horse* at the National Theatre in London, human actors work with magnificent, life-sized puppet animals created by the internationally renowned Handspring Puppet company from South Africa. The touching tale of the bond between a boy and his horse is realized by a team of puppeteers who bring the animals to life.

Other important playwrights have tried their hand at writing plays for puppets, including Belgium's Maurice Maeterlinck (1862–1949) and Spain's Federico García Lorca (1899–1936). Lorca's visit to Argentina from 1932 to 1934 inspired puppet theatre presentations of European classical plays as well as Lorca's own work. Argentine puppeteers traveled through South America, expanding interest in the form.

Puppetry Today

Puppetry's ability to captivate spectators with dynamic visual images makes it a perfect theatrical answer to today's media age, and it is an increasingly popular theatrical tool. Jim Henson (1936–1990), following in the footsteps of Howdy Doody; Kukla, Fran, and Ollie; and Shari Lewis's (1933–1998) Lamb Chop, introduced generations of children to puppetry through television with his Muppets, whose sophisticated humor addresses adults as well. Jim Henson's Creature Shop puts technologically innovative puppets to work on film and television, and the Henson Foundation continues to support puppeteers creating new works for the stage. Director-designer Julie Taymor freely mixes masks with *bunraku*-style puppets, shadow puppets, and other manipulated objects of her own invention in a single production. To call her work simple "puppetry" underestimates the variety of stage images she employs. The success of *The Lion King* (1997) attests to the popularity of

> Today, most Latin American **puppet theatre** serves a social and educational function, but young, **daring artists** are exploring new forms that interact with other **technologies.**

From Puppets to Performing Objects

Puppetry, one of the earliest forms of performance, is becoming a central player in today's world of media entertainment. The term *performing object* is replacing the term *puppet* to describe a wide range of inanimate objects found in theatrical performance and on film, all manipulated either directly by a performer or through a variety of technological means.

Puppeteer Stephen Kaplin[1] describes how performing objects range along a continuum that begins with the actor in costume and moves to the most technologically sophisticated computerized creatures. The farther the object is from the performer, the more technology the performer requires to manipulate it. When actors put on costumes, they are using inanimate materials to help them project character. When they wear masks, the separation of the performer and the performing object is more distinct. A puppet is an object fully removed from the actor. Sometimes the technology is simple—a wooden stick for a rod puppet or a set of strings for a marionette. At a greater distance, the technology can become more complex, such as radio signals or computers to control animatronic or mechanized puppets. Even computer-animated figures can be considered performing objects. They are manipulated by someone projecting character through advanced computer technology. In the first *Star Wars* film, the character Yoda was primarily operated like a hand puppet, by Henson puppeteer Frank Oz. The size of the figure was partially determined by the length of Oz's arm. In his second movie appearance, Yoda was primarily an animatronic or mechanically operated puppet, controlled by a puppeteer working the controls from off the set. In his final appearance, the animatronic Yoda was assisted for two scenes by a computer-animated counterpart, whose every move was crafted in cyberspace. Computer animation draws connections between the ancient skills of puppeteers and the new skills required for technological media.

Any performing object can threaten to displace the actor's central position on stage, especially when it is operated electronically. However, some of the most technologically advanced performing objects have a performer, or several, behind them who give life to what is otherwise inanimate matter. In the past, puppeteers were often masked or hidden on stage. Today, in shows such as *Avenue Q* and in the work of a company such as Royal de Luxe, they are often visible, drawing focus to their skills in performance. By featuring object manipulators in this way, the theatre continues to emphasize the central role of live performers.

[1]Stephen Kaplin, "A Puppet Tree: A Model for the Field of Puppet Theatre," *The Drama Review* 43, 3 (Fall 1999): 28–35.

this form. Performing artists Janie Geiser and Kazuko Hohki combine performing objects with film and video, a match that often works more fluidly than live performers working in concert with electronic media. The Handspring Puppet Company in a joint production with the National Theatre in London have created a spectacular production of *War Horse* (2010), in which giant puppet horses interact with live actors who ride them in a spectacular epic tale.

Today puppeteers experiment with an endless array of performing objects. They use found objects as puppets, they create their own figurative and nonfigurative forms with novel materials, and they blend aspects of every tradition with media technology. Trained as a visual artist, Theodora Skipitares combines video projection with shadow puppets made from synthetic materials, stuffed figures that use the actor's hands as their own, and imaginative visual sights. A give and take between established traditions and new experiments continues to expand the art of puppetry and its theatrical possibilities.

GLOBAL TRADITIONS AND INNOVATIONS

Traditions Evolve

Each of the performance traditions described in this chapter has had a long and colorful history and a large international sphere of influence. Traditions, such as Korean *t'alch'um*, have had less of an impact on other forms but have held deep cultural meanings for their societies. They all reflect how varied theatrical expression can be and how the imaginative and creative spirit can instigate change and challenge seemingly fixed forms. As we look at our own traditions, it is important to remember that they were once innovations. The true theatre artist looks to tradition and sees only possibilities.

Summary

WHAT elements characterize Indian Sanskrit theatre and the performance traditions it inspired? p. 98

▶ Indian Sanskrit drama is a sophisticated poetic tradition whose plays survive but whose codes of performance are lost to us, except for the description in the *Natyasastra*, a more than 2,000-year-old authoritative text on the form that continues to influence Indian arts today.

HOW have mime and the *commedia dell'arte* performance traditions evolved from antiquity to today? p. 100

▶ The mime tradition dates to antiquity. *Commedia dell'arte* was an improvised Renaissance theatrical form with stock characters, whose influence can be felt in theatre, circus, vaudeville, film, and television to the present.

WHAT distinguishes the important theatrical traditions of Japan? p. 103

▶ Japan has several important theatrical traditions. *Noh* is a highly stylized ritualistic form that developed in the medieval court. *kyōgen* is its comic partner. *Kabuki* is a seventeenth-century tradition that evolved dynamic staging, costuming, and acting styles to cater to its popular merchant-class audience.

WHAT are the primary characteristics of Chinese opera? p. 111

▶ The characteristics of musicality and synthesis define traditional Chinese theatre.

▶ Singing is the heart of Chinese Opera, or *xiqu*, a form that combines music, dance, song, acting, mime, spectacular makeup, conventionalized characters, martial arts, and dramatic storytelling.

WHAT are the roots of the Carnival tradition, and how has the tradition adapted and changed? p. 114

▶ Carnival, a theatrical form born in pagan Europe, traveled through colonization to the Caribbean and Latin America, where African slaves transformed it into an expression of freedom.

WHAT roles do puppet traditions play in communities around the globe? p. 119

▶ Almost every culture has a vibrant puppet tradition that serves a ritual function or as popular entertainment. Puppets come in many shapes and sizes and have various modes of manipulation.

MySearchLab®

▼ The Elevator Repair Service's *Gatz* was a six-hour-long performance of the entire 49,000-word text of F. Scott Fitzgerald's novel, *The Great Gatsby.*

Alternative
Paths *to Performance*

Other Authors, Other Texts, Other Forms

Every theatrical performance has a text that provides coherence and form, but that text is not always a play script, and the author is not always a playwright. A theatrical text can come in many guises—a musical score, movement notation, or visual images—and can be created in many ways. The author may be a playwright, or the author may be an actor, a director or designer, a choreographer or composer, a clown or mime, or an ensemble of artists. A theatrical work often defies notions of authorship because its very nature is collaborative.

Plays give rise to a linear creative process that begins with the ideas of a playwright, which are expressed in a script, that is then turned over to directors, actors, and designers for interpretation on the stage. The creative process does not always follow this course from page to stage, however. Often the process is inverted, and rehearsals and performance shape the written text. Sometimes the result of alternative paths to performance is alternative theatrical forms. The forms discussed in this chapter are both old and new; some are popular and easily accessible, while others are unfamiliar, but all are created without a traditional play as the starting point. Understanding how a theatrical text created in unusual ways structures a performance can help us appreciate the variety of experiences we might encounter in the theatre today.

New forms develop when theatre practitioners believe old ones are exhausted or unable to express current concerns. Some artists endeavor to use traditional styles in original ways. Others seek a more personal means of expression. Whatever the impulse, they all search for new ways to create and reinvigorate the stage. This leads to innovations that may defy accepted conventions. Artists who rebel against tradition are referred to as the **avant-garde**, from the French term for the soldiers who march ahead of a military formation. Metaphorically, that is what these artists are doing: scouting out new artistic territory. Many of the forms and artists discussed in this chapter broke new ground, although now their path to performance is well trodden by others who have followed in their footsteps. As you will see, when enough theatre practitioners follow new conventions for a period of time, a new theatrical tradition is established. This continual cycle of renewal through innovation is the process that keeps theatre exciting and relevant.

1. Do all performances begin with a written play text?

2. What prompts artists to create new forms of theatre?

3. What is the avant-garde, and what role does it play in the evolution of the theatre?

CHAPTER 06

Creating Through Improvisation

Many theatrical forms rely on the improvisational creativity of the actor rather than on the playwright's written words. In such forms, actors take center stage as creators of drama, not solely as performers. Such was the case in the

▼ Rebecca Northan reveals the challenges of dating when she picks an audience member at random each night and then carries on a 90-minute improvisational blind date with him.

improvised sixteenth-century *commedia dell'arte* discussed in the last chapter. The demise of the *commedia dell'arte* was hastened by its assimilation into written plays. Because it depended on the spontaneity of improvisation and physical humor, an element that was inherent to its very nature—the freedom of the actor—was destroyed by the written word.

Improvisation is a central element in African culture, where spontaneous interaction with an audience can transform a performance. Many African countries maintain a tradition of theatre that very much resembles the *commedia dell'arte*, with actors working from an outline prepared by the leader of the troupe. The stock characters reflect African types—the aged and crippled female crone, the cocky young stud, and the usual collection of gluttonous servants and tricksters. Most of these companies are traveling troupes, just as their European counterparts were.

Improvisation plays an important role in many Asian theatrical traditions, as performers adapt well-known stories or prepared material to topical events. In the *bhavai* tradition of Gujarat, India, traveling players hone a repertoire of sketches (called *veshas*). These sketches are not written down but are passed on from father to son through practice and performance. When the players arrive in a town, they inquire about current events and issues of importance to the local people. This information helps them choose what *veshas* to perform, so their improvisations will be relevant and filled with topical allusions to which the audience can relate.

> **❝ For me, improv is all about firing up parts of the mind and imagination in new ways. ❞**
>
> —Mark Rylance, winner of the 2011 Tony Award for best actor

GLOBAL TRADITIONS AND INNOVATIONS

Commedia Scenario

Commedia dell'arte performers improvised on a scenario. The scenario shown here is taken from act III of *The Captain*, which was published in a collection of scenarios in 1611 by Flaminio Scala (1547–1624), a *commedia* actor. Scripts like these hung backstage for the actors to look at before performing. On the left we see the names of the characters in the scene and on the right the events that will inspire improvisation.

The Captain: ACT THREE

FRANCESCHINA	Franceschina enters, grieving because she will never again see her husband, Pedrolino.
CASSANDRO	Just then, Cassandro enters, looking for the Captain. He sees Franceschina; recognizing her as the nurse, he begins to berate her, and falling to her knees, she tells him all that has happened to his daughter and where she left her.
DR. GRATIANO	At that moment, the Doctor enters, rejoicing about the wedding. He sees Cassandro, who tells him that Franceschina is the nurse and he now hopes to find his daughter. They go into the Doctor's house.
PANTALONE ORATIO	Pantalone and Oratio enter with jewels for the bride.
PEDROLINO PORTERS	Thereupon, Pedrolino enters with porters who are carrying things for the wedding, and they all go into the Doctor's house.
CAPT. SPAVENTO ISABELLA	Just then, the Captain enters with Isabella, who is dressed as a soldier. They say they want more than anything to stop the wedding, and they hide.
ARLECCHINO MUSICIANS	Arlecchino now enters with the musicians, instructing them that the banquet will be held in a garden at the Tosa Gate. The Captain and Isabella, having heard everything, leave. Arlecchino knocks.
ORATIO FLAMINIA	Oratio comes out holding Flaminia by the hand.
PEDROLINO FRANCESCHINA	Pedrolino comes out, holding Franceschina by the hand.
PANTALONE DR. GRATIANO	Pantalone comes out, holding the Doctor by the hand. The musicians start playing and they all dance off to the garden at the Tosa Gate.

Source: From *Scenarios of the Commedia dell'Arte*, Flaminio Scala's *Il Teatro delle favole rappresentative*, trans. Henry F. Salerno (New York: New York University Press, 1967), 83. Used with permission of Michelle Korri.

Improvisational theatre is also alive and well in the United States and Canada. Second City and Chicago City Limits are long-running theatre events in which actors improvise and create from ideas proposed by the audience. A simple subject or title volunteered by an audience member can serve as the dramatic text and form the catalyst for comic sketches. Many contemporary improvisers draw on a bag of tricks and comic bits that they can insert as they improvise, just as *commedia* actors used *lazzi*. The excitement of the form lies in the spontaneity and virtuosity of the actors as they interact in performance. Improvisation festivals take place every year in cities from Amsterdam to Vancouver. Interesting interactions with the audience can also form the basis for improvisational theatre. In *Blind Date*

(2010), the work's creator, Rebecca Northam, asks a member of the audience to fill in for the date who has stood her up and then proceeds to improvise an entire performance with a stranger on stage.

Improvisation is an inherent part of the theatrical process. Before performances are set, there is a period of rehearsal that usually begins with trial and error, so what appears to be a fully scripted and blocked performance is actually created through improvisation. Discoveries made during rehearsals are often incorporated into published plays. At each performance, actors face a set of unknowns that can alter the playing of the text: an unexpected laugh, a forgotten line, or a malfunctioning prop can trigger improvisation.

The Performance Ensemble and **Collaborative Creation**

HOW does collaborative creation challenge traditional theatrical decision-making hierarchies and methods?

Although all theatre is always collaborative, sometimes traditional decision-making hierarchies dissolve and a group of artists share responsibility for creating a text. Such a group may improvise, discuss, and share ideas. In this process, there may not necessarily be a single author. Collaborative creation is often favored by those with strong political and social beliefs in the power of the community.

During the 1960s, when the social revolution inspired a search for new forms, some theatre artists rebelled against the established written text and the hierarchy of control within the theatrical process. The traditional supremacy of the playwright's words was seen as a metaphor for the social and political power structure that needed to be overthrown. Following the ideas of French theorist Antonin Artaud (1896–1948), for a time even language itself was decried as the source of manipulation of the masses, and the primal expression of sound and movement was given priority. Groups such as Joseph Chaikin's (1935–2003) Open Theatre (1963–1973) and Peter Brook's International Centre for Theatre Research (founded in 1970) searched for new systems of language based on sound and movement that could transcend cultural boundaries. Many theatre companies began rehearsals with an idea or a concept but no written text. The actors, designers, and director joined in a process of collaborative creation through improvisation; the performance text and the dramatic text evolved together, and the creative performance team was the author of both texts.

The idea that a play can be authored by a company of people and that even the audience can claim some part of authorship is a marked departure from the traditional concept of a playwright as the sole author of the dramatic text.

One of the earliest groups to work in this manner was The Living Theatre, whose political work was discussed in Chapter 2. Some of that group's work involved audience

> **"** We find an **idea** that we want to express physically. Then we do what is necessary to realize it. If it requires special **physical** exercises, then we do them. **"** [1]

—Julian Beck, Founder of The Living Theatre

participation, and spectator reaction influenced the dramatic text. Even when The Living Theatre worked with playwrights, some parts of the script were worked out in performance. Its production of Jack Gelber's (1932–2003) *The Connection* (1959) not only used jazz improvisation as a metaphor for the actor's work but also featured jazz musicians improvising with the actors on stage.

Collaborative groups were an international phenomenon. Peter Brook began his work in London and then set up in Paris. Jerzy Grotowski's (1933–1999) Polish Laboratory Theatre used physically based acting techniques to reconstruct and construct dramatic texts; his efforts were an inspiration to many groups around the world.

Today many theatre groups continue to use collaborative improvisation and experimentation to create performance texts. Although dramatic texts may develop out of this work, they are "written" through an active working process on the stage. One important example of this is the collaborative docudrama *The Laramie Project* (2001), a performance about the events surrounding the gruesome murder of Matthew Shepard. Shepard was a young gay man who was severely beaten and left to die on a roadside in Wyoming in the winter of 1998. To create the work, members of the Tectonic

[1] Julian Beck, "Acting Exercises," in *The Twentieth Century Performance Reader* (London: Routledge, 1996), 61

The Open Theatre created works in collaboration with actors and writers, and pieces often developed over two years of experimentation. The script for *Terminal* (1969) is the result of a group expression of cultural attitudes toward death and mortality. Performed with ritual elements of choral movement and chanting, words are evocative of deeper meanings, and images of the transitory nature of the human body are everywhere present as the living and the dying become one. Susan Yankowitz (b. 1941) is credited as the "playwright" for this piece, but she is often not mentioned in publicity or reviews, and she openly acknowledged the awkwardness of being "the author of an 'authorless' piece." She wrote lines for the actors to try out and accept or reject. Sometimes the actors suggested the lines for her to write. Most often, sound and gesture replaced words as the source of meaning.

The Dying Resist

Lights. A circle of actors walk at a brisk, regular pace. When individuals break out of the circle, the others maintain the original size and shape of the circle by adjusting pace and distance. Two Team Members stand outside the circle. One gives instructions. The other drones words of approval, which eventually become empty sounds.

Team Member 1:

Keep moving.

Everyone is part of the circle.

Everyone must keep the circle moving.

Follow instructions.

Don't accelerate or slow down.

Don't stop.

You are each responsible for keeping the circle moving.

Everyone is useful.

You are each keeping the circle alive.

Team Member 2:

Very	good.	Nice.
Very	good.	Nice.
Very	good.	Nice.
Very	good.	Nice.
ery	ood.	ice.
ery	ood.	ice.
ery	ood.	ice.
ery	ood.	ice.

Individuals step out of the circle, or stop abruptly where they are.

First one. Then another. Then more.

Individually, and finally in unison, the Resisters punctuate the drone with the word "out."

Resisters: / Team Member 2:

Resisters:		Team Member 2:		
Out				
		ery	ood.	ice.
out	out	ery	ood.	ice.
	out	ery	ood.	ice.
out			(Etc.)	
out				
out				
out				
out				

The actors continue their circle.

They ignore both the physical obstacles presented by the Resisters and the word of protest.

The circle and the protest exist simultaneously.

The Runner Who Never Gets Started *The Runner crouches over an imaginary starting line on hands and toes. He holds the racing position for several moments, then jumps to his feet, panting. Behind him, a Second Runner runs frantically in place. The First Runner repeats his action.*

The Dying Are Drugged *Several of the Dying sit or lie on the beds. We see them in their drugged condition—vacant, tranquilized, harmless. A high-pitched hum is heard.*

Note: *This fragment should bear a rhythmic and thematic relationship to The Dying Resist.*

▼ Using current events as a springboard for collaboration, actors of the Tectonic Theatre Project portray community members they interviewed to create the text for the Laramie Project, directed by Moisés Kaufman.

Theatre Project served as researchers and interviewers and then as dramaturges, writers, and actors. Director Moisés Kaufman (b. 1963) took actors to Laramie, Wyoming, where they interviewed Shepard's friends and family, the friends and family of the men who killed him, the person who found his body, the sheriff who led the investigation, other gay men in town, church leaders, teachers, and various other members of the community. The actors turned these interviews into short monologues, attempting to reproduce the voices, actions, and words of the people they had interviewed. Actors then performed these vignettes for each other, debating for and against keeping different pieces. In doing so, the acting company became involved in aspects of the production that would normally be left to the playwright and the director. The end result painted a theatrical portrait of Laramie, Wyoming, and examined the various ways its individuals and the community as a whole dealt with issues of prejudice. A written play was not the starting point of this project, but the end, and the program lists the director and all the members of the company in addition to several writers as the authors of the final script.

THINK

Is it possible to objectively portray people who played a part in horrific events?

South African director Mbongeni Ngema (b. 1955) created Theatre of the Ancestors in the 1980s, a political people's theatre of little means and great theatricality. In the community spirit of the African tradition, he brings together an ensemble of untrained actors who live together for many months, building the spirit of *ubuntu*, or brotherhood, out of which collaborative creation will grow. He provides rigorous training for actors as they create performances through improvisation about matters that are of immediate concern to the group. Using the storytelling, dance, and choral song at the heart of African performance, they built a production of *Sarafina* (1987), which tells the tale of a murdered civil rights lawyer. Through impersonation and storytelling, the actors in this group invite the spirit of the fallen ancestor to live within them. Acting becomes a vehicle that combines traditional beliefs with education, personal growth, and creative expression. Ngema used the same method in *Woza Albert!* (1981) to call up the spirit of memorable political leaders and enact them on stage.

❝❝**Black people** are always seen as people who do not have **heroes**. One of the important things I do with my **work** is to **reveal African** heroism.❞❞

—Mbongeni Ngema, director

▼ *Sarafina*, written and directed by South African Mbongeni Ngema, with music by Ngema and Hugh Masekela, dramatizes the struggle of South African youth against the oppression of apartheid. First produced in South Africa, the play later moved to New York, where it was nominated for five Tony Awards.

Mime and Movement Theatre

HOW do mimes create performances?

In many performance traditions, the movement of the actor is the primary conveyor of meaning or story. The literary text is either nonexistent or given secondary dramatic value. For example, most performances that use masks focus on the body and emphasize movement over language. Indian *kathakali*, Balinese masked comedies, Native American performance, African festivals, and *commedia* and clown traditions around the world rely on movement as a primary text. Because mime is recorded only in the actor's body, there are few tangible records of movement-based performance through history. We do have enough evidence, however, to know that such forms seem to have existed in all periods, in all cultures.

Although movement-based theatre is a global phenomenon, the term *mime* usually evokes images of a story acted out without words, as in a *pantomime*. Actors working in the manner of Marcel Marceau to conjure up the existence of unseen objects and people on stage perform *illusionary mime*. Many mime performances are actually *mimodramas*— silent plays with characters, plot, and a story; the absence of language means that they are conceived in the body, and not through dialogue. Less well known are various forms of abstract mime that do not rely on a narrative and whose expression lies in the kinetic energy of the body such as the *statuary mime* of Étienne Decroux (1898–1991). This abstract corporal expression often feels closer to modern dance.

> ❝ Mime **evolves** in **silence** where the word is not yet **permitted**, or no longer permitted. ❞

—Jacques Lecoq

Jacques Lecoq (1921–1999) created a mime school in Paris devoted to the development of a fundamental and natural transcultural mime that preexists language. The Mummenschanz, a company originally formed by Lecoq students, masks not only the face but often the body as well, turning the actors into abstract shapes that express meaning much the way it is expressed in abstract art. Many of Lecoq's students have also applied his philosophy of mime to energize stage movement within more traditional theatrical forms. Geoffrey Rush (b. 1951) is among the many Lecoq students who bring virtuoso physical work to their theatrical roles as he demonstrated in his 2009 performance in Eugène Ionesco's *Exit the King*, which also featured Lecoq alumna Andrea Martin (b. 1947). Directors Julie Taymor (b. 1952), Simon McBurney (b. 1957), and Ariane Mnouchkine (b. 1939)—all former Lecoq students—are known for the physicality of their productions.

Unlike dance, which is structured through rhythm, music, and line of movement, the mime begins with a narrative, an idea, or an image and then gives physical life to that concept. Mime performance is created through improvisational trial and error until a performance text is concretized into fixed patterns of movement. Most often, the author of the movement text is also the performer, creating the same organic link between the dramatic text and the performance found in all performance traditions and particularly in solo work. Some movement texts can be passed on to new generations of interpreters because they are carefully choreographed and notated.

Variety Entertainment

HOW does variety entertainment appeal to both public taste and the avant-garde's artistic sensibilities?

Variety entertainment is as old as recorded theatre history. We know that street performers, referred to as "mimes," performed in ancient times. Aristotle alludes to them in the *Poetics*. The theatre in the late Roman Empire was largely a variety show. Variety entertainment is always high on fun and low on intellectual demands and lacks a sustained narrative. It has appealed to the general public through the centuries by featuring diverse entertainments that are not connected by a single story line.

Clowns and Fools

Clowns and fools are found in most cultures, and as we discussed in the section on comedy in Chapter 4, they serve a variety of social functions. Their performances have in common minimal written text and a dependency on tradition, improvisation, and physical action. Ceremonial clowns of Native American traditions may use texts based on ritual, and circus clowns may develop personal texts based on their individual clown characters. Sometimes daring acrobatic feats may provide the text for circus clowns. Clowns may depend on the knockabout humor of the English pantomime and music hall tradition that extended into silent film. Talking clowns use verbal humor as a nontraditional written text, which has led to a new derived tradition of stand-up comedy.

In certain regions of English-speaking Africa, a form of variety entertainment called **concert parties** evolved in the 1920s, and touring companies have performed all over West Africa ever since. A hybrid combination of African culture and American and European entertainments, concert parties include musical numbers, brief topical sketches, and female impersonators. Comic routines feature clowns and tricksters winning the day in slapstick romps with stock characters out of West African society. The concert party clown, in an intriguing bit of cultural borrowing from early American films, often appears to this very day with the heavy white painted lips of the American **minstrel show**. Today's concert parties continue the blending of traditions, incorporating gospel, rock, and soul music. The Yoruba Opera in Nigeria is similar in form and practice, and it was probably influenced by concert parties.

African performances also included elements of **vaudeville**—a popular American variety show form that incorporated many different kinds of dramatic texts. Vaudeville

◀ The Akan Trio, a Ghanaian concert party, are shown here performing an opening chorus in the late 1950s. Note the use of the exaggerated makeup of American minstrelsy, whose negative racial stereotype traveled the globe and became a form of self-parody in West Africa.

performances relied heavily on the stand-up routines and knockabout humor, which evolved from earlier clown traditions. Vaudeville, which had its heyday toward the end of the nineteenth and the early twentieth centuries, billed itself as family entertainment. Its counterpart was the less family-oriented **burlesque** show, which featured bawdier humor and usually included striptease. Both popular entertainments were eventually eclipsed by movies. To keep audiences in the theatre by offering something for everyone, vaudeville and burlesque might include musical numbers, acrobatic bits, comedy duos, and even animal tricks. The evening usually ended with an extended theatrical scene.

Variety Entertainment and the Avant-Garde

The early twentieth-century avant-garde rejected the art forms of the past as not reflecting the dynamism of the modern technological world. The Italian futurists, in particular, focused on variety show performance as a means of developing a new artistic sensibility. They wanted to destroy the illusionary realistic stage world and the convention of the *fourth wall* and foster an active interaction with the audience. The clown, the acrobat, and the juggler were the perfect performers to achieve this. These performers do not represent anything other than themselves and are not

Blackface Minstrelsy

Sometime in the late 1820s, the white performer Thomas Dartmouth Rice (1808–1860) put burnt cork on his face, dressed himself in rags, and did a shuffle dance while singing "Jump Jim Crow," claiming he had copied the routine from a black slave he saw down South. This marked the beginning of blackface minstrelsy, a popular entertainment of songs, dances, and racist comic routines that portrayed a derogatory stereotype of the lazy, slow, lascivious black man speaking ignorant English that dominated the American stage throughout the nineteenth and early twentieth centuries and continues to haunt American culture.

The iconic makeup of the minstrel clown, a blackened face with white circles around the eyes and mouth, topped off by a wild fright wig, permitted cross-race performance and the construction of black identity by white performers for white Americans. Minstrelsy's romanticized portrayal of plantation life, with cheerful slaves singing for their masters, helped many northern whites imagine an acceptable picture of slavery, even as the abolitionist movement was on the rise.

While the first minstrel performers were white men, around 1865, blacks began performing in their own minstrel troupes, thinking they could cash in by providing a more authentic look at black culture. Ironically, the minstrel stereotype was so strong that black performers also had to cork up and put on wigs to conform to audience expectations. Burnt cork makeup had come to represent blackness on stage more than real skin color.

Although it presented blacks in a demeaning role, minstrelsy permitted black performers the freedom to speak forthrightly on taboo topics such as politics and religion. The great vaudeville and musical theatre entertainer Bert Williams (1876–1922) discovered both freedom and constraint in blackface performance. He developed a character called "Mr. Nobody." The blackface makeup, he claimed, freed him to find himself as a performer and develop his comic style. Although he rose to great fame, offstage he continued to experience the oppression that accompanied a real black face in America. Minstrel acts were popular in vaudeville, and the form traveled the world, finding popularity in England and the British colonies as well. The popularity of minstrelsy gave black performers in the United States an avenue to display their talents and earn a living, but it also enlisted them in perpetuating the very stereotype that oppressed them.

By the mid-twentieth century, the black clown character developed in minstrelsy appeared on stage, film, and television without the exaggerated makeup but preserving its demeaning character traits—a grotesque vision binding black performers to racist stereotypes. In the late 1950s, the civil rights movement took pointed aim at the minstrel clown, replacing the demeaning image it promoted with expressions of "black pride." Black theatre artists appropriated the minstrel mask for political purposes, using it to challenge racial oppression. In Ntozake Shange's (b. 1948) 1979 theatrical choreopoem, *Spell #7*, a large minstrel face hangs as an imposing image over the stage and over the lives of the characters, who strive to free themselves from stereotypes.

◀ In *The Regard Evening* (2003), Bill Irwin spoofs the avant-garde as well as the conventions of realism and variety theatre. Using costume elements as symbols (the baggy pants, ruffled collar, and big shoes of the clown; the top hat and cane of the vaudeville dancer, or hoofer; the goofy hat of the stand-up comic; and a Groucho Marx disguise), Irwin humorously explodes each tradition.

caught up in the illusion of narrative. Their acts rely on a presentation of concrete skills—feats that inspire interaction with the audience.

These old popular entertainments have come back in the form of *new vaudeville* and *new burlesque*. They bring an aesthetic and social self-consciousness that seeks to alter audience sensibilities. These new clowns, comics, acrobats, mimes, and jugglers are distinguished from their antecedents who played for pure entertainment value; their physical humor and movement are part of a dramatic text with other messages and new goals. The best known of these new clowns is Bill Irwin (b. 1950), trained as a circus performer, dancer, actor, and mime, who has extended comic clown routines beyond their pure amusement value. In *Largely New York* (1989), Irwin appeared as a "post-modern hoofer" whose doomed attempts to learn a variety of modern dance styles end up trapping him inside a television. All this was performed with ongoing banter with the audience. Despite his light-hearted veneer, Irwin delivered pointed social and aesthetic commentary.

The Quebec-based Cirque du Soleil uses circus performance as a theatrical text by playing on the inherent dramatic content in feats that defy gravity and the limits of the human body. It has spawned imitators around the world. Performed with attention to every aesthetic detail, from dramatic lighting to elaborate costumes and sound, these circus artists assume theatrical characters as they dazzle us with circus skills. Unlike other circus performances, in which the focus is on the raw energy of the skill and danger, Cirque du Soleil clothes its acts in an air of mystery, mysticism, and the exotic. The Flying Karamazov Brothers, who can juggle almost anything, from meat cleavers and sickles to chunks of tofu, fish, and eggs, engage in an ongoing comic patter with the audience that titillates the mind while their feats titillate the eyes. In their performances, circus is combined with impeccable comic timing.

GLOBAL TRADITIONS AND INNOVATIONS

Futurist Performance

The artistic movement known as futurism dates its inception to the "Futurist Manifesto" written by F.T. Marinetti (1876–1944) in 1909. He followed it, in 1913, with his "Variety Theatre Manifesto," in which Marinetti declared that the theatre of realism and "psychology" did not reflect the modern technological era and declared it passé. Futurists exalted a variety theatre of "madness" and absurdity because it necessitates constant invention to amaze its audience. Futurist performance emphasized the illogical and rejected a narrative based on cause and effect. Some aspects of the *theatre of the absurd* discussed in earlier chapters originated in this aesthetic.

In this short piece by Giacomo Balla (1871–1953), the gibberish of the lines sabotages the narrative thread. The stage is empty and draws attention to itself with red and green lights. This empty space was a novel idea at the start of the twentieth century. The actors come out and perform as variety show entertainers, not belonging to any dramatic context.

Giacomo Balla

To Understand Weeping / *Per Comprendere il Pianto*

man dressed in white (*summer suit*)

man dressed in black (*a woman's mourning suit*)

Background: square frame, half-red, half-green.

The two characters are talking, always very seriously.

man dressed in black: To understand weeping . . .

man dressed in white: mispicchirtitotiti

man dressed in black: 48

man dressed in white: brancapatarsa

man dressed in black: 1215 but mi . . .

man dressed in white: ullurbusssssut

man dressed in black: 1 it seems like you are laughing

man dressed in white: sgnacarsnaipir

man dressed in black: 111.111.011 I forbid you to laugh

man dressed in white: parplecurplototplaplint

man dressed in black: 888 but for G-o-d-'-s sake don't laugh!

man dressed in white: iiiiiirrrrririrrriri

man dressed in black: 12344 Enough! Stop it! Stop laughing.

man dressed in white: I must laugh.

CURTAIN

Source: Futurist Performance, by Michael Kirby, with manifestos and playscripts translated from the Italian by Victoria Nes Kirby. Copyright © 1971, 1986 by Michael Kirby. English translations of manifestos and playscripts in Appendix copyright © 1971 by Victoria Nes Kirby. Reprinted by permission of PAJ Publications, New York.

Storytelling

Storytelling has long been considered an origin of theatre. It contains all the fundamental elements of the form—a performer, an audience, characters, and narrative. Gifted storytellers can even transform into the characters in their tales, turning their narrative into a form of theatrical performance. Storytelling performance has a long and continuing history.

Telling the **Community's Story**

Just as families tell stories about colorful relatives and lessons learned from parents and grandparents, communities tell stories to answer the vital questions that sustain every society: "Who are we?" "Where do we come from?" "What is our purpose?" "How should we live?" In places without a written language, storytelling performances keep a culture's traditions alive.

In many African cultures, storytelling is a vital way of educating the young and entertaining the community. Narration, acting, drumming, and song are interwoven into a participatory art form, and audience response creates improvised moments. Subjects tend to stress the continuity of the community and its values and may include tribal heroics, feats of strength and wit, and tales of magical powers. The legends have morals and imply behavioral dictates. Many African storytellers are talented impersonators who can portray all the characters, human and animal, through alterations in voice and body. Narrative descriptions are recounted with sound effects and expressive intonations.

> **Often stories begin with riddles posed to the children of the community as a teaching device.**

The stories pass from one generation of storytellers to the next, with each adding its own embellishments. The idea of authorship can be an anathema to societies where cultural property belongs to the community and ideas of ownership are not reflected in methods of creation. Often community members interrupt the story to act out particular passages or sing an appropriate song, and the audience may spontaneously enter the playing space to dance and sing and add to the performance. Although much storytelling consists of myth and legend, the *griots*—storytellers of West Africa—provide an oral history of their communities through their recitation of epic heroic tales. These sagas, which can last for hours, are filled with music and songs,

praises for leaders and their ancestors, genealogies that connect the past to the present, and proverbs that ensure the continuity of cultural values.

Storytelling performance traditions exist the world over. Native American cultures have an ancient tradition of storytelling often accompanied by drumming and dancing that involves the community. *Meddahlik* is a Turkish theatrical

▲ An African *griot* woman, Ya Jalahatuma Jabate, performs a song of praise at a gathering to celebrate the installation of the Chief *Griot* of Kita. She is playing the *karinya*. In West Africa, instruments are allocated by gender. Only men can play drums and stringed instruments, while women play percussion.

Staging the Great American Novel

The experimental group Elevator Repair Service has been staging stories written by great American novelists. The group's six-hour-long *Gatz* (2005), a performance of the entire 49,000-word text of *The Great Gatsby*, by F. Scott Fitzgerald (see chapter opening photo), was followed by William Faulkner's *The Sound and the Fury* (2008), and Ernest Hemingway's *The Sun Also Rises* (2010). These are not simply readings. Instead, every word of the novel is given life on the stage. Often when heard in the context of a stage production, new meanings for the text are revealed, as words take on a dimensionality not found on the page. Sometimes the more meditative pace of the novel seems at odds with the theatre's demand for action; this highlights what makes a drama and a novel distinct artistic forms, with different ways of telling stories.

---

form in which storytellers tell ancient legends and romances with songs and jokes and improvise off audience feedback. Sometimes the *meddahs* incorporate allusions to contemporary happenings to provoke discussion. The *Pansori* tradition of Korea is a form of musical storytelling that includes narrative and song often improvised for particular audiences. These storytelling forms and many others fight for survival in a world where the written word and mass media are rapidly replacing storytelling performance traditions as information sources.

Telling **Personal** Stories

Sometimes a storyteller recounts a personal history. Solo performance has become popular in recent years, evolving from several traditions—from stand-up comedy to **performance art**. In performance art, performance is an extension of visual art in time, with more significance accorded to the visual image than the spoken text. Today, individual actors create solo pieces to air their unique talents, experiences, and concerns.

All of today's solo performers owe a debt to Spalding Gray (1941–2004), who was a pioneer with his solo performances in the 1970s. Gray was instrumental in turning solo theatre into a respected performance form. His performances provided an opportunity for personal exploration and confession, and many younger artists cite him as their inspiration. His texts sound and read more like diary entries than traditional theatre pieces. When he performed *Swimming to Cambodia* (1985) or *Monster in a Box* (1990), monologues that related very personal episodes from his own life, he did not just reveal his particular personality on stage; the audience also witnessed his attempt to come to grips with his own life experiences, using the medium of theatre. Although written, published, and available to other interpreters, Gray's monologues are deeply connected to him and his life experiences. After his death, at the inspiration of Gray's widow, *Spalding Gray: Stories Left to Tell* (2007) presented a collection of Gray's monologues performed by actors. While Gray's sardonic wit still soared through the voice of others, the link between the creator and the performer in solo performance was made all the more palpable by Gray's absence. Spalding

Gray continues to speak to us and inspire. *And Everything Is Going Fine*, a 2010 documentary film by Steven Soderbergh, is constructed entirely of clips of Gray speaking.

The growth in the number of performers who have taken to this form reflects a confluence of forces. As producing theatre becomes increasingly expensive, having a single artist sitting alone on stage with few or no set or costume elements is an economical and portable way to create theatre that can be taken to different venues with little effort. On a deeper level, as the world moves toward multicultural awareness, individual voices representing groups that had been largely silent can now be heard and welcomed in the public arena. Performers from marginalized groups often take to the stage to represent the political and social agendas of their communities.

Personal Stories, **Political Agendas**

Early male solo artists such as Spalding Gray and Eric Bogosian (b. 1953) focused on political or social commentary in their work; when women claimed the solo stage for feminist performance, the personal often became political. A few generations ago, it would have been unsettling just to see a woman alone in command of a theatre; now women are not only solo but have created daring pieces that blur the line between public and private acts. Performers such as Karen Finley (b. 1956) and Holly Hughes (b. 1955) use the shock value of nudity, obscene tirades, and sexual images—including Finley's smearing her naked body in chocolate and offering the audience a lick—to raise awareness of their political concerns. Some of the disturbing effects are visual statements, reflecting solo performance's origins in performance art.

THINK

When an artist wants to make a strong statement of social protest, should there be limits to how far he or she can go in violation of social taboos?

Spalding Gray's texts developed out of his performances. To create a piece, he sat at a desk on stage in front of an audience and improvised from an outline. The performance was recorded, and the tapes were transcribed. He then edited and expanded the performance transcripts, continuing this process of performance, taping, editing, and expanding until the written monologue was complete. Early audiences did not hear the completed dramatic text, but rather a text in process. The audience's responses became a collaborative element. Interestingly, many solo performers create in this way. Because the writers and performers of solo texts such as Gray's are the same person and the material is so deeply connected to their lives, the texts are composed organically during the performance process.

Feminist performance paved the way for explorations of class, race, ethnicity, and sexuality. Daring, provocative, and often naked, Tim Miller (b. 1958) challenges audiences to see past his homosexuality to his humanity. In pieces such as *Glory Box* (1999), *Body Blows* (2002), *US* (2003), and *Lay of the Land* (2010), he thrust himself into the American cultural war over gay marriage and immigration rights. Similarly, London-based Muslim performer Shazia Mirza (b. 1976) uses comedy to expose our ethnic and religious stereotypes and fears with jokes about terrorists and the "veil." Solo

artists use their art to probe the nature of identity and social definitions of difference, self, and other, while bringing visibility to the concerns of disenfranchised groups. Their work challenges us to think about how we define ourselves and those we do not know.

Although some solo artists perform themselves, other solo performers create character sketches by imitating or performing people they know—family members or people they have met or interviewed. John Leguizamo (b. 1964) in *Mambo Mouth* (1991), *Freak* (1998), and *Ghetto Klown*

(2011) singlehandedly populates a stage with as many as 39 different characters from the Latino community. Korean American Margaret Cho (b. 1968) explores Asian American identity and crosses racial lines to play characters of various races and ethnicities, forcing us to examine our own social typecasting. Sarah Jones (b. 1973), in her acclaimed show *Bridge and Tunnel* (2004), examines assimilation and identity in her portrayal of a dozen or more New York characters of different races, religions, and ethnicities who reveal their deepest longings at a community poetry contest.

As stand-up comedy turns increasingly "in your face" and agenda driven, it often becomes difficult to draw a clear line between stand-up and other forms of solo performance. Many festivals of solo performance include entertainers who bill themselves as comedians as well as those who consider themselves performance artists. The comic is always looking for laughter as a release, but performance artists often provide no outlet for our shock or outrage. What all these artists have in common is the authorship of texts that require their personal presence on stage. The actor's relationship to the individuals and experiences presented is integral, and unlike a play written as a monologue, these personal performance pieces can't be reproduced by another actor.

Whether driven by the need for personal expression or the economic realities of today's theatre, solo performances have proliferated across the United States, and cities from Seattle to New York host festivals featuring dozens of solo artists. Solo performances festivals organized around political themes, such as the 2009 "Performance of Maternity" festival in Kerala, India, have brought together academics and artists to explore international social issues through theatre.

▼ Tim Miller's *Lay of the Land* (2010) is a personal and political exploration of the issues surrounding gay rights in the United States.

Documentary Theatre

HOW do theatre artists use primary source material as texts?

History has long been the source for theatrical fare. Some believe the events depicted in Greek tragedy are based in fact; Shakespeare wrote history plays; Arthur Miller went to Salem, Massachusetts, to study the court records of the 1692 witch trials before writing *The Crucible* (1953). These documentary records served as the inspiration or backdrop for fictional historical drama. Today we see a new kind of **docudrama**, or **documentary theatre**, in which actual primary sources become the text for a performance. Unlike reality television and its frivolous invented drama, documentary theatre tends to have political and social messages and attempts to address pressing issues with theatrical immediacy. Increasing numbers of theatre companies are using the tools of journalism in the creation of art.

Solo Social Documentarians

Although solo performance is a personal form, it does not have to exclusively deal with personal material. Several solo artists have explored social and political issues through the transformation of material collected from various primary sources. The work of solo artists such as Eve Ensler (b. 1953) and Anna Deavere Smith (b. 1950) can be classified as docudramas.

Anna Deavere Smith's first performances were part of a large project she calls *On the Road* that explores ethnic, religious, racial, and American identities. Her characters are all people she has met in real life, and Smith lets them speak for themselves: The dialogue she uses is taken directly from transcripts of interviews she has done. Performing their words, Smith re-creates the speech patterns and mannerisms

▲ Anna Deavere Smith in her one-woman play *Let Me Down Easy* channels Lance Armstrong telling the story of his comeback from testicular cancer to expose the healthcare crisis in America.

▼ *The Great Game: Afghanistan* (2009) is a series of short plays exploring the cultural and political history of Afghanistan and the havoc wrought by foreign intervention and invasion. The performance is punctuated by verbatim remarks by political and military figures such as Hillary Rodham Clinton.

of her interviewees with great precision. In the process, she changes before our eyes like a chameleon. Race relations are a central focus in her work. *Fires in the Mirror* (1992) is an investigation of the racial and religious attitudes that triggered the riots and murder that took place in Crown Heights, Brooklyn, in 1991 after a car driven by an orthodox Jew hit a black child. *Twilight: Los Angeles, 1992* (1993) deals with the urban unrest following the beating of a black man, Rodney King, by Los Angeles police in 1992. In these pieces, Smith, a light-skinned African American woman, performs men and women of every ethnic and racial background. She moves so seamlessly from one role to another that the characters' ethnicity, race, and gender seem to obliterate her own. Her performances allow the audience to maintain a degree of detachment and objectivity as they encounter volatile issues through emotionally involved characters. Watching Smith, we cannot help but think deeply about how gender and race are portrayed in our culture and on stage. Smith's performance of her characters is an essential and untransferable part of her pieces. More recently, in *Let Me Down Easy* (2009), Smith channeled 20 different characters confronting illness and death against the backdrop of a flawed and inequitable medical system.

Eve Ensler's *Vagina Monologues* (1996), discussed in Chapter 1, contains many documentary pieces about sexual violence against women during the war in Kosovo, where Bosnian women were systematically raped as part of a program of ethnic cleansing. Her piece has opened doors for other artists to continue to explore world events through a woman's eyes.

Heather Raffo, an American of Iraqi descent, assembled 10 years of collected interviews with Iraqi women to create *Nine Parts of Desire* (2003), a collage of personal perspectives on conditions in Iraq before and after Saddam Hussein. The authentic voices of women whose families have been literally and figuratively torn apart by a brutal dictatorship and a brutal war provide a contrast to the distanced portrayal of events we see in the mass media. Raffo wrote *Nine Parts of Desire* as her master's thesis at the University of San Diego out of concern for her family still living in war-torn Iraq. The piece serves as a sharp reminder of the very personal and individual consequences of government policy.

Docudramas

As *The Laramie Project* shows us, docudrama need not be a solo art. The Culture Project produces plays devoted to illuminating pressing social issues. It explored the moral questions surrounding capital punishment in its production of *The Exonerated* (2005), a piece constructed primarily from court transcripts and interviews with six exonerated inmates released from death row after serving prison terms of 2 to 20 years. The performance applies no theatrical razzle-dazzle. Actors sit on chairs, facing the audience, giving testimony to the horrors of a judicial system that could kill in error. The piece has been performed with a rotating cast of stars. The authentic words speak for themselves and, interestingly, heighten the emotional response in the audience. Similarly, journalist and playwright George Packer (b. 1960) interviewed Iraqi translators who, after risking their lives and those of their families to help Americans after the invasion, were betrayed by the American government and denied refugee status in the United States. Their stories were dramatized in *Betrayed* (2009). Increasingly we find dramatists using the techniques of journalists to illuminate the central moral dilemmas of our time.

Documentary work can also take a comic turn. The group Culture Clash, featuring three performers with roots in El Salvador and Mexico, combines the methods of Anna Deavere Smith with wild comic sensibility. Creating portraits of communities through interviews with diverse populations, Culture Clash fashions stinging social satire by connecting the documentary sources with original humorous material. The group's performance of *Chavez Ravine* (2005) described the uprooting of a Chicano community in Los Angeles to make way for the new Dodger Stadium in the 1950s. The Civilians is a New York–based theatre company that does "investigative" theatre based on in-depth research into social and political issues not fully covered in journalistic venues. *In the Footprint: The Battle over Atlantic Yards* (2010) provides an exposé of a controversial development project in Brooklyn that displaced local residents and businesses. Although each show raises the specific issues of particular locations, as seen through the eyes of those who live there, each piece also addresses the general concerns of our urban multicultural society.

Docudrama is not a new form of text. During the 1930s, the Federal Theatre Project, created by the Roosevelt administration, performed "living newspapers" with texts drawn from newspaper articles, speeches, and government documents interwoven with dialogue to dramatize the pressing social problems of the day.

Even medical writings and therapy sessions can be turned into dramatic texts. Peter Brook turned Oliver Sacks's book on neurological disorders into *The Man Who* (1995), an exploration of the boundaries of normalcy. Storytelling workshops with Alzheimer's patients are the basis for a performance of Anne Basting's *TimeSlips* (2001), which depicts the internal confusion of people with dementia.

In each of these examples, the dramatic text is not a traditional play but an assemblage of primary source materials recast in theatrical form. There is no "playwright" creating characters and dialogue; instead, a writer or group of writers may function as interviewers, historical researchers, or archivists to craft the material into an effective piece of theatre. The selection and organization of the journalistic material shapes the meaning the audience takes from the performance.

THINK

If theatre uses the journalist's tools and methods, is it bound by the journalist's ethics to present a balanced picture of the facts?

Reenactments, or Living Histories

Historical reenactments make new theatrical use of documentary materials and are found at historic sites around the United States. At Plimoth Plantation, a reconstructed seventeenth-century village in Massachusetts, actors study the history of the period and are each assigned to take on the identity of one of the original colonial inhabitants. Costumed in period clothes and speaking in the appropriate accent, these actors replicate the social and cultural life of a historic community and interact with visitors. They improvise banter with visitors and explain the colonial way of life, never breaking with their characters or the historic context. Historical documents provide the scenario for this kind of docudrama—a "living history."

Opera and Operetta

HOW does music enhance the dramatic effect in opera and operetta?

Everywhere in the world, music and dance serve as theatrical texts. Blended with other elements, music and dance enhance dramatic effect by permitting sustained heightened emotion and the externalization of profound passion or spiritual yearning. Characters often burst into song when words do not suffice to express their intensity of feeling. Music and dance texts can reveal character, set pace and rhythm, create a mood, enliven, and entertain. Most importantly, music and dance permit us to transcend

> **If you can walk, you can dance. If you can talk, you can sing.**
>
> —African expression

▼ A huge crowd in the plaza of Lincoln Center watches a giant projected video simulcast of Puccini's *Madama Butterfly* at the Metropolitan Opera for free, while the paying audience watches inside the theatre.

Opera in the West

In the late Renaissance period, several Italian performers and theorists, eager to recapture the effect of ancient Greek tragedy, experimented with performances that reintegrated drama with continuous music. By the end of the 1500s, this experimentation had given birth to opera, which soon spread throughout the Western world.

Why should so elaborate and ostentatiously unrealistic an art form have caught on in an artistic climate so concerned with verisimilitude—the appearance of truth? Why is opera more wildly popular today than ever before? Opera is one of the few performance styles in the West that allows its audience something of the expanded theatrical effect of traditional Asian forms, such as kabuki or Chinese opera. Emotionally charged stories become larger than life when performed with continuous, powerful musical accompaniment. Think about the impact an effective soundtrack gives to a movie or television program.

Opera is a fusion of different elements. Poetic dialogue written by a librettist portraying dramatic situations is united with a composer's music, which heightens the emotional content and "interprets" the dramatic events and psychological states of the characters for the audience. When Mimi in Puccini's *La Bohème* (1896) has evocative words to sing to a compelling melody and that melody is enriched by a large orchestra playing along with her, the audience enjoys an overwhelming emotional experience that conventional spoken drama, or nondramatic music, cannot provide. Ironic tension can be created between what the characters are singing and what the orchestra is suggesting by the music it is playing. Mozart in *Don Giovanni* (1787) has the orchestra "contradict" his singing characters in this way and even poke fun at them with wry instrumental commentary.

Opera derives much of its expressive vocabulary from the contrast between lyrical, or melodic, music such as arias and choruses and a style of music referred to as *recitative*. Recitative is "musical speech"—a nontuneful declamatory kind of singing that serves to move the dramatic action forward. Lyrical, tuneful music is used in arias to accent the character's emotional state.

Dramatic action usually stands still for arias to allow the audience to savor the emotional high point. This explains why arias and lyrical music are the most popular features of operatic performance and why an audience may well burst into applause when they are over. In these passages, the drama has been translated into music that talented opera singers are able to bring to life through the beauty and range of their voices, their handling of melodic phrases, and their sensitivity to the meaning of the words they are singing as well as the dramatic situation. Operatic arias act like the freeze frame on a videotape or DVD player. In some respects, this freeze-frame quality is analogous to the posing effect in kabuki performance. Opera is one of the only living Western theatrical forms that allows for a similar manipulation of time and encourages a similar kind of aesthetic savoring.

The German Romantic opera composer Richard Wagner (1813–1883) famously described opera as a *gesamtkunstwerk*, or "total art work," uniting the skills of librettists; composers; dancers; singer-actors; and set, costume, and lighting designers in an artistic unity that thrills, elevates, and moves audiences. The complexity of Wagner's operas contributed to the development of the modern director's role and to innovations in lighting and auditorium design.

The composer is the ultimate dramatist in the opera house. The composer's choices govern the audience's perceptions of what they are hearing and seeing. The important opera composers of history may be regarded as great music composers as well as among the finest theatre artists of their time. Major opera composers include Claudio Monteverdi (1567–1643), George Frederick Handel (1685–1759), Wolfgang Amadeus Mozart (1756–1791), Giuseppe Verdi (1813–1901), Georges Bizet (1838–1875), Modest Musorgsky (1839–1881), Richard Wagner (1813–1883), Giacomo Puccini (1858–1924), and Benjamin Britten (1913–1976). Operas by contemporary composers such as Philip Glass (b. 1937), John Adams (b. 1947), and John Corigliano (b. 1938) ensure that the operatic repertory continues to grow.

Source: Mark Ringer, author of *Monteverdi the Dramatist* (Amadeus Press, 2005), teaches theatre at Marymount Manhattan College.

ourselves and the ordinary boundaries of our emotional lives. Dancing and singing are activities basic to the human spirit through which we directly express our emotions and deepest longings.

In previous chapters we have already studied many Asian theatrical forms that use dance, song, and musical accompaniment to dialogue. All traditional African performance includes dance and drumming. Drama with spoken text and no music is more the exception than the rule in the world of theatre, and it reflects the West's emphasis on verisimilitude and realism.

Opera

Although song and dance were generally removed from the spoken drama in the European theatre tradition, different separate theatrical forms that included music and dance also continued and evolved. Opera, operetta, melodrama, and other entertainments continued to sate the popular appetite for music and dance theatre. Opera is the longest continuous tradition of Western music theatre to sustain popularity. (The history of opera is detailed in the nearby box "Opera in the West.") In 2006 the Metropolitan Opera in New York launched high-definition simulcasts of live performances to venues around the United States. The tremendous response from the public led to expanded broadcasts to theatres and schools around the world, and several other major opera companies have also begun experimenting with simulcasts in an attempt to build new audiences.

To further lure the public, the Metropolitan Opera has increased its emphasis on the theatrical elements of opera—aspects that have often been viewed as secondary to the music. Acclaimed theatre directors such as Robert Lepage (b. 1957), Bartlett Sher (b. 1959), and Julie Taymor provide innovative staging and more refined acting. New productions reconceive well-known operas in innovative and exciting ways that have ignited both wild enthusiasm and vehement protest. Controversy lures audiences, and opera is rediscovering the importance of its theatrical roots.

Operetta

Opera has not held a monopoly on European musical theatre. By the mid-nineteenth century, bourgeois audiences in Paris were demanding new entertainment, and Jacques Offenbach (1819–1880) obliged with the **operetta** form. Operetta borrows many features from opera and incorporates

dance, farce, and clowning to tell a simple story that always culminates in romance fulfilled. Often satiric in nature, it was a readily accessible popular entertainment form. Operetta was later popularized in German-speaking countries by Johann Strauss (1825–1899) and in England by W. S. Gilbert (1836–1911) and Sir Arthur Sullivan (1842–1900). The nineteenth-century *zarzuela* in Spain shares many elements with this form, and operetta was in many ways the forerunner of today's musical theatre.

The lines that divide opera, operetta, and musical theatre are not clear, and it is hard to generalize about the distinctions. Opera is written in the tradition of great European art music; operetta and musical theatre have no such pretensions, yet great music has been written for these forms. In general, opera has less spoken dialogue than operetta and musical theatre, but contrary to common belief, many operas do include spoken text. Operetta always deals with lighthearted subjects, but there are many comic operas as well. Comic opera's sentimentality is replaced in the operetta with a witty and satiric tone whose goal is to amuse, not to move. Thus most operettas lack opera's overt appeal to the emotions, yet here again there are exceptions. Although we often think of opera as highbrow entertainment for the elite, in many places, opera is a people's theatre.

One significant difference between musical theatre and operas and operettas as they are performed today is that operas and operettas are performed by singers who act, whereas musical theatre is performed by actors who sing. This distinction indicates a shift of some of the emotional burden from the music onto the text. Operettas, although still performed, are not written today. Their audience has been claimed by the musical theatre, which borrowed much of its form and many elements from operetta and other popular entertainments. Musical comedy, with its light-hearted stories, has also given way to today's musical theatre, which often treats serious subject matter.

The American **Musical**

HOW has the American musical evolved?

When we think of contemporary musical theatre, we typically think of the form that grew up in the United States and is today embraced by countries around the world. The American musical has always combined textual materials and involved the collaboration of several authors. Music, lyrics (usually in rhymed verse), choreography for a danced

text, and spoken dialogue that fleshes out the story line and comprises the **book** (the written text of the musical) combine to create the musical form. These are created by a composer, a lyricist, a choreographer, and a book writer. Often the roles may be combined, as in the case of Stephen Sondheim (b. 1930), who writes both words and music for most of his work. Although each of these texts can be read separately for meaning (we can listen to a recording of the songs or read the book), the way the various texts interrelate and reinforce each other in performance defines the musical form. The American musical was once a simple story told through song and dance, interspersed with spoken dialogue, but it has become the subject of new experiments that play with the relationships among these various textual elements. The history of the musical is itself one of change and transformation.

In its origins, musical theatre combined elements of American melodrama, dance, popular song, and variety show entertainments such as vaudeville, burlesque, and minstrel shows, in combination with the European operetta. As the importance of story line grew, plots became more complex, resulting in the development of the **book musical**, a story told through spoken text and song. Recent decades have seen a return to the **revue**—a nonstory musical form— as the subject matter in the traditional book musical has become increasingly serious. The British musical, such as *Phantom of the Opera* (1989) and *Cats* (1981), emulates the high art of opera and reduces the element of spoken text. Simultaneously, opera companies are staging American musicals in opera houses not only in an attempt to appeal to a broader audience base but also as a recognition that what was once popular culture has reached the status of high art.

Today, the American musical is ubiquitous. Broadway musicals are performed the world over, and other cultures have created their own versions of the form. American musical texts are combined with foreign books and lyrics. Japanese director Amon Miyamoto (b. 1958) staged a version of Sondheim's *Pacific Overtures* in 2000, that incorporated *noh, kabuki, bunraku,* and *rokyoko* techniques to present the Japanese perspective on Commodore Perry, using the American musical form as a distorting mirror. The Japanese version of the musical then toured the United States. In Singapore, the American musical is the most widely embraced theatrical form, and the homegrown musical *Nagraland* by Dick Lee used Asian themes and written text to create a hybrid cultural piece that then toured successfully in Japan. *Riverdance*, the Broadway musical touring the world since 1995, was performed in the 7,000-seat Great Hall of the People in Beijing, where the legislature normally meets. The play immediately sold 50,000 tickets, and has since had return engagements in China, proving that music and dance texts can transcend culture and politics.

Multiculturalism and the American Musical

Musical theatre was one of the first forms to explore multicultural elements and themes, as if dance and music provided a distancing that permitted contributions from marginalized groups. As early as the 1920s, African American musicals appeared on Broadway, starting with *Shuffle Along* in 1921, by Eubie Blake (1883–1983) and Noble Sissle (1889–1975). But three more decades would pass before serious drama by

▼ Culture clash in multicultural New York City is portrayed in this scene from the 2009 Broadway revival of *West Side Story*.

an African American would receive a Broadway production with a black director and cast. Ragtime and jazz musical texts were appropriated by white composers, and black dance forms were incorporated into the standard dance repertory. George Gershwin's (1898–1937) *Porgy and Bess* (1935) openly uses the sounds and rhythms of African American culture as text.

Musicals daringly explored racial themes before society as a whole was ready to confront such issues. In *Showboat* (1927), Jerome Kern (1885–1945) and Oscar Hammerstein (1895–1960) explored the impact of anti-miscegenation laws on race relations and provided one of the earliest examples of a musical with a complex, tightly woven plot whose drama is heightened by the musical text. Richard Rodgers (1902–1979) and Hammerstein used *South Pacific* (1949) to explore the roots of personal prejudice and *The King and I* (1951) to examine cultural barriers to understanding. In 1957, Leonard Bernstein (1918–1990) and Stephen Sondheim exposed cultural clashes in America through *West Side Story*. *Parade* (1998) with music and lyrics by Jason Robert Brown (b. 1970) and a book by Alfred Uhry (b. 1936) used a historic court case to expose religious intolerance and anti-Semitism in the American South. In each of these productions, the musical and dance texts reflected particular cultural idioms or an outsider's concept of music and dance texts of other cultures, reinforcing the thematic material presented in the written book. The history of the American musical reflects the multiculturalism of our society and its use of music and dance as a tool for assimilation and understanding of difference.

THINK

Is it ever appropriate to employ a racist form to create art, even to fight racism?

HIDDEN HISTORY

Reappropriating Minstrelsy

The composer and lyricist team of John Kander (b. 1927) and Fred Ebb (1928–2004), who had worked together and enjoyed tremendous success with *Chicago* (1977) and *Cabaret* (1969), tackled a disturbing event in American history in their final collaboration, *The Scottsboro Boys* (2010). The musical tells the story of the arrest and conviction on false rape charges of nine young black men and boys in 1931 Alabama and the anti-Semitic rants against the Jewish lawyer from New York who defended them. The trials divided the country along geographic and political lines and helped fuel the civil rights movement.

The Scottsboro Boys took a risky approach to the material, using the minstrel show's racist form as a distancing frame for the events and as a means to decry the racism the story portrayed. Many felt that the caricatures used to portray the white sheriff, southern belles, poor blacks, and Jewish lawyer were offensive and inappropriate for the serious subject matter, while the creators asserted that it provoked a response and highlighted the inequities of the time. The very use of the minstrel form, even in deconstructed self-parody, provoked protest and controversy, and the Freedom Party organized demonstrations outside the theatre. The show closed after less than three months, raising the question of whether Broadway can be the venue for challenging material that fires controversy.

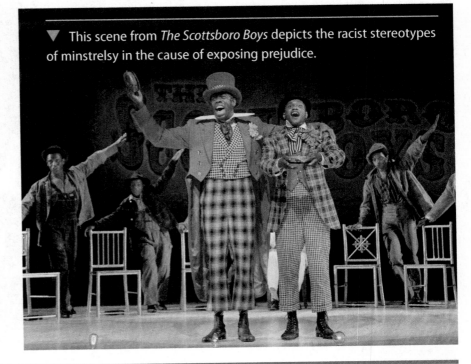

▼ This scene from *The Scottsboro Boys* depicts the racist stereotypes of minstrelsy in the cause of exposing prejudice.

The Jukebox Musical

In a jukebox musical, music not originally written for the theatre is assembled from other sources, and a story is loosely constructed to accommodate the songs. Although the form has been around for decades, currently there are increasing numbers of commercial productions of such shows. For producers, this form is an economical time saver, and the fan base of the songwriter forms an immediate audience, guaranteeing ticket sales. Shows such as *Rain* (2010) (The Beatles), *American Idiot* (2010) (Green Day), *Jersey Boys* (2005) (Frankie Valli & The Four Seasons), and *Mamma Mia!* (2001) (ABBA) have drawn enormous crowds to theatres in recent years. Some critics wonder if this genre is growing due to economic necessity or as a result of the lack of exciting new ideas from musical theatre artists.

Dance Notation

Dance movement is generally passed on directly by teachers or choreographers who model physical work for dancers and students to follow. This process leaves no tangible record of a dance, and the difficulties of transmitting and preserving choreography for new artists has led to attempts to create notation systems that record physical movements the way musical notation records sound.

The Frenchman Thoinot Arbeau's (1520–1595) *Orchesographie*, published in 1588, set out a system for European court dance that remained in use for 200 years. All court dances used one basic posture, so the system was simple. In the early eighteenth century, Raoul-Auger Feuillet and Pierre Beauchamp created a system that accommodated the more complex footwork of court ballet, a developing form at the time. Female ballet dancers of the period wore long dresses that covered most of their bodies, so the system had to communicate only floor patterns and the dancer's feet.

In the nineteenth century ballet costumes became shorter, and ballet became freer, with more expressive upper body movements; these changes rendered the old recording system inadequate. Both the Frenchman Arthur Saint-Leon (1821–1870) and the German Friedrich Zorn (1820–1905) tried systems using stick figures, but these could show only static positions.

Today the most common notation systems are Labanotation and Benesh Movement Notation. Labanotation was developed in the 1920s by Rudolf Laban (1879–1958). It uses principles of space, anatomy, and dynamics to record all kinds of movement, not just dance. Benesh Movement Notation, developed in the 1940s by Joan (b. 1920) and Rudolf Benesh (1916–1975), also aims at a general use and has been employed for physical therapy as well as dance. Because of the complexity of human movement in three-dimensional space, these systems are complicated, and recording a piece of choreography can be a time-consuming process. Most choreographers still create and pass on their dances in the studio and find videotape sufficient for recording and preserving their work. Written notation systems still have advantages, and libraries such as the Dance Notation Bureau in New York commission and preserve choreographic notations for future study and restaging of artistic works.

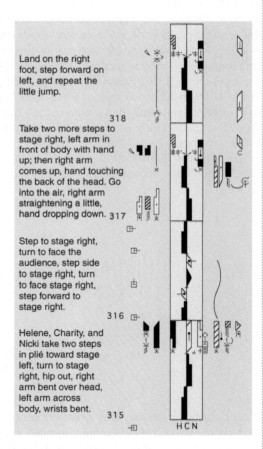

Land on the right foot, step forward on left, and repeat the little jump. 318

Take two more steps to stage right, left arm in front of body with hand up; then right arm comes up, hand touching the back of the head. Go into the air, right arm straightening a little, hand dropping down. 317

Step to stage right, turn to face the audience, step side to stage right, turn to face stage right, step forward to stage right. 316

Helene, Charity, and Nicki take two steps in plié toward stage left, turn to stage right, hip out, right arm bent over head, left arm across body, wrists bent. 315

H C N

▲ This Labanotation was drafted by Billie Mahoney in 1977 for Elaine Cancilla's reconstruction of Bob Fosse's choreography of "There's Gotta Be Something Better" from *Sweet Charity*.

Dance in Musical Theatre

While dance has always been part of the musical form, as musical theatre developed, dance moved from an entertainment vehicle for showgirls to become a vital part of the dramatic text. Starting in the 1930s, dance came to be used much the same way as songs, to further the plot or reveal a character's state of mind or emotions. George Balanchine's (1904–1983) choreography for *On Your Toes* (1936) by Richard Rodgers and Lorenz Hart (1898–1943) brought new stature to the role of dance. The 1940 Rodgers and Hart *Pal Joey* featured Gene Kelly (1912–1996), who famously used dance as an expression of character. In 1943, Rodgers and Hammerstein's *Oklahoma*, choreographed by Agnes de Mille (1905–1995), drew on her classical training. In this musical, dance adds psychological dimension and helps to tell the story. De Mille's dances went beyond the simple narrative to express the character's inner life and unconscious longing. Jerome Robbins (1918–1998) made dance an integral part of the dramatic text and the choreographer the central figure in shaping a musical production with his work on *West Side Story*. He was one of the first director-choreographers; others include Bob Fosse (1927–1987), Tommy Tune (b. 1939), Susan Stroman (b. 1954), and Twyla Tharp (b. 1941). Musicals such as *Bring in da Noise, Bring in da Funk* (1995) now find their drama entirely in the dancing. *Billy Elliot* (2005) is a popular musical whose subject is the longing to dance.

In Matthew Bourne's (b. 1960) production of *Swan Lake* (1999), the music served as the inspiration for a danced dramatic text about sexual obsession and repression. Not one word was spoken; the music and choreography combined with an idea to form the text. Several other danced theatre pieces without dialogue—such as *Contact* (1999), choreographed by Susan Stroman, and Twyla Tharp's *Movin' Out* (2002) and *Come Fly With Me* (2009)—have made their way to Broadway. These works are categorized as theatre, not as dance performances, because characterization, narrative, and dramatic conflict are the departure point for the choreographer's conceptualization of movement. Usually the focus of dance performance is on the quality and line of the movement. In these "dance plays," the dancers may also be working with or against the lyrics of the music as the verbal text that regulates the dance. Innovative avant-garde directors such as Pina Bausch and Martha Clarke (discussed in Chapter 8) have also created dance theatre pieces that push the limits of both arts.

Musical theatre texts sometimes have **no dialogue** or almost none; **dance** stands in for the word or goes **beyond** the word to express pure **sensation** and **emotion**.

The Theatre of **Images**

WHY is the theatre of images a performing art?

During the first decades of the twentieth century, European avant-garde visual artists became interested in performance as a way of repudiating the commercialization and merchandising of art. These artists experimented with ways of expressing the modern aesthetic in forms that incorporated the ideas of time and action. They mixed media, forms, and incongruous images to create performance collages that defied traditional categories. This early work provided the inspiration for American and Asian performance art of the 1970s and 1980s, and new theatrical forms continue to evolve from these roots to the present. Performance art has gone in several directions, including the exploration of solo performance. One of the lingering results of this movement is the idea of a nonliterary visual dramatic text conceived as a series of visual images incorporating mixed media and grand spectacle. Stage pictures, video, film, slides, and even lights are part of the dramatic text and are privileged over the written word, narrative plot, and developed character.

One of the best-known artists working in this image-dominated form is Robert Wilson (b. 1941), who begins each of his works with a visual idea as the structuring element. What little language is used does not necessarily tell a coherent story, and the dramatic action moves from image to image. Actors are manipulated as visual elements on the stage. The images are supported by sound and music, often composed by Wilson's longtime collaborator Philip Glass (b. 1937), whose minimalist style is a perfect complement for Wilson's nonnarrative pieces. Attending a Wilson performance is like sitting before a giant living, moving painting with sound effects and words and music. One assimilates

The document shown here is the visual text for *The Golden Windows*, a performance piece created by Robert Wilson (b. 1941) with music by Tania Léon, Gavin Bryars, and Johann Pepusch, that pre- miered at the Münchner Kammerspiele in Munich in 1982 and later played in Vienna, Montreal, and New York. For Robert Wilson, trained as a visual artist, visual images are the primary text that structure the performance. These story- board sketches show how Wilson envi- sioned the progression of the piece.

part c   teil c
early morning   früher morgen

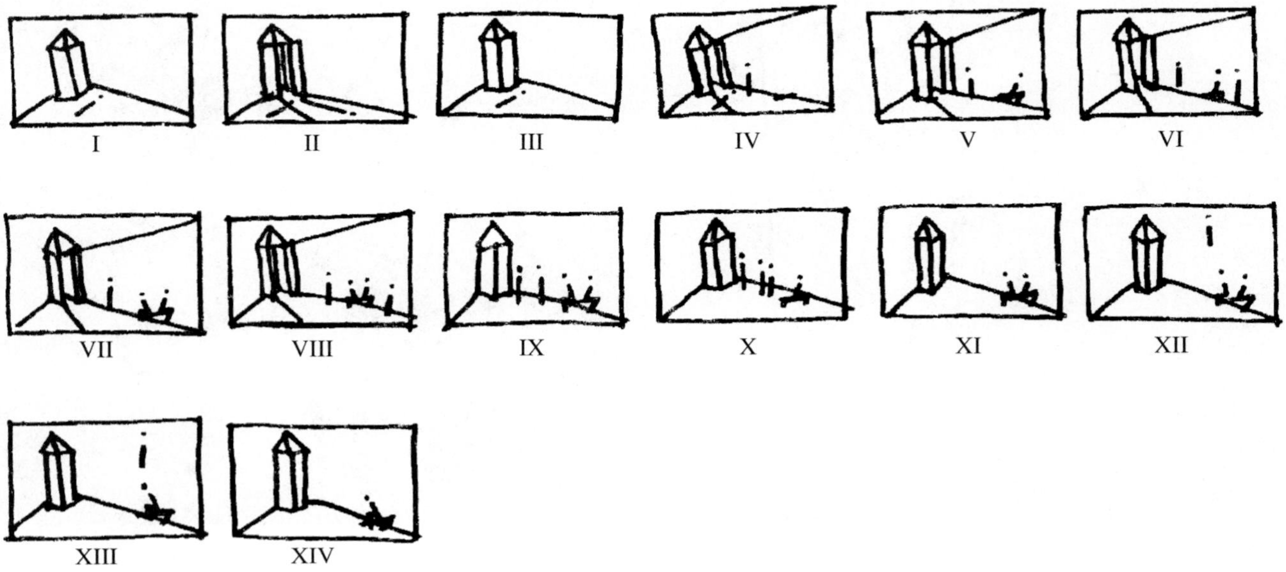

I. 3 lies on floor.		I. 3 liegt am boden.
II. door opens and shadow of figure grows from doorway of house.		II. tür öffnet sich, schatten einer gestalt wächst aus dem eingang des hauses.
III. door closes.		III. tür schlieβt sich.
IV. 4 appears. door closes.		IV. 4 erscheint. tür schlieβt sich.
V. 3 sits on bench downstage right.		V. 3 sitzt auf bank vorne rechts.
VI. 1 enters downstage right.		VI. 1 kommt von vorne rechts.
VII. 1 sits on the on-stage side of bench which is placed stage right. his back is to the audience.		VII. 1 sitzt auf dem linken ende der bank, die rechts vorne steht. rücken zum zuschauer.
VIII. 2 enters downstage right, walking towards doorway of house.		VIII. 2 kommt von rechts vorne, geht auf den hauseingang zu.
IX. 2 stops in doorway.		IX. 2 bleibt im hauseingang stehen.
X. 4 does dance and 1 embraces her.		X. 4 tanzt; 1 umarmt sie.
XI. 2 enters house. door closes. 4 exits.		XI. 2 geht ins haus. tür schlieβt sich. 4 ab.
XII. 2 appears in sky.		XII. 2 erscheint am himmel.
XIII. 3 exits downstage right.		XIII. 3 geht rechts vorne ab.
XIV. 1 sits on bench alone.		XIV. 1 sitzt allein auf der bank.

▲ Robert Wilson's storyboard from *The Golden Windows*, 1985.

▼ Robert Wilson's image text is realized in this performance of *The Golden Windows* at the Kammerspiele Theater, Munich. The moment captured in the photo corresponds to sketch X in the figure in the Artists in Perspective box on page 151.

Oda Sternberg

the total effect as one might look out at a panoramic vista while listening to birds and reading poetry. Audience members simply respond to all the sensory input. We will discuss Wilson's work in more detail in the next chapter.

Sound and Image Theatre

Some theatrical creators think of music as a structuring device for the visual world. Postmodern composer and director Heiner Goebbels (b. 1952) explores the relationship between images and sound. In his work, dazzling stage pictures are juxtaposed with a global array of music and poetry. In *Hashirigaki* (2003) for the Théâtre Vidy in Lausanne, Switzerland, the title was translated from the Japanese to mean "the act of walking, thinking, and talking at the same time." These acts are explored by three performers—Japanese, Swedish, and Canadian—against a background of Gertrude Stein poetry, Brian Wilson's Beach Boys music, and Japanese and original compositions on a cross-cultural collection of instruments, while fantasy set pieces and fabulous lights create visual effects. The actors, who are of diverse physical types and possess different accents, mutate the sound and action much as the repeating language of Stein's poems mutates words. In *I Went to the House but Did Not Enter* (2008), texts by T.S. Eliot, Maurice Blanchot, Franz Kafka, and Samuel Beckett are accompanied by Goebbels'

original score to haunting effect. If Robert Wilson's work resembles that of a landscape artist, Goebbels is a creator of soundscapes. The audience has a sensory experience without connecting narrative line.

Much of the work of Robert Wilson, Heiner Goebbels, and others occurs on a grand scale that requires grants and funding from governments, cultural organizations, and institutions, often contradicting our traditional perception of the avant-garde artist struggling to create with little or no financial resources. In reality, established artists have formed a well-funded institutionalized avant-garde that performs regularly at performing arts festivals around the world.

THINK

Are today's avant-garde artists really pushing boundaries and making countercultural statements if their work is dependent on high-tech creation and requires the support of governments and wealthy institutions?

GLOBAL TRADITIONS AND INNOVATIONS

Staging the Film

While once it was common for plays to be made into films, we are now increasingly seeing the process working in reverse, with films serving as both visual and literary texts for stage productions. The commercial theatre uses this formula to profit from successful motion pictures such as *The Lion King* and *Batman*, but many avant-garde directors are also using cinematic imagery in their theatrical work.

German director Thomas Ostermeier (b. 1968) adapted the 1979 Rainer Werner Fassbinder film The *Marriage of Maria Braun* into a sleek stage production in 2010. Ivo Van Hove (b. 1958) presented *Teorema* (2010), an adaptation of the 1968 Pier Paolo Pasolini film and the *Antonioni Project*, based on three films by Michelangelo Antonioni, with the Toneelgroep ensemble in Amsterdam.

American director Ping Chong (b. 1946) used Japanese film director Akira Kurosawa's *Throne of Blood* (1957), itself an adaptation of *Macbeth* to feudal Japan, as the basis for a stage drama; in doing so, he created an adaptation of a film of an adaptation of a play.

Many of these productions incorporate film footage or projections, either from the original film or of the current stage actors. They are all influenced by the strong visual imagery of film and the idea of the film director as the creator of the text.

▼ The *Antonioni Project* plays the live actors against their video projections in this theatrical production based on the films of Michelangelo Antonioni.

Alternative Paths to Performance **153**

The Diversity of Theatrical Forms

As we have seen, the many methods of theatrical creation have led to a diversity of theatrical texts and forms that defy easy labels. Much of the work we have examined in this chapter is deeply tied to the artists who create and perform them and is not easily transmitted to new generations of interpreters. Some are so rooted in the actual physical body of the actor that they cannot be given to others. Unlike plays, these kinds of texts lack transmissibility, are temporal, and underscore the ephemeral quality of the theatre. The acceptance of alternative texts and methods of creation has led to the era of the director-auteur, a creator who envisions both the written and the performance text. We will discuss the director-auteur further in Chapter 8.

Drama, comedy, and musical are no longer adequate for categorizing the performance forms we see today.

To some degree, however, exceptions to the rules have always existed. Renaissance theorists divided genres into comedy, tragedy, and pastoral, omitting the *commedia dell'arte*—the most vital theatre of their time, perhaps because it had no play text. In other eras, secondary forms have also been given short shrift. The difficulties involved in categorization are highlighted when theatre works are considered for awards and prizes. The Pulitzer Prize committee took back its nomination for "best drama" from Anna Deavere Smith because her work was seen as documentary and not a play. Similarly, in recent decades, disputes have arisen about how to categorize new forms for the Tony Awards. Is an opera musical theatre? Is a stand-up comedy routine a comedy? Is a musical with dance and no book or singing a musical? Is a solo performance a play? To accommodate the problem, in 2001 a unique category was created, called "Special Theatrical Event," and everything that didn't fit neatly into a traditional niche was placed there until the 2009–2010 season, when the award was "retired," further demonstrating the arbitrariness of categories.

These controversies reflect the changing concept of theatrical text. Accepted categories of texts have always been determined by the groups that dominate a particular society. These are the people who award prizes, sponsor festivals, write criticism, or subsidize the arts. As artists push creative boundaries, they force us all to reassess the limits of established theatrical models. Today alternative forms are given a place alongside traditional works, reflecting the more inclusive social power structure and an increasing acceptance of diversity and innovation.

Summary

WHAT role does improvisation play in the creative process around the world?   p. 128

▶ Improvisation relies on the actor's skill to create a performance without a fully written text. Improvisation is central to most theatrical creation.

▶ Improvised theatre created by the performer, exists around the world.

HOW does collaborative creation challenge traditional theatrical decision-making hierarchies and methods?   p. 130

▶ A group of artists can create a piece together, beginning with a concept but no written text. A written text may evolve from collaboration. Traditional decision-making hierarchies may dissolve.

HOW do mimes create performances?   p. 133

▶ The mime begins with a narrative, an idea, or an image and then gives it physical life.

HOW does variety entertainment appeal to both public taste and the avant-garde's artistic sensibilities?   p. 134

▶ Traditions of variety entertainment have used improvisation, clowning, music, and circus skills to appeal to public taste by featuring diverse entertainments.

▶ The early twentieth century avant-garde, used variety show performance to destroy the realistic stage world and foster an active interaction with the audience.

HOW is storytelling a form of theatre?   p. 138

▶ In some societies storytellers pass on the heritage of a community.

▶ Solo performance is a popular way of telling personal stories. It allows the voices of particular groups and individuals to be heard and often expresses political content.

HOW do theatre artists use primary source material as texts?   p. 141

▶ Docudrama uses primary source material as a text and usually has a social message.

▶ Historical reenactments use historical research to create living history.

HOW does music enhance the dramatic effect in opera and operetta?   p. 144

▶ Music and dance are used as dramatic texts throughout the world to heighten the emotional content of a performance.

▶ Opera is a fusion of different elements, featuring poetic dialogue written by a librettist united with a composer's music.

▶ Operetta borrows elements of opera and uses dance, and clowning to tell a simple romantic story.

HOW has the American musical evolved?   p. 146

▶ The American musical combines the work of a book writer, lyricist, composer, and choreographer. It was one of the first American forms to explore multicultural and racial themes.

▶ The dance musical uses dance as the central dramatic text.

WHY is the theatre of images a performing art?   p. 150

▶ In the theatre of images, stage pictures, video, film, slides, and even lights are part of the dramatic text.

MySearchLab®

The Actor
Theatre's Living Presence

The Thrill of Simulation

Imagine a theatre: house lights dim, stage lights illuminate the empty stage, and we, in the audience, wait expectantly. What are we waiting for? We are awaiting the entrance of the actor, without whom there can be no theatre, for the theatre depends on the presence of the live human being. The actor's body, voice, heart, and mind become the embodiment of the human narrative portrayed in the theatre.

In Roman times, a famous actor named Parmenon was renowned for his imitation of a pig. Audiences would journey far to see Parmenon perform his famous sow. One day, a jealous fellow actor leaped onto the stage with a live pig and said to the audience, "You who so idolize Parmenon, what do you think of his acting next to this real pig?" The audience replied, "It's a good sow, but it's still not as good as Parmenon's sow." What does this ancient parable tell us about acting? Acting is more than just imitating the behavior of everyday life. Acting adds artistic interpretation; it produces metaphor and meaning; it captures the essence of a being. Acting is not simply reproduction and imitation.

In fact, it is the very artifice of the performance that thrills us. Things that we would find disturbing, upsetting, or even frightening in real life excite us and give pleasure when we see them acted in the theatre. We would not choose to be at someone's deathbed, or to witness a violent duel or acts of war, but in the theatre, we are permitted the aesthetic distance with which to examine human conduct. No matter how close to life it seems, no matter how real the emotions feel, we are aware that we are watching a simulation, and this fills us with awe. Actors have the power to appear to be living a part, and yet we, the audience, know it is not so.

1. How is the theatre dependent on the presence of the actor?

2. In what ways is acting more than just imitation of everyday human behavior?

3. What does the artifice of theatre permit the audience to experience?

To Act Is **Human**

Acting is a fundamental human activity. You can see this when you watch children at play. Whether it's playing house, or doctor, or soldier, people have a basic need to express themselves through impersonation and fantasy. Aristotle wrote about this in the fourth century B.C.E., and it remains true today. He tells us that imitation is a necessary and pleasurable human activity and a source of knowledge about the world and ourselves. Anthropologists have observed the need for play-acting in every society. Sometimes it is channeled into storytelling, sometimes into ritual drama, festivals, pageants, or parades. While this predisposition takes many forms around the globe, it appears to be present everywhere.

Social psychologists believe we "perform" aspects of ourselves in various situations in everyday life. This daily role-play, however, is quite different from the imaginative, vital transformation required to act in the theatre. Imagine for a moment that you were placed on the stage in any of your various daily roles—student, boyfriend, girlfriend, child, parent, employee, brother, sister. Would the audience find you interesting or compelling? You most likely would not even be audible beyond the first row. The audience would not have the sense of a consciously created and shaped artistic performance. Although you may be playing a role, you are not *acting*. Your behavior would not possess the essential universal qualities required of an actor. Although actors use their own physical and emotional beings, they are not necessarily portraying themselves.

The **Universal Qualities** of Acting in the Theatre

Acting is a special form of behavior. It transcends the everyday and consists of universal principles: energy, control, purpose, focus, enlargement, dynamics, and transformation. Although actors learn various methods and work in ways that accommodate different theatrical styles and traditions, the following special qualities are shared by all performers all over the world:

▶ **ENERGY.** All theatrical performance requires physical, emotional, and mental energy. Harnessed energy gives intensity and vitality to an actor's work and holds the audience's attention. Directed energy creates the quality we have come to call *stage presence*. In life, our energy is a result of our personality, mood, physical state, and environment. On stage, actors must shed their everyday concerns as they work to create a vigorous and radiant stage presence.

The removal of physical and emotional blocks requires work. Many actors study for years techniques that permit them to access and free the channel for energy flow.

▶ **CONTROL.** The actor must be in control of a performance. Even in highly emotional moments or states of ecstatic movement, some aspect of consciousness oversees what happens. Actors study techniques to achieve control. They do physical exercises to increase strength and flexibility, and they do vocal exercises to free the voice. They may study fencing and circus skills

The sociologist Erving Goffman (1922–1982) saw a connection between the way people behave in social situations and the theatre. In *The Presentation of Self in Everyday Life* (1959), Goffman postulated that as we conform our behavior to the demands of different social situations, we behave as actors on the stage in front of audiences, choosing among theatrical elements—the costumes, props, and the social mask we display. We form an elaborate social network of actors and audiences as we perform and serve as audience members for each other. He framed this as a dramaturgical model for social interaction.

In today's digitized world, we have an increasing number of platforms on which to perform. Facebook, Twitter, MySpace, and Second Life all offer us opportunities to construct our identity for others, much the way actors create a character. While under the illusion of sharing authentic experiences, we carefully and self-consciously construct a persona through which to communicate to the virtual world. MIT Professor Sherry Turkle in *Alone Together: Why We Expect More from Technology and Less from Each Other* (2011) explores the social and psychological impact of living through a constructed self and posits that your psychological self risks becoming a performance. With the infinite opportunity for self-dramatization on the Web, have we all become actors in our own lives?

to develop coordination and timing, or dance for grace and flexibility. They carefully analyze the text so their understanding of the role is complete. If they are learning a performance text, they study every gestural and vocal detail. Mastery of all the components of expression enables the actor to achieve a controlled performance.

▶ FOCUS. Acting requires a heightened awareness and level of concentration. The body is on alert in the theatrical environment, and attention cannot wander. Actors are careful to guard against thoughts from everyday life intruding on their creative process. They are aware of the audience and adjust to the audience

▲ Jude Law and Nakamura Kankuro are trained in different traditions, but they both embody the universal qualities of acting: energy, control, purpose, focus, enlargement, and dynamics. Note the dynamisms of their stage presence and the rootedness of their physical postures. Each actor draws us in with the special magnetism of great acting.

response, but they must keep their primary focus on the onstage action. They are constantly selecting and adjusting focus.

▶ **PURPOSE.** All action on stage is purposeful and meaningful. Aimless action can defuse the energy of a performance and confuse the audience. Even the smallest gesture is read by the audience as having significance, so actors develop an awareness that every sound and movement they make has meaning. The famous acting teacher Eugenio Barba (b. 1936) refers to this as "decided" action—determined and directed.

▶ **DYNAMICS.** A performance is like a piece of music. It has dynamics, rhythm, and tempo. It strikes various notes and keys, with moments of rising and falling intensity. Actors shape a performance to have texture and interest and to reflect the cadence and rhythm of the text and their character.

▶ **ENLARGEMENT.** Acting requires the expression of common emotions in an uncommon way. Actors must fill large theatres with feeling and project vocally so as to be heard in the last row of the theatre. Actors must be able to enlarge their movement, voices, and energy field without losing a sense of authenticity. In particular styles, they may need to project heightened imagistic texts or unusual physical expression.

▶ **TRANSFORMATION.** The mask is a symbol for the theatre because it expresses the stepping outside the self that transforms the actor on the stage. Put on a mask, and you can become anyone. In theatre traditions that use masks, the transformation is palpable. In Western theatre, where actors rarely use masks, the actor uses the self—the body, mind, and feelings—to transform the self. No performance is ever an exact replica of who the actor is in real life. Even actors who play themselves, as often occurs in solo performance pieces, are playing the role of themselves. They are heightened, theatricalized, and transformed.

These fundamental qualities form the basis of all acting for the theatre, however diverse the theatrical style. All actors try to find a pathway to these universal principles.

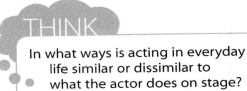

THINK

In what ways is acting in everyday life similar or dissimilar to what the actor does on stage?

What **Does** an Actor **Do**?

WHAT does an actor do?

If you are American and have only limited theatre-going experience, this may seem like a simple question. You might respond, "An actor plays and interprets a character in a play." But, in fact, the answer to this question is complex. Actors in different theatrical traditions actually do different things. Their training is a function of how and what they will be expected to perform.

A great deal of American and European theatre is constructed around a *play text*. The actor is an interpreter of the dramatic text, and actor training involves text interpretation and character analysis and learning the ways to best transmit the playwright's ideas and portray the character.

In contrast, *performance* traditions pass on all aspects of a performance that can be read for meaning. This includes all that an actor does. Specific gestures, movement, and vocal elements, musical accompaniment, mask, makeup and costume elements, and precise staging are determined and fixed. The actor's role is to learn a performance and to preserve a tradition. The training passes on that tradition by teaching rules of prescribed behavior—codified acting. Improvisational theatre demands yet another kind of acting, based on spontaneity and freedom. Training for this kind of performance involves removing blocks to self-expression and freeing the imagination. In traditional African theatre, the actor must sing, dance, tell tales, and manipulate the audience into participatory response. In such traditions, there may be no formal training at all; performers absorb oral and movement traditions, and an entire community can participate. Different traditions and styles pose different technical demands, so technique is a function of what kind of acting is expected.

◀ Actors use their minds and bodies and the aid of makeup and costumes to step outside themselves and transform into characters. In this photo an actor of the Beijing Opera prepares to play a painted face character using traditional makeup.

Presentational Versus Representational Acting

The earliest recorded musings on the art of acting in ancient Greece and Rome identified two approaches to performance. Some actors seemed to truly feel their characters' emotions, as if transported or possessed by another being, whereas others presented their characters' feelings with virtuoso technique that thrilled the audience through overt artifice. The living of the emotions came to be called **representational** acting and is seen in more realistic styles. The openly artificial reproduction of emotion was labeled **presentational** and appears where there is a heightened theatrical style. Almost all ancient performance traditions embrace a presentational style. The modern era has advocates of both approaches.

Through the centuries, the question remains, "Can the actor really feel the emotions portrayed, or is the actor always, through technique, dissembling and presenting the external signs of emotion?" From the time of Plato in the fifth century B.C.E. to today, these two approaches to acting have been presented as polarities—between the rational and the irrational, between art and craft, between mind and body. In eras and cultures in which the rational mind was celebrated, acting that was contrived and virtuosic was acclaimed. In periods that celebrate nature and the natural, a more emotionally driven acting style has been hailed. Today, through neuroscience, we have come to understand that we cannot so easily compartmentalize the mind, the body, and the feelings. All good acting combines both techniques because all our thoughts are recorded in our bodies, just as all our movement has an effect on our feelings and how we think.

The Actor's **Dual Consciousness**

DOES an actor experience genuine emotion on stage?

The question of how an actor can appear to be carried away by emotion and yet still deliver a controlled performance continues to intrigue. What keeps the actor from going mad? The actor's sanity is ensured through the ability to stand simultaneously inside and outside oneself.

Denis Diderot (1713–1784), French Enlightenment thinker, dramatist, and critic, in a famous essay *The Paradox of the Actor*, framed the discussion of dual consciousness for future generations. He believed that the actor presents the "ideal model" of the truth, as created by the actor's imagination, and that a part of the actor's consciousness should always be outside the role, shaping and guiding the presentation of the ideal.

The idea of dual consciousness was present even in ancient times. In ancient Greece, the original word for actor was *hypocrite*. By the third century B.C.E., as the art of acting became the province of professional actors, the word *hypocrite* had taken on the meaning it has today, to characterize a deceiver or dissembler, indicating the ability to stand outside the self to shape an illusion of truth. The other word the Greeks used for actor was *thespis*. A man named Thespis is said to be the first actor in the late 6th century B.C.E. The root of his name—the word *theos*, or "god"—is also found in our word *thespian*. The actor was someone filled with the words of God, reminding us that Greek theatre had its origin in Dionysian ritual and ecstatic dance. Depending on the cultural viewpoint, actors may be considered speakers of divine truths, or they may be divinely inspired deceivers.

> **Diderot's essay raised questions that haunt discussions of acting to this day:**
>
> - How is it possible, if the actor really feels the part, to maintain control of a performance?
> - Is the actor working internally for a real emotional connection or externally, like a sculptor, for a desired effect?
> - Is there a creative process we can outline as a method, or is acting intuitive and instinctual?
> - Can we create controlled illusions of emotional authenticity?
> - What is the "ideal model," and how does it reflect the culture and theatrical conventions of a given time and place?
> - Is the actor's imagination culture bound?

We have all experienced this sense of double consciousness whenever we tell a lie. What makes lying closer to acting than other behaviors is the constant self-awareness that we have when we lie. We know the truth, and yet we are fabricating another reality. We choose how to create this alternative reality, what story to tell, and how to deliver it. We are ourselves, and yet we are outside ourselves.

Acting **Reflects** Culture

HOW is the idea of good acting culturally determined?

Acting has always been considered "special" behavior, outside everyday life, so actors are always set apart from the norm. In some cultures they are revered, and in others they are scorned or reviled, but always they provoke some exceptional response.

The Holy or Profane **Actor**

In many cultures acting is a holy act. Whole theatrical traditions have sprung from religious inspiration, and often the spiritual process of the actor is a primary part of a technique that uses trance, meditation, and ecstatic dance to extol the gods. Actors express their devotion to the gods by delivering themselves as offerings.

In India the tradition of the holy actor goes back to the *Natyasastra* and its account of theatre as a creation of the god Brahma. Recall that Indian theatre was first performed by sages and meant as a ritual sacrifice. Many Indian traditions continue to manifest this sacred view of performance and the actor. The *Rāmlilā* is a cycle play that reenacts the life of Rama and Krishna and is performed throughout northern India during the Hindu festival of Dashahara. Community actors are believed to actually be the gods and goddesses they portray, and spectators worship them by touching their feet, praising them, and participating in postperformance rituals. The *Rāslilā*, a devotional dance-drama about the life of the god Krishna, takes place yearly at temples in Uttar-Pradesh, a region associated with Krishna's life that is also the destination of many devotees and pilgrims. The *Rāslilā* uses music and poetry to bring the spectator to an ecstatic vision of the god. Throughout the performance spectators worship, make offerings, and bow before the performers. The *bhāgavata mela* from Tamil Nadu is performed once a year, in honor of one incarnation of the god Vishnu, a half man/half lion called Narasimha. It is enacted in front of the deity at a temple, where the mask of Narasimha is worshiped as a holy object all year. The actor who performs Narasimha fasts all day before donning the mask. He is then transported into a trance and becomes possessed by the god.

Some cultures see the actor's ability to impersonate the creatures of the natural world as a special power. In these cases, the actor is viewed as a kind of shaman traveling between the world of the spirits and our world to bring back knowledge. Many Native American performances incorporate mime and dance

▶ A member of the Nambe Pueblo, taking in the spirit of the buffalo he has hunted, participates in a celebration of thanksgiving as part of the Nambe Waterfall Ceremonials, New Mexico.

as actors portray revered animals. Similar mimetic-dance performances occur the world over, performed by groups as diverse as the Bushmen of the Kalahari and the Navajo and Lakota of the American Plains.

Although the European theatre derived from ritual acts, it was not long before professional actors were seen as unholy purveyors of entertainment in the Western world. In many eras actors were considered of low moral repute, and actresses were even labeled as prostitutes and courtesans. The Roman Empire found slaves and prostitutes performing in the theatre. It is said the Emperor Justinian first spotted his future empress, Theodora, performing a striptease act. The Elizabethan theatre banned women from the English stage, and from 1642 to 1660, during the era of Puritan rule, the theatre was seen as morally offensive, and public

Acting Conventions and Culture

Audiences come to the theatre with expectations that actors will perform on stage in a manner that reflects their society's values and its view of beauty, emotion, psychology, and behavior. This in turn affects the way actors use the human body to portray feelings on stage. What is viewed as authentic or believable acting is culturally determined and can vary widely. Japanese culture values beauty as an integrated part of existence revealed through subtlety and simplicity, a hidden part of the way things are performed. In contrast to the Western concept of time passing, the Japanese, influenced by Zen, believe that we pass but time is still. Understanding how the Japanese view the world is crucial to understanding the nuanced slow movements of the *noh* actor. Understanding the American focus on individualism and psychological motivation can help someone outside the culture comprehend the authentic emotion sought in most American acting. Around the world today, the wide variety of acting styles reflects these differences. In other periods, actors behaved in very different ways and used techniques unlike those practiced today.

performances were forbidden. When the Restoration period returned the female actor to the stage, she was often of dubious reputation. The famous actress Nell Gwynn (1650–1687), the mistress of King Charles II, was the daughter of a brothel owner. It was not unusual for prostitutes to work the audience, and wealthy noblemen often sought pleasure backstage. The legacy of the profane actor can be found in today's fascination with the lurid details of actors' personal lives.

> Today's **celebrity worship** of actors combines a **sacred sentiment** with **secular activity.**

In the modern era, Jerzy Grotowski (1933–1999), the famed Polish director and acting teacher, united the sacred and the profane with the concept of the "holy" actor, offering himself in an act of humility as a sacrifice to his art. To lead the actor to a state where he or she is freed to release a deep spirituality through art, Grotowski incorporated many of the techniques of ritual performance—trance, meditation, physical endurance, and ecstatic dance, stripping the actor of all personal blocks. The state of "secular holiness" that Grotowski sought to teach reflects the interest in Asian philosophy and religion in Europe and the United States in the 1960s.

Acting **Conventions** in the **European Tradition**

Because the play text has been so central to the European tradition, most Western acting has been about the interpretation of a role. Actors begin with the question, "How can I enter my character's world to understand and portray my character's situation and emotions?" While the question has remained the same through the centuries, the answer has differed in various eras, and individual actors have sought personal solutions reflecting the conventions of their times.

American and European acting until the early twentieth century bore no resemblance to what we think of as good acting today. Actors of the past would appear artificial and melodramatic to us. You have only to look at an early silent film to get a sense of how different acting was just a short time ago. The few films we have of the great star of her day, Sarah Bernhardt (1844–1923), appear almost as parodies to our sensibilities. Early recordings from the late nineteenth and early twentieth centuries of actors performing Shakespeare indicate that vocal technique was exaggerated. Actors intoned their lines and gave what we would call unnatural readings. All this was to change as the theatre increasingly turned to realism and an interest in the new science of psychology during the twentieth century.

For centuries, it was believed that there were universal forms of emotional expression, that everybody expressed a particular emotion in exactly the same way. Emotions were seen to fall into only a few categories. Aristotle wrote of 15 major emotions in his *Rhetoric*. Descartes spoke of 6 primitive passions in 1666; and Aaron Hill (1685–1750), in his *Essay on the Art of Acting* in 1746, described 10 dramatic passions. Such categorization of the emotions continued well into the twentieth century. If each emotion had a set form of physical expression, and there were only 10 or 20 emotions, then actors needed only to learn the standard body positions and facial expressions of each emotion to communicate feeling from the stage. The few manuals we have from earlier periods catalog the portrayal of emotions by positions of the body and facial expressions. Many of the paintings of actors from earlier centuries show them in the poses depicted in these books. Audiences accepted the convention that character and emotions would be portrayed in external and generalized ways.

Not only were emotions generalized, but character types were generalized as well. Actors were hired to play a particular **line of business**—a particular type—from young lover to old miser. Actors made their reputations in these types and brought the same qualities to every role, much the way Hollywood typed early actors as leading men, gangsters, femme fatales, heroes, or ingénues. To some extent, the practice continues today.

These acting styles were well suited to the heightened poetic language that was the written convention of the time. The vocal skills of the actor were most significant. So-called declamatory acting emphasized phrasing, diction, and a mellifluous (sweet or musical) voice. A good voice was vital for the successful performer, who struck the appropriate poses while delivering speeches. Today, it is hard for us to imagine that there was no attempt to make dialogue sound like natural speech or stage movement seem like everyday life. Although some actors talked of developing a more "natural" style starting in the eighteenth century, we would not find their emotionalized acting realistic today. *Presentational* acting reigned, and there was no disguise of theatrical artifice. Actors were openly acting.

> " He who is incapable of **feeling strong passions**, of being shaken by anger, of **living** in every sense of the word will never be a good **actor.** "

—Sarah Bernhardt, *The Art of the Theatre.* [1]

The Development of Actor Training

HOW has actor training changed since the nineteenth century?

Before the twentieth century, acting, like most other crafts, was learned through apprenticeship, and often skills were passed down through families. Young actors joined companies and learned by watching those more accomplished at the art. The first attempt to create a training method came from a Frenchman, François Delsarte (1811–1871), whose system of oratory provided a pseudo-scientific, mystical approach to the subject. Although Delsarte's system was created for public speaking, European actors, whose art was still based on declamation, found his ideas useful.

> " The **soul** of speech is in **gesture.** "

—François Delsarte

Delsarte's system was a revival of the manuals of set positions for each emotion. In his system, however, the instructions were broken down into the smallest body parts and positions and coordinated with speech patterns and inflections, all carefully illustrated on charts. This gestural and vocal code for emotional presentation was to be learned by rote (mechanical repetition). Although Delsarte seemed to understand that an organic connection existed between gesture and feeling, his method was totally external and did not provide links to text or character. The only American known to have studied with Delsarte was Steele MacKaye (1842–1894), who founded the American Academy of Dramatic Art to teach the Delsarte method in the United States. The Delsarte system became the most popular system of actor training in America through MacKaye's work during the first part of the twentieth century.

THINK

What part of an actor's performance can transcend linguistic barriers? (Think about observing people speaking languages you don't understand.)

[1] Sarah Bernhardt "The Art of the Theatre," 1923. In Toby Cole and Helen Chinoy. *Actors on Acting.* (New York: Crown, 1970), 208.

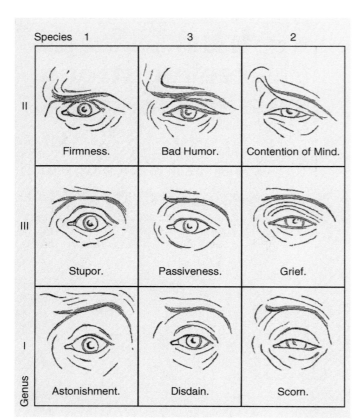

Species	1	3	2
II	Firmness.	Bad Humor.	Contention of Mind.
III	Stupor.	Passiveness.	Grief.
I	Astonishment.	Disdain.	Scorn.

Genus

◀ **DELSARTE'S EXPRESSIONS OF THE EYE**

Delsarte trained actors and orators to take these positions to express specific emotions through outward physical gesture. Each nuanced position of the eye and flexing of the facial muscles around the eye and brow was meant to depict a particular emotion. Delsarte developed corresponding charts for the positioning of the hands, feet, head, and mouth.

Source: Adapted from *Delsarte System of Oratory,* 4th ed. New York: Edgar S. Werner and Co., 1893.

GLOBAL TRADITIONS AND INNOVATIONS

A Universal Language of Emotional Expression

Actors have long searched for a universal language of emotions. The last decades of the twentieth century saw an accelerated interest in expressive forms that could transcend cultural frontiers fueled by globalization and interculturalism. The search for a universal language of emotions that can be understood by people everywhere stands at an interdisciplinary crossroad of art, anthropology, psychology, and biology.

Theatrical experiments motivated by either rational science or romantic primitivism have produced interesting results. Rejecting language as the tool of power and the camouflage of feeling, mystic actor-director Antonin Artaud (1896–1948) called for a primal language of screams, sounds, and movement to take over the theatre and break down the barriers between actors and audience. From rational science came the understanding of emotion as a biological response to the environment shared among all members of our species and even with animals.

In 1970 British director Peter Brook (b. 1925) assembled a troupe of international actors at his Centre International de Recherche Théâtrales (CIRT) in Paris to explore the possibility of intercultural theatrical communication. Through exercises and improvisations inspired by Artaud, Brook stripped his performers of the cultural specifics of their individual training to find a shared theatrical expression. Exercises in voice and movement drawn from international traditions gave the company a shared physical and vocal technique. Using only a series of rhythmic syllables chosen by the company (ba-sh-ta-hon-do) as a vocal language for exercises, the actors searched for a more primal non-verbal communication system.

Brook's most ambitious experiment was *Orghast* (1971), a production commissioned by the Shiraz Festival in Iran. The 12-hour performance, drawn from myths and legends and based on the ancient myth of Prometheus stealing fire from the gods, was performed outside overnight in the mountains surrounding the tombs of Persian kings. *Orghast* was written by the poet Ted Hughes in a mixture of Avesta, a dead language from the time of Alexander the Great; ancient Greek; Latin; and Orghast, a language Hughes invented based on English, using the most evocative sounds possible for each word and idea. The cast played with this new language over a long rehearsal period, using the movement it evoked to discover a more organic emotional eloquence. In performance there was no shared language between cast members and audience, only a primal vital theatrical encounter.

(continued)

Polish director Jerzy Grotowski's (1933–1999) exploration of organic human exchange began in the early 1960s in his Laboratory Theatre, where rigorous physical training for actors was meant to tear down social barriers to free expression. Starting in 1970 his investigations took him beyond theatre to "active culture" and "paratheatrical experiences." He had already rid his theatre of luxuries in costume, makeup, set, and lighting that might overshadow the actor–audience encounter. He now tore away the cultural trappings of daily life that stood in the way of direct human connections. He took small groups to remote locations, where, without the use of language, they could rediscover human communication. Freed from ordinary social rules, participants tapped into previously unexplored emotions and ways of interacting. Grotowski reintroduced songs and ritualized movements in his final work, to discover an essential communion between human beings uncontaminated by false cultural expressions.

Italian-born director Eugenio Barba (b. 1936), who worked with Grotowski in Poland, subsequently started his Odin Teatret in Norway and brought Grotowski's research back to the field of theatre proper. In 1979 he founded the International School of Theatre Anthropology (ISTA) to investigate the shared qualities of physical presence in performers across cultures. For Barba, the performer has three levels of expression. The first is based in the actor's unique persona and gifts, and the second is based in the cultural tradition in which the performer has trained. The third level, "pre-expressivity," is the universal vibrant presence of the physical actor on stage before any culturally specific technique is expressed. This third level has been the subject of Barba's investigations. In *A Dictionary of Theatre Anthropology: The Secret Art of the Performer* (1991), written with Nicola Savarese, Barba defines the pre-expressive state of performers from different theatrical traditions as an altered and often

precarious physical balance, a dilation of the body, an opposition of directions within the body, a direct gaze from the eyes, and a codified intentional use of hand gestures, all of which make actors seem supremely alive on stage.

Psychologist Paul Ekman (b. 1934) offers a more scientific point of view on a universal language of emotions. Ekman codified almost all the possible movements of the human face in his Facial Action Coding System (FACS) and correlated different expressions to different emotions. Looking carefully at films of politicians, criminals, and emotionally disturbed patients who were caught lying on camera, he discovered that there are involuntary transitory facial expressions that spontaneously reveal emotions. These "microexpressions" are generated by a different physiological system than the one that governs our intentional facial expressions, revealing emotions we consciously try to hide. Because they are involuntary, like breathing, they are universal. Ekman also discovered that intentionally making a facial expression, unmotivated by the emotion it displays, creates physiological changes in heart rate and body temperature associated with having the real emotion. Making an angry face can elevate the heart rate. Pixar, creators of *Toy Story*, and DreamWorks, creators of *Shrek*, have both used FACS in their computer animation.

Chilean neurophysiologist Dr. Susana Bloch was developing similar ideas during the 1980s as she produced experiments to record responses to emotional situations. She noticed universal physical patterns of response that she called "effector patterns." Bloch discovered that repeating the posture, breath, and facial expression of these patterns could induce an emotional response akin to a real emotion. Bloch documented the breathing, facial expression, and physical position that could best elicit each of six primary emotions. She called the system Alba Emoting and in the 1990s began working with actors, holding workshops

▲ The actor Ryszard Cieslak (1937–1990) exemplifies Grotowski's intense physical acting style. The fundamental human emotions expressed in this performance can be read across cultures.

all over the world. Although there are many zealous advocates of the system in the United States, there is also a great deal of resistance to a technique that works externally to create emotion.

Ekman's and Bloch's scientific studies echo the prescribed codified positions of early European acting, the Desarte system, and the *rasa*-based acting technique of *kathakali*. Science has now documented the interrelationship between external expression and internal feeling that these traditions advocated.

Constantin Stanislavski and the Science of Psychology

It is hard for us to realize today that the idea of individual psychology was born in the late nineteenth century and is only a little over 100 years old. The psychological approach to acting that we identify with the American theatre is even more recent than that. It is rooted in the work of the Russian actor and director Constantin Stanislavski (1863–1938), who created the first systematic approach to acting that included script analysis and role interpretation and is now taught the world over.

Stanislavski believed that the methodology of science could be applied to acting and that the actor's laboratory was the studio, not the performance hall. With a group of talented actors in his laboratory at the Moscow Art Theatre, Stanislavski searched for a technique that would enable actors to inhabit the new naturalist plays of his time. The ensemble style demanded by these plays, which presented situations close to everyday life and used natural language and a realistic portrayal of character and emotion, required an approach to acting different from the bombastic, melodramatic acting of the period. Stanislavski strove to develop a training methodology that could address psychological realism. This was truly pioneering work—entirely different from any other approach to acting.

Detailed text analysis is crucial to the Stanislavski system. Every play establishes a series of conditions for the characters. Stanislavski called these the **given circumstances**. Actors must comb the play for details about these conditions. If information is not included in the play, it is part of the actor's work to create the missing details. Actors need to ask themselves many questions as they read. The actor asks these questions in the first person to identify with the character's situation and to provoke a personal response. Where am I? What country, location, building, or room am I in? When is it? What period, time of day, and season? Who am I? What is my relationship to the other characters? Why am I here? What has just happened? What is happening now?

Stanislavski observed that imagining these circumstances has an immediate effect on the actor's behavior as people always adapt to the conditions in which they find themselves. If it were a cold winter night in medieval Denmark, and I were on night watch on the ramparts of a castle where yesterday a ghost had appeared, as in *Hamlet*, my walk and bearing, the feeling in my body would all be different than if I were in a small tenement apartment in twentieth-century New Orleans on a sweltering summer day, as in *A Streetcar Named Desire*. Specificity is important. For example, if I said I was in a restaurant, this would not be specific enough. It might be a McDonald's or a four-star restaurant in Paris. I certainly would not behave the same way in each of those places. How I eat, my table manners, and how I sit, talk, and hold myself would completely change.

The Basic Principles of the Stanislavski System.

- **Given circumstances**—The physical and emotional conditions in the play that determine a character's behavior

- **Imagination and the magic *if***—The ability of the actor to act as *if* the fictional given circumstances were true

- **Objective or task**—What the character wants at any moment on the stage

- **Psychophysical action**—What the character does to achieve the objective or task

- **Adaptation**—The adjustment of the character's behavior as circumstances change

- **Units and beats**—Divisions of the script, with each unit or beat representing a single objective or task

- **Concentration of attention**—The focus of the actor's attention exclusively on the reality on stage

- **Emotional or affective memory**—Drawing on the actor's personal experiences to evoke emotion (later abandoned)

- **Communion**—The deep communication that takes place between actors on stage

- **Physicalizing the character**—What the actor does to give physical life—body, voice, mannerism—to the character on stage

Specificity of detail in the circumstances is important for determining specificity of behavior.

Once the given circumstances are outlined, the actor must ask, "How would I behave *if* I were this character in these circumstances?" This **magic *if*** stimulates the imagination. The circumstances cause the character to desire a certain outcome—the **objective**—the goal that drives a character every moment. The actor is launched into *action* to achieve his or her character's objective. This action becomes the source of interesting and compelling stage behavior. As the character moves through the play pursuing objectives, circumstances are altered by the character's actions. The actor/character must make internal *adjustments*, or **adaptations**, to these changing circumstances, each of which

◀ A set of extreme circumstances drives the physical action and is reflected in the bodies and faces of Hope Davis and Jeff Daniels in this scene from Yasmina Reza's *God of Carnage* (2009).

marks a unit or beat of the drama. This pattern of stimulus and response energizes an actor's presence and movement through the play. In addition to the immediate scene and **beat** objectives that they live each moment on stage, characters also have larger **superobjectives** that motivate them throughout the entire course of the play.

Truthful acting for **Stanislavski** meant behaving in a way that was consistent with the imaginary circumstances of the play. Until the twentieth century, it was an accepted European convention that actors faced the audience directly when they spoke, even when their lines were directed toward other characters. To combat this convention, Stanislavski developed the idea of **concentration of attention**, insisting that actors keep a circle of attention with their eyes that did not encompass the audience and that they focus instead on objects and characters within the stage reality. He emphasized the importance of actors not speaking directly to the audience but instead truly talking to each other and communicating on stage to create the deep emotional connection that actors must make to each other. This is the basis of ensemble performance.

After the script is analyzed for circumstances, beats, objectives, and actions, the actor works on the psychological and physical embodiment of the character, answering the most important question: "Who am I?" Stanislavski emphasized the importance of combing a play for buried information to create a complete picture of the character and his or her relationship to other characters. Details allow the actor to play a distinct and unique individual instead of a cliché. This contrasts sharply with the method of playing generalized emotions and types that dominated the European theatre until the twentieth century. Stanislavski also developed exercises for a free and flexible body and voice that facilitated physicalization of the character.

One part of Stanislavski's early technique—**emotional memory,** or **affective memory**, sometimes called emotional recall, remains a subject of controversy to this day. Based on the work of French psychologist Théodule Ribot (1839–1916), the technique requires the actor to focus on the sensory stimuli surrounding an event in his or her personal life that was similar to the situation in the character's life in order to evoke an emotional response. Acting teachers have disagreed about the effectiveness of the use of an actor's personal memories to portray the emotions of the character. Most importantly, Stanislavski himself discovered that it is not easy to call up emotions at will, and he abandoned this technique. During the 1920s he came to believe that emotions need to be stimulated indirectly through physical action. Disputes over how much an actor's personal psychology must enter into actor training continue today.

Stanislavski's later work was influenced by the theories of Russian physiologists Ivan Pavlov (1849–1936) and Ivan Sechenov (1829–1905), who studied conditioned reflex. Stanislavski came to believe that inner feeling and thought are expressed in the body, and physical actions can become a bridge between our inner and outer worlds. When actors

> The bond between the **body** and the **soul** is indivisible. . . . In every **physical** action, unless it is purely mechanical, there is concealed some inner action, some **feelings**. This is how the two levels of life in a part are created, the **inner** and the **outer.**

—Constantin Stanislavski, *Creating a Role*[2]

think as their characters, they are stimulated to perform physical actions that are justified by the given circumstances and objectives; simultaneously, this truthful behavior can actually evoke the appropriate emotions.

Today, almost a century after Stanislavski began his innovative work, the system he pioneered remains at the center of actor training programs on every continent. Various interpreters have expanded or modified the core techniques, and new exercises have been created, but the fundamental concept of purposeful behavior on stage within the imaginary circumstances is key to acting in various theatrical styles. Recent discoveries about the physical basis of emotions in modern neuroscience seem to confirm much of Stanislavski's thinking.

THINK

Because the actor uses his or her own body, heart, mind, and emotions, do we see the real person when the actor performs a role?

Explorations in **Physical Training**

Stanislavski's ideas spread through the tours of the Moscow Art Theatre. Although he had talked about the need for muscular relaxation and physical training for the actor, Stanislavski left behind no set methodology for achieving these goals. Other figures, often with very different views of the theatre, pioneered the work in this area.

[2]Constantin Stanislavski. *Creating a Role.* Trans. Elizabeth Reynolds Hapgood. (New York: Theatre Arts Books, 1961), 227–228.

In Russia, Stanislavski's student Vsevolod Meyerhold (1874–1942) created **biomechanics**, a physical training system for efficient and expressive movement. Biomechanics offered a developed system of exercises, based in organic patterns of movement, that taught the actor complete control over the body and developed the capacity for quick response to stimuli. The training reflected Russian developments in neurophysiology pioneered by Pavlov and others. The system is still studied today.

In France, in the 1920s, Jacques Copeau (1878–1949) founded the École du Vieux Colombier to resuscitate the theatre. The school integrated circus, mask, mime, Asian movement, and *commedia dell'arte* training into the acting curriculum. Modern French mime originated in this school. Copeau's nephew, Michel Saint-Denis (1897–1971), created the Old Vic Theatre School in 1946, followed by the National Theatre School of Canada in 1959, and in 1968 the Julliard School in New York, all based on Copeau's ideas of physical training for the actor. Not until the 1970s were similar regimens of physical training incorporated into the curricula of many American acting schools, and it took almost a decade before such work was widespread in the United States. Today, it is impossible to imagine a professional actor training program that does not provide extensive courses to develop an expressive and articulate body.

Freeing the **Actor's Energy**

The 1960s and early 1970s were marked by a search for new forms of theatre. The revolutionary political atmosphere had a profound impact on the theatre and acting. Social structures were seen as obstacles to freedom of expression. Learned social inhibitions were viewed as obstructing the flow of energy and feeling and blocking the actor from reaching a primal emotional source.

Ideas and techniques drawn from Asian philosophy and religion that emphasized the impossibility of separating the physical from the psychological were applied. From Zen came an understanding of the importance of proper relaxation and breathing techniques. Focus on the breath creates a greater awareness of the whole body, and through awareness comes the control so necessary to acting. The influence of Asian religion and philosophy is evidenced in the idea of a *body center*, or a point in the body where breath, movement, feeling, and thought are integrated through focused relaxation. The process through which an actor reaches this integrated state is called **centering**. Centering permits the harnessed and economical use of the body's physical, emotional, and intellectual energy and results in a dynamic performance. Various approaches to movement training, such as the Alexander and Feldenkrais techniques, focus on proper alignment and body image to free physical movement from muscular tension. Simultaneously, vocal techniques have been developed in the past 50 years to facilitate a free, natural, and fully projected voice. Vocal coaches Kristin Linklater (b. 1936), Cecily Berry (b. 1926), Arthur Lessac (1909–2011), and Patsy Rodenburg (b. 1953) have been at the forefront of this type of voice training, which replaced the old emphasis on elocution.

The Stanislavski System Becomes American Method Acting

Method acting, that distinctly American brand of theatrical performance marked by force of personality and raw emotion, and personified by figures such as Marlon Brando (1924–2004), James Dean (1931–1955), and Paul Newman (1925–2008), evolved from the Stanislavski system. Two actors who had studied with Stanislavski, Maria Ouspenskaya (1881–1949) and Richard Boleslavsky (1889–1937), came to America with the 1923 tour of the Moscow Art Theatre and remained and taught his technique to a group of actors at the American Laboratory Theatre in New York. There, during the 1920s, Lee Strasberg (1902–1982), Stella Adler (1902–1992), and Harold Clurman (1901–1980) learned their craft. Together with Cheryl Crawford (1902–1986), Robert Lewis (1909–1997), Sanford Meisner, (1905–1997), and Elia Kazan (1909–2003), they formed the core of the Group Theatre (1931–1941), where they transformed the American theatre and turned the Stanislavski system into something distinctly American.

Using the Moscow Art Theatre as a model, this passionate ensemble of young actors and directors set out to reform the commercial theatre with socially conscious plays, an ensemble style, and emotionally authentic acting. In time, however, artistic and personal differences brought friction to the Group. Notably, Stella Adler and Lee Strasberg clashed over his focus on emotional, or affective, memory. Adler felt the technique was tearing her up emotionally, which inspired her to travel to France in 1934 to meet with the ailing Stanislavski who had long since abandoned his focus on emotional memory. Even at the time of the 1923 tour, he was already working on the psychophysical approach to acting that took the actor's attention off the personal emotional life. Ouspenskaya and Boleslavsky, who had trained during the earlier stages of Stanislavski's work, had passed on an incomplete system to their New York students. By the time he met Adler, Stanislavski was concerned for his legacy in America. He taught her his new technical approach, focusing on the given circumstances and action, with emotion as a by-product, not a goal. When she returned, Adler shared the method of physical actions with the Group and challenged Strasberg's authority in the ensemble, creating a rift between Adler and Strasberg. Strasberg believed Stanislavski was contradicting himself and that he, Strasberg, had now developed his own method that was as valid as the evolved Stanislavski system.

In 1947, six years after the Group disbanded, several of its alumni—Harold Clurman, Elia Kazan, and Robert Lewis—met to discuss continuing its work. Out of this meeting came the idea to start The Actors Studio, a name that hearkened back to Stanislavski's first studio. Its initial class included many who would become luminaries of American theatre and film—Marlon Brando (who also studied with Stella Adler), Montgomery Clift (1920–1966), Julie Harris (b. 1925), Karl Malden (1912–2009), choreographer Jerome Robbins (1919–1998), and film director Sidney Lumet (1924–2011) among them. In short order, Lewis and Kazan had conflicts. Kazan's landmark production of A Streetcar Named Desire, with Brando in his definitive performance, had led to a busy directing schedule. They needed someone who had ample time to devote to the school. Strasberg, at first kept out because of his difficult temperament, was having little success in his career and was called in for the task. In 1948, Strasberg joined the Studio. By 1951 he had become its artistic director, a position he held until his death in 1982, and the rest is American theatre history. Method acting, Lee Strasberg, and The Actors Studio would become synonymous.

Authenticity of emotion became the focus of Strasberg's work, and actors turned inward to mine their psyches for the experiences and feelings that could translate to the stage. He developed emotional memory exercises and the famous "private moment" that put actors' personal issues into public view as they enacted private behavior that they would normally do only behind closed doors. In private moments, many actors crossed social boundaries with daring nudity and intimate behavior.

▲ Marlon Brando, who died in 2004, exemplified the intensely emotional style represented by American method acting. He burst onto the theatrical scene in 1947, with his portrayal of Stanley Kowalski in Tennessee Williams's A Streetcar Named Desire.

(continued)

(continued from page 171)

Much rumor still circulates around this exercise, although most work was quite tame. In the Studio's early years, little emphasis was placed on the vocal and movement work of British and European conservatories. Without that training, Studio actors rarely developed the skills for character roles and the classics, and one criticism of the method was that it prepared actors only for realism and roles in which they could play themselves in heightened theatrical terms.

Strasberg was at once a dominating force, a bully, and a father figure to his students. He traumatized many young talents and nurtured others. Many who studied with him became the great actors of the American theatre, ensuring his reputation as a guru. Strasberg also spawned a cult of acting teachers who used his method to push young actors to their emotional breaking point. Although Strasberg was well aware that Stanislavski was influenced by behavioral psychology and not versed in Freud, Strasberg's techniques meshed well with the American obsession with psychoanalysis during the 1950s and 1960s. As more and more of the public were examining their inner demons, watching actors wrestle with theirs was a public projection of the American psyche and the hallmark of a new American acting style that would captivate the world.

▼ The necessity of physical training for the actor is evidenced in the staging of this scene from *A Midsummer Night's Dream* at the Linbury Theatre, Royal Opera House, Covent Garden, in London.

THINK

Should there be any limit to what an acting teacher can ask actors to experience during training (e.g., nudity, intimacy, smoking, drinking, pushing actors to physical and emotional limits)?

During the 1960s, the European and American avant-garde moved away from traditional plays or used texts as a basis for improvised action. This placed new demands on actors. Notable European directors of the 1960s created productions that relied on exquisitely trained actors capable of physical and vocal virtuosity. Jerzy Grotowski developed a set of difficult exercises called *plastiques* that could be performed only by physically trained actors. Jean-Louis Barrault (1911–1994) trained as a mime and incorporated elaborate group pantomime sequences into his work. The 1970 production of *A Midsummer Night's Dream*, directed by Peter Brook, serves as an example of the demands of the new theatre. Scenes were played on trapezes, and actors juggled while reciting their lines in perfect Shakespearean rhythm. The performers were required to have all the traditional skills of accomplished Shakespearean actors and be able to do circus tricks as well. Theatre groups in the United States such as the Open Theatre, The Performance Group, and The Manhattan Project worked improvisationally to create performances with the actors as both creators and performers.

It has been almost 100 years since the importance of physical training for the actor was just an experimental idea in Europe. Today new systems of training continue to thrive around the world. The Japanese director and teacher Suzuki Tadashi (b. 1939) developed a technique based on the physical rootedness of ancient Japanese

▲ Member of the SITI company practice the Suzuki training method which focuses on actors receiving energy from the earth to realize their full expressive potential.

acting traditions. Through stomping, the actor coordinates the movement of the upper torso and the feet, creating an awareness of the energy at the center between the upward and the downward forces. American director Anne Bogart (b. 1951) cofounded the Saratoga International Theatre Institute with Suzuki. She uses **Viewpoints**, a physical training system developed by Mary Overlie, which fosters awareness of the basic components of movement—line, rhythm, tempo, and duration. Workshops in these methods are given around the world, providing evidence of the globalization of actor training.

THINK

Should all roles be open to casting with any actor, regardless of ethnic or racial identity? With so few roles available in the commercial theatre for minority actors, should those roles be reserved for them?

An Eclectic Approach

Once acting schools taught only diction, script analysis, and scene study. It is now common for acting schools to offer classes in circus for coordination and strength, mime and mask work for an articulate and expressive body, *t'ai chi* for balance and form, yoga for breath control and focus, Suzuki for centering, African dance for centered control and rhythm, Alexander technique for alignment and "good use," fencing for focus and coordination, Viewpoints for spatial awareness, vocal production for a free voice, diction for clarity of speech, and singing. All these techniques are now seen as vital and reflect borrowings from many different cultures.

Christine Toy Johnson is an actor, writer, producer, and advocate for inclusion in the arts. Her extensive acting career spans Broadway, Off-Broadway, national tours, regional theatres, television, and films. She has been active in the Nontraditional Casting Project, which promotes employment opportunities for minority and disabled actors, and was honored in 2010 by the Japanese American Citizens League.

Can you explain your work with nontraditional casting and its goals?

I became involved in advocacy for nontraditional casting and inclusion in the arts about twenty years ago. At the time the discussions of nontraditional casting were ripe because of the hiring of the non-Asian Jonathan Pryce to play the Asian (later justified as "Eurasian") "Engineer" in the Broadway premiere of *Miss Saigon*. I remember thinking that if Cameron McIntosh could argue that actors (such as Jonathan Pryce) should be able to play other races, then the door had to swing both ways. At the time we were still fighting to get the opportunity to play our own ethnicity. I lost many *King and I* jobs to Caucasian women so it seemed only fair that in plays where race was not germane to the plot, Asian American actors should also be allowed to play non-Asian roles.

Is authenticity important in portraying Asians on the stage?

Given the lack of opportunities that Asian actors have had, I stand firm on fighting for our right to portray Asians on the stage. Unfortunately, Asian roles have often not been portrayed with the dignity, respect, and lack of stereotypical characteristics that most Asian American actors would bring to the same roles. It was vital for us to start portraying our multicultural society through the characters we played on stage. After all, the theatre has always been an educator and a mirror to our society. I have had to explain the abhorrent concept of "yellow face" being the equivalent of "black face" in the eyes of the Asian American community. One would never cast an African American role with an actor who is not African American, yet it is still common to find non-Asian actors in "yellow face" portraying Asian roles on stage.

Why is nontraditional casting important?

The arts and the media have a unique opportunity to influence the way we look at each other. Nontraditional casting has always been about enriching the quality of storytelling, expanding boundaries, portraying the universality of the human spirit. The opportunity to help heal society by highlighting the beauty of both our similarities and our differences is an incredible gift, and this is the power of theatre.

What special efforts, if any, do you make when preparing for a role that is outside your personal racial background?

I prepare all roles in the same way, no matter what their racial or cultural background might be. Trained to examine the text and to mine the details that are there in order to illuminate the life of the character, I aim to understand what makes a character tick, and why they do what they do. In getting to the root of a character, the basic questions I ask are the same: What does she want? What will she do to get it? What's standing in her way? Why is she motivated to do the things she does? I also do extensive research on a person's cultural, societal, and professional background, developing the backstory of a character as much as possible in order to understand the richness of their life history.

▼ An example of non-traditional casting is Asian-American actor Christine Toy Johnson as Ethel Toffelmier in the Broadway production of The Music Man.

The Acting Profession **Today**

The glamour of the acting profession draws many people to the theatre, but, in fact, the actor's life is filled with hard work, endless training, and many disappointments. For minority actors, the road to success may be even more difficult. Still, actors will tell you that nothing compares to the thrill of performing, of feeling all your physical, mental, and emotional energy flowing and focused. It is an exhilarating sensation. Actors need to be emotionally and physically healthy to deal with the technical challenges of training and to have the ability to analyze characters objectively. The knocks of the profession and the constant risk and rejection, along with prolonged periods of unemployment, require a strong ego and sense of self.

In the past, actors joined companies where they performed with a group of people for many years. Actors sometimes even became shareholders in the profits. Shakespeare and Molière, both actors, wrote for their own acting companies and had specific actors in mind for the roles they wrote. Today there are few theatre companies or repertory troupes in which actors stay together for years. Instead, actors are hired for a single role for the run of the play and frequently find themselves unemployed for long periods between engagements. The advantages of ongoing companies are many. Actors have a sense of family and ensemble that does not have to be created afresh after every production; work can be developed that fits with the talents of particular actors; and of course, there is the advantage of not being perpetually unemployed.

Repeatedly, perhaps many times a year, actors seek work through **auditions**, where they perform either prepared material or read from the play being cast for the director. A small number of actors are asked to return for a second audition, or **callback**. They may or may not be cast, even after repeated efforts. After casting, there is a rehearsal period during which actors explore their roles, analyze the text, and develop physical characterizations—a walk, a voice, and mannerisms—for their characters. During rehearsals actors explore actions and objectives with the guidance of the director. Every actor must find a way to have his or her interpretations and choices mesh with the choices of other actors to create a seamless imaginary world. They adjust to costumes, sets, and lights and ready the production for performance.

Sometimes actors begin not with a written play but with a concept and are expected to create the text. Rehearsals in such a case involve improvisation and exploration until a performance text is fully created. We discussed some of the groups that work in this way in Chapter 6.

Over a period of weeks, an actor's performance develops. The intellectual analysis gives way to physical embodiment, and the actual performance becomes second nature. At this point, actors no longer think about the meaning of the piece, the voice or movement or feeling. It all becomes an organic part of the actor's being, an integrated whole.

> All the training of the body, voice, and mind frees actors to transform themselves into imaginary beings with beating hearts.

The Warm-up

Before every rehearsal and performance, all trained actors perform a **warm-up** to relieve tension that could block emotional flow, to loosen and limber, and to get centered and focused. There is no single way to warm up. Actors construct warm-ups that suit the roles they are playing or particular vocal or movement challenges they may face. Some theatre companies warm up together as a way of getting the energy flowing among the actors before they are on stage. An acting warm-up is not unlike a warm-up for an athletic event. Actors, like athletes, must ready the body to give its all.

Stage and Film Acting

The technical demands of the stage are much greater than those of film, although some of the basic principles of acting

THINK

When so many highly trained actors are unemployed, is it right to bring in an actor with celebrity appeal and little stage experience to play a coveted role? Is it justified if it lures new audiences to the theatre?

for these two very different media remain the same. Actors analyze the script, the character, and the circumstances for a film the same way they would for the theatre. They choose physical characterizations, voices, and gestures. Stage actors must also have mastery of vocal technique if they are to be heard in a large theatre without vocal strain; they must radiate physical energy and choose actions that read across space, and they must learn to play off a live audience. On the other hand, film actors are supported by microphones, close-ups, and camera angles. They rehearse for very short periods, in small bits, and often out of sequence so they do not have to create a sustained and developed performance. Ultimately, actors in film have less control over the shape of their final performances than do actors in the theatre because the film director and editor cut, determine camera angles, and shape what the viewer sees. Many actors who work in both film and theatre say that when they work in film, they miss the contact with the live audience and the sense of immediacy and control of the arc of performance. As a result, many, like Jude Law (b. 1972), Helen Mirren (b. 1945), Kevin Spacey (b. 1959), Denzel Washington (b. 1954), and Catherine Zeta-Jones (b. 1969), return to the theatre for challenge and renewal. On stage, there is no safety net, no chance for a retake.

▼ Film star Catherine Zeta-Jones performs here in the Broadway revival of the Stephen Sondheim-Hugh Wheeler musical *A Little Night Music*. Her star power drew audiences to the theatre.

Acting in
Performance Traditions

Performance traditions that involve music, dance, song, masks, and exaggerated makeup demand a very different kind of acting than realism, and exuberance and theatricality take precedence over the quest for emotional authenticity. The style of acting among different traditions varies widely, and the training can be formal or informal. In Africa and among the indigenous peoples of the Americas and Australia, many traditions are passed on through initiation, imitation, and apprenticeship, and the burden is on the student to observe, absorb, and practice techniques. In Asia many codified systems are rigorously taught.

Traditional Asian Acting Styles and Training

Asian theatre traditions revel in the artificiality and artistry of a presentational style. Plays in these traditions often tell tales of gods or legendary heroes, and an amplified style of performance that integrates dramatic presentation with mime, dance, music, and sometimes acrobatics supports the mythic dimensions of these larger-than-life characters. Asian theatre forms use colorful costumes, vibrant makeup or masks, and exaggerated styles of movement. On the Asian stage, to move is to dance and to speak is to sing. Actors do not concentrate on the development of psychologically realistic portraits but instead practice embodying archetypal figures.

Asian actors master codes of performance that previous artists have developed and perfected, sometimes over hundreds of years. These codes typically delineate physical postures and gestures as well as vocal styles for a defined number of role types. They may also determine patterns of stage movement as well as costume and makeup. The emphasis in these traditions is on the accomplished execution of a completely envisioned role rather than on developing a unique interpretation.

Traditional Asian forms were passed down through families, from one generation to the next. From their infancy, future actors were exposed to the art they would later take up as they watched their parents rehearse and perform and listened to the music and stories of the theatrical repertoire. Because changing economic and social realities throughout Asia have endangered these family traditions, special schools now provide training to students who are not from artistic families.

In many Asian traditions, training in the early stages involves the master's manipulation of the student's body.

▲ A teacher at the College of Dramatic Arts in Bangkok helps a student perfect the stance of a vigorous character from *khon*, a Thai classical masked-dance tradition. *Khon* students are matched to role types such as a young man, a young woman, a demon, or an athletic character, usually used for the monkey Hanuman in the *Ramayana* epic. Students train to perform the single role type that best matches their physical potential. Precise physical positioning is an important part of the art, and students learn and repeat their characters' traditional postures and dance sequences before using masks. The college is the major school for training in classical Thai dance and is the descendant of the old palace department of performing arts.

The student's process is marked by intense observation and imitation of the master's movement patterns and then endless repetition until formal perfection is attained. If you have ever studied a martial art, you may have experienced some similarities in approach. Formal training usually starts at a young age, when the body is flexible. Asian theatre forms demand extraordinary physical expression, in which every part of the body, including fingers, toes, and even the eyes and mouth, are fully articulated. The closest parallel in the West is the training of classical ballet dancers, who must start at an early age to develop the strength and flexibility required to master a set repertory of positions and movements. It is common for students to be chosen to study particular kinds of roles based on how well their faces and bodies conform to preconceived ideals. Much early training involves preparing the actor's body for performance.

Kathakali: A Case Study of **Asian Training**

Kathakali theatre from the state of Kerala in India offers a good example of the arduous demands placed on the traditional Asian actor. *Kathakali*, which means "story-play," dates to the late sixteenth and early seventeenth centuries. In *kathakali*, all-male companies of actor-dancers enact tales from Indian epics as well as stories from popular Hindu lore. They are accompanied by percussion music and vocalists singing both narration and dialogue. *Kathakali's* derivation from the Kerala martial arts tradition accounts in part for the

demanding physicality inherent in the form. The actors must also be fit to carry the voluminous skirts and large headdresses that are traditional costuming. It takes two to three hours for the actor to don traditional makeup and costume in preparation for performance (see photo in Chapter 10). They then act, dance, and leap through shows that can last from 6:30 in the evening until 6:30 the next morning.

Kathakali actors traditionally begin their training by age 7 or 8. Class can fill an 8- to 13-hour day that includes both philosophical and text study, as well as rigorous physical training. Instruction concentrates on preparing the actor's body for the physical demands of performance and includes building general strength and flexibility and learning jumping, body control, and footwork patterns. Actors remodel their bodies to the basic posture that is the basis for all *kathakali* movement—head straight with chin tucked in, heels together with knees turned out, forming the shape of a flat rhombus with the legs. The outer edges of the feet are never placed flat on the ground, and yet perfect balance is maintained. The spine is held in a concave curve, with the rear end pointing up, arms out to the side, elbows slightly bent, and hands limp so that from the side the performer looks flat. Starting from this position, the actor must be able to execute all the prescribed dance patterns and occasional feats of physical virtuosity. To attain this stance, young actors lie on the floor with their knees turned out and their teachers step on their backs, molding their bodies into the ideal shape.

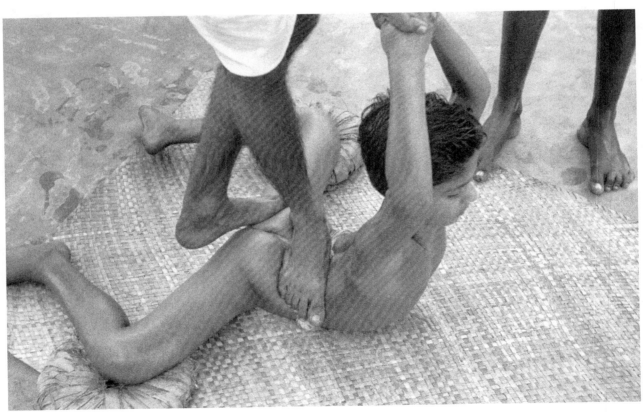

▲ At a training school in Kerala, India, a young student develops the flexibility required for the physically demanding art of *kathakali*. Traditionally artists begin training when they are young and their bodies are supple.

Kathakali actors neither speak nor sing on stage. Both narration and dialogue in *kathakali* are presented by a vocalist who stands with the musicians. Actors communicate the Sanskrit texts to the audience in a language of hand gestures known as **mudras**, whose meanings change in relation to various body postures and facial expressions. As part of their training, *kathakali* actors learn 500 *mudras* and the texts from as many as 18 plays. In the *kathakali* theatre, a variety of role types are defined by their traditional makeup and costuming. Unlike some other Asian forms, in which actors specialize in one role type their whole lives, *kathakali* actors learn all the roles and how to perform each within the entire dramatic repertoire.

Like all other actors, *kathakali* actors embody characters and present their emotional states and experiences. *Kathakali* acting identifies nine basic emotional states, or *bhavas*—erotic, comic, pathos, fury, heroic, fearful, repulsive,

wondrous, and peace—plus a tenth state, shyness, used only for female characters. Actors express these states by executing prescribed facial expressions, with specific positioning for the eyes, eyebrows, and mouth. They also do exercises to render their faces flexible and expressive. In one such exercise, actors sit facing a wall as they listen to their teacher tell a story. They must enact everything the character in the story sees and feels, using only their eyes. When performing, actors place small seeds in their eyes to redden them and make them more remarkable.

Like many other Asian performers, *kathakali* actors play on a mostly bare stage and create the imaginary world around them through physical gesture. An actor's movements will tell the audience that he is mounting, riding, or dismounting a horse.

Mastering *kathakali* performance takes a lifetime of practice. Actors do not truly reach their prime until their 40s,

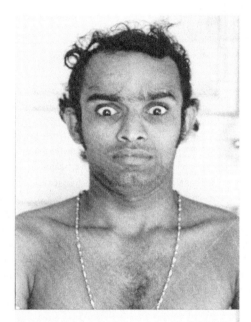

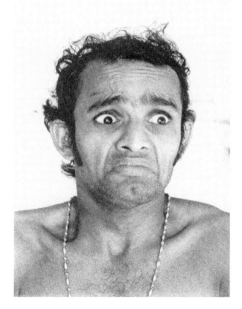

◀ Kathakali actors convey the basic *bhavas*, or states of being-doing through facial expressions that require total control of all facial muscles. The audience savors the corresponding *rasa*, or flavor of feeling, produced by each expression. Pictured here, clockwise from top left, are the emotions fury, disgust, fear, and peace or at-onement. Interestingly, Delsarte, working in nineteenth-century France, developed a system that echoes this late sixteenth-/early seventeenth-century Indian performance tradition, which draws from more ancient roots. Compare these expressions with those in the figure on page 166.

◀ *Kathakali* dancers Amaljeet and Rewati Aiyyer are Lord Krishna and Draupadi in a scene from the *Mahabharata* at a cultural festival in Patna, India. Note the traditional makeup and costumes of the actors as well as the stylized use of the face and hands.

when their technique becomes second nature and can serve as a vehicle for artistic expression. The following often-quoted statement reveals the philosophy embedded in the *kathakali* approach to actor training:

> Where the hand [is], there [is] the eye;
> where the eye [is], there [is] the mind;
> where the mind [is], there [is] the *bhava*;
> where the *bhava* [is], there is the *rasa*.[3]

The term *bhava* means the actor's expression of the character's emotional state, and the term *rasa* means the audience's aesthetic savoring of the theatrical experience.

The **Puppeteer** as Actor

To be a puppeteer is to be a kind of actor. The puppeteer needs to master the ability to create and project character, just as actors do. The difference is that a puppeteer projects performances through the medium of a performing object—a marionette, glove, shadow, or rod puppet, whether of Asian or Western origin—rather than through his or her own body. The close relationship between human and puppet performance provides some insight into the stylized acting found in Asia and may even explain some of the training methodology. The marionette theatre in Myanmar is said to predate live-actor performance forms. Dance postures of human actors mimic the movements of puppets. One frequently performed novelty act pits a marionette in a dancing contest against a human performer. In Indonesia the **wayang kulit**, or shadow puppet, tradition predates *wayang orang*, a masked-dance form with human actors; the two forms share many similarities.

Puppeteers have traditionally trained informally in families or with performing troupes, and this is still the case

for many forms. Today institutions throughout the world offer workshops and courses of study for aspiring puppeteers. They teach the art of manipulating a variety of performing objects. It is relatively easy to learn to manipulate some puppets, such as shadow puppets, whereas operating others, such as marionettes or *bunraku*-style puppets, takes a good deal of patience, coordination, and dexterity. Most programs teach movement and mime to help puppeteers understand their own physical actions and centering, so they can impart physical expression to a performing object. Voice training is also important because vocal characterization helps define a speaking puppet. (Imagine *Sesame Street*'s Kermit the Frog with a low, husky voice, and the character would be transformed.) Also, puppeteers may do the voices of several characters in a single show. Because puppeteers often create their own shows from scratch, many programs teach puppet construction. Some also provide classes in playwriting to help puppeteers develop scripts for performance.

Freedom Within Constraint; Constraint Within Freedom

Western actors often believe that the strictly defined codes of traditional Asian performance hinder the actor's freedom and creativity. Asian performers, in contrast, feel that the constraints of tradition that guide their performances actually liberate them artistically. Freed from having to make new choices in terms of action, characterization, physicality, and vocal placement, they are fully available on stage to execute a role for which a lifetime of practice has prepared them.

Most Asian theatre codes of performance are not as strict as they might seem at first glance, and the actor's creativity may be called on in ways that would seem surprising to Western performers. In Chinese opera, for instance, actors master a single role type, such as the vivacious young female or *hua dan*, which they play their entire lives.

[3]Phillip B. Zarrilli, *Kathakali Dance Drama: Where Gods and Demons Come to Play* (London: Routledge, 2000), 91.

Matsui Akira (**b. 1946**) *is a master actor-teacher of the Kita School of Japanese classical* noh *theatre. He began studying* noh *at age 5 and at age 13 became a "live-in apprentice" to Kita Minoru, the fifteenth generation of* noh *masters of the Kita School. Since age 20 he has been performing and teaching throughout Japan and has been active in disseminating* noh *abroad by training student actors around the world; acting in productions of plays by Shakespeare, W. B. Yeats, and Beckett; co-creating new "English* noh*"; and choreographing* noh*-style dances to jazz ballads and poetry. In 1998 the Japanese government designated him an Important Intangible Cultural Asset. He is an Affiliated Artist with Theatre Nohgaku, whose mission is to share the beauty and power of* noh *with English-speaking audiences and performers through English-language productions, training workshops, lectures, and professional residencies.*

Could you describe your own training in *noh*? How did you become a *noh* performer?

I'm not from a traditional *noh* family. When I was 5 years old and growing up in Wakayama City, I was quite small and my doctor suggested I do *utai* (*noh* chant) to make me stronger. In fact, he was a teacher of chant, and so I started taking lessons from him. My parents had the doctor introduce me to his teacher, a Kita School performer named Wajima Tomitaro. I began to take lessons with Wajima sensei, and he had me occasionally perform *kokata* (child) roles in plays in Wakayama and Osaka. When I was 13 years old, I was very fortunate to have Wajima sensei arrange for me to go to Tokyo to live with the *iemoto* (headmaster) of the Kita School, Kita Minoru. I was one of seven *uchideshi* (live-in disciples) of the *iemoto* and the youngest. We would wake up early in the morning and practice chant and dance for a couple of hours before going off to regular school. After school we would come back and have lessons in

the *hayashi*—the four instruments of *noh*. A different *hayashi* teacher would come every day. Then we would rehearse more chant and dance. Some days we would have performances where we began to learn how to help backstage.

Of course, what we were doing as *uchideshi* was not just learning how to perform *noh*. We were doing what we call *shugyô*, which includes much more than just learning how to perform. It is learning how to live. We had to clean the house, we had to open and close all the house shutters, we had to do the things our seniors told us to do. And of course the most important is learning proper greetings and etiquette in the house and then backstage. Even if you think your senior isn't a particularly good performer, you must learn to respect him. We don't have exams to determine who has the highest score, and we are not like sumo or other sports where you have a winner or loser. It is difficult to determine who is a better performer, but even if one thinks one is better, someone else might eventually be a better teacher. So we always have to show respect for our elders.

What we come to understand in the process is that etiquette is the basis of one's *noh* training. And it becomes important in passing along the art to our own sons. If I died young, who would teach my own son? It really is necessary that my association with other performers is good so they can help in the training of my son no matter what the future.

To many Western actors, the idea of learning a codified performance form can seem constraining. Can you explain how it frees you to create within the form, or how you see your own creativity emerge within the form?

In the West, dance and theatre have become separate things. In both *noh* and *kabuki*, dance and theatre are melded together. When you do dance, you of course have to learn the forms of dance which we call *kata*. But then as you begin to add more levels of theatre, you need to add inner elements of expression. Even with those inner elements, the basis for movement still is dance in terms of how you move or even walk. Classical

▼ Matsui Akira appears in *The Gull,* a new Canadian *noh* play.

(continued)

(*continued from page 181*)

ballet still uses balletic movements as its base even though a theatrical story is being presented. So *noh* isn't theatre in the sense that Shakespeare is theatre. *Noh* has dance that follows rules, which makes it different from Shakespeare. And it also has music, which means that movement has to fit along with the rules of music, and that of course is what dance is.

Kata, the set movement patterns of *noh*, are thus born of dance. How one expresses those *kata* then becomes the source of creativity for the actor. Do you express those *kata* in a large fashion or a small fashion? Do you make them simple or complex? Each *kata* might have its parameters of expression, but there is a lot of freedom within those parameters. *Kata* might have set rules, but the actor has freedom to vary those boundaries. *Noh* actors use *suriashi* "sliding feet" movements to walk, but there is a great variety in how you execute that walk.

If you can execute the *kata*, you can perform. In turn, that might make it difficult to stand out as a performer because you might think that everyone is doing the same thing. But not all actors look the same doing the same *kata*. Some might be very precise, others not so. For the audience members who know *kata*, that difference is interesting. It is up to the actor to take the expression of those *kata* to a higher level to create something that deepens a sense of understanding of the story. And that is what creates the difference between performers and performances.

What do you believe are the most important qualities or skills for a *noh* actor?

For the head of a school, more important than performing itself is passing on the tradition and the performance standards of the tradition. But for other performers in the school, the question is how can one learn the tradition but make it feel new, relevant, and vital to the present. And that is really the most difficult thing for a performer to do. If one just takes the patterns and performs them without giving them new life, they are just antiques, and the actor just becomes a museum of ancient performance.

Source: The interview with Matsui Akira was conducted in Japanese and translated and transcribed into English by Richard Emmert, the founder and artistic director of Theatre Nohgaku.

However, they choose which gestures from the character's physical vocabulary they will use to reflect feelings at particular moments, often varying choices from one night to the next. Chinese opera audiences are sensitive to these changes and judge the actor in part by these creative decisions. Chinese opera singers also help select the music that accompanies a performance. During Chinese opera rehearsals, actors indicate to the musicians what kind of music they feel would be appropriate for a particular moment on stage, and the musicians select a musical piece from a repertoire of known melodies.

In the Japanese *noh* theatre, actors make interpretive statements about their characters through choices in costuming. The appropriate style of kimono for a role might be prescribed, but a performer will decide on a particular design or pattern for the garment, perhaps one with cranes or fall-colored leaves, to reveal his view of the play. In Western theatre this type of choice is made by costume designers and directors rather than performers.

Whatever performance codes exist, however, living traditions are always in flux as they react to the needs of new actors, changing times, and contemporary audiences.

No current performance is a complete replica of any done in the past. In Asia new social, political, and economic realities are continually altering time-honored traditions. *Kathakali* plays once done outdoors in the round by firelight for local audiences are now presented indoors on proscenium-style stages with electric lighting for audiences from all over the world. Such changes inevitably influence performance style and technique.

Just as traditional Asian forms are relaxing some of their strict performance codes, American and European stage acting is becoming an increasingly refined and disciplined art. Whereas once actors took to the stage by whim or passion, today's American stage actor is a highly trained professional who has usually studied the craft intensively for an extended time. Most have been trained in conservatories or MFA programs that often require a minimum of three years of study. Physical rigor and control are demanded and often taught through Asian training systems or mime and mask work. Freedom within constraint and constraint within freedom have been the hallmarks of contemporary acting around the world. Actors achieve this by looking toward tradition for innovation.

Summary

HOW is acting integral to the human experience? p. 158

▶ Acting is not simply reproduction and imitation. The excitement of live acting comes from watching the process of simulation.

▶ Acting is a fundamental human activity around the world.

WHAT are the universal qualities of acting in the theatre? p. 158

▶ All actors transcend everyday behavior through energy, control, focus, purpose, dynamics, enlargement, and transformation.

WHAT does an actor do? p. 160

▶ Actors in different theatrical traditions do different things on stage, and their training is a function of how and what they are expected to perform.

▶ Representational acting is seen in realistic theatrical styles in which actors live the emotions. Presentational acting appears where there is a heightened theatrical style and an openly artificial reproduction of emotion.

DOES an actor experience genuine emotion on stage? p. 162

▶ Actors' dual consciousness allows them to stand simultaneously inside and outside a role they are playing.

HOW is the idea of good acting culturally determined? p. 162

▶ Acting generally reflects a society's views of beauty, emotion, psychology, and behavior.

▶ In the European tradition most acting focuses on interpreting a written role. Before the twentieth century, actors in the European tradition generalized emotions and character types.

▶ In some traditions a heightened theatricality is valued.

HOW has actor training changed since the nineteenth century? p. 165

▶ Before the twentieth century, actors trained through apprenticeship. Beginning in the twentieth century, formal training systems and schools for actors were developed that worked on the psychological and physical development of a role. Stanislavski's system of actor training took a scientific approach based on psychology and dominated American actor training during the twentieth century.

▶ There has been an increased interest in physical training for the actor in the current theatre.

WHAT is the acting profession like today? p. 175

▶ Actors need to be emotionally and physically healthy to deal with the instability of employment and the technical challenges of creating a role.

▶ Stage and film acting differ but share common elements.

HOW do actors train in performance traditions? p. 177

▶ Actor training in performance traditions can be very rigorous, including many years of physical work, vocal work, and practice of the repertoire that may begin in childhood.

▶ Puppeteers project character through a performing object and may train informally or in schools that include physical and vocal work for the actor as well as practice in various methods of object manipulation.

▶ Actors balance the constraints of technique with the freedom of artistic expression, although the balance is different in different theatrical traditions.

MySearchLab®

Robert Wilson's 2009 production of Heiner Müller's *Quartett* features his signature dazzling visual images and slow repetitive movement and sound.

The Director

The Invisible Presence

Where Is the Director?

Actors embody the characters who engage us; playwrights pen the words we hear; designers create the sets, costumes, and lighting we see before us. These are all palpable aspects of the theatrical experience, and it is obvious to us who is responsible for the artistry behind each one. So where is the director?

The director is everywhere! Everything we experience in the theatre is infused with the director's unique style and personal perspective. The director molds each dramatic interaction and movement on stage, shapes the reading of every line, and selects each detail of design. Though absent from the scene during the performance, the director's presence is everywhere.

Directors provide a unified artistic vision of what the world of the production will be. Sometimes it is literally a vision, as a director imagines the stage in concrete theatrical images. Sometimes the director's vision may be about the process of creation. Sometimes it redefines the very nature of a particular text or theatrical style. In any case, there is always a guiding vision, and the director leads the creative process toward its realization.

Although all directors provide production concepts and make the final decisions about what will be seen and heard on stage, directors work in different ways, toward different goals, and under diverse circumstances. There is no single description of the working process of the director. Today directors can be found the world over, working with and without traditional play texts, however the primary role of the director in the American theatre remains the interpretation and realization of plays.

1. What is the role of the director in the theatre experience?

2. How does the director's presence manifest itself in a performance?

3. What is the primary role of the director in the American theatre?

Directors Mold the Theatrical Experience

Directors decide how to manipulate theatrical elements to create meaning on stage. Aware that audience members consciously and unconsciously read significance into all aspects of a theatrical performance—from the color of an actor's shirt to a momentary silence—directors carefully frame and shape the audience's experience. They select each tangible detail of acting, staging, movement, design, sound, and special effects, as well as intangibles that can be felt but not seen, such as mood, rhythm, and tempo. Often directors can determine where the audience sits or

HIDDEN HISTORY

From Shock to Ho-Hum

Even the most shocking confrontations with convention can in time become the norm. So many 1960s avant-garde directors such as Julian Beck (1925–1985) and Richard Schechner (b. 1934) involved the spectator in the performance that eventually it became an accepted theatre practice, and audience participation in the action became a new convention. The same is true of nudity on the stage. Director Tom O'Horgan (1926–2009) created an uproar in 1968 with female nudity in *Hair*; fleeting male nudity followed. By 2003, you could watch an entire baseball team shower naked in director Joe Mantello's (b. 1962) *Take Me Out*. Consider how shocking such a thing would have been in 1965, and you will realize how fast theatrical innovations can evolve into new conventions when directors consistently push the limits.

◀ The naked body, once a taboo in serious drama, is now an accepted stage convention. Here the Nearly Naked Theatre Company in Phoenix performs *Take Me Out*.

how and when the audience enters the theatrical space. A director might put notes in the program or set up a lobby display to help contextualize a piece for the audience. The director chooses curtain music or sound effects that put the audience in the mood of the production. The director's art lies in making decisions about how to use all the means available to create a compelling theatrical encounter. For this reason, directors must understand the possibilities and pragmatics of design, technology, stage effects, sound, and acting to achieve optimum results from the efforts of others.

Every director possesses a vocabulary of theatrical conventions from which creative choices are made. While some directors stay within the traditional stage conventions for particular works and styles, many directors achieve acclaim precisely because they challenge the prevailing notion of how to realize a play or what kind of text to use. Setting a Shakespearean play in Nazi Germany or the American Wild West, having video projections interact with live actors, making the audience change location and seats, basing a production on a painting, or turning an unsuspecting group of people into an audience in a public space are just a few of the ways directors have chosen to defy convention. Today we put a premium on such originality, and directors often resist the traditional to create bold new concepts. Extraordinary directors may create a new vocabulary of stage conventions for others to use.

Directors are artists engaged in creation, but they must also step back from the process and look at it from a distance. They act as the audience's eyes and ears, reading what they have helped lay out on stage, just as a spectator would. They shift back and forth between these two roles of creator and spectator as they make decisions about which elements of the production to keep and which to change.

Directors must possess a heightened **visual** sense and a keen ear for **language** and **phrasing**.

Rehearsal is the director's time. During this period the director, having conceptualized the piece, molds the theatrical work, exploring the text with the actors and designers to construct meaning in every theatrical moment on stage. On opening night, the director's work is done; the stage manager takes over the show and acts as the caretaker of the director's vision. It is then up to the performers and the crew to enact the production that the director envisioned and created with them. At this point the director's omnipotent role is diminished. The director becomes powerless, having bequeathed artistic trust to the members of the company. The arrival of the audience completes the director's process.

Directing, a **Recent** Art

HOW did the current role of the director evolve?

Considering the enormous task of the director, it is difficult to believe that the art of directing is a relatively recent phenomenon in the history of the theatre. The idea of the director, as the role is defined today, began to take shape in the late eighteenth and early nineteenth centuries in Europe, and it was not established in its current form until the early twentieth century.

Of course, the theatre has always needed someone to run the show and organize the performance. In different eras, this role was performed by the playwright, an actor, or a manager. But these were organizational roles, not visionary or interpretive ones. In ancient Greece, the playwright acted in his plays and trained the chorus; in ancient Rome **actor-managers** also often functioned as directors. In the Middle Ages, towns and guilds named **pageant masters** to organize theatrical events. The sixteenth to the nineteenth centuries saw the rise of actor-managers and

stage managers who provided coordination for performances. There was little concern for a conceptually unified production. Performances took place on bare stages or in front of reusable painted backdrops or flats, not specific to any particular play, so no one was needed to coordinate the designers' efforts with a specific concept. Before adequate stage lighting was developed, actors usually stood in set patterns on the front of the stage, stepping forward to speak their lines, so no one was needed to stage a play. For the most part, actors worked on their roles alone and wore costumes they owned. It is hard for us to believe, but actors in Shakespeare's time never read the entire play they were performing; they received only **sides**, actors' individual lines and cues, copied by a stage manager. Beyond a run-through, working rehearsals did not usually take place, so no one was needed to run them or serve as an acting coach. Prompters often saved the day for inadequately rehearsed actors.

"--OR NOT TO BE"!

> "I did not **look** to magnificent scenery, and a brilliant wardrobe, but I looked to good **pieces** . . . . By means of good pieces I **educated** the actors. . . . I attended the readings of plays and **explained** to everyone his part."

—Johann Wolfgang von Goethe, 1785[1]

The Rise of the **Modern** Director

During the eighteenth century in Europe, an increasing interest in "natural" behavior and in scientific precision resulted in a growing dissatisfaction with artificial acting style and the lack of a coherent approach to performance. Some theatre companies began to hold working rehearsals, and theatre practitioners searched for a more organized and natural approach to staging. Several figures made important initial contributions to defining the role of the modern director.

Johann Wolfgang von Goethe (1749–1832), a German playwright, poet, essayist, and novelist, experimented with new methods of theatre production during his tenure as director of the Court Theatre in Weimar from 1791 to 1817. The plays Goethe and Friedrich Schiller (1759–1805) wrote presented an elegant poetic style called "Weimar Classicism" and required acting skills beyond those of the Weimar actors, who were more at home with clownish farces.

Goethe established rules for actors' comportment on stage so the company could form well-composed stage pictures that he modeled on great paintings and sculpture. He had his actors read the text together in rehearsal rather than just memorize their own lines from sides. Using a stick, he beat out the rhythm of each line so the actors would present the verse musically on stage and in a unified style. To control visual composition, he drew grid lines on the stage floor to permit precise instructions about how and where to move. Taking control of all the artistic elements on stage, Goethe became a prototype for the future director.

Georg II, The Duke of Saxe-Meiningen (1826–1914), working out of his own small German court theatre, brought the idea of detailed visual unity in production to new heights. He spared no expense to achieve his goals of historical accuracy in costume and setting and, using

[1] Johann Wolfgang von Goethe. *Conversations of Goethe with Eckermann and Soret*, cited in *A Source Book in Theatrical History*, ed. A.M. Nagler, (New York: Dover, 1952), 426.

GLOBAL TRADITIONS AND INNOVATIONS

Performance Traditions and Master Performers

Performance traditions do not need a director because they have preestablished codes that dictate exactly how a performance should be done. The master performer, who knows every piece of the repertoire by heart, as well as its staging, teaches every detail to others, fulfilling the function of director. What we might consider directorial choices—selection of costume, makeup, and movement—are left to the actor. Even today, the performances of great *kabuki* actors are passed down *in toto* to their successors, with each move, gesture, facial expression, and vocal inflection scrupulously imitated.

the visual arts as his guide, arranged actors in interestingly composed stage pictures. His company was renowned for its crowd scenes in which each actor displayed an individual character yet worked in unison with the others. Between 1870 and 1890, the Meiningen Players made frequent performance tours throughout Europe, disseminating their impressive new staging practices.

The idea of a thematically unified stage work, or *gesamtkunstwerk*, came from Richard Wagner (1813–1883), who asserted a directorial vision for the operas he composed. For Wagner, the musical score unified the theatrical work and set the tone and the mood for each character, each scene, and all the visual elements of the staging. Using music as the unifying force, Wagner offered a prototype for a unified production style that related form and content.

With the publication of Charles Darwin's (1809–1882) *Origin of Species* in 1849, interest in the environmental and hereditary factors that shape human behavior preoccupied the world and the theatre. These ideas gave birth to the social sciences of sociology and psychology, removing the study of human nature from the province of religion and philosophy and putting it squarely in the scientific domain. Writers such as Emile Zola (1840–1902), Henrik Ibsen (1828–1906), August Strindberg (1849–1912), and Anton Chekhov (1860–1904) wrote plays with psychologically complex characters who grew out of particular social milieus. Naturalist plays that examined the social and biological forces that determine human interactions required sets and costumes that reflected the reality of characters' lives specifically and truthfully in order to expose the truth of social ills.

The generic settings of the past were now insufficient for understanding characters within their own dramatic worlds.

Theatre practitioners now saw the need to create specific environments for particular plays and the need for an

▲ André Antoine's 1902 production of *La Terre (The Earth)* in France features naturalistic detail like real hay and live chickens in the farm scene shown here. The actors' mundane activities also stress the naturalism of the scene, as does the natural light of the candles. The set gives the impression that a real barn is presented, with the fourth wall removed.

artistic eye—a director to unify the stage elements with the play text. At the Théâtre Libre, André Antoine (1858–1943) went to great lengths to re-create his characters' environment on stage. In his production of *The Butchers* (1888), he bought the contents of a butcher shop and hung rotting beef on stage, leaving nothing to the imagination. He arranged rooms as you would find them in real life, and during rehearsals he decided which side to open as the "fourth wall." Antoine feared that professional actors of his day, known for heightened emotional ham acting, would ruin the stage illusion, so he engaged amateurs who he believed would behave more naturally in an attempt to make the stage represent a "slice of life."

The modern director as visionary, unifier, and guide to actors was born in Stanislavski's early work.

Constantin Stanislavski (1863–1938) came up with a better and more influential solution to the problem of melodramatic acting in his famous system, which focused on psychologically motivated behavior and ensemble work (see Chapter 7). He integrated the acting with the play, set, costumes, light, and sound to create the seamless illusion of reality on the stage.

Because the contemporary director evolved from the need for a realistic, coherent, unified presentation of the world of the play on stage, the role of the director was originally conceived as an interpreter of the dramatic text. The first modern directors were found in Europe and in cultures that had inherited that theatrical tradition's emphasis on the written play.

The rebellion against realism in the early twentieth century fostered the emergence of influential directors drawn to nonrealistic aesthetics. Before long, it became clear that the unified vision the director gave to realism and the written play could be applicable to any theatrical style and stage creation. Directors carved out expanded roles, usurping both the role of the actor as the guardian of stage technique and the role of the playwright as the author of the text. Many of the alternative forms we examined in Chapter 6 illustrate how directors may begin their creative process in many different ways and take on multiple roles.

Some directors re-envision the process of directing and the very idea of what a director and a theatrical event are supposed to be. Some have carefully planned all aspects of a production and expect the team to fulfill a set concept, while others offer actors and designers the freedom to contribute to the vision. No matter what the process, directors are ultimately in charge of every aspect of a production. In the sections ahead, we will examine some of the ways directors create theatre.

Directors became more than just realizers of plays and turned themselves into wizards of stagecraft and manipulators of conventions.

The Director as Interpreter of a Dramatic Text

WHAT are the steps in the director's creative process?

The director, as the interpreter of a play, guides its journey from the written word to the performed action. Under this model, the director's work begins long before the first rehearsal. Selecting, researching, analyzing, and interpreting the text and determining a concept and stylistic approach all must be done before the hands-on work begins. Sometimes, in the commercial theatre, producers or artistic directors may choose the text and then hire a director suited to the project, based on the director's experience with similar material or because of other talents the director might bring to the project.

Choosing the Text

In the interpretive model of directing, a production begins with a play. The first job of directors is to choose the text.

A play may address an important issue or present themes the director wants to explore, or it may provide an intriguing image or character. When theatres hire directors after choosing a season of plays (a very common practice), directors must uncover inspirational elements of a play before they begin their work.

Many considerations go into play choice. Practical constraints such as budget and working conditions or the availability of performance rights may be influential. A director may want a script that accommodates a particular actor or theatrical space. The intended audience also plays a key role. Directors may think about the needs of their particular community, considering what might provide enjoyment or illuminate issues of concern. At a university theatre, staging a classic play such as *Twelfth Night* or *Waiting for Godot* may be beneficial for training student actors or because students are reading these plays in their classes. Sometimes a director chooses something daring to challenge prevalent tastes and lead the community toward new visions of the theatre and its possibilities.

THINK

Should directors choose plays that appeal to the intended audience's taste, or should they seek to expand audience taste?

Directors also have to know themselves, know their particular talents and abilities. Some directors are particularly good with musicals, others with classical language, still others at staging productions that rely on mime and movement. Although many directors want to stretch their talents, in the commercial theatre, a director is expected to assess what he or she can deliver before committing to the job. In the end, the play must be exciting to the director, who needs to communicate enthusiasm to others involved in the project in order to sustain their efforts through the rehearsal process.

Establishing the **Directorial** Vision

The process of interpreting a play text begins with the first reading. The director's immediate response often serves as an anchor for all the other discoveries that follow. From the first reading, a director will begin to imagine the physical world the play will inhabit. What are simply words on the page to others are relationships, movement patterns, line readings, stage business, and theatrical moments to a director who reads the play over and over again to become familiar with all its nuances, to know the characters intimately, to feel its imagery and structure. A director will search the play for a central idea that can unite all the elements of a production and sum up the meaning of the piece—a thematic statement, a demonstrated lesson, an eternal truth.

▲ The 1959 Broadway production of Lorraine Hansberry's *A Raisin in the Sun*, with Claudia McNeil as Lena Younger and Sidney Poitier as Walter Lee Younger, brought the yearnings and conflicts of a black family to the attention of the general culture and an African American director, Lloyd Richards, to the Broadway stage.

> ❝ What I look for is a play that says to me **YOU** must do this. YOU. Not because it is a good play, or a black play, but I want to do something that **expresses** ME and my concerns. ❞

—Lloyd Richards (1919–2006), the first black director to direct a Broadway production.[2]

[2] Author's 2004 interview with Lloyd Richards.

Directors may do research to broaden their understanding of a piece. The time period in which the play is set or when it was written illuminates its historical context. Information about the playwright can also help unearth a play's hidden meanings. Research on a subject the play deals with, such as AIDS or environmental hazards, makes the director more knowledgeable. Directors may also read critical interpretations of the text written by scholars. Reviews and photos of past productions can show how other directors dealt with the problems the play poses. Some directors, however, scrupulously avoid looking at such material to leave themselves open to a spontaneous response. Some directors work with **dramaturgs**, discussed in Chapter 14, who provide additional research and interpretive ideas that help shape the director's perspective on the script.

When directing a new play, a director works closely with the playwright, who is often in attendance at rehearsals, and the two usually come to an agreement about the interpretation of the text. The director may request rewrites, identifying staging problems in the script that need to be solved, character elements that are lacking, speeches that need to be cut, and even scenes that might be juggled. This, of course, is a delicate process with competing egos, but ultimately it works because of the shared goal of a successful production.

Conceiving a Play for the Stage

Directors imagine the theatrical world the play must inhabit on the stage and develop a clear concept of how they will communicate the central meaning to the audience. The concept will lead to a stylistic approach to the material that will guide all the collaborators involved. Style—the manner in which life will be portrayed on stage—can mean realistic staging that approximates real life, or an abstract, symbolic, or emotionally heightened stage world. The director's chosen style must capture something essential in the play and permit it to realize its full dramatic potential and meaning.

Some directors find a central metaphor that provides a clear image for the actors and designers. For example, a director might conceive of *A Doll's House* (1879) as being about a caged bird trying to fly free. The image might move the actor playing Nora to flit around the stage or speak in a high lyric voice. The set designer might try to find ways to enclose her in her space. Some directors follow Stanislavski's principles and formulate a **spine**, or superobjective for a play, to establish a central line of dramatic action that can guide actors in their choices. Using a strong active verb, they describe the central action in a single phrase that will propel actors through the play. A superobjective for *Romeo and Juliet* might be "To reach for love over all barriers." This is an image that demands physical urgency. Bertolt Brecht (1891–1956) used the term *fable* to describe the heart or lesson of the theatrical story a director needs to grasp. Other directors avoid metaphors and spines and prefer using a personal vocabulary to talk at length with designers and actors about a vision or interpretation.

Different directors will find different meanings, fables, metaphors, and spines for the same play, depending on their point of view.

Shaping the Visual World

In the commercial theatre, producers, who run the business side of the production, or artistic directors may be responsible for putting together the team of designers, technicians, and stage managers to realize the director's vision. In noncommercial ventures, this job may fall to the director. Even when producers select the designers, they usually seek the director's input in assembling the creative team.

Directors seek designers who "can speak their language"—that is, designers who can translate their conceptual language into tangible costumes, sets, sounds, and lights on stage. Partnerships develop, and successful director–designer collaborating teams are often rehired for many productions. Usually, long before actors are cast, the director meets with the set, costume, lighting, and sound designers who will be working on the show. At this first meeting, the director shares his or her interpretation of the play and vision or concept for the production. A dialogue begins between director and designers that continues until opening night. Through a process of discussion and negotiation, the director guides designers in creating sets and costumes appropriate for the production.

Occasionally a director will have a very specific costume or set piece in mind or will be planning a particular bit of staging that will require certain set or costume demands. The designers, drawing on their own training, research, and imagination, invent designs that express their artistic realization of the director's interpretation. It is the director's role to make sure the various design elements come together to project a unified artistic vision on stage.

Although all the designers attend production conferences together, occasionally the set, costume, and lighting designers create conflicting elements—perhaps colors that jar or costumes or set pieces from different eras. It is up to the director to catch such contradictions and to facilitate a dialogue among designers to determine what will be cut and what will be kept or changed.

Working with Actors

Directors generally hold auditions to cast actors for a show. They come to auditions with basic ideas about what qualities they seek for each role. Physical type is often a secondary concern because most directors focus on the predominant personality and presence an actor projects as well as particular talents and technical know-how. If a director knows a role will be physically demanding, it is more important to find an actor who is agile and expressive than one who is tall. A play may require an actor to have good comic timing or an ability to speak poetic language or sing within a certain range. Traits such as a character's age or gender may also be fairly restrictive. Final casting choices are always based on the way the ensemble comes together. A particularly strong audition by an actor who was not the original physical type the director envisioned may lead the director to rethink other casting choices.

Auditions give a director a chance to test actors' ranges and abilities and to see if they are compatible with the director's working style. A director may ask auditioning actors to perform prepared monologues or to read from the play they are casting. A director might have actors try a part in different ways to see how flexible they are or how well they take direction. Amazingly, directors learn to use a five-minute audition to identify exactly the qualities they seek. In the commercial theatre, the producer may have already cast a star in the lead, so the cast will need to be assembled around that central presence. Occasionally none of the actors who audition will match the director's vision of a character, and the director may need to reinterpret the role. At other times an actor's inspired reading may give the director fresh insight into a part. Often a very talented actor is not suitable for any roles in a current production but might be remembered by a director for future projects. Like all other parts of the creative process, casting requires negotiating between ideals and realities.

At the first rehearsal, you can feel the anticipation in the air as the ensemble's creative journey begins. This is the opportunity for the director to set the tone for the project and to explain his or her personal working process. Usually, everyone present sits around a table and takes notes. The director talks at length about an overall interpretation for the play and the way each role fits into the larger picture. The excitement begins when the actors read through the script, many encountering and relating to their fellow cast members for the first time. If the director has done his or her job well, there is a simmering energy and a palpable sense of potential.

" This is not magic but work, my friends. "

—Bertolt Brecht, *The Curtain*

At the next set of rehearsals, smaller units of the play are rehearsed with groups of actors. The director frames each scene within the interpretation of the play and defines the relationships and goals of the characters. Actors have questions about their parts, and early rehearsals are often spent in discussion. Although directors may come into these sessions with fairly strong ideas of what they want, rehearsal is a time of exploration and experimentation. Actors explore the meaning of their lines and the best readings while searching for physical actions that embody meaning, are interesting to watch, and move the play forward. For much of the early rehearsals, the director may serve as an acting coach, often creating improvisations to help actors discover relationships and physical action or to facilitate their ensemble work. The best directors encourage actors to take creative leaps and to try out new ideas. Rehearsals are hard work, but they are also exciting times of discovery and uncovering layers of meaning in the script.

Eventually the experimentation comes to an end, as the director sets the **blocking** (the pattern of how the actors will move on stage at particular moments) and selects the best ideas for action and line readings. The scenes are strung together until the actors are ready to do a **run-through** of the play from beginning to end, without stopping.

▶ Director Ariane Mnouchkine of Le Théâtre du Soleil working closely with her actors during a rehearsal of Shakespeare's *Richard II* at the Cartoucherie de Vincennes.

Bill Rauch the artistic director of the Oregon Shakespeare Festival, talks to staff during technical rehearsals. Computers now play a vital role in light and sound design and in running the show.

Integrating the Elements of Production

The first opportunity the director has to see how all the conceptual pieces fit together on stage is during **technical rehearsals**. Although many directors have **paper techs** (a time when they walk through the technical aspects of the production with the designers and staff), until this point, the total vision of the performance has remained in the director's imagination.

The technical rehearsal is the moment for the director's vision to come alive.

Work with the actors now takes a backseat to integrating other elements of production, including lighting, sound, set changes, and the technical aspects of the play. Much of this time is spent with the director deciding on the exact timing for certain cues. When will a sound effect be heard? How many seconds should it take for the lights to dim? The director, the designer, and the stage manager confer about choices, and the director makes the final decision about what will best support the text, the acting, and the world on stage. Once all the pieces are in place, and the timing has been decided *to the second*, the actors and the crew are ready to run through the play, while the director watches and takes notes about parts of the production that need to be adjusted in some way.

A technical run-through offers a director the opportunity to make sure that all the elements of the production are working together and to test the pace and rhythm of the piece. There may be notes to the designers, to particular actors, or to the stage manager and running crew, as tiny adjustments are made. A **technical dress rehearsal** gives the opportunity to see the costumes under the lights and to make any final changes to actors' wardrobes before the **dress rehearsal**, the last step in bringing together all the elements of production for a trial run.

In the commercial theatre, **previews** give the director an opportunity to try out the production in front of a live audience. Because theatre is essentially about actor–audience interaction, it is only at this point that the theatrical piece can be appreciated fully. The director listens to and watches the audience. Their responses can alert the director to parts of the production that need to be altered. The pace of a scene may be too slow, making the audience restless. If the audience does not get a joke, the director may try to clarify it or remove it. Language that is particularly difficult may need to be slowed down so the audience can follow it more easily.

Previews provide the director with a final opportunity to make changes.

Because of the enormous financial investment at stake in large-scale Broadway productions, shows usually have several months of out-of-town tryouts before they open in New York. During this period, directors may oversee drastic changes, such as rewrites of the script. Often, work continues until **opening night**, when finally, the director's work is done. The director has guided the company in making choices about every element of production. Although the director will not appear on stage, every aspect of the piece reflects the director's artistic hand. Every night the actors and the crew recreate the performance as the director has staged it with them.

High-Concept **Directing**

Many directors believe they can reveal more of a play's themes to a contemporary audience if they challenge conventional interpretations of well-known plays. They may choose to move a play's time period; change its location; invert the genders of the actors; or add music, masks, or puppets. **Deconstruction**, a movement in literary criticism that questions the idea of fixed meanings, truths, or assumptions about texts, is the hallmark of the postmodern aesthetic and has given license to directors to search for new meanings and forms in plays once thought to be confined to particular interpretations and styles.

Lee Breuer's (b. 1937) *Dollhouse* (2003) presented a version of the Ibsen play with female roles played by tall women and male roles played by four-foot-tall men; the miniature set was sized to the male characters (see photo on p. 196). This inverted the metaphor of the play; in this production, women dominated the psyches of men, toying with them as puppets. German director Thomas Ostermeier (b.1968) presented an updated version of *A Doll's House*, titled *Nora* (2002) in which Nora, instead of simply walking out on Torvald, shoots him (see photo on p. 196). Ostermeier believes that contemporary conspicuous consumption and credit card debt were akin to the spirit that placed Nora in financial difficulty in the Ibsen play. These **high-concept productions** can often provide illuminating new readings of well-known works that speak to our own time.

In the 1960s, in the wake of the publication of a book by Polish critic Jan Kott titled *Shakespeare, Our Contemporary* (1961, English translation 1964), it became fashionable to recontextualize productions of Shakespeare. This practice continues and has now extended to additional works in both the classical and modern repertory. Peter Brook, famous for his reimagined Shakespearean worlds, opened the doors for others to push the boundaries of original and classical texts, often to the point where they are free of any formal constraints. The European theatre has a long tradition of adaptation of classic texts. Bertolt Brecht staged his version of Shakespeare's *Coriolanus* and Sophocles' *Antigone* long before the 1960s. From Ariane Mnouchkine in France, to Peter Stein in Germany, to Miyamoto Amon in Japan, prominent directors have been empowered to use plays for their own ends.

Such appropriations of well-known plays stamp a personal imprint on the material and open up interpretive possibilities. The Dutch director Ivo Van Hove (b. 1958) has reinvented classical American works by Eugene O'Neill, Tennessee Williams, and Lillian Hellman. His *A Streetcar Named Desire* (1998) featured a stage with just chairs and a water-filled bathtub, into which characters plunged naked at moments of dramatic tension. He similarly deconstructed Moliere's *Misanthrope* in 2007, in which the characters, in a contemporary setting, revealed their baser sides, including food fights and screaming matches, instead of covering up with hypocritical social niceties.

> THINK
>
> Is there something in the play text— form, convention, style, language— that must be respected, or should the director be free to interpret a play without constraint?

Productions that turn expectations on end can be controversial. Writer Samuel Beckett (1906–1989) objected to director JoAnn Akalaitis' (b. 1937) reimagined *Endgame*. He felt her concept violated his original intentions, just as Arthur Miller (1915–2005) was distressed by Elizabeth LeCompte's (b. 1944) use of portions of his play *The Crucible*. These conflicts raise questions of authors' rights versus directors' rights of free interpretation. Despite some disputes, appropriations of plays by directors have become standard in the international avant-garde; they are less problematic, of course, when the playwright is dead and cannot challenge the director's concept. Traditionalists believe that such liberties violate the sanctity of a playwright's work and that the intentions of the author should be respected. Others argue that it is never possible to know the playwright's true intentions, that a dramatic text is a pre-text for the action on stage and is truly a jumping-off point for the creative leaps of the director.

▶ In *Dollhouse*, director Lee Breuer's high-concept production of Henrik Ibsen's play, Nora towers over her husband Torvald and Dr. Rank. Nora's house and the miniature furniture inside are suited only to the men. Her cute gestures and frilly dress add to Breuer's interpretation of Nora as a grown woman playing at being a child.

▲ Director Thomas Ostermeier's Nora gives us a contemporary take on the same story depicted in the nearby photo of Lee Breuer's Dollhouse. Compare these with the image of Ibsen's original play *A Doll's House* in Chapter 3. Each image shows how a director's concept is manifested.

The French theatre company Le Théâtre du Soleil, founded in 1964 as a collective, is today identified primarily with Ariane Mnouchkine (b. 1939), its director and main artistic force. Between 1981 and 1984, the company's sumptuous Shakespeare productions contributed to interculturalism, becoming an active theatrical idea and subject of debate. Mnouchkine looks to Asian theatrical forms and other stylized traditions, using masks, colorful makeup, and extraordinary movement to help distance actors from psychologically based acting techniques and create a theatre of symbols and archetypes rather than realistic representation. *Richard II* (1981) echoed the imagery and techniques of Japanese *kabuki* and *noh*; *A Midsummer Night's Dream* (1968) took influences from Indian *kathakali*; and *Henry IV* (1984) combined motifs from all of these forms. For *Les Atrides* (1990–1994), a cycle of four ancient Greek plays that included Aeschylus's *Oresteia* trilogy preceded by Euripides' *Iphigenia in Aulis*, the company created a gestural language resonant of the *mudras* of Indian *kathakali* and hand movements of Armenian dance. Jean-Jacques Lemêtre's musical accompaniment fused motifs from musical traditions the world over. Mnouchkine doesn't attempt to replicate performance traditions but uses them as a springboard for developing a unique theatrical idiom.

Mnouchkine's rehearsal process is unusual. (See photo on page 193) Actors rehearse in costume from the beginning and may help develop the characters' costume by adding, changing, and eliminating elements. Final casting of roles may not be settled until very late in the process. Several actors may try out the same role, collectively creating a character that one of them will eventually embody in performance. Mnouchkine works on general actor training during the rehearsal process, and once or twice a year she offers a public acting workshop from which new company members are drawn.

A Théâtre du Soleil production is a total theatrical experience that begins with a trip through the outskirts of Paris to the troupe's home in a converted ammunition factory. In the theatre's large entrance hall, spectators read books related to the theme of the production and purchase homemade food from actors. Mnouchkine is always present before and after the show and at intermission, helping out and talking with spectators.

Interculturalism

Interculturalism has inspired many directors to freely incorporate elements from diverse cultures into their production concepts. Together, deconstruction and interculturalism have opened up the expressive potential of many well-known plays. Ariane Mnouchkine's production of *Les Atrides* (*The Orestia*) (1990–1994) used acting styles, costumes, makeup, and musical instruments and rhythms inspired by Asian traditions. Intercultural borrowings have gone in every direction. Suzuki Tadashi's (b. 1939) interpretation of *The Bacchae*, by Euripides, used the slow movements and sculptural poses of the traditional Japanese theatre to startling dramatic effect, and Ninagawa Yukio (b. 1935) has done stunning *kabuki*-esque versions of ancient Greek tragedies and Shakespeare. Singaporean director Ong Keng Sen (b. 1963) creates productions that mix Western classics with an array of Asian traditional theatrical forms. Borrowing from Asian cultures outside his own, his 1997 *Lear* incorporated artists from Japanese *noh*, Chinese opera, Indonesian *silat*, and Thai dance. The actors each spoke in their native tongues, and the production was supported by an international team of designers. His work has been described as inter-Asian, intra-cultural, and Asia-centric and has aroused both critical praise and controversy.

▲ Ong Keng Sen's *Lear*, performed here in Singapore, uses masks, costumes, music and acting styles from various Asian traditions and is performed by a multinational cast.

Ong Keng Sen **(b. 1963)** *is the artistic director of Theatre Works in Singapore. His Flying Circus Project explores the relationship between contemporary and traditional Asian arts. Born in Singapore of Chinese ethnicity, he is acutely aware of the cultural differences among Asians, and his work questions what it means to be Asian in the twenty-first century. His many productions have toured the world.*

Please describe your work.

I have sited myself in intercultural practice. I am trained in Western theatre, but my work has primarily been negotiating cultures through performance. One of my roles as the negotiator is to interface with the classical traditional arts of Asia. I have been working with traditional masters of Asian forms in Shakespeare re-creations and re-manifestations. I have also been looking at society through the lens of traditional masters. My work has varied from performing documentary to working with conventional texts, such as Lear and Othello, to form a meta-text around the original play.

We study traditional art forms be it *noh* or *kabuki*, but they are hermetic [closed] structures. How do we, the people coming from outside these hermetic structures, access and negotiate with these monumental structures of the Asian theatre. Although I am Asian, I am also outside of these traditions. I use English as my first language and this automatically distances me from these art forms. As an English speaker, English becomes the way you access the world and think about these forms, so you must decolonize your mind. I am not useful to a Japanese audience helping them understand *kabuki* because they have their own codes and language. I am not the preserver of these traditions. My role is to link these art forms to other cultures outside of Japan and bring them close to popular culture.

What do you think is the future for Asian performance traditions?

In Japan, classical forms are still performed, not just to preserve their heritage. They are performed for their pure aesthetics, the way we in the West perform classical music. Despite the Internet, Second Life, virtual realities, and modern media, these classical forms remain monumental. Asian traditions are not dying, but there is a robust reinvention going on and people within the traditions are finding ways to access and reach out to young audiences. Teenage girls are now swooning over young stars of *kabuki*, even the young stars who play the *onnagata* role.

How do you define reinvention?

Reinvention exists on many different levels. Sometimes it is just updating, like doing a Hollywood movie of *Romeo and Juliet*. Sometimes it is entering a dialog with other forms. The way Indonesian *Gamelan* is in a dialog with jazz. There are also conceptual reinventions—taking the costuming, the text, and liberating it from its classical language. Every new translation is a reinvention. In terms of my own reinvention when I bring a *noh* actor into *King Lear*, I am providing a window into the art form that is *noh*, and into its synergy with Shakespeare, but not because *noh* theatre needs reinvigoration through contemporary theatre for survival. I don't believe that. There is a space for pure and authentic classical forms and a reason for insisting on authenticity. There is a space in Japan both for popular reinvention, and for a different kind of reinvention from people like us who are not from the culture.

Can you explain your claim that Shakespeare is culturally neutral?

Anyone who is not English can appropriate Shakespeare to tell the narratives of their own culture. He has become a site on which you can graft anything. You cannot do that with a *kathakali* play, or a *kabuki* or a *noh* play. When you read Zeami about *noh* and its principles rooted in a philosophy, you feel that you need to have begun as a child to learn how to do this 600-year-old text. You don't dare to play with it. Shakespeare does not begin from these types of codes and training methods. So many trajectories have been carved through Shakespeare's work that the original plays become multiplied and transgressed. There is a sense that Shakespeare is not sacrosanct. There have been no gatekeepers of the Shakespearean tradition the way I feel there are gatekeepers of the Asian forms of *noh*, *kabuki*, and *kathakali*.

Can you discuss your docudrama *The Continuum: Beyond the Killing Fields?*

You cannot understand traditional arts unless you look at them in relation to their culture, society, and politics. *The Continuum: Beyond the Killing Fields* is a documentary performance which I made with a Cambodian dancer who was incarcerated in Pol Pot's concentration camps for four years. When I started working with her she was 70, now she is 80. Pol Pot wanted to destroy all the classical artists who worked in the courts. This piece looks at four artists who were persecuted for being classical artists. There are testimonials and oral history, and then the performance of the testimonial. The artists are performing themselves, and what is behind the façade of the role. They were trying to interrogate and document their lives and how their lives actually intersected with the context of their country. It becomes a documentary of their bodies. It is also an anthropology of a community of artists–a lens through which we can study Cambodian society during these four years.

What do you mean by Asian hybridity?

The rural has disappeared in the Asian context. Imagine that smaller Chinese cities will someday have the size and complexity of New York. A niche of older people practice their traditions while other artists are traveling and importing American and European trends and ideas. Pop culture today is expanded because of the mobility of ideas and aesthetics and the quick availability of information on

(continued)

the internet. The younger generation in Asia sees all these ideas and are grabbing them and recombining them.

Is interculturalism still possible after the globalization we have been experiencing in the last 10 years?

We are not yet in a global soup. Suzuki in Japan still provides a systematic look at the body which is different from Stanislavski's actor training methods, or Grotowski's, but all systems have become available to young actors. They are not Russian systems, Polish, or Japanese systems. It is the same with dramaturgy. There are different techniques of storytelling around the world; it depends what you want to school yourself in. Things are no longer the cultural property of a certain group.

Why do you continue to do live theatre?

It is about craft. It is now impossible to find local crafts. Craft is of value in a world where everything is IKEA. Acting is a very specialized craft—just to repeat the same performance every night. The world would lose something very important without theatre. It is a way of thinking about community. The value of putting all of us in one house watching together is not to be underestimated. This is still valuable even if I can more easily click on an internet movie. Theatre still allows us to find ourselves.

Interview with author, New York, February 7, 2011.

ELIZABETH LECOMPTE
Creating with Technology

Elizabeth LeCompte (b. 1944) is best known for her work with the New York–based experimental theatre company the Wooster Group, of which she is a founding member and director.

Why is technology such an important part of your directorial concept? Are you more drawn to its stage effect or to the commentary it makes on human existence in the twenty-first century?

I don't know. I just like having all kinds of technology in the room when I work. For fun. I like to put the real thing next to its copy and have them play off each other. It gives the actors power by amplifying and doubling them, and I can imagine worlds that couldn't be in the theatre 30 years ago, and ideas that inform old texts in new ways.

Do your actors require any particular skills in order to perform with the technological elements you use in production?

No. Only that they like the ideas we are working with. If they come with an opinion already formed that technology is bad, then it inhibits their ability to play. They aren't competing with the technology. It's a tool for them to be creative.

Does the fragmentation of the text undercut the playwright, and can you discuss some of the reactions of playwrights to your work?

Texts for the theatre have always been edited and shaped for the company and/or for the time. I think that's what I do, too. It's a tradition from Shakespeare. To say we "fragment" the text is more radical than what we actually do. Sometimes we only do a piece of a play (a play within a play). The text isn't fragmented, we just use a fragment of the text. This use bothered Arthur Miller—who said he was afraid people wouldn't know that there was more of it. Playwrights I have spoken to (Tony Kushner, Paul Auster, Romulus Linney) are inspired by our work.

Source: Used with permission of Elizabeth LeCompte, director, the Wooster Group.

▼ This production of Tennessee Williams' *Vieux Carré* by is performed by the Wooster Group, directed by Elizabeth LeCompte, and displays LeCompte's trademark integration of technology.

The techno-theatre aesthetic has pushed directors to envision new possibilities for the stage world beyond established texts.

The Techno-Theatre Aesthetic

New technologies have aided directors looking for innovative interpretations of texts. Directors now possess a tool bag through which they can manipulate the stage world through video, projections, film, and the Internet. Elizabeth LeCompte (b. 1944) and the Wooster Group are known for their conceptual staging of well-known plays that have been deconstructed to reveal hidden meanings. These productions often incorporate technological effects to startling

THINK

Does a playwright's insistence on a particular interpretation of a work risk making it a tired cliché?

Think TECHNOLOGY
The Builders Association—Performing Dislocation

The Builders Association makes technology's infiltration and transformation of everyday life the theme of its techno-theatrical pieces. *Alladeen*, a 2003 stage production directed by Marianne Weems, was linked to a Web project and music video directed by Ali Zaidi and explored the philosophical concerns emerging from today's global technology. The piece presents Indian men and women as they train to become phone operators at an international call center in Bangalore, serving American companies and their clients. They learn American pronunciation and culture so they can pretend to be based in the United States. The workers watch episodes of *Friends* as part of their training, and their faces morph into those of the *Friends* characters through video projections. Video fantasy sequences based on Bollywood-style films describe the workers' hopes for the future. The site-specific piece *Avanti: A Postindustrial Ghost Story* (2003-2005), staged in an abandoned Studebaker factory in Indiana, projected images and videos onto moving screens to tell the story of job loss and industrial failure when Studebaker went under. *Continuous City* (2007) examines the dislocation caused when personal relationships are mediated by technology and social networking. Groups like the Builders Association make theatre that comments on technology itself and speaks to our current experiences and concerns.

▼ The Builders Association's *Continuous City* features massive video screens that dwarf the human presence on stage and remind us of the need to assert our essential humanity in a wired world.

results. Their adaptation of Racine's *Phèdre* (*To You, the Birdie*) (2002) depicts a constipated Phaedra receiving enemas from her servants, while male characters engage in an ongoing badminton game and bodies are severed on video screens. In *Brace Up!* based on Chekhov's *The Three Sisters* (1991), live performers off stage appear on video monitors alongside live stage action. Actors alternately speak on stage and from microphones located behind the main playing area. Video segments include the grandmother of an actor trying out the lines of the play's elderly nanny, silverware being dropped again and again, and film clips from Kenneth Branagh's *Henry V*. An image of Godzilla accompanied by a loud sound appears each time the character Solyony is about to speak. The effect is that of a fragmented reality, a collage of real and electronically amplified images and sounds.

Some theatre companies and independent artists envision their work through the active integration of film, video, computers, high-tech sound, and other digital media with theatre's live action, creating a new mixed-media techno-theatrical aesthetic. Film, video, and digital sound can barrage the audience's senses to create a montage effect. These media allow for radical shifts in location and can change a production's pace and sense of movement. They can break up linear stage narratives and provide spectators

with links to outside or distant events as well as glimpses into a character's inner life.

Robert Lepage (b. 1957) brings a combination of film and theatrical sensibilities to his company Ex Machina in Quebec. In *Elsinore* (1996), a retelling of *Hamlet*, Lepage plays all the roles, talking to his own real-time video images and distorting his voice through pitch-shifters. The production disorients the viewer with panels that rotate to reveal new scenes and videos. Infrared and thermal cameras allow spectators to peek behind castle walls. The final duel is projected from a video camera atop the poisoned sword. More recently, Lepage has been asked to bring his stage wizardry to reinvigorate productions at the Metropolitan Opera in New York, including a 3-D production of Wagner's *Siegfried* (2011).

> **A techno-theatrical aesthetic reflects the way technology has infiltrated our everyday existence, transforming how we think about time and space and how we connect to each other.**

The Director as Acting Guru

WHY are directors involved in actor training?

Sometimes the director's vision is so specific that a particular acting style is required to fulfill it, and directors have trained their actors in a particular methodology to carry out their concept. In the most rudimentary way, that is what Goethe did when he set out his rules for actors at the beginning of the nineteenth century. Later directors developed sophisticated training systems to create their ideal actor. Many of the approaches to actor training we discussed in Chapter 7 were created by directors. Perhaps the first director to work in this way was Stanislavski. Confronted with the direction of the plays of Anton Chekhov, he recognized that actors of his time were ill equipped to create the psychological realism he wanted in these works. In his "laboratories," Stanislavski trained the Moscow Art Theatre company of actors in his famous system. The naturalistic acting in his productions was the hallmark of his directorial work.

One of Stanislavski's own students and star actors had an alternative view of the theatre. Influenced by antirealist movements in art, Vsevolod Meyerhold envisioned a

highly stylized directorial art that incorporated sets inspired by Russian constructivist art. The biomechanics training system he developed, which turned the actor into an efficient worker for the stage, making optimum use of body movement and rhythm, was meant to facilitate the actor's integration into his production concepts. His directorial work featured acting with vibrant physicality.

Jerzy Grotowski's (1933–1999) *Poor Theatre* focused on the primacy of the actor in space. Grotowski developed a physical training system that pushed the actor's limits through excruciatingly difficult exercises called *plastiques*. Training with Grotowski was a test of body and spirit, but it was necessary if an actor was to act in his productions, which placed extraordinary demands on the actors. Suzuki Tadashi developed a technique of foot stomping to give proper physical and vocal support to actors to meet the challenges of his highly stylized directing. Anne Bogart (b. 1951) uses the method pioneered by Suzuki with Viewpoints, a training methodology used to orient the actor

Japanese director Suzuki Tadashi (b. 1939) gained international fame for forceful productions of Western classics such as Sophocles' *Oedipus Rex* (2002) and Euripides' *Trojan Women* (1974) and *The Bacchae* (1978). Even in stillness, actors from the Suzuki Company of Toga (SCOT) realize a riveting intensity on stage. Suzuki's theatre is driven by the organic "animal energy" of the actor, which he celebrates in opposition to the machine energy that runs modern society and much modern theatre.

Suzuki's system of actor training was developed as an alternative to the realistic *shingeki* style that dominated Japanese theatre when he entered the profession. His system is physically arduous. Through a series of exercises that involve vigorous stomping and various ways of walking, actors become conscious of how their feet connect to the ground. They discover an inner physical sensibility and create a strong base to support the kind of breathing and dramatic expression necessary for performing classical texts. Although many critics see a particularly Japanese style of expression reminiscent of *noh* and *kabuki* in Suzuki's work, Suzuki feels his training distills the virtues of these traditional forms to create a universal theatre that restores the body's wholeness. His system is now practiced by followers throughout the world.

Suzuki has adopted some aspects of the traditional Japanese *iemoto* family system of teacher and disciple relationships. He takes the role of *sensei*, or master teacher, acting as both a taskmaster and spiritual guide. He is an autocratic force in sessions, in which all company members participate to cement a sense of community and the group's performance aesthetic. Actors are active in every part of running the company, from cleaning rehearsal halls to administration. Theatre technicians connect with the actors' work by participating in the physical training sessions.

The company spends several months a year living and working together in the remote village of Toga when they are not touring abroad. It is difficult for some actors to give complete physical, emotional, and personal dedication to a theatre company in the way Suzuki requires, but many of Suzuki's actors have devoted years of their lives to his work. The actress Shiraishi Kayoko's (b. 1941) performances as Clytemnestra and Agave most exemplify Suzuki's theatrical vision. Her extraordinary physical and vocal control and stage presence are the rewards of her dedication.

Suzuki has collaborated closely with the architect Isozaki Arata to create outdoor theatre spaces that combine spatial values from traditional Japanese theatres with those of ancient Greece and Elizabethan England. In building such theatres throughout Japan, Suzuki and Isozaki have assisted in decentralizing Japan's Tokyo-based theatre world and revitalized the audience's connection to the performance.

Suzuki has helped foster interculturalism in the theatre through the worldwide popularization of his actor training system, his own exchanges with international theatre artists, and his creation of the Toga Festival, the first international theatre festival in Japan.

◀ Playing the title role in Suzuki Tadashi's production of Euripides' *Electra*, actress Saito Yukiko embodies Suzuki's physical acting training, which energizes the entire body through a stance rooted through the feet to the floor. Shown here are members of the Suzuki Company of Toga at the Japan Society, New York.

and direct energy in space to train the group of actors who comprise the SITI (Saratoga International Theatre Institute) company. She believes the shared technical vocabulary creates a true ensemble and enables actors to create boldly envisioned works with spontaneity and speed. These are but a few examples of directors who developed serious training systems for actors. Each of the methods mentioned here has had a significant impact on actor training, but they were all inspired by directors in search of a cohesive company of actors who could fully realize their directorial vision.

Director and Actors as **Collaborators**

In companies with a shared aesthetic philosophy and acting technique, some directors feel uncomfortable with the hierarchy of the traditional structure, with the powerful director controlling the creative process. They prefer a collaborative approach to creation. For this to succeed, the creative ensemble must share goals and expectations about the process and the end product. The ensemble must have a common artistic vocabulary and methodology. Although the image of co-equals working together to create a performance is an appealing one, more often than not, there comes a time in the collaboration when someone steps forward as the leader, or director, to make the choices necessary to finalize a performance. It is almost impossible to arrive at a polished production in a leaderless vacuum, although many groups have attempted to equalize roles. Some directors, such as Simon McBurney (b. 1957), may act in their productions and give the actors free rein during a prolonged rehearsal process, but final creative decisions remain with the director.

Many of the actors in the collaborative groups of the 1960s were committed to particular physical approaches to acting as well, and often the director served as an act-ing teacher for the company. In all these collaborative ensembles, although the rehearsal process is more open and egalitarian, eventually a director steps forward to determine the final text, fix the staging, select the design elements, and set sound and lighting cues.

In **collaborative** groups, **adaptations** of plays or original **performance** texts are created through the **rehearsal** process, as the members of the company **explore** the theatrical values embedded in a **particular** play or improvise on a theme.

Indonesian director Putu Wijaya (b. 1944) founder of Teater Mandiri in Jakarta, draws on the Balinese view of *desa, kala, patra,* believing that every presentation naturally changes in relation to time, place, and mood. Putu formally establishes only some aspects of a piece and concentrates instead on training his actors to respond to each other. In his highly abstract presentations, which include shadow play and loud music, there is always room for new ideas and improvisations and even for unrehearsed performers to jump in and take part. Sound and lighting operators are given license to adjust their artistic elements, depending on how the actors are performing on any given night. Putu himself also takes part in productions, adjusting elements during the show to challenge the actors to connect spontaneously.

SIMON McBURNEY
Collaborative Creation

ARTISTS IN PERSPECTIVE

Simon McBurney **(b. 1957)**, a brilliant and idiosyncratic British director, brings incisive intelligence and a style marked by strong visual images and virtuoso physical acting to all his creations with the theatre company Complicité. Formerly known as the Théâtre de Complicité, the group was founded in 1983 by four actors trained in physical theatre with the mimes Jacques Lecoq (1921–1999) and Philippe Gaulier (b. 1943) in Paris. They brought the collaborative method they had practiced in France to their new company in England, which has since grown to international fame. Complicité collaborates with a large number of actors, directors, and designers from around the world. As the company's work evolves, the key ele-

ment of a Complicité production remains that of an ensemble building on a shared technique and artistic language. Recent productions have blended sophisticated stage technology with the physicality of the performance.

A Complicité production can begin with either a thematic idea or a text followed by a sustained period of research and development. *Mnemonic* (1999) grew from shared memories inspired by a tale of the discovery of the body of a 5,000-year-old man in the Alps. In *Mnemonic*, McBurney also played a main acting role. *The Noise of Time* (2000) used sounds and images to explore the life and work of composer Dmitri Shostakovich, and *The Elephant Vanishes* (2004) was

based on three short stories by contemporary Japanese writer Murakami Haruki. McBurney has demonstrated his ability to work with more traditional texts as well in his remarkable production of Ionesco's *The Chairs* (1998), nominated for six Tony Awards. Each of McBurney's works dazzles in unexpected ways, and theatre connoisseurs look forward to the next flight of his imagination.

No single method is used in the evolution of a Complicité performance. The approach is marked by a general openness to the material, which allows the group to play with ideas and follow where they lead through research, improvisation, discussion, and artistic exchange. The group sometimes fills the rehearsal
(continued)

(continued from page 203)

space with videos, images, clothes, and objects that inspire them and that later may be incorporated into their improvisations. The long rehearsal process can lead to many dead ends, but at other times it culminates in serendipitous and compelling theatrical images that could only emerge from collaborative experimentation. The work may be highly intellectual in its premise. *A Disappearing Number* (2008) explores cultural tensions between East and West through the metaphor of mathematics as it explores the minds of two mathematicians from opposing cultures. McBurney traveled to India for his research on the Indian mathematician Srinivasa Ramanujan (1887–1920).

As a director in a collaborative process, McBurney chooses the point of departure for each creation, guides the work so it continues to yield new insights, and makes final decisions about how to stage the performance. In rehearsals, he keeps the feeling of childish play that allows the imagination free reign, and pushes the performers toward dynamic discoveries. All the while, McBurney must inspire confidence that this long period of theatrical exploration will yield an engaging piece of theatre.

▼ Simon McBurney's *A Disappearing Number* uses mathematics to expose cultural difference.

The Director as Auteur

WHAT is a director-auteur?

When the origin of the idea for a performance comes from the director, not the playwright, we call that director an *auteur*. In French, the term means not only author but also the originator of a concept. The term *auteur* was first applied to film directors who created and controlled every aspect of a work, from inception to realization, creating the screenplay and the film. Stage directors can envision a total project in much the same way. The original idea may come from their own imaginations, not from a playwright, and they can set about creating the production as a reflection of their personal viewpoint.

The director-auteur creates a **performance text** that records all that will happen on stage. A performance text is born as part of the directorial conception and cannot easily be handed to others because the text and the staging are conceived as a unified whole expressing, a distinct and personal point of view. Because this kind of work is so personal, it is not unusual for these directors to have their own theatre companies where they can exercise complete control over their artistic vision.

▲ Performed in French, English, and Mandarin, Robert Lepage's *The Blue Dragon* depicts the collision of Asian and Western values and exposes the hypocrisy of both. Lepage's work is known for its ingenious special effects and stunning designs.

Director-auteurs exercise much more control and authority over all aspects of the production, and performance is the realization of a complete and personal vision.

The development of the director-auteur followed a natural progression. The acceptance of high-concept productions liberated directors from basing their work on prevailing assumptions about either the form or content of the dramatic text or expected stage conventions. As directors felt free to adapt a play for their own ends, it was a short step to the director as the creator of the text. In fact, many high-concept directors also work as director-auteurs. Figures such as Robert Lepage, Simon McBurney, and Ivo Van Hove move back and forth between traditional play texts and works they have envisioned as author and director. Richard Foreman (b. 1937) was an early representative of this kind of director-auteur-playwright. He wrote his own works for his Ontological-Hysteric Theatre

in New York, where his quirky texts and performances represented a unique and personal vision; he has now decided to focus on film. Lee Breuer is also a director-auteur; when he is not reinventing traditional plays such as his *Lear* (1991), with reversed gender roles set in the American South, or his *Oedipus at Colonus* (1984), staged as a gospel musical, he does much the same kind of personal exploration in the texts he has written for Mabou Mines, a theatre collaborative.

In recent times, the director-auteur has become a phenomenon of the international avant-garde. Today, at any major international theatre festival, the majority of the productions present the director as author or adapter of the dramatic text. We no longer speak of seeing the new *Hamlet* or *Oedipus* but speak of the new Lepage, McBurney, Van Hove, or Ostermeier production.

Although much of this kind of work is intellectually difficult for mass audiences, Mary Zimmerman (b. 1960) has shown that the director-auteur can create works that appeal to a more general public. Her adaptation of Ovid's *Metamorphosis* (2002), with a text based on Greek myths, was created collaboratively with the actors. It played on Broadway for two years, and she won the Tony Award for its direction.

◀ The paintings of Hieronymus Bosch served as inspiration for this dance-theatre piece, *Garden of Earthly Delights*, conceived and directed by Martha Clarke. Story and image are presented through the dancers' physical postures and gestures.

The work of director-auteurs should not be confused with that of traditional playwrights who elect to direct their own work. Playwrights Douglas Turner Ward (b. 1930), David Mamet (b. 1947), Irene Fornes (b. 1930), George C. Wolfe (b. 1954), and Sam Shepard (b. 1943) are among the preeminent American playwrights who have acted as directors for their own plays. Unlike director-auteurs, these playwrights create works that are not uniquely tied to a particular and personal directorial concept and can be passed on to others.

Alternative Beginnings

When directors find inspiration for theatrical projects in sources other than plays, they begin their creative journey in a variety of ways. Directors may assemble texts not originally written for the stage—poetry, novels, diary entries, historical documents—and create a collage of the material for dramatic effect. They may write an original text or create one with a group, or they may envision the text in nonliterary terms (see Chapter 6), creating an alternative form of performance text.

Directors may also create out of nontextual elements of performance. Their visions emerge from images, sounds,

movement, dance, music, stage technology, or other theatrical elements. Some of this work does not resemble traditional theatre experiences and may appear as hybrid forms—theatre crossed with dance, rock concerts, music video, opera, mime, and the visual arts. Alternative forms always require new ways of conceiving a performance.

Many directors come to the theatre from other artistic disciplines, and those biases are reflected in the way they create. Choreographer-directors Martha Clarke (b. 1944) and Pina Bausch (1940–2009) created dance-theatre pieces that mix dance, dialogue, and striking visual design with theatrical and nontheatrical texts and music. In Clarke's *Garden of Earthly Delights* (1984) reimagined in 2008, she used a painting by Hieronymus Bosch (1450–1516) as the central text she brought to life through mime and danced enactment of stories she imagined from the canvas. Using a dance vocabulary and theatrical elements, the piece defies simple categorization. The theatre encompasses many art forms—writing, design, painting, sculpture, acting, mime, dance, music, and media—and each can provide a starting point for the performance text. Whatever the point of origin, as adapter, writer, designer, or collaborator, these projects sometimes follow alternative creative processes for the director.

Director as Designer

Some directors come to the theatre with a strong visual aesthetic of their own that can govern their creative process and the way they work with a design team toward the final production. In Chapter 6 we looked at the image text of Robert Wilson (b. 1941). Wilson has paved the way for other artists. Director Ping Chong (b. 1946) also came to the theatre from the visual arts, so he thinks about space and light as primary elements in his creations. He focuses on visual storytelling and is keenly interested in the intersection and interaction between Western and Asian culture. He features puppets and dance in his work because of their sculptural qualities, and he has done original puppet works using the techniques of various Asian puppet traditions. Ping Chong has created environmental art installations and videos, as well as theatre work. His 2010 *Throne of Blood* was based on the Japanese film adaptation of *Macbeth* and took place in feudal Japan with a mostly American cast.

Julie Taymor (b. 1952), the first woman to win a Tony Award for directing in 1998, works with traditional texts in nontraditional ways. She is a director-designer, puppet- and mask-maker, mime, and choreographer who employs her design skills to tell a story. Because she controls all aspects of the production, her work provides an integrated artistic vision, with emphasis on visual storytelling. Taymor studied mime in Paris and traveled extensively through Asia to study various puppet and masked theatres. Her work often provides a synthesis of intercultural theatrical traditions. A strong visual text was used in Taymor's famous production of the popular *Lion King* (1997), in which Taymor served as mask and puppet designer as well as director. Although Taymor mixes puppets with live actors, she relies on the talents of actors to support the fantastic masks she creates. The atmosphere of the performance and

> **THINK**
>
> In the theatre of images, where language is less important than the visual elements, do we lose something vital, discover something new, or both?

ROBERT WILSON
Visual Auteur

ARTISTS IN PERSPECTIVE

Trained as a visual artist, Robert Wilson (b. 1941) brings these talents to bear in all his work for the theatre (see the chapter-opening photo). Although he has imprinted traditional plays and operas with his signature style, he is best known for his conceptual work as a director-auteur. Wilson functions as writer, designer, and director; controls every detail of his staging; and structures his directorial concept with a strong visual picture. That picture is extended through a series of thematically linked images and associated meanings. Sample storyboards he creates as texts for his work constructing the progression of the theatrical event through images are shown in Chapter 6.

Wilson's stage pictures may include human figures and set pieces that may or may not have realistic dimensions. When working with actors, Wilson gives very precise instructions about where they need to be on stage and how slowly or quickly they must move to create visual moments he envisions. Wilson manipulates actors as pictorial elements, and he does not play the traditional directorial role of acting coach. Language, far from providing a cohesive narrative, functions as background music for the visual images.

The experience of time and space in the theatre is a focus of Wilson's work, and time is deeply felt in his slow-moving images. His seven-day-long piece *KA MOUNTain and GUARDenia Terrace*, performed in Shiraz, Iran, in 1972, ran day and night for a week, erasing the boundaries between art and life. Fame came to him in 1976, with *Einstein on the Beach*, a five-hour uninterrupted opera with minimalist music by Philip Glass for which he did a series of drawings that Glass set to music. Wilson described their process: "We put together the opera the way an architect would build a building. The structure of the music was completely interwoven with the stage action and with the lighting. Everything was all of a piece."[3]

Einstein on the Beach established Wilson as the preeminent American artist in this genre, but his epic productions and spectacular stage pictures necessitate opera-house scale, and he has often more easily found funding for his work in European government-supported venues. When Wilson turns his hand to more conventional plays, such as his *Woyzeck* (2002), with music by Tom Waits (b. 1949), they are always unconventionally staged, mixing unexpected elements and music, and always giving preeminence to the visual realization. They may mix live actors with puppets and speech with recorded sound; they play with rhythms and scale, challenging our perceptions. The Wilson style has reached wide audiences in the United States and Europe and inspired many followers. Wilson spends summers at the Watermill Center in New York developing new works with international artists in a spirit of collaboration.

[3] www.glasspages.org/eins93.html.

her directorial concepts are embodied in her designs for a show. She collaborates with lighting, set, and costume designers who work with her to create a seamless visual world on stage.

Designers were directors in earlier generations as well. Gordon Craig (1872–1966), a pioneering director and theorist who developed abstract sets and understood the importance of light, color, and sculptural elements, directed actors in ways that would complement his visual designs. He envisioned a perfect actor, free of psychological realism, highly trained and capable of symbolic gesture. Until such an actor appeared, he put forth the idea of a marionette that could substitute for the fallible human actor on stage. The Polish artist and designer Tadeusz Kantor (1915–1990) worked as a set designer and then moved into performance art and happenings. His later work was a theatre of living images with actors manipulated like mannequins. His art was influenced by the atrocities of World War II, which demonstrated that human beings are not always on a higher plane than objects.

The Director's Personal Qualities

HOW can the director's temperament affect the creative process?

Directors have been described as coaches, trainers, mother hens, psychoanalysts, midwives, and confessors, as well as tyrants, despots, and mad geniuses. A director's temperament can range from maniacal control freak to open egalitarian. Despite this gamut of possibilities, some general qualities are required of all directors. Leadership and organizational skills are necessary to guide and coordinate an artistic staff of actors, crew members, and designers in realizing an artistic vision on stage. Directors need to have the same qualities as any other good leaders, including self-confidence, interpersonal skills, and good problem-solving capabilities. Because the theatre relies on collaboration and engages its artists' intellectual, emotional, and physical faculties, each individual's contributions must be valued to hold an ensemble together and elicit the best work possible.

While some mavericks still see themselves in a godlike role, most directors working today approach their jobs in a collaborative spirit. The image of the dictatorial director is mainly a relic of past eras. Some directors are authority figures, but most strive not to be authoritarian and encourage others to follow creative impulses. So much of the rehearsal process is spent in exploration that a director must be a good listener, be open to questions, and know how to ask just the right questions of others to open new pathways to expression. Because so much of artistic creation requires risk, the director must inspire trust. All artists must feel that their efforts will be respected and that the director has created a safe environment for experimentation. Simultaneously, directors must build confidence in their creative process and its results, so that all participants are fully committed. When a strong artistic and intellectual vision is combined with the personal attributes that enable others to reach their full creative potential, a director becomes inspirational.

Summary

HOW do directors mold the theatrical experience?   p. 186

▶ The director molds every moment of performance and provides a unified vision of the production.

▶ Directors manipulate theatrical elements and stage conventions to create meaning on stage.

▶ Directors shift between the roles of creator and spectator, acting as the audience's eyes and ears during rehearsals.

HOW did the current role of the director evolve?   p. 187

▶ The role of the modern director as we define it today is only a little more than 100 years old. In the past, playwrights, actor-managers, or company stage managers helped organize the performance but did not determine the vision of the production.

▶ The role of the modern director emerged with the rise of stage realism, which elicited the need for an outside eye to bring all the elements of production together to create a complete, unified environment on stage.

WHAT are the steps in the director's creative process?   p. 190

▶ Some directors interpret a play, taking it from the page to the stage through a process that begins with choosing and analyzing a play and developing a production concept.

▶ Directors guide designers and actors through the rehearsal process and, in the final stages of rehearsal, integrate all the design and technical elements into the production.

WHAT is a high-concept production?   p. 195

▶ When directors break with established conventions and impose a personal vision to elucidate hidden meanings in the text, we call these high-concept productions.

▶ High-concept productions may call upon various cultural traditions and the latest technologies to realize their vision.

WHY are directors involved in actor training? p.   201

▶ Sometimes a director's vision is so specific that a particular acting style is required to fulfill it, and the director trains actors in a particular methodology to carry out his or her concept.

▶ If directors and actors share a common technique, the work may often develop through collaborative effort.

WHAT is a director-auteur?   p. 204

▶ Director-auteurs begin a production with a personal vision rather than with the work of a playwright. They may assemble texts not originally written for the stage, write an original text, create one with a group, or envision the theatrical text in nonliterary terms, sometimes creating hybrid theatrical forms.

HOW can the director's temperament affect the creative process?   p. 208

▶ Whether dictatorial or collaborative, all directors must possess leadership skills and present strong artistic vision that can inspire the work of others.

MySearchLab®

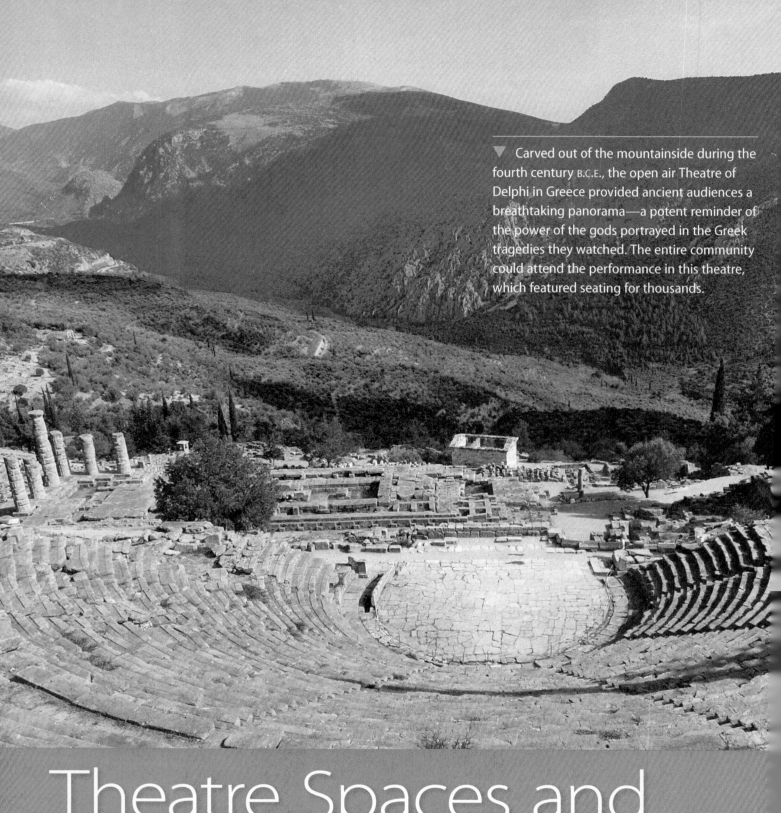

Carved out of the mountainside during the fourth century B.C.E., the open air Theatre of Delphi in Greece provided ancient audiences a breathtaking panorama—a potent reminder of the power of the gods portrayed in the Greek tragedies they watched. The entire community could attend the performance in this theatre, which featured seating for thousands.

Theatre Spaces and Environments *The Silent Character*

Space Shapes the Theatre Experience

All theatrical encounters occur in time and space. Space determines the nature of the relationship between the performers and the audience and among audience members. It affects the nature of the performance and its reception. It may be planned or determined spontaneously, but space is always a silent character in the series of interactions that characterize performance.

Some spaces have been constructed to be theatres; others have been converted or co-opted for theatrical use. In some performance spaces the relationship of the audience and the performers is predetermined by architectural design. In others, this relationship is flexible and can be reconfigured to meet the needs of particular performances. In every case, the way the artists perform their work is affected by the nature of the space and its impact on the theatrical aesthetic.

Often, we are not conscious of the way theatre space works to create meaning and context for an event. When we attend the theatre in an ornate opera house with opulent lobbies and bars serving champagne, we develop certain expectations for a lavish production, meticulous detail, and star performers. When we venture into a fringe theatre behind a storefront, in a warehouse, or in a church basement, we expect experimentation, provocation, and minimal visual or technical elements. In an African village where the entire community is assembled in a circle with drummers and musicians, we expect celebration and participation. We measure what we see against what we expect, and we make sense of a performance accordingly. The next time you attend the theatre, take note of how the location and space affect your expectations and interpretations.

1. How does space determine the nature of the relationships between performers?

2. How do theatre spaces and environments affect the nature of performance and its reception?

3. How does space play the role of a silent character in theatre performances?

CHAPTER 09

Space and Theatrical Conventions Evolve Together

The theatrical space encompasses the world of the actors and the world of the spectators. Every spatial arrangement is a negotiation between protecting the magic of the actors' domain and meeting the audience's need to connect to each other and the world of the performance. Theatre spaces develop within a cultural framework that establishes the rules of the encounter between these two worlds. The tacit understanding among participants of how these two worlds relate is one of the basic conventions of theatre. Consider how rarely a spectator willfully violates the actors' space,

even when it would be easy to do so. When performers invite us to enter their world, we know that stepping into the playing space changes us from observer to performer and brings with it burdens, responsibilities, and power. A nontraditional use of space can surprise the audience and alter the dynamics of a performance. Space contributes to the regulation of the actor–audience relationship.

Theatre spaces evolve organically to serve the needs of performers, audience members, and the larger community. Gathering in a circle to watch an event is the way human beings naturally congregate when a public presentation occurs. In city parks, on college campuses, and in small villages—wherever performers set up—spectators form a circle around them. No one orchestrates this audience formation; it is the natural result of a desire to see up close and feel the energy of the performance. Encircling the performance provides optimum proximity and **sight lines**—clear vision for the greatest number of people. Whether we are in Tibet or Ghana, Greece or Mexico, theatrical spaces find their origins in these spontaneous circles.

As the needs of actors and audience grow in complexity, more elaborate spatial arrangements develop. Spaces for the actors behind doors or curtains are created to conceal the actors' magical transformation and to house props, prompters, and costumes. Elevated stages, moving stages, or **raked seating** on an incline provide

◀ Spectators naturally form a circle around street performer Whistler eating fire at this beautiful outdoor performance site in British Columbia, Canada.

solutions to sight line problems for growing audiences. Performance forms define their spaces, just as spaces can delineate performance forms and possibilities.

Theatre Space Evolves with Technological Change

As theatre artists incorporate new technology into their artistic process and audiences accept new conventions facilitated by these advances, theatre spaces must accommodate change. In ancient Greece, spectators gathered on hillsides to watch choral dances, taking advantage of the sight lines provided by the natural elevation. Later, tiered seating was carved into the slope of the hill (see the chapter-opening photo). At first these tiers were fitted with wooden benches and then with stone seating. In the Roman era, engineering advances such as the arch and vaulting permitted large freestanding theatre structures.

The development of perspective painting in the Renaissance led to painted perspective scenery and ensuing changes in theatre architecture. One of these changes was the creation of a picture frame stage through which the illusion of a perspective painting could be achieved on a grand scale. When a system for changing painted perspective wings was invented (see nearby THINK Technology box), the stage area expanded to hold a series of painted panels, called **flats**, on the side of the stage, and stage depth increased. The area beneath the stage was expanded to include machinery to move these painted panels.

Once electricity was in common use, it became necessary for theatres to adapt to the needs of lighting instruments and overhead hanging grids. Developments in sound and lighting created the need for a control booth from which to operate equipment. Some older theatres have lights and sound operated from an open place behind the orchestra seats. Newer theatres consider current technology in their architectural design and create spaces to house technical equipment and the staff needed to run the show.

THINK TECHNOLOGY

The Operation of Giacomo Torelli's Pole-and-Chariot System for Simultaneous Scene Changes

Giacomo Torelli (1608–1678) perfected a system for instant set change. A series of flats along the side of the stage are painted to create a receding perspective. The scenic flats are placed in tracks on the stage and are attached to pole supports that fit through slots on the stage floor. These supports are attached to "chariots," a system of interconnected ropes and pulleys below the stage. Every flat of a set can be attached to a single winch. When the mechanism for running the pulleys is turned, one set of flats slides out and another set with a different design rolls in simultaneously, creating rapid scenic changes that dazzled seventeenth-century audiences. This remained the standard method of achieving set change for more than 200 years.

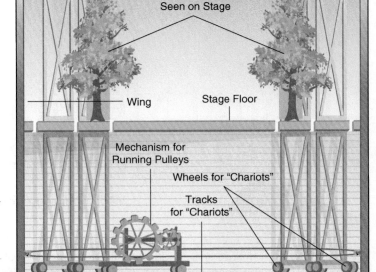

► This illustration depicts the Operation of Giacomo Torelli's Pole-and-Chariot System for Simultaneous Scene Changes.

The Boundaries
of Theatre Spaces

WHAT are the boundaries of theatrical space?

Many of us think we enter the theatre space when we walk into the auditorium where the performance will take place. But if we consider our experience, we see that we enter the theatrical environment long before taking our seats. The moment we break with our everyday lives and are enveloped by the aura of the event, we enter the realm of the theatre. If we have read or seen anything about the performance, we may have formed a mental picture of the space before we arrive that will be an emotional orientation point. As we approach the theatre, we start to feel a sense of anticipation and excitement that prepares us for the event.

If the theatre is in an unusual setting, just getting there can become part of the performance. Journeying from Manhattan to a residential area in Brooklyn can turn the trip to the theatre into the first entry into the environment of the drama. Audience members were not informed of the theatre location when they reserved tickets to *I'm Gonna Kill the President! A Federal Offense* (2003) and were told to show up on a street corner in the East Village section of Manhattan. There a contact sent them to meet up with another contact around the corner, where they were subject to a security check before being led to the theatre several blocks away. This set up the subversive themes of the performance.

Outdoor summer theatres often have an atmosphere of festivity that transports us into the theatrical environ-ment and its excitement. At Broadway theatres, with shows appealing to tourists, lines form down the block, whereas at serious dramas, attended by New York theatre regulars, patrons continue the tradition of milling under the marquee to soak up the atmosphere before curtain. We look around to see who else is in attendance and what kind of people have chosen this show. We may listen to conversations about what people are expecting or share our own expectations with companions. These interactions are already shaping our audience response.

Today, theatre architects spend a great deal of time thinking about how the public will arrive at the theatre; they conceive of the atmosphere as a part of the theatrical environment. The recent renovations to Lincoln Center in New York have turned a cultural enclave, once decried as an elite fortress insulated from the neighborhood, into an environment that invites the public to enjoy the space and the events it hosts. The addition of a new atrium with information center, discounted tickets, and café with Wi-Fi access make the center's offerings feel accessible to the general population. On summer evenings, there are free open-air events. Theatres around the world are attempting to lure the public by creating inviting environments in and around performance spaces.

Cultural Meanings
of Theatre Spaces

WHAT does performance space tell us about the values of a culture?

The location of performance spaces within the larger community says something about the nature of performances and the way each one is valued by its society. The tribal celebration in West Africa is rooted in the community's daily life and is performed in the center of the village or inside the chief's home. The ancient Athenians placed their theatre

The Last Supper: Home Theatre

To reserve seats for *The Last Supper* (2002), you telephoned the playwright-actor Ed Schmidt at home and left a message on his personal answering machine. You were told that dinner would be served and then given only the street address of a brownstone on a quiet residential street in Brooklyn. The building appeared no different from the other houses on the block and had no external signs of theatrical activity. Once on the stoop, you discovered a small marker sending you to the basement entry. You entered and crossed a low-ceilinged unfinished cellar and exited into the backyard. Although there were no signs, the only place you could go from the yard was up a back stairway

that led to a door opening into a comfortable family kitchen. The programs on the church pews in the small dining area were the only sign that a performance was about to take place.

Schmidt appeared and began to prepare dinner, interrupted by his six-year-old son who was hushed and sent upstairs to bed. The actor's opening monologue commenced, until he discovered that he had not defrosted the fish. You were then sent to the living room to chitchat with other audience members and eat cheese and crackers while the host made other dinner arrangements. By the end of the performance, the line between fact and fiction was successfully blurred; the reality of Schmidt's home, child, and food underscored his theme that truth is an illusion.

In 2010, Schmidt used a similar formula to disrupt the audience's sense of reality with *My Last Play*. Schmidt is now divorced, and his new home is less cozy. His living room is now the site for yet another unusual theatrical adventure. He tells how the play *Our Town* failed to provide the solace he sought in the wake of his father's death and, as a result, he is bidding farewell to his life as a playwright. Proclaiming that he has given up on the theatre, he dismantles his personal theatre library and invites spectators to each take a volume as they exit. The journey to a residential neighborhood and the intimacy of the setting combined with the personal confessional makes the theatrical experience unsettling for audience members who struggle to discern fact from fiction.

▶ Ed Schmidt, in a very personal farewell to the theatre, gives away his home library. Here he is seen holding the books selected by his audience members during a performance of *My Last Play*.

next to the temple of Dionysus, underscoring Greek theatre's ritual origins. It was built on public land, into the slope of a hill just below the Acropolis, the seat of government and power, emphasizing the civic role theatre played in Athenian life. The public theatres of Elizabethan England were constructed in the rough neighborhoods on the outskirts of the city, reflecting general moral disapproval of theatrical activity. Under Louis XIV in France, state-sanctioned theatres

were built close to the king's palaces, elevating the status of theatre-going and reflecting the king's love of the arts. Compare the *kabuki* and *noh* theatres of Japan. *Kabuki* developed in the "pleasure quarters" of cities, where brothels and courtesans operated, reflecting the outcast position of actors at that time. In contrast, the earlier *noh* theatre took shape within the samurai courts. It was performed in palaces and temples and was considered to be a poetic, refined tradition.

◀ At Garnier Hall, home of the Monte Carlo Opera in Monaco, the late Prince Rainier III and his entourage watch the show from the theatre's lavish royal box, positioned to give the monarch the best view of the performance and his subjects the best view of the monarch.

Theatre **Spaces** and the **Social** Order

Theatres reflect the social hierarchy. Where you sit and how you enter and exit confer status. In highly stratified cultures, a protected space, from tents in Tibet to the royal box in London, is often created for the ruling classes, reflecting the social structure outside the theatre. For centuries, the nobility used one set of entrances and the rabble another. Opera houses and theatres were constructed with locked boxes that "insulated" the elite from the general public and provided a private domain within the public performance space. Kings were often placed where they could be seen by the audience, performing their royal roles as the actors performed on stage.

When the Industrial Revolution brought people to cities, large theatres replaced smaller houses to seat growing audiences. With the democratic revolutions of the eighteenth and nineteenth centuries, more egalitarian seating arrangements developed. However, even today, audience members may enter through the same doors, but they are segregated by the economics of ticket prices.

It is interesting to look at the space allotted to actors in various theatres. Often dressing rooms are small and cramped and meant to be shared, reflecting the social status accorded actors. Today, the union Actors' Equity sets minimal standards of accommodation, in an effort to make actor comfort more of a consideration. The theatre's social order is customarily reflected in dressing room assignments. Around the world, star performers are traditionally given quarters closest to the stage. In Japan, some of the lowest-ranking actors are the *sangai. Sangai* translates as "third floor," referring to the faraway location of their dressing rooms.

The tradition of the **green room**—a space where actors socialize and audience members greet them after a performance—developed during the late seventeenth century in England, indicating the increased fraternization between performers and their public. We have some evidence that these spaces were originally green, but today the term refers to rooms of any color that serve this function. European theatres developed similar artists' salons, or conversation rooms.

Theatre **Architecture** as **Symbolic** Design

Ritual acts sanctify the places where they are performed—and delineate symbolic spaces where gods and humans participate in an exchange between two worlds. Theatre forms that evolved from religious practice occurred in spaces that contained spiritual meaning. Traditional African theatre, so closely linked to its ritual origins, occurs in a circle that permits physical and psychological contact between actors and celebrants and the divine.

The architectural space of early theatres was itself an expression of the dominant values of the culture. Because the architecture provided a universal backdrop for the dramatic action, specific scenic environments and designs for every drama were unnecessary. In fifth-century B.C.E. Athens, the performance space provided a metaphor for the Greek worldview expressed in the plays. The theatre was adjacent to the temple and even contained an altar to the god Dionysus. The orchestra, the circular playing space on the lowest level, was the province of the chorus, who often represented the voice of the people. The *skene*, the retiring house where actors would prepare for their entrances, featured doors that symbolized royal power. The province of the gods was on the upper level from which a *deus ex machina*, a god figure descending from above, could appear. (Take a virtual tour of the Theatre of Dionysus at www.theatron.co.uk/athens.htm.) The audience, seated on levels carved out of a hillside, often looked out on spectacular natural vistas behind the action.

The ancient Greek theatre space reflected both its ritual origins and dramatic themes, while serving the structure of the plays.

▶ **THE ANCIENT GREEK THEATRE** In the ancient Greek theatre, the chorus entered the orchestra, the area where they would sing and dance, through the *parodos*, or large aisle. The *skene*, or scene house, served as both a backdrop and a place from which actors entered. No one knows exactly what the *skene* looked like during the fifth century B.C.E.; one possible configuration is rendered here. The doors at the center of the skene represent the entrance to a palace and were wide enough to allow the *ekkyklema*, a platform on wheels with a scene displayed on it, to be pushed through. The stage behind the orchestra was at or close to ground level, although the stage was elevated several feet off the ground in later periods. The audience sat in steeply rising rows of seats set into the hillside.

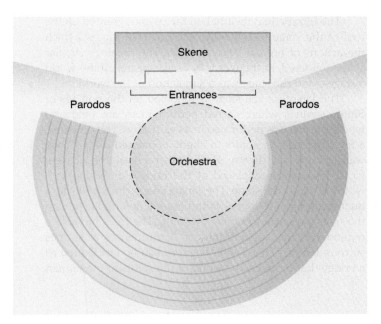

THINK TECHNOLOGY

Stage Devices in Ancient Greece

The ancient Greeks did not make extensive use of technological devices in their productions. The few they did use clearly reflected the cultural attitudes and aesthetic sensibility of the times.

The mēchanē was a large hand-powered crane that hoisted actors above the *skene*. The flying actor usually portrayed a god, and the *mēchanē* suggested the gulf between human and divine power. It captured the philosophical issues at the heart of Greek tragedy in a visual theatrical metaphor.

The ancient Greeks also made use of an ekkyklema, a platform on wheels that rolled on stage displaying actors in a pre-arranged tableau—a staged picture. The Greeks did not like to depict violence on stage, and the *ekkyklema* allowed them to show the aftermath of violent action without showing graphic brutality. Aeschylus probably used the *ekkyklema* in *Agamemnon* to reveal the dead bodies of King Agamemnon and Cassandra after they had been stabbed to death by Queen Clytemnestra off stage. The *ekkyklema* allowed the

Greeks to contemplate tragedy as an idea, rather than a sensational, bloody spectacle.

It is impossible to know whether the Greeks first brought these devices into the theatre to accommodate already completed plays or whether playwrights introduced ascending gods and offstage action in their works because they knew the *mēchanē* and *ekkyklema* were available. What we do know is that both devices were part of Greek theatrical convention and today inform our understanding of that tradition.

▶ **STAGE DEVICES OF THE ANCIENT GREEK THEATRE** The *mēchanē* was a crane used to lift actors above the skene. The *ekkyklema*, a platform on wheels, could be rolled out of the central doors to display a tableau—a visual scene depicting the aftermath of an offstage event.

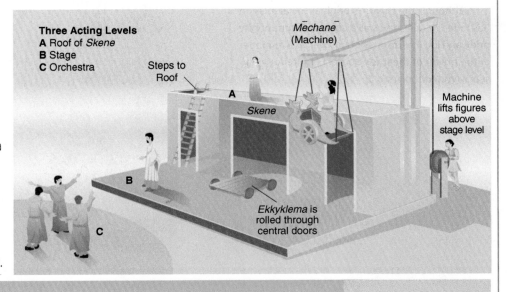

Three Acting Levels
A Roof of *Skene*
B Stage
C Orchestra

Steps to Roof

Mēchanē (Machine)

Skene

Machine lifts figures above stage level

Ekkyklema is rolled through central doors

The Elizabethan theatre had the cosmos painted on the roof of the stage to symbolize the universe against which the actions of human beings played. The theatre's circular shape rendered, in the words of Shakespeare, all the world a stage—and the stage was a simulation of the world.

The Japanese *noh* stage is modeled on the porches of Shinto shrines where sacred performances are held and where the *noh* was performed in its early days. The pine tree, a favorite place for spirits to alight, is painted on the back wall of every *noh* theatre. Real pines representing heaven, earth, and man are placed at the bridge, or *hashigakari*, which leads to the stage. The Japanese word for *pine* has a dual meaning and implies faithfulness and long life, giving the trees' presence symbolic meaning. The trees are also a reminder of the original outdoor performances at shrines surrounded by pines. The *hashigakari* can be interpreted as a bridge that connects the world of the spirits to the human realm; the actor's slow entrance across this bridge is a journey from the beyond to our world.

Analogously, early Indian dramas took place in temples, and early European passion plays grew out of Christian ritual in churches, where the religious architecture provided emblematic background for the theatre. Symbolic elements were part of the permanent theatre architecture, and the space was filled with multilevel meanings that expressed the values and beliefs of the culture. The drama was staged against an unchanging backdrop representing a seemingly universal worldview.

Once the idea of a single world order and an entrenched cultural value system gives way to individualism, subjectivity, and social fragmentation, spaces and environments were needed that expressed varying perspectives and values. As that happens, theatrical environments moved from the symbolic to the representational.

HIDDEN HISTORY

The Smallest Opera House in the World

In the tiny village of Montecastello di Vibio in the Umbria region of Italy sits the smallest opera house in the world. It is a miniature horseshoe-shaped theatre with boxes, velvet seats, and ceiling frescoes. Opened in 1808, it was meant to provide a place where, through theatre, opera, and music, the rival leading families of the region could end disputes and find peace—and so it was named *Teatro della Concordia*.

Although the theatre's original social mission has faded, it still serves as a source of community pride and local performances, as well as a reminder of the power of theatrical space. For interior views see: *www.teatropiccolo.it/*

▶ The Teatro della Concordia is wedged between buildings on one of the small village's narrow winding streets.

Times Square: The Transformation of a Theatre District

New York's Times Square, at Forty-Second Street and Broadway, has been synonymous with theatre since 1895. At that time, developer Oscar Hammerstein, grandfather of the lyricist Oscar Hammerstein II, opened the Olympia, a huge entertainment complex housing three theatres. The Olympia's success led Hammerstein to build several more theatres in the same locale, which in turn attracted other theatre developers.

A theatre district sets a tone for its offerings, and success or failure of the whole community outweighs the fortunes of any single production. During World War I, Times Square experienced its first real boom time, producing 113 shows in a single season, despite the war. But the Great Depression forced many theatre owners to transform their establishments into movie houses to provide inexpensive entertainment. In the 1960s and 1970s, Times Square's legitimate theatres competed for space and attention with the X-rated movie theatres and shows that crowded the district and brought with them seedy and illicit activities. Theatregoers who lingered to dine or drink after a show were greeted by the area's alternative nightlife—prostitutes looking for clients and drug dealers pushing their wares. The area had one of the highest crime rates in the city.

Since the 1990s, Times Square has undergone a guided transformation. Spearheaded by the Walt Disney Company's refurbishing of the New Amsterdam Theatre and supported by the City and State of New York, the Forty-Second Street Development Project has worked to make the Times Square area an inviting place for out-of-town tourists. Most of the X-rated shows in the area have been closed down, replaced by wholesome entertainments, including several Disney productions, as well as large commercial enterprises, an enormous Toys "R" Us housing a full-size Ferris wheel, and a Disney Store. Times Square's streets now bustle all night long with crowds of tourists going to shows, watching the blaze of neon lights and huge video screens while spending their money.

What has been called the "Disneyfication" of the area pleases some and leaves a good number of New Yorkers and theatre aficionados unsettled. While the old Times Square may have had a high crime rate, its legitimate theatres still catered to the taste of seasoned and discerning theatregoers. Today's theatrical fare is noticeably less challenging. Local businesses have been pushed out by chain stores, and much of the area resembles an urban version of the suburban mall.

Times Square is losing its unique cachet and becoming a carbon copy of other commercial developments. Many fear that the area is being turned into a theme park with only children's fare and family-friendly entertainment. Under "Disneyfication," what will happen to local culture and the ability of Broadway theatres to address important and controversial issues? Will there be a place for challenging productions in New York's theatre district?

THINK

Is a cleaned-up neighborhood worth the price of a loss of local culture and challenging theatre?

◀ The Disney Store and Disney's stage version of *The Lion King* dominate this view of the revived theatre district around Times Square, New York, where once peep shows and porno films dominated the urban landscape.

Akwasidai Festival's Symbolic Space

The Akwasidai Festival is a ritual celebration of the Akan tribe of the Ashanti clan in Ghana. It takes place every 40 days, 9 times a year, in a never-ending cycle, reflecting the Ashanti view of time. The enactment honors dead ancestors and secures their blessing. In this ceremony of purification and thanksgiving, art, ritual, and politics merge; the entire rite serves as a prelude to a town meeting. The space, the seating arrangement, and all the props have symbolic value and reflect the central values of the culture.

Drumming starts the night before the festivities, while the chief prays to tribal ancestors. He prays in his "palace," the largest building in the town with a central interior area that can accommodate the entire population. The next morning, all the townspeople and guests assemble in the courtyard of the palace—the source of spiritual, ancestral, and political power for the community.

All the villagers dance, stopping abruptly upon the chief's entry. The chief, in all his gold regalia, receives the homage of his people, surrounded by dancers, praise singers, and horn-blowers. He takes his seat upon the Akan-Ashanti golden stool, the symbol of nationhood, the embodiment of ancestral spirits and of the chief's authority. An umbrella with a tribal symbol at its point is held overhead as protection. Two rows of elders surround the chief in two rows to his left and right. On his right are also linguists—who speak the chief's words—and court criers. Next to the elders are the town's children, symbolizing the connection between the living and the dead, the old and the young, through endless cycles of ritual and renewal.

The elders engage in narrative dance, and the chief accepts their dedication by touching a dancer's head with a golden sword that symbolizes ancestral authority. Many of these dances portray the chase of women by men and are meant to ensure the continuation of the community and fertility. The chief then dances with the sword raised toward him, followed by the subchief. They resume their seats in state as the villagers rejoice in song and dance. The drumming subsides, and one drum softly beats the rhythm of the town meeting while the town criers bring the villagers to order. The chief speaks to his people through the linguists who enact his words. The world of the ancestors and the world of the present are brought together through song and dance in the ancestral palace.

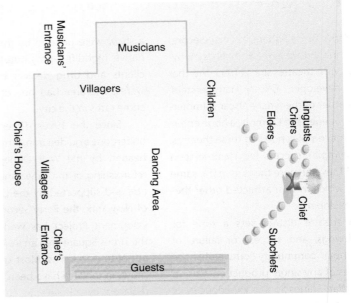

GROUND PLAN FOR AKWASIDAI CELEBRATION The chief's home in the center of the village features a communal space used for celebratory dance. Before taking his seat on the throne, the chief walks through the area where his people sit.

During the Akwasidai festival, the Ashanti king sits in state surrounded by tribal elders and criers and wears a robe of kente cloth reserved for chiefs. Symbols of Ashanti belief are everywhere, from the painted stool to the elaborate gold medallions.

The Spiritual Space of *Kutiyattam*

India's sacred *kutiyattam* performances take place in open-air rectangular wooden structures found in the compounds of Kerala's Hindu temples. Sacred temple grounds are open only to practicing Hindus, who are therefore the only spectators. Spectators must purify themselves by bathing before entering the temple to witness performances. The performances take place from late in the evening until sunrise, by the light of a single oil lamp. Performers drawn from a special cast of temple servants are charged with specific rites, among them, acting *kutiyattam*. Unlike most other performances in India, *kutiyattam* takes place in relative quiet; the vendors and stalls that usually spring up for outdoor performances are not allowed within temple compounds.

The nine *kutiyattam* stages found in the region of Kerala are the only surviving examples of permanent theatre structures from ancient India, and they conform more or less to the descriptions of ideal performance spaces set out in the *Natyasastra* (see Chapter 5). Only three of these sites remain in use. The largest, the stage at the Siva Temple of Trichur, can seat around 500 spectators and is used only once each year, on a highly auspicious day.

The slightly raised, square *kutiyattam* stage is set facing the temple deity. Because performances are an offering, actors play toward the deity. A roof supported by pillars covers the stage. Its underside is usually highly decorated with paintings and carvings that are not visible to the audience, presumably serving ritual purposes of their own. Before setting foot on stage, actors, like those throughout India, put their right hand to the floor of the stage and then to their eye and head to acknowledge the sanctity of the space and the performance and to entreat blessings for the event.

▲ In this *kutiyattam* temple theatre in Kerala, India, the space is bare; audience members sit on three sides. The interior of the roof is highly ornate.

Traditional Theatre Spaces and Environments

WHAT are the advantages and disadvantages of staging in proscenium, arena, thrust, and black box theatres?

Today, there are a number of spatial arrangements specifically designed for theatre buildings. They reflect established traditions and accepted spatial conventions. Each of these configurations brings a set of advantages and disadvantages to staging practices. Some are better suited to particular types of texts, performance styles, or scenic designs. During the course of the twentieth century, black box theatres became common because they permit flexible configurations of space, so that theatre artists can decide what best fits a particular project and concept. Today practitioners in search of spaces hospitable to new theatrical forms can pursue flexibility within designed theatre spaces as well.

In this section, we look at how proscenium, arena, thrust, and black box theatres play a role in the creative choices artists make. We also explore how each space affects the actor–audience relationship.

> **A theatrical concept demands a particular scenic arrangement, just as, and even more so, architecture calls forth, demands, and informs a theatrical concept and style of presentation.**

—Jacques Copeau, *Registres I*, 1941

Proscenium Stage

Most of the theatre you have seen has probably taken place on a **proscenium stage**, or **picture frame stage**. In this arrangement, the audience sits facing a raised stage. During the Italian Renaissance, a **proscenium arch**, sometimes in the shape of a rectangle, was constructed over the front of the stage, separating the audience from the performance space and forming a frame for painted perspective stage scenery. Spectators had the impression that they were looking into a framed living picture, and the perspective painting could give the illusion of great distance behind the actors. The **stage curtain** is usually just inside the frame and is raised to reveal the stage action and lowered to conceal set changes. In some eras before electrical lighting, a large **apron** (a raised extension of the stage) protruded past the proscenium arch and was often used as the major playing space for the actors. Actors were lit with **footlights** at the front of the stage, and the arch framed the scenery behind them. Today, the apron is usually small, and actors perform behind the proscenium arch. Sometimes an **orchestra pit** below the apron of the stage houses musicians. Sometimes the pit is elevated to form an extended apron when an orchestra is not required.

To the left and right of the playing area are **wings**, empty spaces that can be masked to hide actors, technicians, props, and scenery that moves laterally onto or across the stage. Scenery that once moved mechanically can now be moved electrically and can be run by computers. Some proscenium theatres have very high ceilings behind the arch called **fly spaces**, or **lofts**, containing painted scenery that is literally "flown" up and down on a system of pulleys to change the sets. These lofts must be at least twice as tall as the proscenium opening so scenery can be completely concealed. Proscenium theatres provide the possibility of rapid set changes through both horizontal and vertical movement of scenery, creating illusory magic to thrill audiences. Even today in our technologically advanced world, audiences "ooh" and "aah" at scenic wonders and may even applaud the new set. The descent of the helicopter in *Miss Saigon* (1991) provided such an effect.

Directly facing the stage is the large raked audience seating area we call the *orchestra*, named for the space in the ancient Greek theatre. **Balconies** in proscenium houses usually overhang a third to a half of the orchestra when they are facing the stage, or they may form horseshoe-shaped tiers around the periphery of the auditorium. The horseshoe shape was the dominant form in European theatres and opera houses during the seventeenth and eighteenth centuries because it permitted private **boxes**. As democratic revolutions overturned the rigid class structure, the architecture of the theatre accommodated egalitarianism with open balconies facing the stage.

A proscenium theatre creates a clear boundary between the world of the audience and the world of the actors. The audience in the proscenium theatre is farther from the stage action in this arrangement than in other traditional theatre spaces. Spectators are positioned as voyeurs peeking into another world. For this reason, the side of the stage closest to the audience is referred to as the *fourth wall*. Watching a proscenium performance, you feel as if the fourth wall of a room has been removed to allow you to see what is happening. The audience views the action from only one side, so actors play frontally toward the audience and **cheat out**—that is, avoid turning their backs completely toward the audience by remaining on an angle even when talking to someone slightly behind them.

When an actor is standing center stage facing the audience, the area of the stage to the actor's right is called **stage right**, and the area to the actor's left, **stage left**. The area of the stage closest to the audience is referred to as **downstage**. The area of the stage farthest from the audience

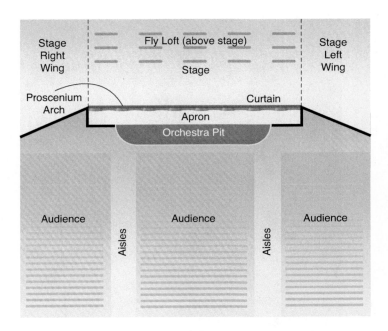

▲ A GROUND PLAN OF A PROSCENIUM THEATRE

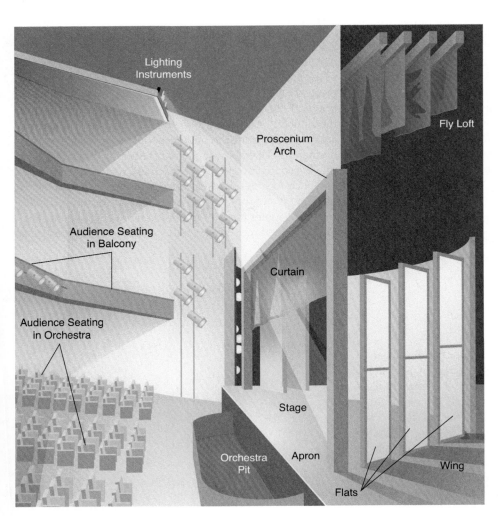

◀ A CROSS-SECTION VIEW OF A PROSCENIUM THEATRE

◄ Note the proscenium arch that frames the stage of the Mayflower Theatre in Southampton, England.

is **upstage**. This terminology is a reminder of the seventeenth and eighteenth centuries, when the stage was raked upward. During a performance, one actor may walk upstage of another, forcing the downstage actor to turn away from the audience to address lines. The first actor thus claims the full attention of the audience. When this happens, we say the downstage actor is **upstaged**. To upstage now also means to steal the spotlight.

Realistic sets work especially well behind a proscenium frame. The separation of the stage world from the auditorium increases the illusion while focusing the audience forward toward the stage. Performances requiring elaborate special effects and scenic changes are also natural for proscenium houses.

Musicals that require an **orchestra** and multiple sets usually are staged in proscenium **theatres.**

Theatre-in-the-Round, or the **Arena** Stage

Many scholars believe that Greek tragedy and the European theatre tradition originated in rituals enacted in a circle. Once theatres moved indoors and became a formal tradition, arena staging all but disappeared until the twentieth century, when it was reborn as a reaction to the proscenium's separation of audience and performer. In the arena configuration, the audience sits on all four sides of a round or rectangular performance space. Actors enter through four or more **voms**, aisles named for the *vomitoria*, or entryways of the ancient Roman amphitheaters. Because there are fewer rows, this arrangement brings more spectators closer to the stage action and permits a sense of intimacy with the actors. Simultaneously, audience members can see each

other across the playing space and are aware of being part of the event. This creates a sense of heightened theatricality and awareness of the fragility of the theatrical illusion.

Arena staging places demands on directors, actors, designers, and the audience. Large pieces of scenery cannot be used because they would block sight lines from some part of the audience. Set designers must develop clever small set pieces that serve the needs of the play and suggest location without any backdrop or flat. Lighting designers have the difficult task of directing the light to keep the playing area separate from the audience without any architectural boundaries. Directors' staging must keep the physical action moving so that no actor has a back to a particular side of the audience for too long. Actors must invent justifications for movement and turns to play to all sides of the house. Unlike the single-point focus of the proscenium stage, arena staging does not direct the spectators' attention in any particular

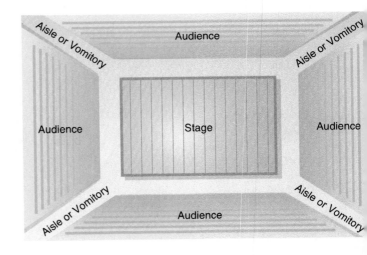

▲ **ARENA THEATRE GROUND PLAN**

► The Fichandler Arena Stage at the Mead Center for American Theater offers multiple entrances through voms. No spectator is ever more than eight rows from the stage. This proximity creates an intimate relationship between the audience and the drama.

direction, and audience members must select focus. Despite all these difficulties, many artists enjoy working within these constraints and believe the arena pushes the imagination to find inventive solutions and the forced movement enlivens a production. Actors also often love the intimacy with the audience. Audience members enjoy this too, as well as the sense of community.

Of course, many plays would be extremely difficult to stage effectively in the round. Bedroom farces, in which the timing of slamming doors and entrances and exits hold the play together, require great skill to stage in arena spaces, as do plays that require enormous realistic detail. Imaginative the-

atre artists often find original ways to overcome the obstacles, and many directors even elect to do plays that would more naturally lend themselves to other spatial arrangements in order to conceive the play in fresh new ways.

Thrust Stage

The thrust stage provides some of the intimacy and theatricality of the arena and some of the practical solutions offered by the proscenium. In this configuration, the audience sits on three sides of a performance area that projects into the audience. The fourth side provides a backdrop for the action and an area for concealment and scene and costume changes. Actors enter from the backstage area or through aisles or voms.

The thrust stage was one of the first arrangements to be used in formally designed theatre spaces. Ancient Greek and Roman theatres are, in fact, thrust stages. Through the centuries, wherever itinerant actors set up stages on their wagons, audiences would gather on three sides to view the action, creating an impromptu thrust stage. During the Middle Ages, when theatre moved outside the church, **platform stages**, with a **scene house** or curtained area at the back for concealment and costume changes, were set up for outdoor performances. Often the platform was on wheels and formed a **wagon**, or **booth stage**, that moved throughout the town performing in different locations, creating a mobile thrust stage.

The theatre buildings of renaissance Spain and England grew out of the idea of the medieval platform stage. The Elizabethan theatre (such as London's famous Globe theatre—see nearby figure and box) was an essentially circular structure open to the sky, with a roofed, raised platform stage on one side and three floors of gallery seating built into the outer walls of the theatre. Around the three sides of the thrust stage was an area called the **pit** in which spectators could stand. On the level of the stage, two doors

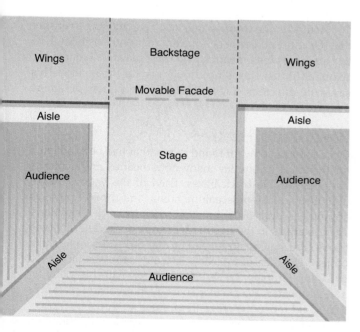

▲ **THRUST THEATRE GROUND PLAN**

The Maclab Theatre at the Citadel Theatre in Edmonton, Canada, accommodates 686 spectators on three sides of a thrust stage. It is reminiscent of the ancient Greek theatre.

on either side at the back were used for entrances and exits. It is believed that a small balcony at the back of the stage provided the roof for a curtained **discovery space** where events or items could be concealed or revealed. The balcony provided a second-story playing space that could represent high places such as turrets, windows, or balconies. Interest in the Elizabethan theatre provoked a resurgence of the use of thrust stages in the twentieth century.

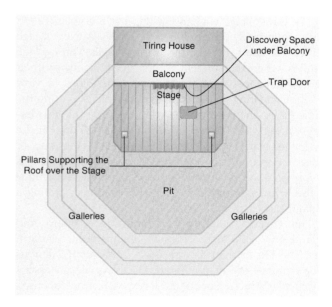

Tiring House

Discovery Space under Balcony

Balcony

Trap Door

Stage

Pillars Supporting the Roof over the Stage

Pit

Galleries

Galleries

▲ **THE GROUND PLAN OF THE ELIZABETHAN GLOBE THEATRE**

The thrust stage has been adapted the world over. Many Asian theatre traditions used some version of the thrust configuration. The *noh* stage of Japan, established in the seventeenth century, is a modified thrust. It has a roofed platform stage that resembles the shrines where the *noh* was originally performed, with audience seating on two sides. The *kabuki* first used the basic *noh* stage until its growing use of elaborate scenery and effects required a curtain and other aspects of the proscenium stage.

Actors on the thrust stage must keep moving to ensure that the entire audience gets maximum frontal visibility. Unlike actors in arena theatres who must play to all four sides, actors on thrust stages need only play to three sides. This eases the director's staging problems and offers designers many options.

Black Box Theatres

Once common only for found spaces that had been adapted for theatrical use, today many new theatres are architect-designed flexible black boxes. Each of the various stages described so far—proscenium, arena, and thrust—presents advantages and disadvantages, options and restrictions. Theatre artists in the twentieth century desired flexibility to choose the staging arrangement that best suits a particular project. The idea of a flexible space theatre was pioneered by Walter Gropius (1883–1969) in 1926, with his plans for a "total theater"—a circular space with revolving platforms that could move the stage from arena to thrust or proscenium, or encircle the audience with scenic projections on surrounding screens.

The Reconstruction of the Globe Theatre

William Shakespeare was one of six original shareholders in the first Globe Theatre built in 1599 to house the performances of the Lord Chamberlain's Men, the acting company responsible for the premieres of the great writer's most significant works. Here Hamlet, Macbeth, Lear, and Othello first strutted across the stage in a disreputable district just outside the then city limits of London.

Burned down in 1613, when an ember from a stage cannon set the thatched roof on fire, the Globe Theatre was rebuilt a year later, only to be torn down in the 1640s by the Puritans, who condemned the immorality of theatrical activity. For centuries the Globe existed as a theatre of legend, living only in panoramic London drawings, maps, building contracts, and written accounts of Elizabethan theatre-goers.

All this changed when American actor and film director Sam Wanamaker (1919–1993) came to London in search of the Globe, only to discover that there was no lasting monument to the theatre's greatest writer. In 1970 he created the Shakespeare Globe Trust to raise money for a reconstruction of the original theatre, based on the existing records, drawings, and accounts, as well as archeological excavations and extant structures from the period. From 1987 to 1997, construction proceeded on a site 200 yards from the original building. Using materials such as oak timbers, handmade bricks, thatched roof, bright paints, and lime-washed walls, the builders of the new theatre approximated as closely as possible the first Globe. The painting of the heavens is re-created on the roof of the stage. Unfortunately, Wanamaker died in 1993 and never saw the completion of his dream.

Since 1997, summer performances at the Globe of period plays have been produced with attention to historical accuracy in costume, props, set pieces, music, and sound. Musicians are placed on the stage itself or on the stage balcony. No recorded sound is ever used. An all-male cast performs the plays as in Shakespeare's time, and **groundlings**, lower-class spectators who could not afford seats, still stand for the duration of the performance, rain or shine, in the open pit area in front of the stage. There are still many unknowns about the acting and pronunciation of the period, as we have no tangible evidence to reproduce.

The limited backstage dressing room and storage areas pose challenges to the actors and theatre personnel, but the only concession to today's needs has been in issues of safety. There are twice the number of entrances, illuminated exit signs, and a sprinkler system, lest the fire of 1613 be repeated. The contemporary audience need only cast off their modern attitudes and expectations to experience history.

▲ The New Globe Theatre in London

THINK

Even in a historically accurate reconstructed theatre, how much of the original experience can be recaptured by a contemporary audience?

Gropius believed the theatrical space itself should feed the imagination. Although the construction of this ingenious space was halted when Hitler took power in Germany, the plans sowed the seeds for later flexible configurations. Today, **black box theatres** that permit the rearrangement of seating and playing areas for every production

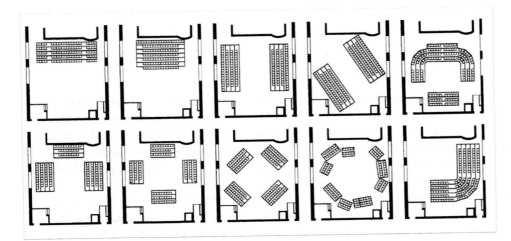

are an accepted convention found everywhere. They require only a large room (painted black, of course) and permit not only the traditional proscenium, arena, and thrust arrangements, but corner stages, L-shaped stage or seating areas, and audience-surround performances as well as environmental and multifocus performances.

Created and Found Spaces

HOW do created and found spaces serve the needs of performances?

Sometimes traditional theatre spaces are not desirable to theatre artists for aesthetic or economic reasons, and they find and adapt spaces not originally conceived as places of performance. Anywhere actors and audience can be accommodated—lofts, churches, basements, warehouses, or factories—can serve as theatre spaces. This often leads to improvised spatial configurations dependent on the parameters of the found space.

And cyberspace has opened up new possibilities for found space. Once it was thought that theatrical space, whatever its size, shape, or nature, had to encompass the performers and the actors, but technology now permits us to transcend this limitation. Theatre artists can now perform in one space for an audience in another, or they can work with artists in remote locations.

> **I can take any empty space and call it a bare stage.**
>
> —Peter Brook, *The Empty Space*, 1984

Street Theatre

The ultimate noncommercial space is public space. Often used by theatres with political or social agendas, **street theatre** brings the performance to the people. Because the spectators are sometimes coerced into becoming audience members, they may resist their role, obliging street theatre artists to use compelling theatrical devices—music, spectacle, masks, costumes, dancing, or confrontation—to engage with the public. Such theatre is limited in its use of text and mostly comprises simple short scenes. Political action theatre in the street is called guerrilla theatre because it sneaks up on audience members where they least expect it and aggressively exhorts them to engage. Street theatre frequently concerns itself with the interests of a particular community; performers hope the public will focus on their work because its subject is of immediate concern.

Multifocus Staging

At every moment in life, many things are going on around us, and we choose where to direct our attention—to the television, a phone call, noise on the street, or a conversation. In a reaction against single-focus realism, some theatre artists feel that multifocus theatre, in which several playing areas are set up simultaneously, gives the audience the same choice they exercise in daily life. The demands on the actor are high in this kind of presentation because they are actually competing with their fellow performers for the audience's attention. Sometimes multifocus staging requires that the audience move from place to place to follow the action. It may also use moving instead of stationary stages, and the audience can choose to follow a particular moving stage or wait for the next wagon stage to appear as part of a processional stage, with new elements of the performance appearing on each subsequent rolling platform. African festivals in which characters are carried through the crowd on hoisted litters use this form, and many medieval performances employed a moving wagon stage. During the 1960s and 1970s the processional stage was resurrected by experimental artists. Companies such as Bread and Puppet Theatre staged large outdoor and indoor multifocus events.

THINK

Should the audience's comfort be a consideration when selecting found spaces, or is discomfort part of the experience?

Environmental Staging

In the 1960s the avant-garde theatre movement viewed the proscenium as promoting a passive audience. The politically active experimental theatre of the period sought a new and vital kind of performance that would engage the audience more completely. Influenced by the writings of theorist Antonin Artaud (1896–1948), work that involved audience participation eventually led to the idea of removing all the boundaries between performers and spectators, to allow them to share space.

Jerzy Grotowski (1933–1999) in Poland and RichardSchechner (b. 1934) in New York experimented with configurations that permitted various kinds of

◀ The use of multiple stages for the Théâtre du Soleil's 1970 production of *"1789" La Révolution Française* permitted the audience to wander among the various playing areas. The actors even invited spectators to follow them to different scenes. This enabled each audience member to construct a personal history of the French revolution. The theatre space was created by members of the troupe who refinished the floors and walls of an old factory.

Large-Scale Puppet Theatres Claim Streets and Meadows

Bread and Puppet Theatre, founded in the 1960s, used huge political puppets that were visible symbols of protest at anti-war rallies throughout the decade. Today, the company still performs in city streets, open fields, and unusual large indoor spaces. At political rallies and marches, the group's enormous puppets—designed by Peter Schuman, built by a community of volunteers, and carried by contingents of 10 or more—are visible for blocks. These processional figures disrupt our usual sense of scale and proportion. Their rough papier-mâché features bring a humanizing presence to industrialized urban environments. The company's slow-moving, silent procession of giants can transform their surroundings, halting the hustle and bustle of traffic and demanding the attention of passers-by unwittingly transformed into spectators.

Bread and Puppet performed its *Domestic Resurrection Circus* every summer from 1975 to 1998 at the company's home in Glover, Vermont. At Cate Farm, grassy fields, pine trees, majestic mountains, and open sky provided a natural backdrop. The final part of the performance, a grand-scale pageant, stretched across the fields, a panorama integrating theatre and nature. At the annual bonfire, which brought the performance into the realm of primal ritual, the year's ills were burned in effigy to make way for Mother Earth. This symbolic puppet of resurrection reconnected participants to the cycle of life, death, and rebirth.

Royal de Luxe, founded in 1979 in France by Jean Luc Courcoult, is a renowned puppetry company that uses claimed space for its performance events. The company's giant marionettes dwarf those of the Bread and Puppet theatre, even competing with urban monuments and buildings in scale. Some puppets are so large that they are manipulated by cranes and can require more than 100 puppeteers. Performances recount fantastic stories and fables, often with political metaphors. Royal de Luxe has performed the world over, claiming the streets and parks of various cities, performing for free. The company's aim is to tell a story to a city, and, wherever it goes, the general population participates in a festival atmosphere.

▲ The French theatre company Royal de Luxe celebrates German Reunification Day in 2009. As two giants enter the landmark Brandenburg Gate, the streets of Berlin become a stage.

Trilogie des Dragons: Location and Space as Theatrical Experience

For the production of Robert Lepage's *Trilogie des Dragons* for the Festival des Ameriques (2003), the audience journeyed far from public transportation through rail yards on the outskirts of Montreal to a huge abandoned railway maintenance building on the waterfront. No attempt was made to convert the space into a theatre, and evidence of its original use refitting railcars was everywhere—from old pipes on the walls to obsolete equipment notable only for its decrepitude and filth. The cavernous space had a large central rectangular playing area 64 feet long by 28 feet wide. Two sets of steep bleachers were constructed facing each other on the opposite long sides of the ground-level stage. These were furnished with flimsy folding chairs that provided seating for the six-hour performance.

No acceptable accommodation was made for the spectators' needs. Approximately a dozen portable toilets were set outside in the yard for the large audience, who often needed to wait in the rain for a turn. Two water coolers were provided. Refreshments were sold at intermission.

All the performances were sold out, and Lepage's imaginative staging of this collaboratively developed piece made it worth the inconvenience. The large space permitted special effects and dramatic lighting not achievable in tighter locations. Characters rode in on mopeds, video projection screens were set up on the short sides of the rectangular playing area, and a wheelchair was set ablaze. The scale of the space was a perfect backdrop for the thematic sweep of the production tracing the Asian immigrant experience from China to Canadian cities, via the world of fantasy and dreams. In some sense, the out-of-the-way place, the strange space without any cosmetic enhancement, even the endurance of uncomfortable seating and lack of facilities made the audience feel part of a special event for those "in-the-know."

---

performer–audience interactions. Schechner's production of *Dionysus in 69* (1968) was an adaptation of *The Bacchae* staged in a garage with large open areas on the floor and scattered scaffolding. The audience could choose to sit anywhere in the space, and each night the actors adjusted their performance to the way the audience had arranged themselves. Certain scenes were performed practically in the laps of some spectators, and lines were whispered in audience members' ears as the actors moved through the space. This created a multifocus environment where the audience could choose not only where to sit, but also where to look and listen. No two audience members had the same experience of the performance. You might be seated near one scene and out of earshot of another. During the performance, the entire audience was invited to join in a bacchanalian dance with the actors, erasing all boundaries.

Revolutionary at the time, environmental staging freed more traditional theatres to experiment with audience involvement in performance by seating the audience on the stage or close to the action. Although the audience may seem to be in the same space with the actors, in a sense there is never a complete sharing. The actors bring with them a halo of energy, an invisible space that surrounds them and empowers them in their interactions with the audience.

Site-Specific Staging

Often theatrical environments are specifically connected to the content of a performance. Staging a play about prison life inside an actual prison, or performing Reverend Billy's *Church of Stop Shopping* in an actual church are ways of creating a hyper-reality. Many historical reenactments take place on original historic sites. In 2001, director Joanna Settle set two short Beckett plays in site-specific locations in Chicago. *Rockaby*, which reveals the internal thoughts of a woman in a rocking chair, was staged in the bay window of an apartment for audiences of fifteen to twenty people, and *Play* was staged in a store window at a busy Chicago intersection. This unconventional theatrical venue, at a busy three-way intersection, brought a new public to Beckett's esoteric work. The isolation of the characters, each confined up to the neck in an urn, was underlined by their encasement behind the store window and the eerie reflection on the glass. Actors had microphones in their urns; their voices were piped to the street through speakers.

Deborah Warner's (b. 1959) *Angel Project* (2003) actually provided audience members with guides to various sites around New York, where sometimes just being in the site itself was the performance. The Old Lincoln School in Brookline, Massachusetts, served as the site for a production of *Sleep No More* (2010), an interactive *Macbeth* in which audience members could follow the cast of characters through the rooms and corridors of the building. Punchdrunk, the British theatre company responsible for *Sleep No More*, has also staged similar site-specific performances in London and New York.

John Gould Rubin staged *Hedda Gabler* (2010) in a swank New York City townhouse. The small living room audience watched Hedda's drama unfold in close proximity. The sense of being voyeurs in a private space was enhanced as the theatre company did not release the address of the performance to ticket holders until the day of the performance.

The Angel Project: Site-Specific Staging

Deborah Warner's *Angel Project* (2003) took spectators on a tour of New York that framed the city spaces in unusual ways, some populated by actor-angels, others with unusual props. Warner considers the urban architecture she revealed as the text for the production. It provides a new kind of visual space where the familiar is made strange through the heightened awareness created by solitary exploration. A quotation from *Paradise Lost* in the program and bits of Christian imagery scattered through-

out the sites, such as religious books and objects in an abandoned porn theatre, feathers floating to the ground, and a nun reading the Bible in Times Square indicate that the work had thematic unity. Spectators picked up a guidebook at the first site and were guided on their way through the city. The timing of each tour was staggered so that each ticket holder traveled alone, turning the usual theatrical dynamic on end with its lone audience of one wandering through open public space.

When you look at the world through the eyes of an audience member walking the streets, everyone appears to be performing. For much of the time, the spectator is deciding where to focus, what image to seize, and what meaning to construct. Each audience member, in a sense, becomes the author, director, designer, and actor of the theatrical space as he or she decides which site-specific spaces to frame in his or her field of vision.

◀ In a moment in *The Angel Project*, conceived and directed by Deborah Warner, a country landscape of flowers pushes through the snow at an indoor venue, where windows provide a new perspective on the urban cityscape outside.

The Actor in Space

The theatrical environment can be created in many ways, in many places. There is not always a need for an architecturally designed theatre building. All that is required is a space that facilitates the interaction between the performer and the audience and

serves the content of the event. Each of the environments discussed in this chapter imposes expectations on the audience and constraints and freedoms on theatre practitioners. The impact of the theatrical environment, however, is felt most directly by

actors, who must fill the theatrical space each and every performance with their physical energy. Although aided by designers and directors, the actor must ultimately build the invisible channel through the theatrical environment to the audience.

Summary

HOW do theatre spaces evolve as theatrical conventions change?   p. 212

▶ Space determines the nature of the relationship between the performers and the audience and among audience members.

▶ Location and space influence the audience's expectations and interpretations of a performance.

▶ Theatre spaces evolve to serve the needs of performers, audience members, and the larger community.

▶ Theatre spaces evolve with technological developments.

WHAT are the boundaries of theatrical space?   p. 214

▶ The boundaries of the theatrical space go beyond the walls of the playhouse to its geographic location and may include the journey audience members take to the site.

WHAT does performance space tell us about the values of a culture?   p. 214

▶ The geographic location of theatres reflects how a culture values its theatre.

▶ Theatre spaces reflect social hierarchies.

▶ Theatre structures and stages can embody symbolic ideas through their spatial configurations, design elements, and unique architectural features.

WHAT are the advantages and disadvantages of staging in proscenium, arena, thrust, and black box theatres?   p. 222

▶ The proscenium stage, with the audience sitting on one side of a picture frame stage; the arena stage, with the audience encircling a central playing space; and the thrust stage, with the audience sitting on three sides of the stage are all common theatrical arrangements that can be architecturally predetermined and offer different advantages and disadvantages for staging.

▶ Black box theatres offer flexibility because they can be arranged in many spatial configurations.

HOW do created and found spaces serve the needs of performances?   p. 228

▶ Found spaces, multifocus staging, environmental staging, and site-specific staging can provide more flexible and unusual arrangements between the audience and the performers.

▶ The size, shape, and arrangement of the theatre space must always permit the actor to reach the audience.

MySearchLab®

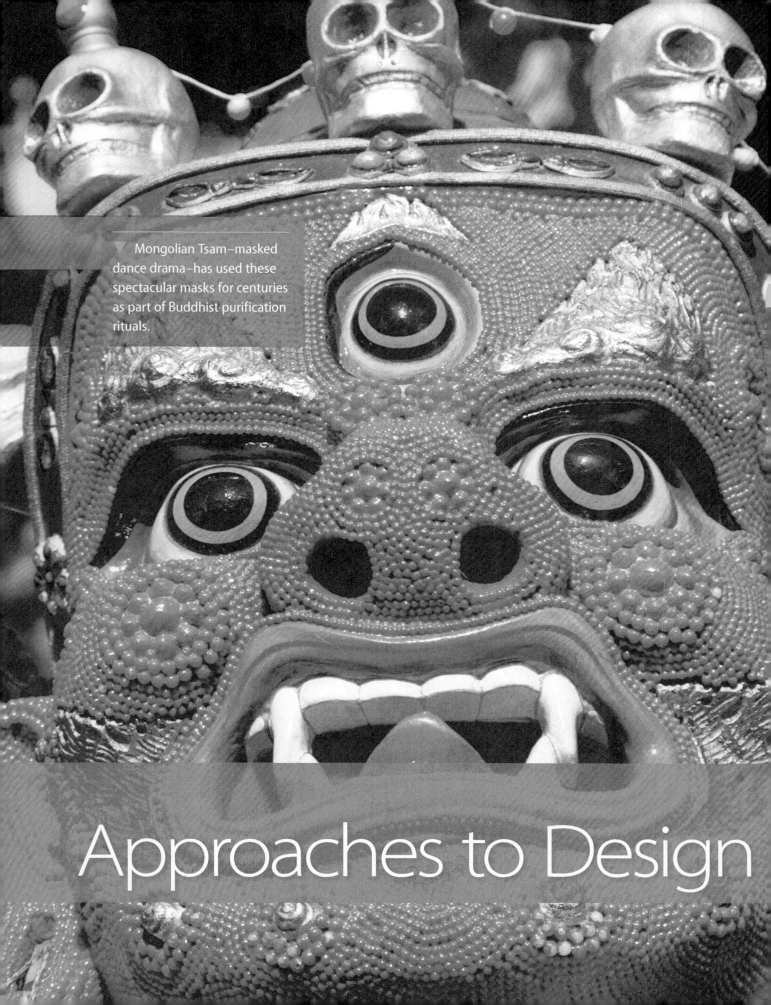

Mongolian Tsam–masked dance drama–has used these spectacular masks for centuries as part of Buddhist purification rituals.

Approaches to Design

Theatrical Design: Art and Technology in Partnership

Drumbeats, music, and cymbals. A shaft of golden light. A blood-splattered glass wall. A grotesque painted face. The theatre is a world of sights and sounds, textures, tones, and atmospheres that permeate our being. Around the globe, whatever the culture, theatre captivates the audience through the elements of sound and spectacle. The sensory world of the theatre speaks to us directly, and we interpret it more quickly and more viscerally than we do the spoken text.

Although the live actor and audience are the basic theatrical elements, it is almost impossible to see theatre unadorned by design. Some theatrical designs have come down to us through long and venerable traditions that continue to inspire the contemporary world. Performance traditions inherit design conventions that are relatively fixed and are passed down from generation to generation evolving slowly over time. Once we are familiar with these performance forms, we may only need to glimpse a costume or mask to identify what kind of performance we are about to see.

Designers in the interpretive tradition imagine the world of the stage afresh for each new production, so we may attend different productions of the same play and be constantly surprised by the visual and sound design. Designers work unfettered by tradition and are limited only by their own imaginations and the practicalities of the stage.

It is impossible to describe the world of theatrical design in the absence of technology. A theatre without technology would consist of a naked actor performing outside without costumes, props, sets, or musical instruments, in front of a group of naked spectators seated on the ground. All aspects of theatrical design, from simple props, lights, sets, sound, makeup, and costumes to elaborate special effects depend on technology at some level. Because design develops in a constant partnership with technology, innovation in design is often tied to technical advances.

Whatever its source, design can be subtle or dazzling and can draw us into the theatrical event. In the instant before a performance begins, we feel the mood of the piece before any action occurs. We read the sounds, colors, and textures and prepare emotionally for what will transpire on the stage. In the chapters ahead, we will look at theatrical design and its role in shaping the theatre experience. In this chapter we begin our discussion with the role of design in performance traditions.

1. In what ways does theatrical design affect audiences?

2. How are technology and theatre design connected?

3. How does the role of the designer differ in interpretive and performance traditions?

CHAPTER 10

Costume, Makeup, and Masks in Performance Traditions

WHAT role do costume, makeup, and masks play in performance traditions?

Performance traditions often highlight the sensory provocation of the theatrical event and are associated with particular visual and aural elements that are essential to understanding their dramatic world. When we see a *noh*, Chinese opera, or *commedia dell'arte* performance, we can identify the tradition immediately by its stage setting, costumes, sounds, masks, and makeup. Although these design features may have originally emerged from individual invention, they are now emblematic of the forms themselves.

Because the actor is so central in performance traditions, costumes, masks, and makeup are often the primary visual elements on stage and serve to enlarge the actor's presence. Chinese opera is a realm of rich colors and elaborate details, as seen in its brocade costumes and painted face characters. *Noh*, by contrast, is minimalist even in its silk kimonos that, despite their beautiful woven patterns, are relaxing to the eye. *Noh* reveals its essence in sublime wooden masks with slender painted lips and eyes. *Commedia* displays its earthy spirit in rough leather half-masks with grotesque features. Balinese performances are dynamic; masks can feature bulging eyes, enormous fangs, bold lines, and vibrant colors. The performers wear large headdresses and wide ornate collars over long robes. They perform with animated physical movements barefoot on the hard ground in or in front of open outdoor Hindu temples. These elements are more than mere adornment; they form a visual, symbolic language that describes the characters and their roles.

Costume

Traditional costumes convey important information about a character's age, temperament, social status, and relationships. They may differentiate young from old, peasants from nobility, and good from bad through conventions of color and style. In Iranian *ta'ziyeh*, discussed in Chapter 1, characters who support Hoseyn dress in green, and those who are against him wear red. The lighthearted patterns of *kyōgen* costumes, bearing images of peaches, radishes, turnips, dogs, and monkeys, reflect the servants' earthy qualities and contrast with the somber costumes of their masters and the rich, dignified robes of *noh*. *Commedia*'s Arlecchino (Harlequin) is immediately recognizable by the diamond-shaped pattern of his suit, which evolved from a patch-covered outfit reflecting his poverty.

▲ In this modern *commedia* recreation by the Picolo Teatro in Milan, Arlecchino (Harlequin) wears his traditional leather half mask and the diamond-patterned suit which has become the emblem of this character. The pattern is said to be reminiscent of the servant character's original patchwork garment of rags.

In *kabuki* a change of costume can indicate a change in a character's temperament or a moment of magical transformation. In *Narukami*, the title character, an ascetic, has ensnared the rain dragon and caused a drought. A seductive princess distracts him and frees the rain dragon, ending the drought and leading to Narukami's transformation into the Thunder God. Narukami's costume is transformed by stage hands who deftly pull out threads from the top of his pristine white kimono so that it falls forward to reveal a design of red flames. This trick, called *bukkaeri*, or "sudden change," is used in many *kabuki* plays to accomplish startling transformations in order to display a new dimension of the character before the audience's eyes. *Hikinuki*, or pulling of the threads, is a similar technique to effect onstage costume change.

Makeup and Masks

Makeup has been with us since antiquity and is seen on ancient artifacts in many cultures. Its first use seems to have been linked to religious ritual, and many theatrical forms that evolved from ritual use elaborate formal makeup patterns. Facial designs in performance traditions are often spectacular and draw the audience's focus to the actor's face, reinforcing the overt theatricality of the performance style. Conventions of color and pattern allow the audience to read the most abstract or ornamental designs. *Kathakali*'s imaginative, detailed makeup follows strict protocol, with the most refined, "green" characters—gods, kings, and heroes—identifiable by their green makeup base (see photo). *Katti*, or knife characters, are of a noble class but have an arrogant or evil nature, indicated by an upturned red mustache. There

▲ On the left, we see *kabuki* actor Danjuro XII in the title role of Narukami, before his transformation into the Thunder God and, on the right, afterward. Notice the metamorphosis of the hair, from tame to wild; the makeup, emboldened in the second picture; the costume, from plain white to flame-patterned; and the actor's gestures, from constrained to expansive. Narukami's costume is transformed by stage hands who deftly pull out threads from the top of his pristine white kimono so that it falls forward to reveal a design of red flames.

are also white-, red-, and black-bearded characters, whose colored beards communicate their status and dispositions. In Szechuan opera, painted face designs, already startling, create an even more dazzling effect when actors change from one design to another. Actors accomplish this change in the time it takes them to do a flip or turn, sometimes making several changes in a row.

The elaborate facial makeup of Chinese opera finds its roots in primitive religious rites in which participants donned animal skins and feathers to drive away spirits and disease. Such practices are thought to have contributed to the use of jackal, bear, and dragon masks during the warring states period (475–221 B.C.E.). These rites developed into theatrical performances, and during the Tang dynasty (618–907), actors wore masks to play ordinary people as well as gods, demons, and animals. During this period some performers began using makeup instead of masks to adorn their faces. Sometime between 960 and 1130, face painting overtook the use of masks in comic plays.

Early Chinese opera facial designs fell into two basic categories: simple makeup for basic male and female roles and more dynamic "parti-colored" painting for strong male roles such as generals and clowns. During the Yuan dynasty (1206–1368), the art of using makeup to emphasize character traits developed, and the Ming dynasty made facial patterns more complicated. As folk operas flowered throughout China during the nineteenth century, the dazzling and intricate facial designs of "painted face" characters fell into the more specific classifications used today.

Masks can refashion the face to the very limits of the imagination and make possible the portrayal of an entire cosmos of beings: people, animals, ghosts, gods, and devils.

Half-masks, like those of the *commedia dell'arte*, leave the mouth uncovered, allowing the actor to speak clearly. Some masks cover the whole head or the entire body, blurring the line between mask and costume. Traditional masks can be made of wood, papier-mâché, grass, or leather. The texture of the mask determines how an actor performs and how much it blends in with the human figure. Leather molds itself to the actor's face, while wood maintains its shape, putting more constraints on the actor's movement.

One set of wooden Chinese opera masks given as a gift to the emperor contained 800 masks, each with a unique design.

In Bali, only people considered ritually strong are chosen to wear the mask of the witch Rangda. These performers are blessed with holy water to protect them from Rangda's power, and the masks themselves are also empowered by religious rituals. In the past, at the end of Korean *pyolsandae* (masked dance performances), the players burned the masks. Perhaps this ritual originated as a way of exorcizing their spirits. Today the masks may be sold to tourists.

Throughout Africa powerful masks are used in ritual performance and have found their way into more secular theatrical activity. In West Africa, to achieve social unity, masks are often used satirically to depict members of outside tribal groups, and animals and spirits are often portrayed by masked actors, sometimes to comic effect.

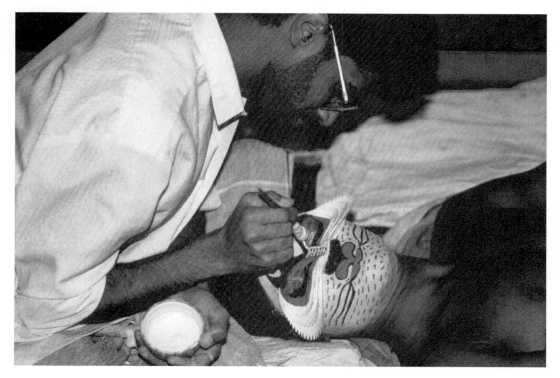

◄ A *kathakali* performer in Kerala, India, has makeup applied to his face as he prepares for the role of a lion-god. This makeup type falls in the category of *tēppu* or "special," designs used only for unique characters or animals. Like *kathakali* beards, the lion's white ruff was traditionally made of rice paste and today is cut from paper.

Chinese Opera Face Painting: Characters Revealed

Face painting in Chinese opera reveals character traits through patterns that divide the face along various lines and principal and subsidiary colors. In "principal color" patterns, used for positive characters, the face has one main color (red, black, or white) with minor touches added to the eyes, eyebrows, nose, and lips. Other basic face patterns include the "vertical-cross-front" pattern, in which a bold black cross organizes other design elements; the "three-tile pattern," which brings attention to the forehead and the cheeks; and the "saddle-shape" pattern or "half-face," usually used for low-class characters, which divides the face in two by focusing design around the eyes and eyebrows. "Parti-colored" pattern is the most complex; it expresses vileness or ferocity. "Clown pattern" uses only black and white and features a white patch between the eyes. "Animal-image" patterns depict the qualities associated with the animal, such as a rat image on a low-life thief.

Clowns with martial skills use one kind of pattern, "date-pit," while others use "bean-curd." "Abnormal-face" patterns distort the facial features and are used for odd or repulsive characters.

The colors in Chinese opera face painting reflect moral qualities and derive from traditional color associations. Red indicates loyalty and bravery; blue, valiance; purple, honesty; green, righteousness; black, uprightness; yellow, cruelty or sinisterness; and white, wickedness and deceit. Pink is used for elderly characters, and gold and silver are used for gods, demons, spirits, and monsters. These characters have some of the most fantastical designs, expressing their supernatural qualities.

Facial designs were developed for particular roles and often display the unique features of a specific character. Yang Yansi, a powerful black tiger god, has the Chinese character for "tiger" on his forehead. Cao Cao, a sinister figure, has a sword on his nose, showing his murderous intentions.

The hundreds of face painting patterns in Chinese opera are used in the over 300 forms of opera throughout China. These beautiful images are an art unto themselves, and molds of opera face patterns adorn the walls of Chinese homes and businesses.

▲ **Makeup patterns from the Chinese opera.** Four traditional makeup patterns from the Chinese opera are shown above. The aged clown is a *chou* role, while the other three designs fall under the category of *jing*, or painted-face characters.

Clowns Across Time and Culture

Clowns, iconic figures throughout the world, wear traditional costumes, masks, or face paint that herald their foolishness and irreverence. The very unconventionality of their dress is itself a convention codified by tradition. Particular clowns are immediately recognizable within their own societies. In America the word *clown* brings to mind the white face, red nose, big shoes, and baggy pants of the circus clown. The image is so well known that the red nose alone can be enough to transform an actor into a clown. Many Native American tribes recognize a clown mask by its crooked nose. Members of the Iroquois False Face Society wear wooden masks with a crooked nose and a twisted half-smile to perform exorcisms of demon diseases, while the Pueblo Indian clown is identified by black and white stripes painted across his entire body. In Medieval Europe, court jesters wore ass ears with bells and multicolored outfits. The *chou* clowns of the Chinese opera wear makeup with a white patch around the nose and eyes and a few black marks. Great performers leave their marks on clown types. Groucho Marx's bushy eyebrows, enlarged nose, painted mustache, and thick-rimmed glasses became the *commedia* Dottore mask for our time. The outrageous nature of their masks, makeup, and costumes allows clowns to comment on social norms by placing them outside normal behavioral expectations.

The clown or fool has existed in almost every society as far back as recorded history. These figures exist across time and cultures because they respond to the universal human need to be free of the constraints of social rules. Clowns always stand outside of mainstream society. From that position, they can comment on or transgress society's rules. We laugh at these transgressions, and this laughter provides us with a release valve for pent-up emotional energy. Often clowns are part of rituals that cement a society's value system. They can teach by bad example. Their very ability to break the rules also affirms the rules and values that govern normative behavior. The clown is free to express our profound longings and deepest anxieties—our need for love and companionship and our fear of death. The clown provides the wisdom that is beyond reason and the knowledge that is only obtained through instinct, intuition and proximity to the forces of nature. A clown can provide an ironic commentary on our lives, and the greatest wisdom often comes from the mouths of fools. Many Shakespearean fools see when wise men are blind.

▶ Many Native American tribes have ceremonial clowns who perform comic exorcisms. They might dance, whistle, sing, shake rattles, or throw cinders or water to chase away evil spirits and cure disease. Pictured here is an Iroquois Native American wearing a false face fright mask, as he kneels in the snow outside a reconstructed traditional Iroquois longhouse. These masks are carved from living trees and are thought to be inhabited by the spirits of the forest with the power to frighten away demons in order to cure illness.

(continued)

▲ Groucho Marx's clever wordplay makes a show of false erudition, while his anarchic spirit turns society's order on end. Marx took his clown character from vaudeville to Broadway, Hollywood, and television.

▲ A chou performer from the Jiangsu Provincial Opera performing for locals in Qufu, in Shandong Province, China. Clowns in Chinese opera speak more directly and colloquially to the audience than do other characters, and many are trained in martial arts and have a repertoire of martial and acrobatic stunts. Clowns can be traced back to some of the earliest Chinese performance traditions.

▶ At the International Clown Theatre Festival in Philadelphia, a clown from the Russian mime group Litsedi in Saint Petersburg wears the traditional red clown nose and makeup. Openly expressing his deepest yearning, this clown wears his heart on his sleeve.

Masked Enactments

The Dogon people live in a remote area of central Mali where a landscape of high cliffs makes travel difficult. Their rituals have therefore remained largely untouched by outside influences for hundreds of years.

The Dogon have a complex system of religious beliefs dominated by ancestor worship. Danced memorial ceremonies and funerals are held to allow the peaceful passage of the dead into the ancestral realm, which is viewed as necessary to ensure the security of the community. Master carvers create a variety of symbolic masks to be used in these ritual danced dramas.

Many cultures around the world use symbolic masks as part of religious ceremonies. These often evolve into secular dramatic enactments.

◀ Dogon men wear traditional Dogon masks to perform a dance in Sanga, Mali.

Sets, Lighting, and Sound Design in Performance Traditions

HOW do set, lighting, and sound conventions support the styles of different performance traditions?

Performance traditions have some of the most sumptuous, artistic, and tasteful stage designs in the theatrical world. Sets, lighting, and sound complement each other to create a singular theatrical environment. The design elements in these traditions have evolved a distinctive aesthetic each with its own dramatic impact.

Sets in **Performance** Traditions

Set elements tend to be sparse in actor-centered performance traditions, but every form has a particular kind of frugality and is governed by its own set of conventions. The two chairs, one table, and rug that are the sole set features of Chinese opera don't represent a particular setting, but the way actors use them can define almost any location from a room, to a mountain, to a temple. The rug can serve as padding for the benefit of acrobats or help establish the boundaries of the acting area. These simple portable pieces, which transform into any Chinese opera set at a moment's notice, suit the needs of this once itinerant tradition. *Commedia dell'arte* solved transportability issues and accommodated its outdoor venues with modest, elevated wooden platforms and a few painted backdrops. The stage of the *noh* theatre reflects the architecture of Shinto shrines with beautiful polished wood floors and an elegant roof. The few set pieces the *noh* does require—a tomb, a hut, or a cart—are made of natural materials and shaped into simple structures, preserving the open airy feeling of the stage. In each of these performance traditions, a few simple stage elements or props serve a variety of purposes.

The *kabuki* theatre, by contrast, has flamboyant sets, an exception within performance traditions. Its vast stage boasts vivid painted backdrops, constructed interiors, and even rotating platforms. Yet *kabuki* set design, however extravagant, is also based on established conventions. Specific designs are customary for particular plays or types of plays, and all highlight the performer. The actor's three-dimensional figure stands out against backdrops, which are intentionally painted with two-dimensional images that provide a background, but don't upstage the actors. When a large number of characters enter at once, stagehands may remove the sliding doors behind the actors to reveal an expansive landscape. The visual transformation makes the stage appear less crowded. Small set pieces, such as trees and rocks, appear only if actors interact with them, never just to decorate the space or indicate location. The *kabuki* stage, with its flower path jutting out into the audience, stretches beyond its scenery. It does not represent a realistic place, but presents a theatrical space appointed for the actor's use.

Lighting in **Performance** Traditions

Performance traditions predate electricity, and they have made use of natural light, candles, lamps, and torches for visibility and special effects. Only recently has electric stage lighting replaced some traditional practices, affording new options, but often at the expense of a form's inherent dramatic impact. At its inception in the seventeenth century, Indian *kathakali* drama took place outdoors at night, by the light of only a single oil lamp. The flickering of the flame in the dark cast eerie shadows and illuminated the actors' colorful makeup in magical ways that helped establish the mythic world of gods and heroes. Today, when *kathakali* performances take place in modern indoor auditoriums with electric lighting, that other-worldly quality can be lost. Traditional shadow theatres, such as those found in India and Indonesia, also take place at night, with only a single light source to project shadows on the screen. The surrounding darkness, the solitary flame, and the fluctuation of the shadows themselves lend these performances a sense of the supernatural. Some of this feeling has been lost today with a crisper electrical light.

In Indian *bhavai*, male actors playing female roles create provocative highlights and shadows on their faces. They attach candles inserted in a paper cup to the ends of the index and middle fingers. By moving the candles back and forth as part of their seductive dances, they serve as their own lighting designers and operators while they perform. With sari material covering their heads, their challenge includes not catching on fire while they dance. Other lighting sources for these performances included torches, now often replaced by halogen lights attached to poles or rooftops that weaken the effect.

One Table, Two Chairs: Innovating with Tradition

Zuni Icosahedron, a cultural collective in Hong Kong developing alternative theatre and multimedia performance, created the 1998 One Table, Two Chairs project. It invited directors to make new performances using the simple setup of traditional Chinese opera. Each director extracted a different theme from these basic elements. Hugh Lee, director of the Taiwan Pin-fong Acting Troupe, suspended the chairs and table from the ceiling where they rotated and evoked the instability of a shifting political situation. Movie director Stanley Kwan used these furnishings to tell the story of his relationship with his deceased father. One chair was placed behind a white screen and the other in front of the screen where rolls of film fell on it from above. A voice-over evoked the image of the father and son in the empty chairs. Hobin Park of JoBac Dance company saw "one table, two chairs" as embodying the smallest social unit. This theatrical experiment demonstrated how the basic unit of a venerated tradition can be transformed through innovative directorial concepts.

▼ In this scene from *In the Name of Lee Deng Hui...Dust to Dust, Ashes to Ashes,* directed by Hugh Lee in Taipei, the traditional Chinese theatre scenic elements of one table, two chairs are put to imaginative new use. Journey to the East 97" Festival– "One Table Two Chairs" Theatre Series.   *Curator: Danny Yung © Zuni Icosahedron*

Sound in **Performance** Traditions

The sounds of performance traditions are as iconic as the visual elements. They alert spectators to the beginning of a show, establish the mood of a scene, provide musical accompaniment for singing and dancing, and create aural effects that reinforce stage action. In France, the *trois coups* (three knocks of a stick against the stage floor) have alerted the audience to the start of a performance for centuries. Spectators can anticipate the opening of a *kabuki* performance by the clap of wooden sticks, which accelerates until it explodes in a crescendo of beats as stagehands run the curtain across the platform to reveal the stage. These wooden clappers also punctuate the actors' movements at climactic moments, just as the clang of cymbals and other percussion instruments underscore the physical actions of Chinese opera performers. In *commedia*, Arlecchino's flat wooden sword—his slapstick—helped him provide his own sound effects for the beatings he habitually received and gave. Drumbeats set the tone for all traditional African festival performances.

THINK

Do traditional forms need to adapt to new technologies to appeal to contemporary audiences and meet modern safety standards?

Specialized vocal techniques in performance traditions help actors establish and differentiate characters and aid projection. Each tradition has a distinctive sound. *Noh* performers chant in a low guttural hum, and Chinese opera singers employ a high-pitched nasal sound. A range of pitches and tones withvin each unique oral style allows for differentiation; the strong male characters of *kabuki* have deep, booming voices, and the female characters have high falsettos.

▲ *Kabuki* performances are punctuated throughout by the sound of *tsuke*, or wooden clappers, struck onto boards. Increasing beats alert spectators that the show is about to begin, and a *battari* sound accompanies the actors' *mies*, or dynamic poses.

Stanley Allan Sherman is a master crafts-man mask maker who specializes in leather masks for theatre, opera, dance, and wrestling. His masks were shown in a long-running exhibition at Lincoln Center Library of the Performing Arts in New York.

How did you become a mask maker?

I am self-taught. When I trained in mime at Ecole Jacques Lecoq in Paris, one of the assignments was to make a mask. After I graduated, I needed masks for my own shows and made them. A friend asked me to make him a leather *commedia dell'arte* mask. I said, "The only one who knows that skill is in Italy and he's dead." He guaranteed me payment, but I did not have to guarantee him a mask. I asked everyone I knew for advice. Carlo Mazzone-Clementi gave me many insights, and at two international leather conferences with leather craftsmen and artists from around the world, we all traded techniques, tips, and secrets of working with leather.

What kinds of masks do you make?

I make leather theatrical masks and am known for my *commedia dell'arte* masks as well as pro wrestling masks. I make masks for live performers and performances, opera singers, dancers, clowns, and films. That is very different from making decorative masks that exclusively hang on a wall. My masks come alive when a person puts them on. They are designed that way. So a somewhat unimpressive mask on a wall will become very powerful and amazing when a performer puts it on.

Can you describe the steps in your process?

I write a list of character elements, the emotions and colors I want the mask to express. Then I sketch the mask on paper. I then create a clay sculpture from which I make a mold that will shape the leather. Once the basic shape is given to the leather, there is drying, cutting, gluing, coloring, adding hair, and elastic.

How much innovation is permissible before you have violated a tradition?

When making *commedia dell'arte* masks, I am sculpting in a certain style. To be in the tradition, you must know the characters and have an idea of how they are performed. I base my mask making on the character and its range of emotion.

My biggest transformations or innovations have been in my pro wrestling masks. I developed what I call a free-floating-moveable-jaw so the characters can do anything they want and the mask stays on. When I developed the Mankind Mask for the then WWF, I saw from watching the performer that the performance was at least 65 percent talk, so sight, air flow, comfort, wrestling safety, and the mask staying on when wrestling are all issues. But I also drew upon *commedia dell'arte*. Only a handful of people know this, but the Mankind Mask I made is basically a form of a modern Arlecchino.

Since you are also a performer, do you physically become the character as you work?

Being a performer is a major advantage to a mask maker. I know how the mask works; I know what needs to be added and not added to the design. I know what to avoid. But the only way to make a great mask is to become the character. I must move around, jump, talk, sing, walk, and whatever else this creation that I am giving life to will do. I am the first person to be any of the mask characters, and I perform it before that mask has ever taken a shape. I become the mask and live as the mask in whatever world that mask is going to be as I am creating.

Source: Used with permission of Stanley Allan Sherman.

◄ Maskmaker Stanley Allan Sherman puts the finishing touches on a leather *commedia dell'arte* mask.

Master Artisans in Performance Traditions

In performance traditions, set, costume, and mask designs have generally developed over time, so there are no designers creating new costumes and sets for a particular production based on their own unique interpretation. Instead, we find craftspeople building the sets, props, masks, and costumes, bringing the visual elements of living traditions to the stage. In some forms, master artisans bring a lifetime of study and artistry to their work.

In Bali, talented mask makers gain a reputation on the island, and performers seek them out and commission their masks. The masks sold to tourists do not generally have the same artistry or sturdiness as those made for performance, which entail ritual practices as part of their construction to give them power. Because Balinese masked performance depends on improvisation, new masks can find a way into performance, such as the recent addition of a mask of a Western tourist. These new characters invite mask makers to develop their own visions, but they must first master traditional forms.

> **Masterful execution of established designs is of greater value than originality in all these forms.**

Within the world of *kabuki*, every job is highly specialized, and many years of training are required for those making *kabuki* sets, props, costumes, and wigs. Both the masks and kimonos of *noh* are made by master craftspeople proficient in the art who pass down their skills and artistic reputation. *Commedia* mask makers also study special techniques for crafting leather masks on a carved wooden mold; would-be mask makers learn as apprentices.

In performance traditions there are also personnel who take care of the material objects of the performance. Some are in charge of setting up the stage, replacing items that have been damaged, or cleaning and caring for items between productions. Amateurs, trained professionals, or the actors themselves may take on these tasks. By preserving the stage artifacts, they preserve their traditions.

Western Stage Design Before the Interpretive Model

WHAT traditions characterized Western stage design before the interpretive model?

In Europe, before the mid-nineteenth century, established conventions governed set and costume choices. These design conventions have not been passed on to us as performance codes, but they were part of the expectations of audiences of the time. Theatrical designers adhered to these conventions and did not see themselves as interpreters of a specific play. Often design choices were left to actors and company managers and resulted from practical necessity more than specific artistic choices.

In ancient Greece and Rome, the architectural wall behind the actors served as a stage set for every play. For example, in Roman comedy the plays were set outside, and the permanent architectural portals on the theatre's back wall represented the doors of the houses where the action took place. It is believed that entering from stage right indicated that a character had come from the town, and entering from stage left indicated that the character had come from the harbor. Actors wore everyday Greek dress for plays set in Greece and daily Roman dress for those set in Rome. Their masks, wigs, and costumes depicted stock characters who were immediately recognizable to the audience. Slaves wore red wigs, old men wore grey wigs, young men wore black ones, and courtesans wore yellow.

In the Middle Ages, costume and set elements for religious dramas were based on iconic imagery from painting and sculpture. The Virgin Mary always wore a blue robe; devils had horns, tails, and other beastlike features; the shepherds of Bethlehem dressed like their counterparts in the European countryside; and God wore the regal robes of an emperor. The sets for productions, placed inside churches for liturgical dramas or on outdoor pageant wagons for religious cycle plays, used stage elements that evoked familiar biblical stories—an apple tree for the Garden of Eden or a cross for the crucifixion—rather than detailed locations.

During the Renaissance, when theatre moved indoors, Italian stage design adopted artistic innovations learned from new experiments in perspective drawing. Professional artists painted detailed wings, drops, and stage floors to create the illusion of a three-dimensional world receding toward a central vanishing point beyond the limits of the actual stage. These sets were visually impressive and functioned as a backdrop for the actors. If performers stepped too far upstage, they could easily disrupt the illusion and scale. These designs were not text specific: The front of a palace suited any tragedy; a city street suited any comedy. Lighting was of course limited by the technology of the times to candles and oil lamps and for the most part was used only for general illumination of the stage and the performers. Actors in comedy and tragedy wore contemporary fashions on stage and usually supplied their own costumes. When appropriate, togas or tunics and helmets evoked the classical world, and exotic costumes represented Asia and the Americas. European court performances and the entertainments that evolved from them were more fanciful, reflecting courtly opulence. Courtiers or kings often participated, dressed as Greek and Roman gods or allegorical figures such as Power or Sovereignty. Sets might represent the heavens, and some sets had special effects that were accompanied by music and sound.

These basic conventions of stage design with generic sets for particular genres continued to be the norm in Europe through the eighteenth century. Many theatres maintained a stock of sets and costumes that were reused for many plays. During the seventeenth and eighteenth centuries in Europe, spectators often sat on the stage—their presence making it impossible for actors to perform in a realistic environment. Experiments in multiple vanishing points, mood painting, and greater historical accuracy did begin a movement toward more specificity in visual elements, but for the most part, calls for the truthful portrayal of everyday life were ignored until the nineteenth century. On the whole, costume and set were only loosely connected to a play's time and location or to particular characters and themes.

Interest in greater realistic and historical detail grew during the nineteenth century. Painted wings and backdrops gave way to a three-walled box set with three-dimensional set pieces that could actually be used by actors. Midcentury theatre managers engaged designers to create sets, costumes, and wigs for particular plays. Improvements in lighting—first gas and then electrical—allowed actors to recede into the stage environment instead of playing in front of it. Ultimately, naturalistic plays and the rise of the director demanded increasing specificity in the stage world. By the twentieth century, European and American stage designers were creating specific designs that interpreted a director's vision of a text and unified all of the production elements. Today, set, costume, lighting, and sound designers collaborate in an interpretive model of stage design, realizing a complete and unique concept for every production.

Contemporary Western Stage Design

As we have seen throughout this book, in every era and in every society, people construct a vision of the world that reflects cultural beliefs and values, and the theatre captures these changing constructs. In some periods, one particular set of stage conventions dominates the theatre, and as a result we say that that period had a particular style. The design conventions we discussed in the previous section were accepted as natural or truthful in their own time. Nowhere is theatrical style made more tangible than in the elements of design, so the history of design reflects the changing ways people view the world and the human condition.

Illusions of Reality

The two photos on this page show a transition in design from naturalism to selective realism. In the photo from the 1905 production of *Girl of the Golden West*, a female saloon owner plays poker to save the man she loves. The environment—the fully delineated walls, floor, furniture, clothing, fur pelts, and bric-a-brac—so completely represents the location and time that we could mistake it for a room in the real world. The set is evocative of the replication of reality in early films, and the growth of film partially explains the shift away from detailed naturalism in the theatre, as film could of course capture every photographic detail of the real world better than any stage set could. In the second photo we see a 2004 staging of *Joe Turner's Come and Gone*. The play is set in 1911 Pittsburgh. In this production, we find realistic details in the wooden table and the floor treatment, but the bric-a-brac in the room only suggests some of what we might find in such a home. The frame of the house is visible; the floor is not fully covered; and the walls are merely

▲ *Girl of the Golden West* was written and directed by David Belasco in 1905 and featured Blanche Bates and Frank Keenan. Belasco was known for his naturalistic stage effects.

skeletal structures. These features allow us to see beyond them to the adjacent room, and beyond the house to the outside world, where industrial smokestacks, symbolic of the social change that dominates the characters' lives, can be seen in the background. Rather than slavishly reproduce every feature of a scene, realistic design in theatre today selects key elements to telegraph significant information about the world of the play.

◀ This 2004 performance of August Wilson's *Joe Turner's Come and Gone* at the Saint Louis Black Repertory Company was directed by Andrea Frye. *2011 Stewart Goldstein*

Identifying a style enables us to understand the theatre of other times and places and the forces that shaped a particular world view. Style provides a conceptual and aesthetic frame for the events on stage and offers us convenient labels for describing the stage world and the way actors behave within this artificial "reality." Today, actors, directors, and designers explore texts and choose from a multiplicity of stylistic approaches so that each production finds its own visual language. It is perhaps this freedom to mix an eclectic visual vocabulary that best defines contemporary style.

Realistic Design

When all that we see and hear on stage closely resembles the natural world, we are in the presence of a style called *realism*. In realistic designs, set, costume, light, and sound are used to depict a specific location, time, and social milieu that explains the behavior of the characters. Solid three-dimensional elements such as furniture, trees, and boulders are part of a habitable environment in which characters can conduct themselves seemingly as they do in life. The concrete reality of a play's universe is expressed in every sensory element on stage, and the psychology, temperament, habits, and tastes of characters are further conveyed in the costumes actors wear. All is seen under stage lights that attempt to reproduce naturally occurring light sources. The dramatic action is accompanied by the sounds of the real world. Of course, despite the imitation of reality, realism is not any more real than any other stage design and is actually a created environment composed of carefully selected elements that communicate meaning.

THINK

If you lift all the elements of a set from real life, is it designed? Is the simple act of selection an act of design?

During the late nineteenth and early twentieth centuries, a detailed and heightened realistic style called *naturalism* was used to create vivid replicas of the real world on stage. These productions and their designs were intended to scientifically expose the truth about social ills. They were influenced by the new field of sociology and by Darwin's ideas about the effect of the conditions of life. Often actual rooms were moved from stores, restaurants, and houses to create precise environments for particular plays. Eventually naturalism was replaced with realism. Realism incorporated purposefully chosen representative elements of the natural world, rather than trying to replicate every detail of a setting. We identify both naturalism and realism as *representational* styles because they both attempt to represent or re-create the real world on stage. These representational styles contrast with *presentational* stage worlds that make no attempt to disguise their theatricality or create an illusion of reality.

Abstract Design

As a reaction to naturalism and its detailed literal depiction of reality, artists in many fields began to assert that there was a beauty beyond the objects of the everyday world, and a higher truth—that could not be found in the objects of real life. They believed that sensory provocation could lead to meanings and associations not found in the concrete objects of life, much the way the words and images in poetry can lead to a more profound sense of the world than narrative text. Designers influenced by these ideas began to conceive of the stage as a symbolic realm of evocative meanings and sensory provocation. *Symbolism* became the first theatrical movement to embody these concepts, using color, texture, and light and sometimes even smells to express the essence of a play. For example, during the last decade of the nineteenth century, aided by advances in lighting, early symbolist designers sometimes presented scenes through veiled gauze and colored lights, in a perfumed theatre which gave the impression of entering a realm of dreams and was intended to connect

"A good scene should be, not a picture, but an **image."**

—Robert Edmund Jones, *The Dramatic Imagination*, 1941.

the audience to unconscious feelings and ideas, a world beyond the real.

In the first decades of the twentieth century, Adolphe Appia (1862–1928) and Edward Gordon Craig (1872–1966) developed the work of the symbolists in their expressive use of light and shadow on stage. Appia saw the actor as a three-dimensional object that moved in a three-dimensional world, and he designed sculptural sets (see the nearby box Modernism in Design). This was in marked contrast to the flat painted backdrops of the past. Appia saw light as the force that could unite the actor with the stage environment. Craig further developed these ideas, working with textures and colors. He designed sets made of movable screens that could move with the actors and scenic changes. These ideas are still part of the design vocabulary of contemporary set and light designers.

Expressionism was a movement related to symbolism that reached its high point between 1910 and 1925. It captured emotional force through its dramatic use of angles, lines, and distortions to portray the world as perceived by the inner character. This reflected contemporary developments in psychology, particularly the work of Freud. Many expressionists believed truth was found in the mind's perceptions, not in the objective external world. Expressionism influenced films of the times, and its aesthetic can still be felt in the subjective use of camera angles and focus.

Expressionism and the collection of artistic movements and styles that developed in the early twentieth century had roots in the nineteenth century's rejection of realism. These movements and styles are sometimes collectively referred to as *modernism*. The hallmarks of modernism are a belief in progress, a celebration of innovation and the materials of the industrial world, and a rejection of art that simply attempts to reproduce objective reality. Modernists proposed that color, texture, and pure form could directly express emotions and even the intangible truths and hieroglyphs of the unconscious mind. Set designs that suggested meaning through nonrepresentational forms emerged. Eventually even human beings were reduced to abstract forms, and many early Modernist movements experimented with costume design that turned performers into geometric objects moving through space. Constructivist designers, inspired by industrial structures, created functional sets using scaffolding, wooden platforms, and metal pipes, turning the stage into an abstract machine in which actors worked like cogs in a wheel (see the photos on page 252–253).

> **The hallmarks of modernism are a belief in progress, a celebration of innovation and the materials of the industrial world, and a rejection of art that simply attempts to reproduce objective reality.**

The high point of modernism in theatrical design occurred when the Ballets Russes engaged a group of renowned modern artists as the creative team for the production of *Parade* (1917). Pablo Picasso (1881–1973) created the set and costumes. The surrealist Jean Cocteau (1892–1963) wrote the scenario, and the impressionist Erik Satie (1866–1925) composed the music. This inspired many other great modern painters—Henri Matisse (1869–1954), Georges Braque (1882–1963), and Juan Gris (1887–1927), among others—to apply concepts from artistic movements in the fine arts to theatrical design. The influence of this work can be felt today in the sets of many contemporary designers who continue to use color, line, form, and movement beyond the confines of realism.

During the 1920s, the impact of the European modernist movements was expressed in the United States in what came to be known as the **new stagecraft**. Robert Edmund Jones (1887–1954), Lee Simonson (1888–1967), and Norman Bel Geddes (1893–1958) were the most influential American designers calling for a renewed theatricality in the visual world. The naturalism that had dominated the American stage gave way to more modernist approaches. Eventually, realistic and abstract design borrowed from each other's vocabulary. Many American theatrical designers followed a theatrical realism, while others continued to design in more abstract forms.

> **"Scenography is the seamless synthesis of space, text, research, art, actors, directors and spectators that contributes to an original creation."**
>
> —Pamela Howard, *What Is Scenography* (London: Routledge, 2002), 130

Collaboration and the **Evolution** of Contemporary **Design**

Today designers are free to borrow, combine, and juxtapose elements from various conceptual movements, traditions, and cultures. Stylistic eclecticism is the hallmark of postmodernism and defines a shift in sensibility from earlier periods. New technologies have opened up untold design possibilities with mixed media. With access to images from every culture past and present and the benefit of global cultural exchanges, designers have a varied palette of visual vocabularies and stage techniques from which to draw. These can merge and cross-fertilize or remain distinct. Designers are called on to realize a written play text as well as alternative forms of performance. The result is productions with their own visual styles, unique unto themselves and the designer's imagination.

Today, many designers call themselves scenographers. They take a holistic approach to the production and see themselves as creators and orchestrators of the entire visual world—sets, costumes, and lights—and co-creators of the production concept. This challenges the traditional hierarchy of the theatre, which typically features a director at the helm of a creative project, aided by a team of designers who realize the directorial concept. Often scenographers cross over into directing. In Europe the title *scenographer* is more common than it currently is in the United States. American theatre for the most part perpetuates the model of directors working with separate set, costume, and lighting designers. However, many stage design training programs in the United States now insist that design students study all visual aspects of a performance.

Modernism in Design

Painted pictorial realism dominated theatrical design from the Renaissance through most of the nineteenth century. Illusions of perspective were rendered on flat surfaces. Actors did not interact with their stage world but performed, for the most part, in front of a painted set. As stage lighting improved, first through gas and later through electricity, actors were able to move away from the front of the stage.

Adolphe Appia, the Swiss designer, sought a way to unite the three-dimensional actor with the two-dimensional scenic design. He started by envisioning the stage space in three dimensions and considering its volume and mass as he designed. To achieve his goals, he employed steps, ramps, and platforms that were usable by the actor. There was minimal painted detail. The resulting sculp-tural set could then harmonize with the sculpted body of the actor. He underscored the importance of lighting as the art that could unite the actor with the space. Today we take for granted the idea of three-dimensional sculptural sets, but it was revolutionary in the 1890s.

During the early decades of the twentieth century, many great visual artists were actively involved in designing for the theatre. Pablo Picasso, Henri Matisse, and Georges Braque are just a few of the many painters whose work graced both the stage and art galleries. This group of avant-garde artists brought the new aesthetic of modernism to the theatre, replacing pictorial realism with pictorial abstraction. These early abstract works were still based on objects in the real world. Cubism, seen in Picasso's designs for *Parade*, attempted to capture multiple perspectives on the same object simultaneously by breaking the subject down into basic geometric shapes.

Eventually modern art moved away from abstractions of objects found in the real world to pure abstraction. Geometric shapes and colors and architectural forms replaced any attempt to render reality. Sculptors began to use a variety of unusual materials—wood, glass, tin, cardboard, nylon, plaster—juxtaposing materials and textures as well as shapes and colors. The great Russian director Vsevolod Meyerhold (1874–1940), who developed an intense physical training system to make the actor an efficient worker in the theatre, saw these sculptural pieces as the ideal set for his stage direction. Lyubov Popova (1889–1924), a leading female artist of

▲ Note the absence of any realistic detail and the three-dimensional use of space that allows the actor to work within the sculptural set in Adolphe Appia's design for the descent into the underworld from Christoph Willibald Gluck's *Orpheus and Eurydice* in 1912.

(continued)

the Russian avant-garde, designed her set for Meyerhold's production of *The Magnanimous Cuckhold* (1922) with wheels, steps, catwalks, ramps, and windmills, to capture the dynamism of the new age and its new actor. As you will see in Chapter 11, the ideas of these early pioneers in modernism are still present in scenic design today.

◄ Lyubov Popova's design for Vsevelod Meyerhold's production of *The Magnanimous Cuckhold* in Moscow in 1922 was an abstract sculptural composition with moving elements that could act as a functional machine for actors.

▲ Leonide Massine's ballet *Parade*, originally produced by the Ballets Russes in 1917, is shown here in a reconstruction by the Joffrey Ballet. The costume, which covers the actor in the photo, was over 10 feet tall. The production captured the "new spirit" of modernism.

The Lion King: Integrating Tradition and Invention

Julie Taymor's visual conceptualization of *The Lion King* (1997) is an example of stage design borrowing elements from different traditions and cultures to create something unique, dazzling, and fresh. In this production, the design inspires the movement and the acting, and the entire event becomes a visual feast in which costume, set, lighting, and performance become an integrated form.

The lion masks mix African mask features with Taymor's own sculptural style. African geometric motifs decorate the bodies of jungle animals. Textures such as fiber, wood, grass, and cloth lift the characters out of their cartoon world and integrate them into the natural environment. The yellows of the savannah setting, the greens of the jungle world, and the grays of the elephant graveyard are the colors of the African landscape. The scene at times comes to life with an explosion of colors and forms drawn from African festival designs. Other aspects of Taymor's design—such as the shadow puppets, the *bunraku*-style puppets, and the streamers pulled from the eyes of masks to represent tears and grief—are influenced by Asian theatrical forms.

Taymor's emphasis on the human dimension of the story of *The Lion King* creates a stage world in which actors play both flora and fauna and in which the human presence is visible in every costume, mask, and puppet. Dancers in striped leotards blend into the zebra figures they carry, their own legs serving as the animals' front legs. Performers portraying giraffes walk on stilts, supporting headdresses that are the animals' long necks and tiny heads. Singers wearing palettes of grass on their heads rise out of the stage floor, bringing the savannah to life; Timon, a comic meerkat, is a life-size puppet operated by a performer in a green outfit and green makeup. His costume gives the character an ever-present foliage backdrop. Dancers adorned with leaves lie on the floor or hang like vines from above to create the jungle setting.

Highly mechanized effects, operated by sophisticated computer consoles, play alongside less elaborate, but equally theatrical, displays. Pride Rock, the lion king's throne, is a large ramp that rotates in a spiral as it rises from the stage. Daybreak is depicted by a large unfolding cloth sun that rises from the stage floor to loom over the savannah. Its blue mirror image on the floor is a watering hole; drought is indicated by pulling it down through the stage floor from its center.

Rich saturated lighting, designed by Donald Holder, transforms the sets with deep oranges and yellows for the heat of a savannah sunrise and purples

THINK

When borrowing design elements from traditional forms, must the cultural significance they carry be acknowledged, or can they simply be recontextualized within new forms?

for a cool jungle evening. At a crucial moment in the story, lighting, props, and dance all come together to produce the image of the dead lion king's face emerging from the starry sky. The production combines Elton John and Tim Rice's pop tunes with the South African vocal music of Lebo M. Time-honored theatrical tradition, new popular forms, the latest technology, and creative invention merge in *The Lion King*.

Summary

WHAT role do costume, makeup, and masks play in performance traditions?   p. 236

▶ Performance traditions feature inherited design conventions. Each performance tradition is associated with particular visual and aural elements that have become emblematic of the form.

▶ In actor-centered traditions, colorful dress, masks, and makeup convey important information about character through a visual, symbolic language. Set elements tend to be sparse.

HOW do set, lighting, and sound conventions support the styles of different performance traditions?   p. 243

▶ In performance traditions the set, lighting and sound often evolved with the needs of the actor.

▶ In performance traditions master craftspeople build the sets, masks, and costumes. The skillful execution of established designs is often of greater value than originality.

WHAT traditions characterized Western stage design before the interpretive model?   p. 247

▶ Europe had design conventions that characterized the theatrical design style of certain periods.

▶ In Europe, in the late nineteenth and early twentieth centuries, naturalistic plays and the emergence of the director gave rise to the interpretive design tradition. In the Western interpretive tradition, the world of the stage can be imagined in a new way for each new production.

WHAT conventions characterize contemporary Western stage design?   p. 248

▶ In realistic stage design, all that we see and hear on stage closely resembles the natural world.

▶ Modernism reacted against realism's search for truth in everyday reality. The impact of European modernist movements was expressed in the United States in the *new stagecraft*.

▶ Today designers borrow, combine, and juxtapose elements from various conceptual movements, traditions, and cultures. They work in a collaborative process to create the world the characters will inhabit.

MySearchLab®

▼ Walt Spangler's 2009 award-winning set for *Desire Under the Elms*, directed by Robert Falls, with its 9-ton levitating house and 200-boulder set, was a perfect metaphor for a troubled family with hardscrabble lives.

Setting the Stage

Designing the Characters' World

The idea that production design should be unique and specific for each theatrical event emerged from the Western theatrical tradition. Today, the set designer as the visual interpreter of a particular play or performance text is common around the globe. A good set design is not just aesthetically interesting or pleasing for its own sake, but functional, evocative, and deeply connected with a total production concept. The set is a kinetic element through which actors move and the audience's eye travels. If the set itself moves, it can establish performance rhythm, and it always both surrounds and inspires the actors' actions.

In life we enter rooms and hear sounds without responding to each detail. But place your bedroom on stage, and it suddenly becomes full of hidden meanings. What book is on the night table? Is the bed unmade? Are clothes neatly folded or thrown on the floor? Are there bottles of pills on the dresser? Are the blinds or shades up or down? All that we take for granted, when placed on stage, fills with import. As audience members, we start asking ourselves questions about the characters that inhabit the space. Who is the person who lives in the messy room with shuttered windows and empty junk food packages strewn about? Suddenly we hear the screech of car brakes and that familiar sound of urban life becomes a signal—a portent of dramatic action to come.

Although most of the time the world around us is assembled haphazardly, at particular moments we decide to take control of the messages our world communicates about us. You may have chosen a piece of music to play when a date arrived to create a particular impression or mood. Perhaps you left an interesting book open, rearranged furniture, or cleaned the room. You may have turned down the lights or lit candles to create a romantic atmosphere. We have all chosen items of clothing to express aspects of our personality or to indicate how sexually appealing we are. Just as you try to set a mood and create a portrait of yourself and your world through the deliberate selection of visual and sound elements, in a similar fashion, designers create a portrait of an imaginary world inhabited by characters through the careful selection of visual and aural signals of meaning. These signals serve as clues that the audience will read as they interpret the action on stage.

1. From what theatre tradition emerged the idea that production design should be unique and specific for each theatrical event?

2. What determines the elements designers place in the imaginary world on stage?

3. How does set design contribute to the totality of the theatrical experience?

Goals of **Set** Design

A set designer's first encounter with a dramatic text is much the same as what we experience when we read a play and imagine the world the characters will inhabit in our mind's eye. But designers must take those mental images and turn them into concrete forms that serve all the needs of the text in real three-dimensional space. To turn words into images and arrive at a completed design, set designers must excel at script analysis. They must unearth the details of the characters' lives and environment, and they must create a shared vision of that world with the director and the other members of the design team. They must also make sure this world is habitable by the actors, possible within the architectural constraints of the theatre, and realizable within the production budget.

Set designers are communicators, sketch artists, researchers, drafters, model-makers, technicians, and leaders. Every step of the way, they must remember that the audience will read every visual element for significance and that each choice they make as designers contributes to the theatrical experience and the telling of a story. To that end, the set design process has several goals, which we describe in this section in some detail.

such as the number and placement of entrances and exits, changes in location, and important set elements that take part in the action. In Georges Feydeau's (1862–1921) farce *A Flea in Her Ear* (1907), the fast-paced action of more than 200 comings and goings of characters trying to catch each other in a sexual encounter while escaping discovery by spouses and lovers requires a number of doors and corridors. Molière's *Tartuffe* has a character hiding in an armoire to eavesdrop, so the position of this set piece is crucial to the action. In Sarah Kane's (1971–1999) *Blasted* (1995), the first act takes place in a hotel room; explosions later tear apart the walls of the room to reveal a civilization in ruin. Therefore, the set designer needs to create a set that can be completely destroyed each night and yet be easily reconstructed for the next performance. (Read about Louisa Thompson's solution to this problem in the "Artists in Their Own Words" box on page 264.) The requirements of the dramatic action become part of the set designer's vision and often are the source of inspiration for the actors.

> **"**I began to read a **script** as though I were going to direct it **myself**. This did not turn me into a **director**, but it did make me a better **designer."**
>
> —Jo Mielziner (1901–1976), Tony Award–winning theatre designer

Goals of set design:

- Facilitates the dramatic action
- Establishes time and place
- Provides an environment that embodies the characters' lives
- Tells the story
- Presents a visual metaphor
- Creates mood
- Defines style
- Determines the relationship between audience and action

Facilitating the **Dramatic Action**

A set must *serve the text and the performance*. Every set should provide a playable space that allows actors to move about and make their entrances and exits freely. Since the set will either limit or open possibilities for physical action, set designers consider a text carefully to make note of all special needs,

Establishing **Time** and **Place**

The set can tell us *when* the action is unfolding—the era, the time of year, and the time of day. A medieval castle, a high-tech office, and a flourishing garden all relate information about time. Sometimes set designers strive to remove the play from any particular time period by deliberately avoiding any defining elements. *Waiting for Godot* is often placed in a no-man's-land outside traditional time periods to express the continuity of the human condition.

The set can also tell us *where* the action is happening—what part of the world and what kind of environment we are in, indoors or outdoors, in a natural environment or an urban setting. Design can tell us what type of building, home, or room we are in. In *The Lion King* the African settings include the open savannah with its jutting Pride Rock, an elephant's graveyard infested with vicious hyenas, and a lush jungle for carefree characters. The cramped urban apartment of *A Streetcar Named Desire* sets the scene for the explosive events in that play, just as aging Russian country estates set the scene for the declining aristocracy depicted in many of Chekhov's plays.

Providing an **Environment** That Embodies the **Characters' Lives**

Set designers enter the characters' world and express in visual terms the religious, political, economic, or social rules that govern it. Federico García Lorca's (1898–1936) *House of Bernarda Alba* (1935) depicts a world imprisoned by Spanish Catholic doctrine. Bernarda Alba holds her five daughters at home under lock and key for an eight-year period of strict mourning. Forbidden social activities and intimate relationships, the daughters watch their youth recede inside the house that has become a jail cell. A set that expresses this feeling of oppression helps the actors live the reality of their situation and gives the audience a sensory experience of the characters' longings.

> **Whether the stage environment is historically accurate, invented by the playwright, or redefined by the director, it determines how the characters act and whether they are constrained or free.**

A set immediately relays information about the people who live within it. Class, taste, education, personality, and occupation are all revealed by the physical environment. The characters' emotional state can be captured by the placement of walls and objects. Realistic sets try to capture the specific details of the environment that can enable us to understand the characters' actions and desires (see "Designing the Character's World" on page 258). In David Lindsay-Abaire's (b. 1969) *Rabbit Hole* (2007) , the characters' comfortable upper-middle-class home is seen in contrast to their emotional world turned on end by personal tragedy. *Brighton Beach Memoirs* (1983), by Neil Simon (b. 1927), takes place in 1937, so the set design must reflect the economic hardship and the aspiration for better things to come at the end of the Great Depression.

> **The designer must mine the play for information about the characters and their environment that can be translated into a visual world on stage.**

Telling the **Story**

The set can chart the characters' physical or emotional journey. In Chekhov's *The Cherry Orchard* (1904), an aristocratic family facing financial pressures and changing times is forced to sell its estate to a former servant. Returning from a trip abroad at the start of the play, they pull the dust cloths off the elegant furnishings that fill their home. In the final scene, the family has lost its estate, and the set, reflecting that loss, is almost bare. The set thus provides the visual expression of the characters' changing circumstances.

Presenting a **Visual Metaphor** for the **Director's Concept**

The set captures in concrete form the abstract ideas present in a work that govern the director's choices. David Rockwell's set design for *Hairspray* (2002) framed the set with a

▶ Timothy Brown's set for Henrik Ibsen's *The Master Builder* at Yale Repertory Theatre (2009) uses an iconic house as a metaphor for an architect's failed dreams. Costumes are by Katherine Akiko Day, with lighting by Paul Whitaker, and sound and original music by Scott L. Nielsen.

metaphorical curtain of hair. In the set for *Thoroughly Modern Millie* (2002), David Gallo provided a backdrop of the city that shapes the characters' dreams. Walt Spangler's 2009 set for *Desire Under the Elms* (see the chapter-opening photo) levitates the house over the action, as a menacing presence and reminder of the strained family ties. The rough-hewn set piled high with boulders becomes a metaphor for the hard-scrabble lives of the characters and the insurmountable obstacles they face to escape their destiny, just as the house that dominates Timothy Brown's 2009 set for Ibsen's *The Master Builder* (1892) becomes a metaphor for the architect's dreams and failures.

Creating **Mood**

Design elements can capture the emotional tone of a production. We often know in an instant whether we are at a comedy or a tragedy by the feeling of the stage environment. Somber, heavy architectural elements create a different feeling from light, airy, open space. Edward Gorey's somber neo-Gothic sets for *Dracula* (1977) were filled with motifs of skulls and bats to set the tone for the horror tale. Scott Pask's 2003 set for *Little Shop of Horrors* featured angled buildings and off-kilter walls (see the photo in Chapter 13), giving us the sense of something amiss in the world. Walt Spangler's 2009 set for *The Importance of Being Earnest* (see the photo on page 266) clearly let the audience know immediately that they were watching a stylized comedy.

Defining **Style**

The set designer manipulates stage conventions to create a visual style—or look—for the set that reflects the director's concept and approach to acting and movement. The set designer can choose to use the conventions of realism by creating the appearance of real rooms and places for actors behaving in seemingly natural ways. Or the stage can be a place of abstraction, using ramps, platforms, and geometrical or symbolic objects, where actors can behave in an artificial, exaggerated, or aestheticized manner. The angled house in the 2009 production of *The Master Builder* (see the photo on page 257) represents the worthlessness of what the architect has attained and the castles in the sky that he will never build, and it sets the mood and style for the play's symbolist drama. Its unusual placement tells us we are not watching a realistic play and enables the audience to accept the strange events in the play. Sometimes directors request a particular stylistic approach to the visual design and direct the actors in a style that contrasts with the design to heighten certain meanings in the text. The very familiar bourgeois living room of the absurdist play *The Bald Soprano* is set off by the anomalous behavior of the characters to reveal the deeper truths of our daily lives (see the photo on page 57 in Chapter 3). Style also reflects genre. The colors and proportions chosen for a comedy are different from those for a serious drama, so the set prepares us visually for the dramatic content. Walt Spangler's set for *The Importance of Being Earnest* (see the photo on page 266) captures the whimsy and lighthearted spirit of the comedy with its giant flowers and set the style while creating the mood.

Determining the **Relationship** Between the **Audience** and the **Dramatic Action**

Creating a set that regulates the relationship between performers and spectators is an integral part of the set designer's work with the director. The set designer can move everything to a distance by framing the action behind a proscenium arch or can draw the audience into the action by using entrances through the audience and the front apron of a proscenium stage. In a black box theatre, in which the seating is flexible, the director and set designer determine the spatial configuration that will work best for the director's concept. These choices will affect every aspect of the production—staging, lighting, and acting—as well as the interplay with the public.

Think TECHNOLOGY

Special Defects in *Spiderman: Turn Off the Dark*

Spiderman: Turn Off the Dark (2011) has proven that dazzling design, special effects, aerial stunts, and a $65 million price tag cannot create exciting theatre in the absence of a coherent story. Director Julie Taymor's work has always prioritized brilliant visual images over strong narrative, but this time the storyline and character development—the soul of theatre—were sacrificed to awe-inspiring stunts created by a Hollywood stunt coordinator and aerial designer. Broadway has increasingly felt the need to compete with digital media to capture audiences accustomed to high-tech entertainment. Yet audiences have found themselves bored, despite spectacular sets and actors performing in-flight battles overhead. When a cinematic aesthetic is applied to the theatre, it succeeds only if it can master the demands and limitations of live performance. The many accidents and show-stopping technical glitches that occurred during the unprecedented number of preview performances underscore the risks of human error that every actor courts each night. The difficulties the production has encountered are a potent reminder that theatre is the place where we explore what it means to be human—not superhuman.

Designing the Character's World

The two sets pictured on this page tell us much about the characters' lives and set the time and place for the action, yet their approaches are quite different. How a set expresses the world in which the characters will live is the result of a collaborative process in which the designer and director determine what visual style will work best with the directorial concept for the text. John Lee Beatty's set (top photo) for John Lindsay Abaire's *Good People* (2011) embodies the poverty of south Boston and its trapped working-class inhabitants, who search for a way out of their limited lives. *Man from Nebraska* (2003) is about a man in a midlife crisis of faith and his search for meaning. Todd Rosenthal's set (bottom set) with 20 different locations simultaneously visible, gives a sense of the journey the lead character takes toward self-discovery. Each box on the grid is three dimensional, except for a few backgrounds, such as the road, which were printed onto backlit vinyl.

Expressing the Director's Concept

These two photos of designs for *The Three Sisters* (1901) reflect very different directorial concepts for the same play. The 2003 Olaf Altmann design (bottom) is clearly focused on the isolation of the characters and the seemingly insurmountable barriers to happiness and fulfillment. The Scott Pask 2009 design (top) focuses on the physical and social conditions that hold them prisoner. The designs reflect very different directorial approaches to the same text and demonstrate how much a set designer contributes to the productions point of view and style.

The **Set** Designer's Process: Collaboration, Discussion, Evolution

HOW do collaboration, discussion, and research evolve into a stage set?

With the exception of director-designers such as Robert Wilson or Julie Taymor, or those working in creative teams, set designers are usually engaged after a production project has been selected. They begin their creative process with several careful readings of the text, or if they are designing for a work evolving through collaboration, they attend rehearsals.

> Set **designers** might ask
> themselves: What
> kinds of **images** does the work
> bring to **mind**? What
> **feelings** are evoked? What
> **elements** are necessary to the
> **dramatic** action?
> What **visual** ideas stand
> out or seem most **important**?

Discussion and **Collaboration**

Although set designers may have many immediate responses to their reading of the text, they do not start designing until they have had lengthy discussions with the director. During the initial meetings, there is an exciting exchange about the text, the concept, and how particular staging problems the director has noted will be solved. Designers stimulate new ideas and can help the director by asking questions about the concept that may clarify the director's vision. They discuss significant set needs the text may require and special moments to highlight. Because set designers are always reading a play with the visual elements foremost in their minds, they can note potential problems adapting the text to particular theatre spaces and see specific needs for the dramatic action that the director may have missed. A good designer also finds unexplored opportunities for the design to create interesting moments and serve the text. Some designers make sketches during these conversations to help the director visualize ideas.

THINK

How much autonomy should a set designer have? At what point should artists subsume their creativity to the collaborative experience?

◀ The Renaissance-style painting on the backdrop of the set demonstrates how researched images can make their way onto the stage to provide atmosphere for a production. Pictured in this staging of Shakespeare's *The Winter's Tale* are Keith David and Aunjanue Ellis; director, Brian Kulick; set, Riccardo Hernández; costumes, Anita Yavich; lighting, Kenneth Posner. The Public Theatre/New York Shakespeare Festival, Central Park.

Research

A set designer may do research to find images—photos and drawings—that reflect the time, place, or directorial interpretation of the production. Such images provide inspiration and are typically presented to the director to see whether they capture the concept the director has in mind.

Set designers' research takes place on three levels: the objective world of the play—its historic moment, sociology, and period style; the subjective level—the history and sociology and style of the director's concept; and the inspirational level—images that are not necessarily specifically related to the play but can spur the designer's imagination. For example, if the director were setting a seventeenth-century French play like Molière's *Misanthrope* in twenty-first-century New York City, the set designer would need to research both periods. The seventeenth-century images would give a feel of the original period and help the designer translate that feeling into contemporary terms. Researched images offer a tool for clarifying ideas in discussion and are vital to formulating a shared vision of the visual world. Old magazines, art books, or historical photographs are all good sources. Most set designers keep files of images to sift through when they begin work on a new production.

> **Research takes place on three levels:**
> - The objective world of the play text
> - The subjective level of the director's concept
> - The inspirational level

▲ Todd Rosenthal's model for *Man from Nebraska* (2003) demonstrates the amount of detail a designer may put into a model to show the director, cast, and technical director how the set should look when completed. Compare the model to the actual completed set shown in "Designing the Character's World" on page 258 to get a sense of how ideas develop in the design process.

THINK

Does reassembling researched images constitute an act of design?

Creating a Design

Once they have an understanding of the vision of the production as a whole, set designers start to imagine the set in more concrete terms. They may ask: What does the audience need to see? What is essential to the visual expression of the text? Synthesizing the director's ideas with their own and taking into account practical considerations about the theatre space, budget, and building time, designers translate their ideas into concrete visual images. Sketches serve as the basis for further discussion. Several sketches may be presented for the director's response, and they may be modified for the final design. A designer may even do a **storyboard**, a series of sketches showing how the set changes to tell the story through time. This technique is often used to solve practical problems. Out of this process, a **ground plan** emerges that gives a view of the dimensions of the stage and the placement of set pieces.

Most set designers build a scale **model** of the set. This three-dimensional model gives the production team more specific information about how the design will actually look and work in the space, as well as a sense of the viewers' angle on the action. Some set designers prefer to develop their ideas through multiple models. Directors may use models in rehearsal to give themselves and the actors a better sense of the environment and to help adjust movement patterns. A scaled human figure is always placed in the model to help everyone visualize the actor in space. Models can reveal how ideas that looked good on paper may not work in reality, precipitating changes before the set is built. Models of rooms often have movable pieces of furniture and scenery so directors and designers can toy with placement for best effect. The designers who work on the other visual aspects of the production, such as costume, lighting, and sound, usually use the model to help guide their choices.

Discussions between set designers and directors take place throughout the production process in production meetings and during informal exchanges. Costume, lighting, and sound designers are part of these exchanges because the design elements need to complement each other and work together. A lamp that needs to turn on in performance raises problems for both the set and lighting designers; a stereo that plays music involves the set and

Think TECHNOLOGY

Computers in Design

Computers offer artists new ways to visualize their work in three dimensions before setting foot in an actual theatre. Set and costume designers use **computer-aided drafting** (CAD) programs such as AutoCAD or Vectorworks to help them draft precise and uniform drawings. Computer sketches allow designers to visualize and modify colors, textures, and forms as they contemplate different design options. Use of a scanner or design programs such as Photoshop and Illustrator can be helpful tools in creating backdrop images, designs for props, wallpaper, and signs on stage. Lighting designers use these programs to test lighting effects on virtual sets and costumes. Computer models are employed to solve technical problems and make aesthetic choices before carpenters

and costumers begin building actual sets and costumes.

Designers and directors also explore virtual reality equipment to experience a stage space in three dimensions before the set is built. Using systems developed by NASA to simulate environments for astronaut training, theatre artists can create an imaginary fully equipped performance space to see how staging ideas will work and how set designs feel from the inside.

Computers help artists communicate at a distance as well. Theatres e-mail blueprints of the theatre space to designers, and designers send computerized images of their ideas for sets and costumes to directors for review and then to the shops for construction. Today it is possible for designers to work at theatres all over the country without

being on site. Computer-generated designs can also be converted into software that programs the power tools used in the construction of scenery. Computerized routers can cut wood and metal to the exact specifications of a design blueprint without the human labor of interpreting and measuring; this ensures accuracy and saves time and money.

Many designers, however, still refuse to design with the aid of a computer. Some older designers were simply not trained in this way, and others claim that the computer hampers their creativity and removes them from the physical connection they have to the materials of their craft and the artistic work of designing. Although computers can be efficient for many tasks, some feel that they jeopardize the artistic integrity of theatrical design.

sound designers. In *The Lion King,* costume elements form the set, requiring coordination between costume and set design. Open channels of communication are vital to coordinate practical and aesthetic needs.

For most commercial productions, the basic designs will be completed before the first rehearsal and then refined through part of the rehearsal process to accommodate the discoveries of actors, directors, and designers. For this reason, set designers must be flexible. They attend rehearsals to get a sense of how the stage is being used in the action. The set design must be finalized and signed off upon long before the first performance to allow time for construction.

The set designer drafts construction drawings to send to the shop. These are first shown to the lighting designer for a check of any lighting difficulties the plans might present. Today, more and more of these drawings are being done on computers because most shop technicians prefer receiving computer-drafted plans. Computer-drafted designs can also be used to program computerized machinery in the scene shop. Set designers may visit the shop to see how things are going, but they are not around to supervise. Therefore, their drawings need to be extremely accurate and contain as much information as possible about the shape, size, function, and look of every set piece. Paint elevations show the application of color to all stage surfaces and are also provided with sample colors for the scenic artists. Set designers need good drafting skills to execute these documents. They rely on the technician's knowledge of materials, carpentry, or engineering to find solutions to design problems, and designers often make changes based on the technical director's suggestions. They work closely with technical staff to make the set design a reality that fulfills the artistic promise originally set out in discussion and sketches.

All props used on stage are chosen by the set designer and approved by the director.

ARTISTS IN THEIR OWN WORDS

LOUISA THOMPSON

Louisa Thompson (b. 1971) won Obie and the Hewes Awards for the set of the critically acclaimed Off-Broadway production of Blasted (2009) and the Hewes award for [sic] (2002). She was also the designer for Gatz in 2010 (see the Chapter 6 opening photo). Her work has been seen in New York and elsewhere around the country. She holds an MFA from the Yale School of Drama and is currently on the faculty of Hunter College in New York.

How much do you think about the entire theatrical space—both that of the audience and that of the performer—when you design?

When I work in any type of theatre—proscenium, thrust, or black box—I am always thinking about the entire space; this includes both where the performance is happening and where the audience is sitting. For me, the relationship between these two spaces is always echoed in the architecture, so the architecture of the space must be included in the design. I can use the architecture to help the production or use it in an unexpected way to change the relationship between the actor and the audience. In both cases, the audience grasps when they enter the theatre that their relationship to the performance is specific in terms of the way the architecture is either highlighted or reconfigured, and this makes the relationship of the spectator to the event feel more immediate.

I am always interested in placing the audience in an unusual position within the space because it awakens the audience's relationship to the performance and the performer and heightens the awareness of the self as an audience member. Sometimes this can be uncomfortable; potentially it is challenging; ideally it is done in a way that serves a specific project. Take the 2004 production of Suzan Lori Parks's *Venus* at Hunter College, where the audience was on swivel chairs surrounded by the performance; the audience was also on stage performing as they negotiated the performance and each other and which way to look. This reinforced the episodic nature of the play, and an unexpected and exciting demand was placed on the audience.

When you read a play, does it call out for a particular space?

Yes, some speak to me as flat and presentational, and I feel that the actors are on display. This evokes a proscenium and is difficult in a thrust or arena space, where the actors can be seen front, back, and side—sculpturally, but not pictorially. You can't make flat pictures when the audience is on more than one side.

Can you talk about the relationship between space and set pieces?

The world of the play is always my starting point, and as soon as I begin to imagine that world, I see it within a specific space, and when I do that, I am dealing with architecture. Architecture is a framing device that helps us focus and block out the distractions of our lives. Sometimes you want to use it; at other times you want to acknowledge it and let it drift away. Sometimes set pieces help to do this. Set pieces can define the performance and the audience space; sometimes they do more than the architecture, when you construct the space within which the pieces fit. As a designer,

(continued)

I am interested in making the relationship between set and architecture as active as possible.

Please discuss the special challenges of designing your Obie-award-winning set for *Blasted*.

The first act required a realistic world followed by an explosion that creates the visual disintegration of that world. How do you represent the unrepresentable? You can't blow up the theatre. How do you compose two entirely different visual worlds, with one containing the remnants of the other, and give the audience a truthful experience? You are forced to confront the theatre space's architecture and limitations. Part of the effect was achieved through synchronized light and sound effects. I saw the set as an actor telling the story of the destruction of a world.

Author's interview 2011. By permission of Louisa Thompson.

▶ In a designer's sleight-of-hand, within a matter of seconds and before the audience's eyes, the neat hotel room seen above was transformed into the bombed out world seen below.

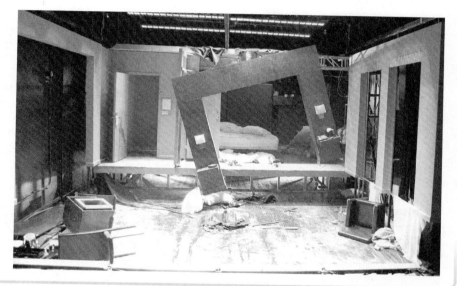

Prop Lists

Early in the rehearsal process, the set designer works with the director and stage manager to create a list of the objects necessary for the stage action; these items are referred to as *properties*, or *props*. Items may be added to or deleted from this initial list as the actors' blocking is developed and fixed. Some props are set out on stage; others are hand props carried on stage by actors. Personal props carried by actors, such as a briefcase or an umbrella, may be part of costume design. Set designers select items for use on stage that conform to the style of the set. There is always discussion with the director about how each object should look and how it will be used. For example, a bowl of fruit can use artificial fruit unless actors eat it as part of the action. Set designers may transform everyday objects with paint, varnish, finishes, and ornamentation, perhaps antiquing an aluminum bowl, distressing a wood box, or bejeweling the handle of a cane. Some props may be built from scratch. Sometimes antique replicas or other original objects are purchased or drawn from a theatre's stock. Set designers may attend rehearsals to see exactly how a particular prop is used by actors to help in their selection process.

When all the pieces are built, the set is *loaded in*. With the set in place in the theatre with actors working on it, the set designer can see how the set looks and functions. Except in the case of very well-funded productions, it is too late to make major changes. Designers can make minor adjustments for visual quality, functionality, and safety. They may oversee or do scenic painting to create textures and finishes, and they may **dress the set** with final touches: upholstery, small objects for tables and shelves, pillows, and curtains.

Set designers supervise the creation of the set from conception to implementation. Their ideas may be modified along the way so the final stage image fits the director's concept, the space, and the stage action. The set's ultimate realization, however, takes place only when the performers bring it to life.

Principles **of Composition**

Spectators rely on stage composition to orient them within the visual world of the stage. *Composition* is an artistic term that refers to how visual elements relate to each other. Set design composition directs the audience members' gaze and guides their interpretation of the visual elements. How we look is actually informed by how we read, whether we go from left to right or up to down. The composition of the stage elements—how they sit in relation to each other—plays on our visual habits to create meaning. Traditionally, certain design elements are considered basic to composition. These include focus, balance, proportion, rhythm, and unity.

Focus

Design elements direct the audience's focus toward parts of the stage that have theatrical, practical, or metaphorical value. The arrangement of objects on stage orients the audience within the space. The lines of a set draw spectators' eyes in particular directions, as do certain colors, textures, and relative masses. Set designers have many ways to bring focus to a particular point on the stage. To rivet our eyes to the palace doors where Queen Clytemnestra lures King Agamemnon to his death, designers might put the doors center stage, paint them bright red in an otherwise dull-colored set, make them appear of massive sculptured bronze, place them on a bare stage, or have all the lines of the set point toward them. A designer might create several smaller frames within the frame of the stage itself, with a window or some other kind of border. Set designers can even take our eyes on a journey through the set, with circular lines that move our vision from one side of the stage to the other.

▲ Walt Spangler's set for *The Importance of Being Earnest* at the Guthrie Theatre in Minneapolis (2009) plays with proportion to create both metaphor and mood for the period comedy.

Balance

If you draw a line down the middle of the stage and the two sides mirror each other, there is symmetry. If more set elements are gathered on one side than another, there is asymmetry. We tend to associate balance with stability, excessive symmetry with rigidity or artificiality, and imbalance with disorientation. By manipulating balance, a set designer can portray a point of view on the world the characters inhabit.

Proportion

Proportion refers to the scale of the set elements in relation to each other and to the actors. Large set pieces can dominate the space and tower above the human figures, while unusually small ones may seem like toys, as in the example from Lee Breuer's *Dollhouse* (see the photo of *Dollhouse* on page 196 in Chapter 8). The relative scale of objects may reflect reality or distort the world for stylistic or metaphorical purposes. The imposing machine that dominated the 1923 set of Elmer Rice's expressionist play *The Adding Machine* served to underscore the dehumanization of people in the modern industrial era. The large flowers in Walt Spangler's set for *The Importance of Being Earnest* (see the photo on page 266) create a visual metaphor for the flowering of love. Scale also tells audiences where to look, as their eyes are drawn to large objects on stage.

Rhythm

The visual world of the stage has a rhythm. Visual statements can repeat in a regular manner or shift abruptly and disjunctively. They can impart a sense of calm or frenzy. In his 1926 production of Nicholai Gogol's *Inspector General*, Vsevolod Meyerhold's production put 13 doors in a line across the stage. Officials emerged from each one to bribe the inspector. The visual repetition of the doors and the repetitive action on stage reinforced the thematic exposition of the machinelike workings of government bureaucracy. Robert Wilson's set for *Einstein on the Beach* (1976) used a scaffolding to create a three-dimensional grid of square spaces. A performer in each frame reinforced the sense of repetition but with variations because each one had a different physical stance.

Unity

The words *harmony*, *unity*, and *integrity* describe a set in which all the elements are in agreement with each other. Often dissonant notes are deliberately struck to drive home a point about the world in which the characters live. A play set in an undeveloped land might present a hut with a satellite dish to demonstrate the reach of globalization. Discordant elements always assume meaning and are carefully selected. However disproportionate or asymmetrical individual set pieces may seem, in a unified design, the composition is justified and meaningful. The characters see their world as whole, and the set should reflect this world with its own integrity.

The **Visual** Elements of Set **Design**

WHAT are the visual elements of set design?

All objects have line, mass, texture, and color, properties that convey meaning through their artistic use. Designers manipulate these elements to accomplish the goals of set design while composing the space. Our ability to read a set is informed by the general visual culture, the associations we have with certain colors or shapes, and how these make us feel.

Line

The visual world is constructed of lines—straight, curved, and zigzag—set horizontally, vertically, or diagonally. These lines give definition to walls, furnishings, and every object on stage, and they impart a particular feeling to the viewer. Straight horizontal lines can convey a sense of rigidity or confinement, reminiscent of a jail cell, or they may convey

▲ In Charles L. Mee's *Big Love*, the padded floor covered in pink vinyl by set designer Annie Smart, serves as a trampoline for the play's dramatization of the battle between the sexes. Actors rejected in love are literally on the rebound.

stability and security. Vertical lines can convey a sense of soaring and power, like the columns on a stately building. Curved lines give a feeling of freedom and openness or of instability, like waves on the ocean. Zigzag lines can create a topsy-turvy world. Expressionist sets of the early twentieth century often used steeply angled lines to express an emotionally charged world seen through the eyes of the central character of the drama.

Mass

Mass refers to the shape of objects on stage, their size and weight, and the way they occupy space. The balance of mass in the stage environment set against the figure of the actor imparts a sense of our human value and power in the stage world. Heavy objects can create a dense, oppressive space and even give a sense of mental weight or claustrophobia. Light ones can create an airy, open space, unleashing a feeling of freedom.

Ornamentation is a related idea that refers to the quantity of objects and detail on a set. Every inch of the set can be filled with patterned textiles, small objects, and set pieces, or the stage may be relatively bare and open. Each creates a different stage world and places different demands on the actors inhabiting the space.

Texture

Audience members don't usually get to touch the objects on stage, but the textures of the design speak to us nonetheless through the play of light on surfaces. Sets often have fake textures—wooden pillars painted to resemble marble or Styrofoam carved to look like brick. Whether real or false, these textures give a particular feel to the environment. Marble can be cold and stately on a government building. Wood can be rustic and homey like a log cabin. Steel is cold and harsh; velvet is soft, luxurious, and inviting. In Les Waters's 2001 staging of Charles Mee's *Big Love*, the stage floor was a springy trampoline. Actors repeatedly threw themselves on the floor at emotional moments and bounced back while speaking about the vagaries of love. The springy floor reflected how relationships can literally send you reeling.

Color

Color can have a powerful effect on us. Simply changing the back wall of a theatre from black to white or yellow completely alters our sense of the space and the associations it draws from us. Set designers think of the play of colors in relation to the actors' skin tones. There are warm colors—those in the red and yellow families, including pinks and oranges—and cool colors—those in the blue, green, and white families. Warm colors tend to create empathy for the characters, while cool colors distance us. A bright, garish red can be disturbing, just as a deep, lush gold can be welcoming. Edward Gorey's 1977 design for *Dracula* conjured up the count's castle using only black etched lines on a white surface and the occasional splash of red. In Chen Shizheng's *The Orphan of Zhao*, performed at the Lincoln Center Summer Festival in 2003, the main playing area was a white square surrounded by a moat of red paint. The actors, barefoot, walked through the pool of red and painted the white stage floor with their red footprints. The final red-splattered canvas was an appropriate visual metaphor for this tale of bloody revenge.

▲ For Chen Shizheng's new staging of Ji Juanxiang's revenge tale *Orphan of Zhao,* from the repertoire of Chinese opera, actors walk barefoot through a blood-red moat as they enter the square white playing area. Through the course of the show, players besmear the pristine white with streaks and pools of red from their feet. By the end, the area where the revenge murders have taken place is visually awash in blood. Set, Peter Nigrini, in collaboration with Michael Levine, Lincoln Center Festival, New York.

The **Set** Designer's **Materials**

WHAT are a set designer's materials?

Set designers draw from a number of materials to create new worlds on stage. They first consider the architectural features of a theatre and the natural environment and how they might contribute to or hinder a design concept. They can then create sets using flats, platforms, drapes, drops, scrims, furniture, and properties. Theatrical design has always drawn on whatever existing technology afforded, from film to treadmills. Today, new technologies have opened up endless design possibilities using digital computer projections.

▲ Tim Hatley's fanciful sets and costumes use color and line to create the irreverent and fun-filled atmosphere in Mike Nichols's production of Monty Python's *SPAMALOT*. Pictured here is the London production with Tim Curry.

The **Architectural** or **Natural** Space

The theatrical space itself is always a component of the set designer's process. It defines possibilities and dimensions, and a set designer always works within some limitations. A theatre with a low ceiling has no fly space and cannot have flying backdrops. A theatre without any wing space cannot house set pieces for multiple scene changes. A black box allows the set designer to play with spatial configurations by manipulating seating and shaping the playing area; a proscenium fixes the relationship of the set to the audience. An arena stage limits the use of walls and massive objects that would obscure sight lines. Sometimes set designers know a production will go on tour, so they design scenic elements to travel easily and be adaptable to different theatre spaces.

The architectural features of a space can become the unadorned design. In 1913, French director Jacques Copeau was the first person in the modern era to look back to the iconic stage spaces of ancient Greece and Elizabethan England and revive the idea of a bare stage to showcase the actor and reconnect the theatre to the performer's vocal and physical power.

A theatrical space may also have architectural or decorative elements that can enhance a set and become incorporated into the design. Peter Brook first staged his 1985 version of the Indian epic *The Mahabharata* outdoors in a stone quarry. When he moved it indoors, the bare, distressed back walls of the Bouffes du Nord theatre in Paris worked as an expressive backdrop. Transferred to New York, the distressed walls of the Harvey Theatre at the Brooklyn Academy of Music matched those of the Paris space and remain one of that theatre's identifying features. When churches are transformed into theatres, the architectural Gothic arches are often incorporated into set designs.

In an open space, the body's expressive power takes center stage.

Many of the New York Shakespeare Festival productions at the open-air Delacorte Theatre in Central Park include the lake and the surrounding greenery of the park as a backdrop for their designs, an apropos depiction of the world of many Shakespearean plays. Some set designers search for preexisting settings in which to place a production. Several companies have made use of the New York urban environment as a stage set.

Some of the more interesting uses of new technology appear center stage, alongside actors, as an integral part of the production concept. Since the invention of film in the late nineteenth century, theatre directors have used projections to create scenery and provide visual and factual support or counterpoint to stage action. Erwin Piscator used projections and film sequences in his political theatre in the 1920s to draw connections between recent historical events and the dramatic action and to distance the audience emotionally from the play.

Creating a workable interplay between live action and recorded action is challenging because film and video images often upstage actors. A slick media projection inevitably grabs the audience's attention. In 2003, *Ubung*, a production from the Netherlands, contrasted videos showing adults involved in decadent behavior—drinking, smoking, wife-swapping—with the same actions played live on stage by children.

In this case, the live action commented on the video, ultimately drawing equal focus to each component. The audience's attention was first directed at the projected film because of its scale; thus it took a while for the audience to adjust its focus to include both the projected and live action and to grasp the thematic interplay between the two.

Today we see increasing use of digital imagery on the stage, often to dazzling effect. Never have projections been more magnificently integrated into a production concept than in the 2008 revival of *Sunday in the Park With George*. Projections interacting with live actors enabled audience members to witness the artist's creative process as they watched the famous Seurat painting *Sunday Afternoon on the Island of La Grande Jatte* come to life.

Some artists are now experimenting with creating scenery by projecting virtual computer models on stage. In the work of San Francisco director George Coates, actors move through projected environments that continually change around them, transforming their world in the blink of an eye. In his 1996 piece *Wings*, head-mounted displays allowed audience members to watch actors and 3-D virtual scenery at the same time. In *The Crazy Wisdom Sho* (2001), at points in the performance onstage actors were directed by online participants submitting wisdom seen on teleprompters. In some productions, Eyeliner, a unique high-definition video projection system, allows freeform three-dimensional moving images to appear within a live stage setting so that an actor can now appear in a 3-D projection beside his live self, or offstage live actors can magically appear and disappear onstage.

In response to the increasing demand for digital designers trained specifically for the theatre, the Yale School of Drama began an MFA program in Projection Design and will graduate its first class in 2013.

◄ The Roundabout Theater Company's 2008 stunning revival of *Sunday in the Park With George*, by Stephen Sondheim and James Lapine, seamlessly integrates design and technology. David Farley's set and costumes, Ken Billington's lighting, and the projection design of Timothy Bird and the Knifedge Creative Network blend levels of reality.

THINK

When a set is nothing more than an arrangement of the space—seating and playing areas—in what way can we consider this a complete design?

Flats, **Platforms**, Drapes, **Drops**, and Scrims

Set elements do not need to meet the building codes of real objects for everyday use, but they must meet many fire and safety codes, as well as union regulations. They need to be as fully constructed or as sturdy as production use requires. A variety of special scenic elements are habitually used as modular components. Set designers can completely transform the theatrical space by using flats, platforms, drapes, drops, and scrims that mask the architectural elements of the theatre as they configure a new environment.

Flats have traditionally been the building blocks of stage construction. These single units of canvas or other material stretched over a wooden frame can be connected to each other to create walls that outline a room or building. They can be painted any color and made to resemble any number of textures and materials. With flats, set designers create structures that are light enough to move into the space but strong enough to last for the run of a show.

Platforms give dimension to the acting area by providing different levels and isolating locations. A platform brought into an empty space can itself serve as a stage.

Drapes can be used as decorative elements on stage. Fabric panels hung across the upstage wall can turn the theatre into a neutral space. Drapes can also be used to outline the playing area. Black drapes can mask lighting or scenic elements and conceal actors before they make their entrances.

Drops are large pieces of painted canvas hung at the back of the stage. They are used to set particular locales. The Cheek-1by-Jowl Company's production of *Duchess of Malfi* (1995) used a bare stage with narrow fabric panels to delineate various scenes and locations.

A **scrim** is a special kind of cloth or gauze that allows light to pass through it. When light shines on it from the front, the cloth appears opaque. When light shines on it from the back, it becomes transparent and can magically reveal scenic elements it once obscured. This provides a clever means of creating magical transformations. A painted scrim can reveal different settings and scenes with a simple lighting change.

Furniture and Props

Furniture and props make spaces specific and relate the scale of the actor to the set. A set depicting a realistic apartment or a store may require extensive furnishings and props and a great deal of dressing to make it reflect the lives of the characters who live and work in the space. Furniture can also be used in a symbolic manner.

▲ Ming Cho Lee's set for Eugene O'Neill's *Ah, Wilderness!* uses only a few pieces of furniture, a light fixture, and a skeletal architectural structure to suggest a spacious, comfortable, early-twentieth-century house. Lighting brings color, dimension, and depth to an otherwise minimal white set.

A throne can evoke an entire palace, a cot can indicate a jail cell or an army barracks, and a giant flower can suggest a garden.

Technology

The newest technologies have always found a place in theatre design, and today high-tech equipment is becoming an ever-more-integral part of set design, from the conceptualization and visualization of design ideas to the construction of set pieces and the regulation of their stage movement. The set designer's ability to use technical tools—from turntables and treadmills to screen projections and interactive computer imagery—for scenic effects continues to grow.

Other Materials

Set designers adopt many materials for the stage, drawing on their evocative qualities. Natural elements such as water, earth, and fire reconnect us with our organic nature. They are manipulable but don't necessarily conform to the dictates of a director. Their very reality captivates us with its potential for surprise and subversion of the theatrical frame. Mary Zimmerman used a pool of water as the central image and playing area of her 2001 *Metamorphosis*, based on tales from Ovid. Actors could dive into its depth, wade across it, and float over it on plastic floats. The pool represented transformation, rebirth, and the power of the gods to create chaos and offer redemption, as expressed in the ancient myths.

Peter Brook's *Carmen* (1983) created a metaphorical bullring and filled the stage with sand. Constructivist designers in the 1920s used steel and wire to create sets that spoke of technology and industry. For Ralph Lemon's dance piece *Geography* (1997), set designer Nari Ward (b. 1963) used wooden pallets within a structure of plastic for a backdrop that reflected the idea of commerce and transport. In each of these cases, the material of the design was a source of meaning and significance within the production concept.

Set designers create a world where the director's vision can be realized. Never before have they had such a broad palette from which to draw. Today, their images may be transcultural. Their materials are both natural and synthetic, and their styles may be traditional, eclectic, or innovative. Their collaborative role has grown. Whatever the result, the set always awaits the live actor to breathe life into the design.

> ### THINK
> In various eras, audiences were drawn to the theatre primarily because of its visual spectacle. In today's visual culture, can set design exist alone as an art form?

HIDDEN HISTORY

Dogugaeshi: Set Transformation as Performance

Through his own artistic pursuit of nonlinear, abstract puppet performance, American puppeteer Basil Twist encountered a Japanese theatrical tradition. After seeing a performance at a puppet exhibit in Paris in 1997, where a black-and-white monitor played a brief film of Japanese screens opening and closing, Twist traveled to Japan to visit those who still perform this endangered art and then created his own performance titled *Dogugaeshi*.

Dogugaeshi means "changing stage sets" in Japanese. Developed on the island of Awaji and in nearby Tokushima prefecture, it is part of a broader regional folk tradition of puppet performance. Large puppet figures play in front of beautifully painted sliding screen backdrops, which move along tracks set into the stage at various levels of depth to reveal new

> In the Dogugaeshi tradition, watching sets change is the main attraction.

scenic backgrounds.

At intermission, the movement of sliding screens and revealed sets is offered as its own entertainment, accompanied by candlelight, the music of the three-stringed *shamisen*, and the pounding of wooden clappers.

In *dogugaeshi* up to 88 screens move in and out of a small puppet stage, in various configurations, opening on to new images, receding upstage, or advancing downstage. One of the most startling effects is produced by a series of screens that act as wings and backdrop to create a perspective view of a large *tatami* room. The number of heavy and intricately painted mulberry paper screens used in a performance expresses the theatre troupe's prosperity and reflects the overall sense of illusion created by the puppet theatre. In the half-light of evening, *dogugaeshi* brings the spectator to a dreamlike state of demi-consciousness, much as Japan's *noh*

(continued)

(continued from page 275)

theatre does, by providing a plane of associative images—plums, cherry trees, dragons, and phoenixes drawn from Japanese myth and poetry.[1] The Inukai Theatre, declared an important tangible asset in Japan in 1998, holds the largest

[1] Jane Marie Law, *Puppets of Nostalgia: The Life, Death, and Rebirth of the Awaji Ningyo Tradition* (Princeton, NJ: Princeton University Press, 1997), 199–200.

collection of painted screens for puppet shows, or *fusuma-e*, with 132 pieces, some reportedly 100 years old.

Twist's *Dogugaeshi*, which premiered in November 2004 at the Japan Society of New York, reenacts the form's near demise during World War II, when puppeteers sold off sacred puppets and performance equipment to stay alive or burned them to keep warm. It also documents the

tradition's recent rejuvenation. Through the visual beauty and movement of panels and screens, the audience is taken on a journey through the recent history of *dogugaeshi* and into a realm of dream, imagination, and memory. The addition of video footage gives a contemporary turn to this tradition of visual imagery as theatrical spectacle.

▲ Screens opening one after another show a continually receding perspective in Basil Twist's *Dogugaeshi*, Japan Society of New York.

Summary

WHAT are the goals of set design?   p. 258

▶ The set designer is the visual interpreter of a performance text. A good set design is deeply connected with the total production concept.

▶ A theatrical set facilitates the action of the play, establishes time and place, creates mood, provides an environment that embodies the character's lives, helps tell the story, presents a visual metaphor for the director's concept, defines style, determines the relationship between the audience and the dramatic action, and expresses the director's point of view on the text.

HOW do collaboration, discussion, and research evolve into a stage set?   p. 263

▶ Set designers collaborate with the director and other designers in developing a theatrical design. The process begins with a careful reading of the text, discussion, and research.

▶ Set designers imagine the set in concrete terms, creating sketches, storyboards, ground plans, and a scale model.

▶ Set designers work closely with technical staff to make the design a reality on stage.

WHAT are the principles of design composition?   p. 268

▶ Focus, balance, proportion, rhythm, and unity in the stage composition direct the audience's gaze and guides their interpretation of the visual elements.

WHAT are the visual elements of set design?   p. 269

▶ Set designers manipulate line, mass, texture, and color to convey meaning and compose the stage space.

WHAT are a set designer's materials?   p. 271

▶ Set designers create sets using the architectural features of a theatre, flats, platforms, drapes, drops, scrims, furniture, properties, and new technologies.

MySearchLab®

Fabio Toblini in his whimsical costumes for *The Two Gentlemen of Verona* (2007) uses wigs, color, and line to set the mood for this fun-filled production at The Old Globe Theatre in San Diego.

Dressing the Character

The Magic of Costumes

Costumes have seemingly magical powers. Where would the wizard be without a cloak, the judge without a robe, the soldier without a uniform, the angel without wings? From the time we are children at play, we learn the power of costume to transform us and shape our identity. Costumes are a major part of role-play in the theatre, and actors rely on their magic. Actors use important costume pieces—a suit jacket, a long skirt, or a tight corset—to feel the character in their bodies. In some situations they rehearse in costume elements or makeup, so that their performances grow out of a psychophysical understanding of character.

We've all had the experience of putting on a piece of clothing and feeling transformed. Slipping into a sexy dress inspires us to walk in a sultry manner; a suit and tie make us more aware of posture and bearing; a certain pair of shoes can make us feel athletic or restrained. Clothing changes the way we inhabit our bodies and consequently alters the way others perceive us.

What we wear tells others who we are: our tastes, habits, social class, profession, gender, and sexuality. When we dress for work or a night out on the town, we are making choices, often unconsciously, about how we want to present ourselves and what we hope our clothes will say about us. In the theatre costume designers make such decisions for imaginary characters. Each choice they make must look like something the characters would have chosen for themselves. Costumes define the character for the audience and the actor while contributing to a unified production style.

1. How do actors use costumes?

2. What makes costumes magical?

3. What information do costume designers give the audience?

CHAPTER 12

Goals of **Costume** Design

WHAT are the goals of costume design?

The living, moving actor is the canvas on which costume designs are realized. The actors' body shapes, size, and skin color, as well as their physical mannerisms and feelings, affect how a costume will appear and be worn. Costumers therefore work more closely with performers than do other members of the design team. Sometimes costume reveals or supports the actor's own physique, and sometimes it attempts to transform it. In either case, the actor's body is always at issue; it is the material substance that must work in concert with costume design.

Actors, of course, are not just brute material; they are psychological beings with deep feelings about their own bodies. They have strongly expressed preferences about what makes them look good or feel comfortable, as well as what clothing inhibits or frees their movement. When creating characters, they formulate strong opinions about what those individuals would wear. Costume designers assist in bringing the director's vision and the actors' personal sentiments into harmony, so performers can act with ease and confidence, while being faithful to the production's artistic goals.

▼ American musicals travel the globe as we can see here in this German production of *Wicked*. Whatever the language, the characters of Elphaba (Willemijn Verkaik) and Glinda (Lucy Scherer) are easily differentiated; costume color and style tell us all we need to know about them.

Costumes help actors express character through gesture. Actors play with their clothes and accessories, integrating them into stage business and body language. Specific details, such as a scarf, a tie, or the placement of buttons, can offer actors the character-defining choices of tossing a scarf flamboyantly over a shoulder, loosening a tie, or undoing a constricting or revealing button.

For designs to be both expressive and functional, costumers need to consider not only the director's concept but also what physical actions the actor will be performing on stage, the psychological nature of the character, and the limitations and potential of the actor. Costume designers must also consider what the audience needs to know about the characters, the environment in which they live, and how the story can be revealed through costume.

◄ David Zinn's period costumes for the world premiere of Sarah Ruhl's *In the Next Room or the vibrator play* wittily comment on the suppression of women's natural sexuality. The excess of buttons, bustles, ruffles, and frills confine and hide the female body. This production, starring Maria Dizzia (left) and Hannah Cabell, was directed by Les Waters at the Berkeley Repertory Theatre with a set by Annie Smart and lighting by Russell H. Champa.

Revealing the Essence of Character

Clothes are very personal and can become a second skin. They are worn close to the body and are transformed through movements and habits. Costumes become a part of who characters are. Costumes define a character's identity for the audience. Consider the dress of Stella and Blanche, the sisters in *A Streetcar Named Desire* (1947). Stella's acceptance of her working-class life is reflected in every article of her clothing and accessories, just as Blanche's flamboyance and desperate need to be perceived as wealthy and desirable is reflected in hers. Similarly, the opposing characters Glinda and Elphaba in *Wicked* (2003) are defined by the costumes they wear (see the photo on page 280), the cut and color. These details tell us about their relationship and the role they will play in the drama.

> "The main job of **costume** design in a production is to provide **physical** and **emotional** support to every actor through the **clothing** he or she will wear to enhance **characterization.**"
>
> —Judith Bowden, costumer

Costumers express what is distinctive about each character through the smallest details. A simple business suit is transformed by the cut, color, lapel size, vent, number of buttons, and cuffs. The addition of accessories such as shirts, ascots, and jewelry can make a statement about each character's personal psychology. Clothing, wigs, and makeup can reveal the character's age for the audience. Fabric texture, pattern, and color can reveal personality traits.

Establishing Time and Place

Clothes can immediately suggest the period in which a scene takes place and with it the feeling of a cultural moment. A long skirt with a tight corset points to the sexual repression of the Victorian period, while a miniskirt reflects the more permissive 1960s. The costumes for Sarah Ruhl's *In the Next Room or the Vibrator Play* (2009) clearly placed the play in the repressive 1880s, when women's clothing permitted them little freedom or sexuality. When a director chooses to set a play in an era other than the one indicated by the author, clothing helps situate the production. Stalinesque uniforms and 1940s dress placed director Rupert Goold's 2007 production of Shakespeare's *Macbeth* in the World War II era (see the photo in Chapter 4), although the language remained Elizabethan.

Although designers research historical costume detail, they are rarely completely faithful to period style. Stage fashion seeks a compromise between accuracy and contemporary audience tastes and knowledge. Particular aspects of a costume may be exaggerated to depict class and social role in an unfamiliar world. Compromises are made for the actor's comfort and to facilitate the stage action.

Stage dress also indicates the time of day and the time of year, reflecting social and seasonal conventions. Tuxedos and long gowns suggest evening; business clothes and briefcase evoke the workday. Sweaters, scarves, and gloves tell us it is winter; bathing suits, shorts, and sandals bring thoughts of summer or the tropics.

> When sets are **minimal,** costuming often fills in information and **enables** the **spectator** to **imagine** the setting.

Costumes can tell us if we are in Mexico or China, in a hospital or a hotel. Bowling shirts and shoes set the scene in a bowling alley, even if there are no lanes or pins. A silk kimono can place a scene in Japan, even if the stage is bare.

Setting the Social and Cultural Milieu

Costumes are always read within a social context. Presentations of social and economic class, of sophistication and innocence are particular to time, place, and situation. Class distinctions are more significant in some parts of the world than in others, and designers must take this into account. Designers don't conceive of a costume in isolation but attempt to describe an entire world and what it considers normal, outrageous, delightful, or suspicious. A character in an old T-shirt and torn jeans is unremarkable at a baseball game but conspicuous at a corporate board meeting; the audience could read much into such an appearance. A character's costume says volumes about that individual's position and emotional state. In productions of *Hamlet*, the king, queen, and courtiers are often costumed in splendid regalia, whereas Hamlet is in simple black mourning clothes, setting him emotionally apart from other members of the court. William Wycherly's (1633–1688) Restoration comedy *The Country Wife* (1675) puts Pinchwife, a Puritan from the countryside, in the midst of fashionable, libertine London society. The conservative dress of the spoil-sport Pinchwife separates him from the fun-loving social world. Ann Roth's costumes in the photo from *The Book of Mormon* (2011) tell us that there is one set of characters out of place within the cultural context of the play and set up the story.

We need only look at Ann Roth's costumes to know that characters are out of place. The costumes set us up for the comic turns to come in the 2011 Broadway production of *Book of Mormon*. Actors seen here are (from left) Rema Webb, Andrew Rannells, and Josh Gad.

Telling the Story

Sherlock Holmes could look at an ink-stained glove or a pair of mud-spattered boots and trace a person's path on a particular day. Clothing and accessories all tell a tale: A character's threadbare coat in the first act and elegant dress in the second indicate a change in fortune. A tear in a shirt may be the outcome of a barroom brawl. A lipstick stain on a collar is proof of an illicit affair. Garments and the state they are in tell us where characters have been, what they have been up to, and how they have fared. Eliza Doolittle in

The sophisticated music of Cole Porter, the 1934 setting, and the brashness of the lead character Reno Sweeney, played by Sutton Foster, are all captured in Martin Pakledinaz's stylish costumes for Kathleen Marshall's 2011 Broadway revival of *Anything Goes*.

Pygmalion (1912) and in the musical version of that play, *My Fair Lady* (1956), appears at the start of the play as a ragged cockney flower girl. As she is educated and learns to speak proper English, her clothes improve with her pronunciation, until she can pass as a grand lady. The costumer needs to chart the character's course through a series of costume changes accordingly.

Costumes chart changes in the character's circumstances.

Demonstrating **Relationships** Among **Characters**

Costumes articulate social hierarchies, family connections, political antagonisms, emotional relationships, and other distinctions (see the photos in the "Artists in Their Own Words" box on page 291). Costumes can imply union, separation, or shared status. Members of a club, an army, or a gang might wear the same jacket or colors. Complementary colors or patterns can emotionally unite two young lovers in the spectator's eyes before the script ever brings them together. Characters in conflict might wear clashing colors or patterns. For example, a production of *Romeo and Juliet* might dress the Capulets in one color or pattern and the Montagues in contrasting colors or patterns, with Romeo and Juliet somehow connected by color, pattern, style, ornamentation, or design. Military uniforms with medals and stripes imply rank status and relationship. We can tell the mistress from the maid by their costumes.

Specifying **Characters'** Social and **Professional** Roles

Costumes can define profession or occupation. The elements the costumer selects to depict social and professional roles is the result of established social and theatrical conventions and the costumer's interpretation of these easily recognized symbols. We identify doctors by their lab coats, police officers by their blue uniforms, and chefs by their puffy white toques. Such dress can be realistic or iconic—representing a category of people. Careful selection of costume elements can say more about who a character is and what he or she does than many lines of expository dialogue.

Defining Style

Costumes can create a representational or presentational stage world. They may be realistic or fantastical or exaggerated. They can stimulate associations with historical periods or help to create a mood and point of view. Because actors comport themselves differently in realistic dress than in elaborate theatrical clothes, costumes affect their acting and help them contribute to a production's unified style. Costume designer Fabio Toblini sets a production style and brings a sense of comic whimsy to his designs for *Two Gentlemen of Verona* (2007) pictured in the chapter-opening photo. The dissonant elements in Jenny Mannis's designs for *Animal Crackers* (2009) sets up the audience for an irreverent comedy (see the photo on page 296), just as Martin Pakledinaz's sophisticated 1930s costumes set the tone for the music of Cole Porter in the 2011 production of *Anything Goes*.

> **"Ordinary** clothes automatically become **extraordinary** on the **stage** or screen. The frame around the events invites intensified **attention** to what is being worn; we know it is there **intentionally** even though it represents something worn casually.**"**
>
> —Anne Hollander, *Seeing Through Clothes*, 1993

Meeting the **Practical** Needs of the **Production**

A text may call for a particular costume piece to take part in the action: a locket to display a picture, a pocket to conceal a letter, a hood to act as a disguise. Designers accommodate these needs so that clothes can play their parts. In Eugène Labiche's (1815–1888) *The Italian Straw Hat* (1851), the madcap action revolves around a hat; when a horse eats one, it places a young wife's fidelity in question; when a replacement hat appears, it puts her jealous husband's mind to rest. In *Twelfth Night*, Malvolio reads a forged letter expressing Viola's desire to see him in yellow stockings worn "cross-gartered." His costume must fit the description in the text to serve the comic action.

The physical demands of a production are a primary consideration in costume design, and all choices must facilitate the actors' blocking. Costumes need to move with the actors, allowing them to bend or stretch, do dance or acrobatics, or any other movement required by the staging. Costumes are three-dimensional objects that travel with the actors across the stage and must offer the audience views from all angles. Some stage costumes need to accommodate quick changes or comic stage business and are designed to facilitate split-second timing.

Cross-Dressing

What does it mean when a man appears on the stage dressed in women's clothes or a woman in men's clothes? This simple question opens what has become in recent years a library's worth of criticism about how different cultures in different times and places have understood and represented gender. Because theatre is a place where we engage in role-play, how we play at being male or female on stage reflects how we define and understand gender roles in society at large. **Cross-dressing**, by its very nature, implies crossing the boundaries of what is accepted as appropriate for one gender or another. Today's costumers need to address social expectations as they select and design clothes that portray gender on stage.

The theatre can replicate commonly held social ideas about males and females or put them into question.

Throughout the world, cultural views about how men and women should behave are portrayed in the clothing they wear. Sometimes cross-dressing on stage presents a complete disguise. For example, this is the case for male *on-nagata* performers in *kabuki*, who present idealized female characters (see the photo on page 00). The image they create through makeup, costuming, and studied movements is so complete that it is impossible to discern the male actor inside the kimono. Tradition asserts that female *kabuki* characters are presented so perfectly that no real woman actor could do justice to the roles. The female form portrayed by men on stage, although astonishingly unlike the male actors themselves, is also unlike any real woman.

The tables are turned on *kabuki* in Takarazuka, a twentieth-century Japanese theatrical company, popular for its musicals, in which women play all the roles. Female Takarazuka performers play such idealized, romantic male leads that they are the true box-office draws for devoted fans, who are primarily women.

Instead of allowing an actor's gender to dissolve inside the role, cross-dressing can also juxtapose the gender of the costume and that of the performer. This is the case for the tradition of the "drag queen," whose presentation of "female" is so exaggerated it is denaturalized. Audience members watching drag queens are continually aware of the tension between the costume and the actor, the role and the player. On stage it is not always the case that "the clothes make the man"—or woman.

At different periods in history, cross-dressing on stage has channeled different kinds of sexual desire. In Elizabethan England, the belief that it was immodest and immoral for women to display themselves publicly led to young boys playing all the female roles. Recent scholars have examined the homoerotic tension that existed in these performances. This tension was furthered when boys played women who disguise themselves as men, such as Viola in *Twelfth Night* or Rosalind in *As You Like It*, allowing male homoerotic relationships to be played out openly on stage.

During the English Restoration, women appeared for the first time on the public stages of England. Beautiful young actresses were often called on to play **breeches roles**, in which they played young men dressed in short pants, or breeches. These roles allowed male audience members to ogle actresses' alluring ankles, a taboo sight outside the theatre.

Although several contemporary theatre companies and directors, such as Edward Hall and Declan Donnellan, have experimented with all-male casts in Shakespearean productions, the experience of Elizabethan cross-dressing cannot be fully re-created in the modern era. Today when women are permitted on stage, the sight of men in women's costumes brings with it different associations and values.

▼ Propeller, the all-male British theatre troupe, has revived the Elizabethan stage convention of having men play all the roles. Seen here is Edward Hall's 2011 staging of Shakespeare's *The Comedy of Errors*, designed by Michael Pavelka.

The Costume Designer's Process

Costume designers are usually engaged after a project has been selected. Like set designers, they come to an understanding of the characters and their world through a close analysis of the text, discussions with the director and the rest of the production's creative team, and through research. They ask themselves what needs to be revealed about the characters through the costumes and what demands the dramatic action makes on the clothing the actors will wear.

Discussion and Collaboration

Before the first meeting with the director, costume designers carefully read the text, come to an understanding of the facts of the plot, and analyze characters. They may highlight the text for any details about the costumes or the characters that may influence the designs. They try to figure out what makes each character tick and how each person functions in the text. They think about the relative importance of each character in the drama and the relationships among the characters. Costumers note any practical requirements for clothing or personal props and any information that reveals location, period, time of day, and season. They may make a rough **costume plot**—a breakdown of the play by acts or scenes and a list of the costume requirements for each character in the scene. Costumers also note the number of costume changes required for each character as well as any potential challenges.

> A **costume plot helps designers keep track of all the items each character wears in every scene.**

At the first meeting with the director, costume designers and directors share their character analysis and trade ideas about how story and characterization can be realized through costume. Directors discuss their concept and how costumes can help bring that concept to fulfillment. Discussions may be informed with specific images that the director or the costumer supply through research—photos and paintings that suggest the feeling they want to capture on stage. Sketches help designers communicate ideas to the director. Simple *thumbnail sketches* of each character help determine a direction for evolving costumes.

Once the director and the costumer have reached an agreement about the look, style, and demands for the costumes, there is a design conference with the director and the entire design team. Costume designers think about the entire visual world of a production—how a particular color or texture of fabric will look under certain lights and how different choices will mesh with the set, lights, and directorial style. Sketches can give a clear idea of how the actors will look together on stage and how costume will help define their relationships. Costumers will bring a sample color palette and fabric swatches to spur discussion. The costume and set designers discuss the coordination of colors between the set and the costumes. They trade notes on the needs of the production, talking about any practical demands that the set might impose on the actor, which the costumer must take into account, such as stairs, ramps, narrow or low doorways, and so on. For example, the costumer might tell the set designer that he or she is planning a high wig and the doorway must accommodate the added height. They might talk about the surface of the floor and its traction, the furniture, and the upholstery to ensure that shoes won't slip and fabric won't fray.

THINK

When dressing someone in traditional dress, must costume designers abide by all the codes of dress, all the costume elements? Is it disrespectful to take only the elements one needs from another culture?

Research

A costume designer's visual research serves as a springboard for discussion and the inspiration for ideas that develop over time. The research parallels the set designer's and also exists on three planes: The world of the play text, the director's concept, and the search for inspirational images.

▲ The researched images attached to the sketch of Maggie Morgan's sketch and final costume for Claudia Shear's *Dirty Blonde* show Mae West's actual garb and serve to inspire the design. The attached fabric swatch gives a precise sense of the color, texture, and ornamentation of the fabric intended for the dress.

Designers consult books on period style, artworks, magazines, and other visual resources. They may visit museums. Today, a lot of research may be done on the Internet. Research can reveal specific period details, the range of a style, and images that stimulate new ways of thinking about the production's look or visual motifs. For designers, visual research is an important part of exploring and exchanging ideas with a director. For period productions, the amount of historical research required is substantial. Costume designers must have a basic knowledge of costume history, as well as social and cultural history. While costumes are fantasy and complete historical accuracy is not necessary, costumers try to avoid historical errors to give the feeling of the period.

Creating the Costume Design

The *thumbnail sketches* used to inspire discussion and demonstrate the direction of the costumer's ideas to the director become the basis for more detailed renderings. *Final sketches* show each costume in detail and present all the clothes and accessories the designer envisions. *Fabric swatches* attached to the sketches for the director's approval communicate the color, pattern, and texture of the fabric the designer intends to use.

Costume designers usually attend a rehearsal as soon as the cast is set so they can adjust designs to the performers' body types. At rehearsals, costumers note the blocking and physical demands on the actors; a designer may rethink a tight short skirt or billowing coat if an actor has to climb a ladder or engage in a physical fight. Costumers provide rehearsal garments such as a long skirt or high heels to simulate restrictions on movement or to help an actor work out the timing of stage business such as getting dressed during a scene.

Costume designers work closely with the actors throughout the process. They take and chart performers' measurements and conduct fittings. Actors share their views on their costumes and express the need for changes or additional items. If actors are particularly uncomfortable with an item of clothing, costume designers usually try to accommodate their needs. Sometimes dealing with demanding actors can be a challenge, so costume designers need to call upon personal diplomacy to smooth out disagreements.

Once designers and directors finalize designs, the costume designer begins to assemble the costumes, working closely with costume shop personnel, who carry out the designs. Costumes can be *built* from scratch in a costume shop, *bought* from a store, *pulled* from the company's stock, or *rented* from a rental house. Building new costumes for all the actors in a production can be costly and time-consuming. For many productions, costumers build one or two special items and create others from existing pieces, adapting them by tailoring, dyeing, distressing, or removing or adding ornamentation to reflect the original design concept. The costumer is expected to have a complete understanding of costume construction, even if the labor is being done by a shop person. The costume designer is responsible for managing the time, labor, and cost involved in costume construction and for overseeing the purchase of materials and the progress of work in the costume shop. The amount of assistance the designer has in this process depends on the financial constraints of a particular production.

After a series of fittings, the costumes are finished. A **dress parade** offers the director and designer an opportunity to see all the costumed actors together under stage lights. Costume designers make sure the clothes fit, move well, and look good together. Dress rehearsals put the costumes into action, often revealing where practical problems might arise. At dress rehearsals costume designers take notes on final adjustments they must make before opening night. Actors are usually anxious to complete their character portrayal through costume, and this is an important moment for pulling the production together. The costume designer's work is finished once the show opens, but a wardrobe staff remains on deck during the run of the show to help launder and repair the clothes for each performance.

THINK

Do costumes need to reflect the designer's and the audience's social stereotypes in order to communicate?

LINDA CHO

Since graduating from the Yale School of Drama, Canadian designer Linda Cho has designed for opera, theatre, and dance, working at venues such as the New York Public Theatre, the Arena Stage in Washington, DC, the Old Globe Theatre in San Diego, the Dallas Theater Center, and the National Theatre in Taipei, Taiwan. Her work has been nominated for several important awards.

Please discuss the role of research in your process.

Research is the backbone of any design. In addition to the look of any period, I try to understand the basic political, social, and economic landscape of the time. I find this is helpful in putting the characters in context and in better understanding their relationships. Other resources I find useful are paintings to find popular colors of an era, or cultural interests like the interest in Orientalism at the turn of the century. Sculpture provides insight into line and texture, and crafts like quilts or stained glass give you a feel for materials. Photographs of actual people help to understand how the garments were worn

and how people moved in them, which is sometimes even more interesting than the actual garments themselves. Armed with images and information, I can take the next step in the design and tailor the costume to the characters. Sometimes the research is a point of departure and the design is abstracted from the original. Even if the intent is a fantastic made-up world, I try to ground the design in concrete research.

How do you deal with racial and ethnic stereotypes when they provide a visual shorthand for the audience?

In our twenty-first-century global village and particularly in North America's multicultural society, I think the average audience member has been exposed to many different cultures and is able to identify the differences between different racial groups. Having said that, I think that there is no need to portray characters as broad stereotypes unless of course the play calls for some sort of parody. I think it is very important when dealing with ethnic characters in a production to research the nuances of that culture and

to get it right. Authenticity just makes the design more interesting and may even serve to educate the audience.

How do you negotiate your ideal costume design with the reality of the actor's body type?

I consider the costume sketch a first step, not the final step in a design process. The sketch is a general framework, and it is open to change, depending on the situation. Whenever possible, I try to get a general idea of the actor's body type before I render the final designs. When I do not get that information, if I can manipulate the body with padding, corseting, and such, and if it is appropriate and the actor and director want to go in that direction, we essentially change the appearance of the actor from the inside out. In some instances I will work from the outside in by tweaking the design, perhaps changing hem lengths, necklines, or adding sleeves to best suit the actor. Sometimes body type is not the motivating factor in changing a design. If the actor who has been cast is different from how I had imagined the character and brings something new

(continued)

and different to the table, I will speak to the director and actor and adjust accordingly. On occasion, I have completely redesigned a costume to work with how the actor is playing a particular role. Ultimately, this is a collaborative medium and if I cannot get the actor to a place of comfort and confidence either through conversations or adjustments, I feel I am not doing my job.

Do you feel a designer brings his or her personal psychology—including race, ethnicity, and gender—to the design process? If so, how?

I don't think you can help but bring who you are into a design. I think the influences are endless. In terms of race, I was born in Korea and was brought up in Canada in a multicultural environment, and certainly that had an influence on my tastes. I have a keen interest in Asian culture. I have borrowed ideas from sources such as Japanese *kabuki*, Korean *ponsori*, and Chinese opera on numerous occasions, even for non-Asian productions. For example, in a production of *Orpheus and Eurydice* at the Virginia Opera, set in Europe circa 1910s, I used the *kabuki* technique of *hikinuki* (which is a way of transforming a kimono instantly on stage by removing basting threads along the sleeves) for Eurydice's gown when she comes back to life.

What advice would you give to young prospective designers?

I think it is important to remember to treat all your collaborators with the utmost respect—not just your director and fellow designers, which goes without saying, but also your drapers, wig masters, craftspeople, and actors, who are experts at what they do. If you can listen to suggestions and welcome input, it can only make your designs better. The sketch, as I mentioned earlier, is a starting place; there are many steps and people involved in getting a costume to the stage.

We are lucky to be theater artists. We chose to be costume designers because we love what we do, and very few can truly say as much. However, this is a world that will probably not pay extravagantly and will require sacrifice and hard work, so try to truly enjoy what you do, for at the end of the day the privilege of doing our art is the ultimate payoff. I remember in graduate school, someone in our class cried (which we all did at least once) over a brutal critique. Ming Cho Lee, our professor, patted her on the back and said, "Don't cry; it is only theatre." Words to live by.

Source: Used with permission from Linda Cho.

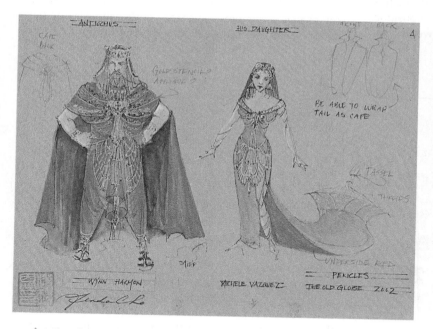

▲ Sketch and final costumes of Antiochus and his daughter designed by Linda Cho for Shakespeare's *Pericles*, directed by Darko Tresnjak at the Old Globe Theatre in 2002, San Diego, California. The costumes define the characters as a pair through the inversion of the red and gold color scheme and through the parallel details and ornamentation. The daughter's long train is made even more regal when draped along the steps of the stage, a connection between costume and set that helps express character. The sketch includes notations about how the tail of the costume can be used as a cape and other notes on color and construction to help the designer communicate her ideas fully to the director and costume shop personnel.

Principles of Composition in Costume Design

The principles of composition discussed in the set design content in Chapter 11—focus, balance, proportion, rhythm, and unity—are applicable to costume design as well. A costume designer composes on different levels. Each costume is a unique composition. The series of costumes an individual character wears composes the character. Finally, the relationship of the costumes of all the characters in the play to each other and to the theatrical space represent a larger composition. The costumer must reflect the production concept, the meaning of the play, the importance of each character, and the relationships among the characters at every level of composition. Principles of composition guide the creation of each character's dress as well as the ensemble of costumes.

> **Principles of composition** guide the creation of **each** character's **dress** as well as the **ensemble** of **costumes.**

Space

Costumers need to think about the actual space of the actor's body, the size of the stage space, and the actor in relation to that space. The size and configuration of the theatre may also influence the scale of detail used in a costume. If the actor is on an arena or thrust stage, the costumer must think three dimensionally or sculpturally about the costume and how it will look from all sides. The proscenium presents a more frontal, two-dimensional view.

Focus

Costume composition directs the audience's attention to particular parts of the body. A ruff at the neck draws attention to the head. Trim on the sleeves sets off the hands. A low-cut neckline pulls our eyes to cleavage. Composition also tells us whom to look at on stage, perhaps bringing our focus to central characters over secondary roles with the use of proportion, color, pattern, or adornment.

Proportion

Proportion is the relationship of parts to the whole. Costumes can change our impression of the body's natural proportions and play with the body's natural symmetry. Proportion in costumes is linked to the silhouette of the period. In the sixteenth century men wore puffy sleeves that gave bulk to their torsos and stockings that emphasized the trimness of their legs. Women, who wore wide sleeves paired with wide skirts, had a more symmetrical look. Empire dresses are slender, with high waistlines that divide the body in two unequal portions just under the breasts rather than at the natural waist. Bustles create the impression of an arched spine and a protruding derrière. Proportions of individual character's costumes, when seen in relation to each other and the stage can give us information about the content of the drama. The queen's dress might be fuller than those of her maids, for example.

Rhythm

When creating a world of costumes, designers consider the relationship of different costumes within an overall scheme. A costume or set of costumes can show repetition or variation in motifs to create a rhythm. Touches of lace at the neck, the sleeves, the waist, and the hem can unite the various actors on stage. An absence of complementary elements can create a tense stage world. Gradations of color or line can heighten the rising dramatic action.

Unity or Harmony

Costumes must create a unified feeling of mood and style. The characters must all belong in the same visual world. There must be a sense that all the different costumes are consistent with the production concept and the other design elements.

Modern Design and the Ballets Russes

The Ballets Russes was founded in Saint Petersburg in 1898 by Sergei Diaghilev (1872–1929). Breaking from the storytelling tradition of classical ballet, the troupe presented a dance form capable of evoking pure emotion through form and movement. Set, costumes, movement, music, and dance worked together to induce specific emotional states. Their work provided an inspirational source for today's modern dance.

To compliment these abstract ballets, designs moved away from the conventional pictorial realism of painted perspective wings, drops, and flats into the realm of abstract art. Many of the greatest modern painters of the day— Pablo Picasso, Henri Matisse, Juan Miró, Georges Braque—among a host of other luminaries of the art world participated, as did the great Russian designer Léon Bakst (1866–1924). By calling on such dazzling new talents to create sets and costumes, Diaghilev hoped to move away from the staid tradition of nineteenth-century European stage design. The stage technology for the scenic work of the Ballets Russes was, with the exception of a few sculptural sets, not revolutionary. Old-fashioned wings and drops were the standard, but what was painted on them was revolutionary. Artists who were revolutionizing the art world provided painted backdrops using vibrant color, stylized composition, abstraction, geometric forms, and either forced or flattened perspective that made these drops unique works of art.

As dazzling as the sets were, the company's designers were most revolutionary in the realm of costume. These costumes not only clothed the human form, they transformed it into sculptural elements of abstract art. Never before had costumes been so specifically rendered to unite with the other elements on stage in the creation of mood, form, and feeling.

Bakst's designs for a series of ballets based on ancient Greek themes used images from ancient Greek vase paintings that also served as the inspiration for the choreography. *Afternoon of a Faun* (1912) featured the electrifying dancer Vaslav Nijinsky (1890–1950), who was instructed on the angular poses and two-dimensional rigid stances of ancient Greek painted images by Bakst. The ballet looked like an animated ancient Greek urn painting. Bakst's costumes were modern vibrant renditions of these earlier images whose colors harmonized with the set. In a similar unified manner, designer Natalia Gontcharova (1881–1962) created sets and costumes for *Le Coq d'Or* (1914) using motifs from Russian crafts and folk art. The style of sets and costumes was characterized by primary colors, distorted perspective,

▲ Nijinsky in the Blue God costume designed by Leon Bakst for the Ballets Russes. Nijinsky's gestures and costume show an Orientalist influence, as do the stylized positions of his hands and feet. These do not quote any single tradition and remain a fanciful interpretation.

(continued)

(continued from page 291)

and stylized floral patterns, reflecting the dynamism of the Fauvist movement in modern art.

The Ballet Russes toured internationally and provided wide exposure for painters and a new venue in which to experiment. Picasso created sets and costumes for the ballet *Parade* (1917) (see the photo on page 253). Henri Matisse was the designer for *The Song of the Nightingale* (1920), set in China, in which the visual world became a European fantasy of the exotic Orient. Matisse saw the costumes as an opportunity to turn the dancers' bodies into architectural blocks—mobile modern sculptures. Matisse commented that painters have always been "choreographers," creating compositional groupings of the human form. Dynamic and

experimental costumes that masked the curves of the body to create a generic building block of shape also inspired the choreography. The visual and performing elements of every production were united by a common aesthetic.

The early decades of the twentieth century were marked by Orientalism, which romanticized the Far East. Following the Paris Exposition Universelle in 1900 and tours of theatre performers and dancers from Siam, Cambodia, India, China, and Japan, Europe was intoxicated with Asian arts. A period of intercultural borrowing began, although few Europeans truly understood the cultural context of the forms they were appropriating. Art, fashion, fragrance, and every form of design

reflected this fascination. The impact of the Ballet Troupe of the Royal Siamese Court on the Ballets Russes was marked. Siamese gesture and technique were incorporated into performances and training and were reflected in the visual motifs Bakst created for sets and costumes. Nijinsky tried to master Siamese hand movements and the use of the upper torso. Bakst created a series of costumes that borrowed heavily from Siamese forms, using short skirts and headdresses with geometric designs. These early intercultural efforts saw culture as fashion and expressed a superficial exoticism. Nonetheless, they provided us with some of the most striking costume designs of the period, if not the century, and elevated costume design to the highest of art forms.

JUDITH DOLAN

ARTISTS IN THEIR OWN WORDS

Designer-director Judith Dolan is best known for her work with director Harold Prince, including the Broadway productions of Alfred Uhry's Parade *(1998) and* Candide, *for which she received a 1997 Tony award for best costume design.* Candide *was revived at the New York City Opera in 2005. After an extensive design career beginning at the Abbey Theatre in Ireland, Dolan earned a Ph.D. from Stanford University in directing and design. As a director-designer, she has mounted productions of the work of Bertolt Brecht, Tennessee Williams, and August Strindberg. She is currently professor of design and associate dean of Arts and Humanities at the University of California at San Diego.*

What is the key to developing your total concept for a production?

As a designer-director, I approach my work as an exercise in poetry where word and image work together cooperatively. As such, the images that the play suggests to me are as vital as the words of the text.

My method is to discover those images and begin to interpret them through physical experiences.

What specific design techniques do you apply as a director?

The chart of character/scene breakdown is the first step through which a costume designer brings the words on the page into a physical reality. It suggests entrances and exits, costume changes, what characters are on stage together, and begins to lift the flat experience of the page onto the dimensional stage. Making the organizational decisions for the chart begins the commitment to the play that reflects my own directorial focus. From the early reading erupt images, questions, prejudices, and physical needs, which become a structural springboard to the textures of the world of the play. Ultimately, the chart becomes for me a time/space document—a visual orchestration of the rhythms and music of the play.

To this I add storyboarding, image research, and collage, other means of visually interpreting the text as a designer-director. The storyboard drawings (the figures are often stick figures) keep the work focused on how the narrative relates to the spatial demands of the production. The storyboard is intentionally "not pretty" so that visual choices are not prematurely made, but in a graphic way, it provides me with the first concrete step into designing the set. The shape and structure of the play is then directly linked to the space of performance.

If the play is a period piece, I research the period from dramaturgical and historical viewpoints, and acquaint myself with the architecture, artifacts, and art of that period. I leave myself open to all sorts of possibilities from contemporary sources to capture the textural qualities of the play for contemporary audiences.

The research period allows me to wander in many potential artistic directions,

(continued)

The sketch contains handwritten notes including:

Parade
Mill Girls
Horrid Little Throwaway Ragdolls

NOT PRETTY
NOT SENTIMENTAL — as if

pigtails pulled back in different ways

clothes should feel brutalized but now just feel good but now just remnants of some lost childhood. A PERVERSION OF THE IMPULSE OF MARY'S PARTY DRESS

meandering parts in hair

braids wrap to join at CB

touches of lace are so faded & limp, worn they seem like faint texture

Old check bib apron pinned to bodice of dress

man's shirt under pinafore dress

Sleeves a bit short

false hem to lengthen skirt

Dark cotton stockings + work boots

35

36

34

Judith Dolan 1998

& this dress feels like an older sister's hand-me-down

THERE IS A SENSE OF VIOLENCE HERE

Sketch 34/35/36

◀ Judith Dolan's sketch and final costumes for *Parade*. The three mill girls on the right of the photo are treated as a group by the director and designed as a group in the sketch. Dolan's sketch is full of detailed notes about costume and hair. The costumes capture period, class, and occupation.

in order to choose the images that are most vital to the collage that will be the world of the production. The collage includes not only two-dimensional images, but also three-dimensional textures. It should reflect the dynamics of the play—whether brutal or lyrical, lighthearted or heavy. This struggle with editing images and then assembling them with other newly introduced textures is an anchor to the preproduction design process, as I become increasingly involved in directing during the rehearsal process.

How does your experience as a costume designer affect your work with actors as a director?

Casting decisions affect the visual nature of the world being created on stage. The actor's singular presence, his or her style—face, body, movement, voice, and internal rhythm—suggest the boundaries of the world. Casting choices related to age, race, size, gender, and nationality contribute to the human texture in performance. My design work has been significantly centered on costume design, and the actor, for me, has always been an important collaborator. My experience as a costume designer has allowed me to operate as a bridge between the world of the design and that of directing. It gives me as a director an opportunity to unite the details of the costume with the interpretation of the character as the performance evolves in rehearsal. It also collapses the boundary between actor, director, and designer and can enrich the work of all three collaborators.

Interview with Judith Dolan. By permission of JD.

Visual Elements of Costume Design

Costume designers articulate compositions through their use of line, texture, pattern, and color displayed on the body in motion. These elements draw on the audience's personal and cultural associations and sensory reactions. Styles and fashions of different periods suggest particular visual elements that may circumscribe the costume designer's work.

Line

Line refers to the **silhouette**, or overall shape, of a costume. We associate silhouettes with specific historical periods, but inherent in particular silhouettes are associated social ideas. In the 1950s, American women wore either pencil skirts or long flair skirts with layers of crinoline petticoats, pointed bras, and high heels that impeded freedom and movement. The line emphasized almost to the point of caricature the hourglass shape, depicting an imposed idea of femininity that imprisoned women in traditional roles. Compare that profile with the short flapper dresses of the liberated 1920s that marked women's newly acquired right to vote and with the miniskirts of the late 1960s and early 1970s, worn during the women's liberation movement. Women's silhouettes can express social restraint through corsets, high necklines, long skirts, and bustles. Costume line can also draw our eyes in a particular direction. Elizabethan men's garments drew the eyes to the codpiece, and the fashion of seventeenth-century Europe enhanced women's cleavage.

Texture

Tactile texture is the feel of the surface of a costume; texture results from the material from which a garment is made, its weave, or what is applied to the surface of the fabric. Texture affects how a costume catches the stage light and can accentuate form and style especially if folds are featured. Thick textures such as velvet absorb light, while smooth ones such as satin reflect it. Texture also influences how garments move on stage, whether they are flowing like silk or stiff like felt or burlap. In turn this affects the actors' physical actions. Textures help define the character's social, emotional, and physical state. The actor's skin is set against the feel of the fabric, so the audience reads the two textures together, eliciting cultural and sensory responses. Satin and velvet seem opulent and give a sense of wealth. Wool can feel cozy and warm and may remind us of sitting by a fire on a snowy evening. Burlap is rough and scratchy and may bring with it an association of poverty, earthiness, or discomfort. Polyester can seem kitschy.

Pattern

Pattern is a kind of visual texture made up of the elements of line, form, color, and space. Patterns can be used on stage to create motifs that create relationships among characters. A costumer may use harmonious patterns, to connect characters or use dissonant patterns to contrast them. After color, pattern sends the strongest visual message to the audience. Pattern can be used to add visual interest to the composition and to give a heightened sense of a character's personality. Bold geometrics indicate a dynamic and extroverted type; florals may be seen as feminine. Pattern may also indicate social status. Loud brash patterns are usually seen on lower class characters, more subdued patterns may reflect more refined and educated taste.

Color

Color is one of the costume designer's most powerful tools. Color provokes a direct physical response in the audience. We interpret color through sensory experience and cultural conventions: Red signals danger and passion in Western culture, yet to the Chinese, it represents happiness and celebration. White stands for innocence and purity in the West, but in Japan it is a sign of death and mourning. Psychological studies indicate that red, yellow, and orange are sensory stimulants, while blues and greens can have a calming effect. The impact of color is modified by its intensity. The deeper the hue, the more it attracts the eye. While light blue may calm, royal blue may arouse. Costumers manipulate our responses to characters by playing with our cultural associations and sensory responses to color.

The way colors are combined or set against different backgrounds affects the way they are read, so costumers must consider the set and lighting design and the way various characters will appear in relation to each other as they select costume elements. They may lay out a palette of color for a production and then assign particular colors and hues to different characters. Through color, costume designers can make relationships among characters immediately apparent and help tell the story: In *Romeo and Juliet*, the Capulets might wear gold while the

▼ Emilio Sosa's costumes for Edwin Lee Gibson's Oedipus in *The Seven* at the New York Theatre Workshop use texture and color to portray the character as a rapping pimp.

Montagues wear silver, or one family might appear in hues of burgundy and the other in hues of green. Personality is evoked through color, so choices reflect an interpretation of character. Would Juliet wear red? Would Hamlet wear yellow? The colors of an individual costume need to work with the actor's skin tones so that the actor's face stands out. Designers specify a palette of costume colors for a show within a scale of color values that coordinates with the colors chosen for the sets and lights that provide the environment for costumes.

The **Costume** Designer's Materials

Costume designers rely on many materials, including fabric, ornament, and accessories; hairstyles and wigs; and makeup and masks to add interest to their designs, to give information, or to add elements of style.

Fabric, Ornaments, and Accessories

The costumer's most basic tool is fabric. Its color, elasticity, movement, and texture all influence how actors move and feel on stage and how the audience understands the characters and the world of the play. Certain historical periods are associated with particular kinds of fabric. Before the twentieth century, only natural fibers were used, but costumers today use synthetics that can approximate the feel of period fabrics. Fabrics can be adapted through dyeing, painting, stenciling, aging, and distressing. Costumers also use other materials, such as metal or plastic, along with fabric, to shape, disguise, and reveal the human form.

Ornaments are the elements costumers add to clothes to give them extra detail and style, such as lace, buttons, tassels, embroidery, and sequins. Each of these decorations can evoke a period, style, social class, or personality. Aunty Mame might wear sequins, large buttons, and jeweled collars, while Juliet might have some tasteful lace or embroidered trim.

◀ Jenny Mannis' ludicrous costumes perfectly suit the zany humor of *Animal Crackers* at The Goodman Theatre, directed by Henry Wishcamper in 2009.

Making Up Race

The civil rights movement led to awareness of the offensive nature of blackface makeup and the racist legacy of performing "black" for white audiences. In subsequent years, in a reversal of the established power structure, plays using "whiteface," in which African Americans wear white makeup or play "white" to comment on white culture, have drawn attention to racial stereotypes.

Douglas Turner Ward's (b. 1930) 1965 one-act comedy *Day of Absence* is a reverse minstrel show in which a black cast dons whiteface to portray a Southern community that wakes up to find that all the blacks in their town have mysteriously disappeared, sending their lives into chaos. Eddie Murphy's 1984 *Saturday Night Live* sketch "White Like Me" demonstrated the privileged position of whites in our culture and brought the idea of whiteface to national consciousness. In Suzan-Lori Parks's 2001 play *Topdog/Underdog*, one of her two black characters has a job at a carnival, wearing white makeup to portray Abraham Lincoln; patrons are invited to shoot at him while he is in character.

The idea of whiteface went commercial in the Wayans brothers' 2004 film *White Chicks*, in which the black comic duo masquerade as rich blond women, using latex masks, blond wigs, and blue contact lenses, to poke fun at white values. In these and other productions, African American culture successfully appropriated a makeup of oppression as a force for power and the affirmation of positive identity.

Although the racism implicit in blackface makeup was brought to national consciousness decades ago, the use of yellowface—makeup and prosthetics to create Asian characters—continues. There seems to be little awareness that Asians find white actors performing "Asian" just as demeaning as whites performing "black" was to the African American community. Hollywood, from the days of silent film to the present, has consistently used white actors to play Asian roles. Stars such as Marlon Brando, Mickey Rooney, and Anthony Quinn donned yellowface apparently without a thought about its offensive nature. In contrast to film, the theatre was more open to Asian actors and often mixed Asian actors with actors in yellowface when productions required Asian roles. The practice has largely stopped in the commercial theatre since the controversy over the casting of white actors to play Asians in the Broadway production of *Miss Saigon* in 1991. Playwright David Henry Hwang, who spearheaded the battle against yellowface productions, has written plays such as *M Butterfly* and *Yellowface* that explore the nature of appropriated Asian identity.

The presence of blackface, whiteface, and yellowface makeup continues to make us question how much racial identity is something we perform according to socially imposed stereotypes. It reminds us that performing racial identity on stage, whether our own race or another's, determines how we as a culture think about race.

▼ Actor Jonathan Pryce wore eye prostheses and bronzing cream to look more Asian in the London production of *Miss Saigon*, which drew comparisons to a minstrel show in the United States. The American protests led to Pryce performing without the perceived racist makeup in New York.

Just as we might accessorize to bring finishing touches to our own wardrobes, costumers fill out the details of a character's costume with hats, scarves, shoes, jewelry, canes, and handbags. Some accessories help actors create character mannerisms: bracelets to jangle, a cane to point, a scarf to twist. Some participate in the action, such as the bowler hats the tramps exchange in *Waiting for Godot*.

Hairstyles and Wigs

Hairstyle completes the actor's visual image and falls under the costume designer's purview. Designers use wigs and hairpieces to reflect a historical period, to reveal a character's personal habits or taste, or to reinforce the overall style of the production. They often alter the actor's own hair through dyeing, cutting, shaving, and styling, or they might ask an actor to grow a beard. In the Broadway musical *Hairspray*, large bouffant wigs sum up the campy style of the piece and comment on attitudes toward female beauty in the 1950s.

Makeup and Masks

Almost all actors wear some kind of makeup. Actors transformed through makeup feel their character develop within when they look in the mirror. Stanislavski wrote much about makeup as a tool for literally getting into a character's skin. Makeup can be divided into three categories: straight makeup, character makeup, and special effects.

Straight makeup can enhance facial features, especially the eyebrows, eyes, cheeks, and mouth, to keep them from washing out under stage lights, allowing the actor's expressions to be read at a distance. Makeup can define a character, create old age, accentuate character traits, or reshape the face completely. Elements such as beards, mustaches, bushy eyebrows, and fake noses permit actors to make amazing transformations. Certain kinds of characters wear traditional makeup, such as the Restoration fop's rouged cheeks and the beauty mark or the Pierrot's white face. Special effects makeup can create bruises, scars, and other infirmities. Teeth can be stained or blackened to create a toothless look. In highly stylized performances, a wide palette of makeup colors and designs can totally transform and even camouflage human features. *Cats* (1982) used makeup to transform an entire cast into animals.

Masks immediately set a presentational style for both the visual elements and the acting and demand a heightened theatricality in all the accompanying stage elements. Masks provide the opportunity for even greater alteration of persona and imaginative flights of fancy than makeup as they enlarge the face. They can turn a group into a chorus with similar faces, reveal a fully defined unique character, or create figures of fantasy. Because masks cover the face, performers compensate by enlarging movement. Robert Wilson's 2004 production of *The Fables of la Fontaine*, staged at the Comédie Française, used fantastic masks to bring these animal allegories to life. Actors who normally worked in the declamatory style of French classical theatre were free to leap, hop, and prance, croak, and roar. The pairing of animal masks with human clothing supported the thematic symbolism of the allegorical material. Because of the demands masks place on actors, rehearsals began with movement exercises as the key to the embodiment of the masked characters.

Costume designers turn the director's vision of the world on stage and the relationship among the imaginary people who inhabit it into a tangible reality. They translate psychological traits into visual language that telegraphs the essence of character to an audience. Ultimately, they are the actor's silent partner in the creation of a vibrant physical character portrait.

▼ Director-designer Robert Wilson uses a combination of animal masks and elegant evening wear to create the anthropomorphic characters of La Fontaine's moral fables in *The Fables of la Fontaine* at the Comédie Française, Paris.

Summary

WHAT are the goals of costume design? p. 280

▶ The power of costume to shape identity is a major part of role-play in the theatre.

▶ Costumers consider the director's concept, what physical actions will be performed on stage, the psychological nature of a character, and the actor's physique.

▶ Costumes help tell the story. They establish time and place and the social and cultural milieu. They reveal the essence of character and express relationships among characters while defining the production style and meeting its practical needs.

HOW do collaboration, discussion, and research evolve into a costume design? p. 286

▶ The costume designer's process begins with a careful reading of the text, discussion with the director, and research.

▶ Sketches help costume designers communicate ideas to the director and other designers. Costume designers consider the other visual elements when making choices and think about how all the costumes will look together.

▶ Costume designers work closely with the actors and with costume shop personnel to make the design a reality.

WHAT are the principles of costume design? p. 290

▶ In costume design, principles of composition take place on the human form.

▶ Space, focus, balance, proportion, rhythm, and unity are the principles that inform costume composition.

WHAT are the visual elements of costume design? p. 294

▶ Costume designers draw on the audience's personal and cultural associations and sensory reactions as they display line, texture, pattern, and color on the body in motion.

WHAT are the costume designer's materials? p. 296

▶ The costume designer's materials include fabric, ornaments, and accessories; hairstyles and wigs; and makeup and masks.

MySearchLab®

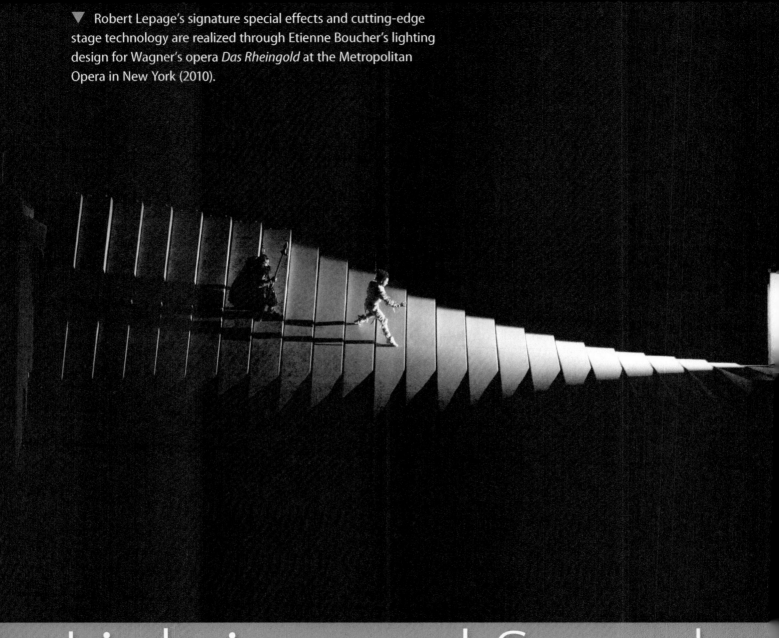

Robert Lepage's signature special effects and cutting-edge stage technology are realized through Etienne Boucher's lighting design for Wagner's opera *Das Rheingold* at the Metropolitan Opera in New York (2010).

Lighting and Sound Design

Technology and Art in Partnership

Although lighting and sound have always been taken into account in performance, they are the newest arts to be fully integrated into the theatre. As technology has advanced, the roles of lighting and sound have expanded, demonstrating how artists take advantage of invention to find new modes of expression. Nowhere is the partnership between art and technology more in evidence in today's theatre than in lighting and sound design.

Lighting design is a vital aspect of every theatre production today, but it is rarely the first thing we think about when we watch a performance. We do not think of light as something we see, but rather as *what we see by*. Light illuminates the theatrical world, and it is in and through light that things are revealed to us.

While we may not think consciously of the sound in a performance, like lighting, sound is always present, affecting our experience. The theatre is as alive with sound as the rest of the world around us and has always appealed to the ear through the resonance of the actors' voices, live music, and sound effects both on stage and off. In Elizabethan England people would say they were going to "hear" a play rather than "see" one. Only recently, however, has sound design emerged as a theatrical art in its own right.

Advances in digital technology now afford a greater ability to create, control, and amplify every kind of sound. What was once the art of creating realistic sound effects to support the dramatic action has evolved into an art of composition that supports the performance emotionally, thematically, and practically.

1. How does lighting design affect the mood of a production?

2. What role does sound play in theatrical performance?

3. How have sound and lighting artists taken advantage of new technologies to enhance the theatre-going experience?

CHAPTER 13

Stage Lighting

A lighting designer must consider both the physical and emotional qualities of light. Many of the good feelings we associate with springtime—warmth, the promise of renewal, the approach of the end of the school year—are evoked subliminally by changes in illumination. The dwindling light of autumn, by contrast, may bring on feelings of melancholy or the desire to huddle indoors and hibernate. Natural light and the way it changes with the time of day, the weather, and the passing of the seasons affects people both physically and emotionally. Since the discovery of electricity, we have become more conscious of the power of

artificial light. We may be drawn to the warm lighting of a cozy, romantic restaurant, and we may want to quickly leave the harsh neon and fluorescent lights of a fast-food joint.

Lighting designers master the art of controlling light. They think consciously about how natural and artificial light connect us to the world, and they specialize in translating that understanding into lighting effects for the stage. Some lighting designers use light conspicuously, allowing it to become a character within the drama itself.

Light often affects us unconsciously. We attribute our emotional reaction to a theatrical moment to the acting or

▲ When the silhouetted showgirls singing "We Are What We Are" are revealed to be men, the lighting makes an ironic commentary on the theme of *La Cage aux Folles*. Nick Richings' dramatic lighting captures the ambience of the night club through its intensity and color in the 2010 Broadway revival.

dialogue and often ignore the supporting role of a lighting effect. However, lighting creates the emotional atmosphere for a theatrical event and plays a crucial role in unifying the visual elements on stage.

Technological **Advances** and **Design** Innovations

The development of lighting design as an art is closely tied to technological advances. Theatre in ancient Greece and Rome and the religious pageants of the Middle Ages all took place outdoors, with sunlight illuminating both performers and spectators, uniting them in a shared physical and social environment. A passing cloud or a dynamic sunset might provide a natural special effect, and torches added illumination as the daylight faded, but generally the control of light was minimal. For indoor court performances during the Renaissance, visibility was a greater concern, and this led artists to experiment with lighting effects in creating theatrical illusions. Chandeliers set with candles or oil lamps illuminated both the stage and the auditorium. Footlights strengthened the light on stage, and mica or tinsel basins placed behind the lamps as reflectors increased their intensity. Stagehands brightened and darkened the scene by lowering or raising cylinders over the lamps or turning lamps on rotating poles to or away from the spectators. Containers filled with colored liquid or colored glass placed in front of lights gave a colored tint to a scene; a crystal orb filled with colored liquid made a glowing moon.

In the nineteenth century, gas lighting allowed directors and producers to control both the intensity and distribution of light across the stage. The *gas table* was the precursor of the modern *lighting board* (the dimmer control panel for all the lights in a theatre). With the gas table, a technician could manipulate all the lights from a single spot, making light changes more efficient. Philadelphia's Chestnut Street Theatre was the first to use gas in 1816. Gas lighting was found in many urban theatres by the 1840s. Other lighting options included the arc light, an early experiment in electric lighting, which produced an extremely harsh and bright light, and *limelight,* in which gas, hydrogen, and oxygen heated a column of lime (calcium-oxide), rendering it incandescent. Limelight, which remained popular until World War I, created an effect of sunlight or moonlight and was most often used as a spotlight.

Today, we use the expression **"in the** limelight**"** metaphorically **to mean that someone is the** focus **of attention.**

Lighting design became an essential theatrical art in the twentieth century, with the development of safe, efficient electricity. Edison's invention of the incandescent lamp in 1879, the first lighting source without an open flame, saved theatres from the plague of fire and also permitted control of intensity. New lighting instruments designed specifically for stage use enabled lighting design to develop as an art.

THINK

Is our theatre richer today because of controlled lighting, or have other aspects of the theatre, such as language and acting, been diminished by the use of sophisticated lighting design?

Artists quickly learned how to exploit each new invention. In England, Henry Irving (1838–1905), known for extravagant theatrical spectacles with massive moving sets and many actors, was one of the first to contrive innovative lighting effects for his productions. He darkened the audience to give full focus to the stage, used lacquered glass for coloring gaslights, and put up black masking to prevent light from spilling into unwanted areas. His fantastic lighting effects often upstaged the actors. In 1902, David Belasco (1853–1931), another innovative producer, built a light laboratory in the dome of the Republic Theatre in New York, where he and Louis Hartman, an electrician, experimented with new techniques and invented devices such as the "top hat" to control the spill of light. The famous sunset scene Belasco created for his production of *Madame Butterfly* (1900) produced a nuanced naturalistic effect of gradual change that extended over 14 minutes. In 1911, Munroe Pevear contributed to lighting design with advances in lighting color theory. Adolphe Appia (1862–1928) theorized that light could unify the actor, the stage set, and the floor of the playing area (see Chapter 6 and Chapter 8), and this concept has influenced lighting design ever since.

Goals of lighting design:

- **Provides selective visibility and focus**
- **Creates mood**
- **Defines style**
- **Establishes time and place**
- **Tells the story**
- **Presents a visual metaphor**
- **Defines style**
- **Reinforces the central image or theme of the play**
- **Establishes rhythm**

Spotlights have been used for nearly a century to provide selective visibility and focus on stage. Follow spots move with an actor, maintaining a constant pool of light. The expression "being in the spotlight" has become synonymous with being a star. In this scene from the 2003 Broadway production of *Gypsy*, the spotlight captures Mama Rose (Bernadette Peters) dreaming of fame. Note the circular lights on the stage floor that repeat the visual theme established with the spotlight in Jules Fisher's and Peggy Eisenhauer's lighting design. This production was directed by Sam Mendes.

Goals of Stage Lighting

The most beautiful set, sensational costumes, and virtuoso acting and directing all mean nothing if they cannot be seen. All the artists of the theatre depend on lighting designers not just for visibility but to enhance their work through the unifying effect of light. The lighting designer is the last member of the visual design team to work his or her magic and create an intangible atmosphere that will set the emotional tone of a production and tie everyone's efforts together.

Providing Selective Visibility and Focus

Lighting illuminates the stage, revealing colors and forms. There must be enough light on stage and enough coverage of the stage so any area that needs to be seen *can* be seen. What must not be seen must be hidden. Lighting can emphasize one part of the stage over another, open up the entire stage area at once, or break up the stage into different sections of brightness and shadow. Light marks the limits of the theatrical environment and establishes the visual composition of the stage. Because lighting tells audience members where to look, it focuses their attention.

Creating Mood

The mood created by lighting evokes a visceral response in the audience and sets an emotional tone for the performance. Lights coming at odd angles can lend an eerie feeling to the stage, while low rose lights can establish a romantic atmosphere. The mood that lighting suggests must provide a logical surround for the characters' behavior. Since light strongly affects feelings, it can help define and justify the character's psychological state and actions.

Serious dramas are often performed in stark or dim lighting; comedies, in brightness and color.

Defining Style

Lighting can impart a sense of reality or of the unreal and echo the stylistic approach of the other visual elements on stage. A realistic play may work well with effects that reproduce light the way we experience it from natural sources, whereas an expressionist piece may benefit from saturated colors at harsh angles to produce a nightmarish quality. A poetic piece can be enhanced through dramatic changes in color that support the images in the text and its inherent theatricality.

Establishing Time and Place

Creating an environment that expresses the location and time of the dramatic action is an important role of lighting. The color and angle of light can convey the time of day, whether it is early morning, late evening, or mid-afternoon; it can also indicate whether it is summer or winter and whether the characters are indoors or out. Lighting can also evoke specific interiors, from the low lights of a tavern to the brightness of a department store at Christmastime.

▲ In *Red*, by John Logan, Neil Austin's lighting permeates the stage and captures the artist Mark Rothko's obsession with red. Rothko is played here by Alfred Molina.

Telling the Story

Lights follow and express the dramatic action. The dimming of the houselights in the auditorium and the raising of the stage lights open a performance. Lights create a transition from scene to scene as they change in brightness or color, perhaps **cross-fading**—gradually diminishing one lighting cue while adding another to transition from one scene to the next. They punctuate the end of an event, with a **fade**—a gradual dimming—or a quick **blackout**. They move our interest from one location on the stage to another and from one character to another, telling us where to look to follow the story. These changes can express an emotional movement as alterations in colors and intensity indicate the changing circumstances of characters.

> **Light coming up, whenever it occurs, inevitably gives a sense of discovery and a new beginning, whereas lights going down suggest closure.**

Reinforcing the Central Image or Theme of a Play

Lighting can embody the very idea of a theatrical work. In *Metamorphosis* (see the photo on page 310), the constantly changing dramatic colors and patterns of light captured the image of the pool of water in which the action took place, extending the feel of the watery surface to the set and reinforcing the theme of transformation. Samuel Beckett's *Not I* (1973) features a spotlight focused on the mouth of an actress. The isolated beam of light echoes her stream-of-consciousness monologue expressing isolation and dislocation. The alienation and loss of self in Beckett's plays is often achieved through lighting effects. The order in which things are revealed as the lights go up can fix a central idea in spectators' minds and give the components of the set relative levels of importance. The shell of a house might be illuminated before the furniture to make a statement about the emptiness of the family living within.

Establishing Rhythm

The speed and frequency of light changes set the pace of a show. Lights going on and off with a bump can startle, enliven, or underscore dramatic impact, whereas gradual fades may extend an emotional moment. Short scenes paired with light changes can create a sense of movement through time. Often light changes can be almost imperceptible, so that the audience feels the result without actually perceiving it. A gradual sunrise or movement of artificial sunlight across the stage during the course of a performance can give us a subliminal sense of the passage of time.

◀ Playwright Samuel Beckett's precise directions for lighting *Come and Go* are nearly the same length as this short play itself, emphasizing the importance of light in his conceptualization of the text. Following Beckett's directions, light isolates the actresses' hats and dresses, leaving their faces dark, and reinforces the play's thematic concerns of human isolation and the interchangeability of identity. This image is from the Dublin's Gate Theatre 1996 production of *Come and Go*, directed by Bairbre Ni Chaoinh; lighting design by Alan Burrett; scenic and costume design by Simon Vincenzi. Lincoln Center Festival, New York.

▶ Kevin Adams's brash lighting and the repeated glow of dozens of video screens complement the driving rhythm of Green Day's music in *American Idiot* (2010) on Broadway.

The Lighting Designer's Process

Lighting designers go through a process similar to that of the other members of the design team; however, their contribution comes later in the production process, and many of their choices are dependent on the set and costume design. A lighting designer must be able to compose the sequence of lighting changes in his or her imagination before actually entering the theatre.

Discussion and Collaboration

Lighting designers begin by reading the text and thinking about what kinds of design elements the production requires as they develop a concept for a performance. They look for specific indications of time and place and any important references to light and its influence on the characters and the mood of the play. They hunt for **motivated light** cues specifically indicated in the text, such as a lamp being turned on, and make lists of the basic requirements. Lighting designers then meet with the director and discuss the director's vision for the production, desired special effects, and the way lighting will function to tell the story or express the concept. Lighting designers make suggestions as to how light might serve the production, enhance a moment, or solve a problem. These collaborative discussions lead to decisions about *unmotivated light cues*—cues that are not specifically required by the text that serve the director's concept.

Unlike other members of the design team, lighting designers do not usually bring sketches of their ideas to the first meetings. Since the lighting designers' goal is to unify all the elements of a production, they must wait to see the set and costume designs to know what they will be lighting. Their presence at early meetings is essential because they can spot potential problems in set design, such as tall structures that might block an angle of lighting, an area of action on a part of the stage that may be difficult to light, or the choice of a reflective surface that might cause the light to blind the audience.

These issues are more easily resolved while designs are still on paper than after they have been built. If the production is a musical, lighting designers listen carefully to the mood of the music and to the feelings evoked by the sound design that must be expressed in the lighting.

Creating a Design

Lighting designers research the historical period of a play. They study architectural features and lighting fixtures of the time. They gather information about the visual images the director is seeking. They look at photos, read about previous productions, and research the text. They may study period paintings and how light functions to illuminate the subject.

Lighting designers keep apprised of the development of costumes and sets. Set placement determines where they hang lights and what parts of the stage they must illuminate. The colors and textures of the set and costumes absorb or reflect light and are of vital concern to a lighting designer in the angle and placement of instruments. White costumes and sets, sequined costumes, mirrors, or shiny surfaces reflect when lit. Lighting designers watch rehearsals and run-throughs of a show to get a good sense of the placement and movement of the actors on stage so they know how the lights should follow the action. With all this information and their understanding of the play, they create a design for the show on paper before hanging and focusing the lights in the theatre.

A lighting designer creates a **light plot** (Figure 13.1)—a blueprint of the stage and auditorium with the **lighting grid** (the metal pipe structure from which the lights are hung). The location of each light to be used for a production is specifically marked on the plan. Lighting designers give each light an identifying number and chart the different instruments they intend to use and their locations. An **instrument schedule** (Figure 13.1) lists each instrument by its number and specifies its location, its purpose, the wattage of the lamp inside, the color of the **gel** (a colored film inserted in a slot in front of the lighting instrument to color stage lights), and other important information about its use. Computer software now aids in the creation of the light plot and the instrument schedule. The **master electrician** uses the light plot and instrument schedule to oversee the crew's installation and electrical connections. During the technical rehearsal, the lighting designer can refer to this chart to know which light to adjust.

Once the set is complete, lighting designers focus the lights in the theatre. A significant part of their task occurs during technical rehearsals, after the blocking (the actors'

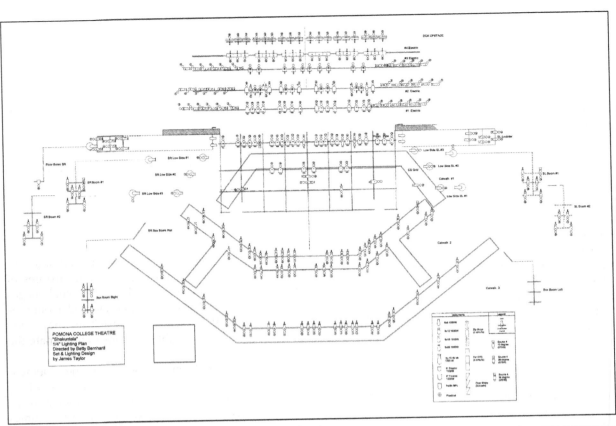

Lighti	"Sh aku		Fall 2003		Desi gn	
1	Front Warm A/D/E	48	Back Warm T	95	Spot SL	142	SR Tree
2	B	49	Back Cool A/D/E	96	Spot Sr	143	Bench
3	C/G/H	50	B	97	Cyc Bottom Lt. Blue	144	Throne
4	F	51	C/G/H/	98	Dark Blue	145	Heavenly Ashram
5	I	52	F	99	Red	146	
6	J	53	I	100	Cyc Top Lt. Blue	147	"Magic" Tree SL
7	K	54	J	101	Dark Blue	148	SR
8	L	55	K	102	Amber	149	Vedic Light
9	M	56	L	103	Kanva Warm Front	150	Vedic Light
10	N	57	M	104	Back	151	River Front
11	O	58	N	105	Side SL	152	River Sides
12	P	59	O	106	Side Sr	153	River Back
13	Q	60	P	107	Kanva Cool Front	154	Clouds
14	R	61	Q	108	Back	155	Menaka
15	S	62	R	109	Side SL	156	
16	T	63	S	110	Side SR	157	Mountains
17	Front Cool A/D/E	64	T	111	Cool Leaves DS SL	158	War Dance A
18	B	65	Side Warm SLIn1	112	SR	159	War Dance B
19	C/G/H	66	In 2	113	Cool Leaves Mid SL	160	Signer
20	F	67	In 3	114	SR		
21		68			Cool Leaves US		

▲ **Figure 13-1: LIGHT PLOT AND INSTRUMENT SCHEDULE** Lighting designer James P. Taylor's light plot (top) and instrument schedule (bottom) for Kalidasa's *Sakuntala* at Pomona College Theatre, California in 2004. The plot shows the placement of lighting instruments on the light grid and throughout the theatre. The key on the lower left identifies the different kinds of lighting instruments on the grid. Notice how lights are placed over the audience, on the stage, and offstage in the wings to allow the designer to control light from a variety of angles. *Reprinted with permission from James P. Taylor.*

▲ The Demon Dance performed by the noted *kathakali* artist Sasidharan Nair, as the action moves to a hermitage in the sky. Figure 13.1 is the light plot and instrument schedule for this performance. Lighting designer James Taylor chose colors to correspond to the wild demonic quality of the dance and music. Directed by Betty Bernhard and Kailash Pandya; choreography by Sasidharan Nair; set and lighting design by James Taylor; costume design by Sherry Linnell. Pomona College Theatre, California, 2004.

movements on stage) is fixed and sets and costumes are finished. The lighting designer and the director now observe all the production elements under the lights. This is a time for setting final lighting levels, making adjustments to focus to make sure all the action is clearly illuminated, and changing gel colors, if needed. The most complex part of the process is setting the timing of light cues—changes in light settings—with the director and the actors. Often this is a time of experimentation. The director may want a slow fade at the end of an act; the lighting designer may suggest that a blackout would be more effective. In such a case, the scene is run both ways, and the best result becomes the final cue. Each lighting change is examined in this careful manner until all the cues are set. The lighting designer coordinates with the stage manager to make sure each cue is properly noted in the **prompt book** (see Chapter 14), which serves as a guide to changes in light and sound during the performance. The work of the lighting designer, like that of the other designers, ends on opening night.

A **simple** show may have 20 **cues**; complex events can have **hundreds** of **lighting** cues that all need to be **carefully** timed.

Jennifer Tipton (b. 1937) was named a 2008 MacArthur Fellow, in recognition of her achievements in "pushing the visible boundaries of her art form with painterly lighting that evokes mood and sculpts movement in dance, drama, and opera." Among her numerous recognitions are two Tony Awards. In demand by notables in the dance and theatre worlds, Tipton still finds time to teach at the Yale School of Drama.

What inspired you to change paths from dancing to lighting?

I began lighting theatre after lighting Jerome Robbins's *Celebration, the Art of the Pas De Deux* at the Spoleto Festival in Italy 1972. Several theatre directors asked me to work with them after seeing that production.

Do you believe having been a dancer yourself has given you a distinct consciousness or sensibility toward the human form in space that influences your lighting?

I am sure that I light space because of the people moving in it rather than because of any text or music.

How does your approach to lighting dance, opera, and theatre differ? Is the source of the inspiration different when working with a spoken text, or pure movement, or the music and singing of opera?

My approach to anything that I do is more or less the same. I try to make the story clear and to respond to the dynamics of the space and the timing. I feel that each production is specific, and I try to find the lighting language or vocabulary that best expresses that production. Of course my approach is often determined by the scenery, by the time given for lighting, and by the circumstances of the production.

How does your lighting for the Wooster Group have to negotiate with the many other technological elements the company uses on stage?

In my first production with the Wooster Group, *BRACE UP!*, I was very aware of "competing" with the sound and video technology. At the time I realized that there was no way. Sound and video are show pieces and very much in evidence in Elizabeth LeCompte's aesthetic. Light takes a quieter place—totally important but following my rules of making the story clear and the rhythm dynamic.

What advice would you give to aspiring designers today?

My best advice for aspiring designers is to respond to your passion. Theatre is a very difficult profession, and you have to be sure that you are madly in love with it. There are dozens of ways to make a better living. If you don't absolutely adore lighting, do something else.

Source: Used with permission from Jennifer Tipton.

▼ Jennifer Tipton's lighting for *In the Penal Colony*, directed by JoAnne Akalaitis, perfectly captures the unsettling feeling of Kafka's words on the stage floor.   ©Dixie Sheridan

The Visual Elements of Light

Look at any panorama over several days at different times. If you are truly observant, you will see that things look different at different times of day and under various weather conditions. The objects you are looking at have not changed; what has changed is the pattern of light, the highlights and shadows that play across these objects and alter your perceptions and, in turn, change your emotional response to what you see. How are these many effects achieved with something as elusive as light? Light has four basic qualities that designers manipulate for various effects: intensity, distribution, color, and movement.

Intensity

Intensity is the degree of brightness of a light. The most fundamental and controllable level of a light is whether it is on or off. Dimmers on a lighting board control power and allow the designer to adjust intensity gradually, just as you do with a dimmer switch at home. Because our eyes continually adapt to lighting conditions, simple changes in the relative brightness of two different light cues can produce a new effect.

Distribution

Distribution refers to where light falls on stage and from what direction, the angle of the light, and the texture or edge of the light. Light can fall in a single stark beam or be diffused in space. Lighting designers control the angle and coverage of a beam of light in the way they position lighting instruments. Theatre lights come equipped with either shutters or flaps called *barn doors*, which close over a beam of light to give a narrow or wide focus. *Spill* refers to light that flows beyond the area of desired focus. A spill may indicate a need to refocus the instruments, or it can sometimes be used intentionally for artistic effect.

Color

A lighting designer uses the color of light as a fundamental expressive element. All light has color. White light contains the entire spectrum of colors that we see. Looking carefully at the white lights we encounter on a daily basis will reveal that some are more orange, yellow, pink, or blue than others, and these different light colorings elicit different associations and feelings. Recall that thin, colored films called *gels* are used to color stage lights. Some gels are lightly tinted and help create the slightly orange or pinkish-white lights to which we are accustomed; others are more saturated and turn the stage a deep blue or red. Lighting designers mix colored gels to create a broad palette of tones. Focusing two lights with different colored gels in the same stage area produces a textured effect of color. Mixing colored light is a different process from mixing paint. Mixing the three primary colors of paint (red, blue, and yellow) yields something close to black, whereas mixing the primary colors of light (red, blue, and green) yields white. Color is essential in creating mood on stage.

Movement

Lighting designers create movement by having lights come on, go off, and shift from one side of the stage to another. These changes may follow developing action, character movement, or changes in scenes or locations. The placement and duration of light on stage are essential elements in lighting design because the audience's eyes will follow the light.

Composing with Light

Although light is intangible, it is a central organizer and unifier of the visual elements on the stage. The stage is a black void until light composes the stage picture as it reveals objects in relation to each other and the actor. The visual elements of design—line, mass, texture, color, and scale—are revealed through light.

Lighting designers achieve these compositional goals through the use of several techniques that permit flexible effects. A **special** is a light with a unique and singular function. Specials are useful for bumping up the light on a particular area on stage that requires extra focus or attention. A **practical** is an onstage light such as a lamp or a fire in a fireplace that needs to appear to be controlled from the stage. Usually the light produced by a practical is supplemented by a special overhead to heighten its effect. Some lights create special effects, such as an eerie light accompanying the appearance of a ghost. Light coming from below is useful for such effects. This is why a flashlight under your chin at Halloween works so well as a cheap, portable special effect. **Backlighting**, light coming from behind the actor, creates silhouettes. **Sidelighting**, light coming from the side of the

▲ These six images demonstrate how the direction and angle of light mold the actor's face. *Top row:* left—high side light from left; center—front light hitting the actor straight on; right—high side light from right. *Bottom row:* left—front light filled out with lights from other angles to give a more three-dimensional view; center—high diagonal light; right—uplight coming from below creates an eerie effect. Model; lighting technician, Vanessa Rundle; lighting consultant, James Taylor.

stage, can provide accents and highlights. It is used in dance and musical theatre to highlight the dancers' legs.

There are many ways of conceiving the lighting design for a specific production. Because it is impractical to think about lights and cues individually, lighting designers think comprehensively about the variety of effects they want to create, how they want to sculpt the actors in space, and what areas of the stage will be used. They then accommodate a range of lighting options within an overall design.

In the 1920s, Stanley McCandless (1897–1967), a professor at Yale University, developed the first comprehensive method of lighting the stage. His system is no longer the only one designers use, but it continues to provide a basic approach. The first step is to divide the stage into areas 8 to 10 feet in diameter. Two lights coming from each side of the stage at 45-degree angles light each area, one with a warm amber- or pink-colored gel and one with a cold or blue-colored gel. This *area lighting* ensures that each part of the stage is covered and has the option of a range of color variations, from warm to cold. The areas overlap so the actors don't end up in dark spots as they move across the stage. *Double hangs* or *triple hangs*, with more than one light on each side for each area, offer an even greater

▲ Low, rich, saturated red stage lighting along with the flickering flames of the candelabra held by Aphrodite set a romantic mood in this scene from the 2001 production of *Metamorphosis*. Directed by Mary Zimmerman; scenic design by Daniel Ostling; costumes by Mara Blumenfeld; lighting by T. J. Gerkens. New York.

Lights focus attention on the lone actor on stage and provide emotional intensity for a theatre of little means and no set. This production of *Being Harold Pinter* (2011). by the Belarus Free Theatre, directed by Vladimir Shcherban and produced by Natalia Kaliada and Nikolai Khalezin, attracted world-wide attention after members of the company were arrested for political protest in Belarus.

variety of color options and coverage. Backlight and sidelight are then added to this plan for greater three-dimensionality. The designer then fills out this general lighting with other instruments used for more specific purposes. A *color wash* that bathes the entire stage can then be layered in.

Other systems of lighting include dividing the stage in horizontal zones rather than areas to create a layered effect with a lot of sidelighting. This method separates the front of the stage from the background and is useful for dance performances and in productions in which scenery flies on and off. *Jewel lighting* is common in Broadway productions. It emphasizes paths of strong light and adds other lights to fill in the stage along with specials. Each of these systems provides general illumination of the stage, some areas of emphasis, and the ability to create special lights for more particular purposes. Lighting designers also create new approaches to solve the problems posed by specific productions.

Think TECHNOLOGY

The Lighting Designer's Tools

The two main types of lighting instruments used in the theatre are the fresnel or spherical reflector spotlight, which gives a soft edge to beams of light, and the ellipsoidal reflector spotlight, which projects a sharper, more clearly defined edge. Follow spots have clearly defined beams and can follow an actor in movement across the stage. PAR (parabolic aluminized reflector) lamps are smaller, less expensive, more portable alternatives that can generate different types of light beams. Remote-controlled moving lights are increasingly part of a lighting designer's arsenal of instruments.

Gobos are small metal plates with stencil-like shapes cut out of them that slide into a slot on the front of an ellipsoidal reflector spot, allowing light through in selected areas to create a specific shape or pattern on stage. Gobos come in many shapes and can create the dappled effect of light shining through the leaves of trees, or the bars of a prison indicated by vertical lines of shadow and light. Designers can also create gobos for specific effects.

Lightboard operators execute lighting cues on dimmer boards and control boards. A dimmer board actually controls the intensity of the light, and the control board tells the dimmer board the timing and level. Today the majority of theatres use *computer control boards* to control the lights. Every light cue—which lights are to go on and off, to what levels, and at what speed—is programmed into the board. In the past, lightboard operators set up each lighting cue on the dimmer board individually and performed cue changes by manually moving dimmer switches on careful counts. This required split-second timing; a minute slip of the hand could change the cue. The number of lighting cues and the speed at which they could change was limited by the number of boards and operators. Computerized boards have made possible the elaborate and dynamic lighting effects we see today at rock concerts and big Broadway spectaculars.

The rapidity of technical advances has expanded the lighting designer's possibilities. Fiber optics and new light sources broaden the designer's palette, and new computer programs give assistance with the design process.

Sound Design

Theatrical sound creates an aural world that reflects the visual world of the stage, drawing many composers to the profession. Theatre has joined other forms of entertainment, such as film, television, radio, and rock concerts, in which designers and technicians thoroughly craft sound to enhance the totality of an experience.

The science of acoustics dates back to ancient times.

Sound Practices in the Past

Theatre has always been attentive to sound, with audibility always a central concern. Greek open-air theatres built into the hillsides had exceptional acoustics. At the Theatre of Epidaurus, originally built in the fourth century B.C.E. and still used for performances today, you can sit at the top of the 55-row auditorium that seats 14,000 and hear someone speak from the stage. Ancient Greek and Roman actors projected their voices from wide mouthpieces in their masks that functioned as megaphones. They intoned their speeches, often to the accompaniment of musical instruments, which allowed their voices to carry. The Romans built a shallow roof over the stage and placed large shallow basins around the playing area that also helped in vocal projection and amplification.

Sound effects have long played a role on the stage. The Romans created the sound of thunder by pouring stones into copper jars; the Elizabethans and their successors achieved a similar effect by shaking sheets of metal or rolling heavy balls down a machine with wooden channels. In modern times stagehands have dropped crash boxes filled with broken glass to produce the sound of an accident or collision or clapped together two pieces of wood to imitate the sound of a gunshot.

In the early twentieth century, Constantin Stanislavski's productions of the plays of Anton Chekhov included everyday sounds—barking dogs, croaking frogs, and clattering dishes—as a vehicle of stage realism. Some thought this naturalistic use of sound was excessive, and even Chekhov doubted its effect. Ever since, the re-creation of the sounds of everyday life has been part of many realistic productions.

In the past, live music would often accomplish the goals of sound design by entertaining the audience before the show and between acts, setting the mood, pacing the action, and accompanying the singers. Today's theatrical soundscapes include traditional and nontraditional use of actors' voices, live music, recorded music, synthetic sound and stage effects, and specifically composed sound scores that clarify the story and heighten the emotional impact. Much of theatrical sound is created, played, and adjusted by digital and computerized sound systems.

> **Goals of sound design:**
> - Is audible
> - Establishes the environment
> - Tells the story
> - Defines mood and style
> - Aids the action and provides rhythm
> - Reinforces the central image or theme of the play

Goals of Sound Design

Most of us seldom take notice of the sounds in the world around us, but in the theatre, the smallest noise is pregnant with meaning. Sound shapes our expectations, sets a mood, and reinforces the narrative. Often sound is used to provide practical solutions to scenic problems such as changing sets. Sometimes it is required by the action in a play. If we imagine an actor shooting a gun that makes no noise, we can see immediately the importance of sound.

Audibility

One of a sound designer's tasks is to ensure that the audience can hear the actors, the musicians, and both onstage and offstage sound effects. Sound designers use microphones, amplifiers, and speakers for amplification. Sometimes sound designers create effects to camouflage unwanted noise such as the thud of set pieces falling into place. Contemporary theatre design and changes in artistic expectations have made today's performers increasingly dependent on technology for amplification and less reliant on their natural ability to project.

THINK

What is lost and gained through the amplification of actors' voices in the theatre?

Although some new technologies live and interact on stage, others take the breath of life from the stage, replacing or mediating the live performance. Sometimes this intervention occurs without audience awareness. Most actors today in large theatres use stage microphones, small devices attached to their clothes or worn around the ear that are almost invisible to the audience. What spectators hear is a digitized voice reproduced by a speaker rather than the actual human voice of the performer they see live on stage. These voices can seem eerily disembodied. Musical productions in particular rely on microphones, even in small houses, because their clear digitized sound reproduces vocal qualities audiences have become accustomed to from CDs and music videos.

The unmediated human voice often has trouble competing for our attention next to amplified sounds, but it can express a direct connection to the heart, mind, soul, and spirit that

may be lost when digitized. The ability to project has separated stage acting from film acting. In film, microphones capture every vocal inflection, and voices are redubbed if they are unclear. In the future, even stage actors may no longer need to train as they did in the past, when they gave special attention to vocal projection as a way of reaching out to the audience.

As artists rely increasingly on the microphone, the audience is forgetting how to listen to the text of a play and the subtle interplay between melody and words in musical theatre. In 2004, as a reminder of the emotional intimacy lost through the miking of the human voice, the show *Broadway Unplugged* featured 20 star performers singing show tunes without the aid of electronic amplification. The performance demonstrated that the emotional immediacy of direct contact may be the price of technological progress.

In a 2011 *New York Times* article, "In Musical Theater, Where Are Those Pipes?"

critic Charles Isherwood bemoaned the loss of great voices in today's musical theatre. He attributed this loss to placing Hollywood and TV stars in Broadway musicals as box office draws, with celebrity now trumping singing talent as a casting requirement. This phenomenon is possible only because sound designers can work their amplification magic.

In 2003 a musician's strike on Broadway closed shows for several days and brought to the fore new concerns about sound technology replacing live music on stage. Theatre producers wanted to reduce the minimum number of live musicians required by the union's contract. They claimed that using fewer musicians would help reduce Broadway ticket prices and allow artists more creative freedom in determining musical accompaniment. Of course, such a move would result in job loss for musicians and the replacement of live music with electronically produced sound. Music is an interactive element that must live and breathe with the

(continued)

◀ Kia Glover, NaTasha Yvette Williams, and Dwayne Grayman wear mikes that are barely visible from the audience in *Ain't Misbehavin'*, the Fats Waller musical conceived and originally directed by Richard Maltby, Jr. Directed and choreographed by Kent Gash; music direction by Darryl G. Ivey; costume design by Austin K. Sanderson; set design by Emily Beck; lighting design by William H. Grant III; sound design by Peter Sasha Hurowitz.

performers. Musical directors adjust the orchestra's timing to the rhythms of the actor's nightly performance and to audience response. They also cover up for missed cues and other unexpected occurrences. Recorded music is frozen; its tempo is unchangeable. Faced with the specter of performing to canned music, actors joined the musicians' picket lines, and Broadway musicals were shut down for the duration of the strike. The union eventually accepted a compromise that diminished orchestra size, though not as drastically as first proposed.

The eventual eradication of live music in the theatre had never before been such an imminent threat. The Council for Living Music is an organization devoted to the preservation of live music. You can read about the history of this controversy at savelivemusiconbroadway.com and even get involved in the preservation movement.

Establishing the Environment

At the 1952 debut of *4'33"*, avant-garde composer John Cage (1912–1992) had his pianist present 4 minutes and 33 seconds of silence. He wanted audience members to focus their attention on the naturally occurring sounds of their environment, to which they usually pay little heed. In this case, the audience became aware of the patter of raindrops, the wind through the trees, and the murmur of puzzled spectators. Cage wanted to demonstrate that silence does not exist in the natural world. Every environment is alive with its own acoustic symphony: crickets chirping, car engines revving, footsteps falling and echoing. Such sounds evoke particular settings and can even indicate a specific time of day. Many of our associations with sounds may be unconscious; like Cage's audience, we often simply block out ambient noise. The sound designer, by contrast, studies and reproduces the aural specificity of times and places to help create a world on stage.

Just as set and costume designers use a specific palette of colors to create a visual identity for a play, the sound designer chooses from a specific sonic palette to create an aural identity for a play.

Telling the Story

Tires screech. A crash. Silence. Then sirens from a distance. Hearing these sound effects, we have already constructed a narrative in our imagination. Theatrical texts often require sounds to set the scene, give exposition, or help define the action. Events taking place off stage can be given life: The clop-clop of hooves announces an unexpected visitor; a steam whistle signals an imminent departure. Motivated sounds like these have an identifiable source and immediately give concrete information to the audience and work the same way as motivated lighting.

Sound can affect the way the audience experiences a story, and often this is achieved with abstract rather than realistic effects. Sound designers consider the emotional arc of the plot and create its aural embodiment. Rhythmic pulsing increasing in tempo can underscore the tension in a scene. The wail of a violin can signal an emotional change. A crescendo can alert us to an explosive moment to come.

Whether concrete or evocative, sounds tell stories and tell us how to relate to the narrative.

Defining Mood and Style

Sounds can establish the mood of a scene: The tick-tock of a clock underlines the lateness of the hour and produces a feeling of suspense. Distorted eerie sounds of chanting can unsettle the audience and prepare them for a strange experience to come. The hustle and bustle of a fairground—carnival music, the hum of the crowd, laughter, and shouting barkers—suggest excitement and a carefree mood. If the music becomes too slow and the laughter too loud, the feeling can change to one of discomfort or apprehension. Exaggerations and distortions can shift the style from realism to heightened theatricality.

Sounds that an audience hears that are outside the characters' world can also establish an atmosphere. Musical scores, like those in films, draw on our emotional responses to indicate the moods dominating various scenes. This practice, reminiscent of nineteenth-century melodrama, has long been part of the theatre. Today recorded rather than live music often achieves the effect. Preshow music, played as audience members arrive and take their seats, sets a tone before the show even begins and plays with audience expectations. Exit music, played as the audience leaves, reinforces a feeling for the audience to remember.

Aiding the Flow of the Action and Providing Rhythm

Sound designers can punctuate dramatic action with sounds or music that herald the beginning or the end of a scene. Sound can cover a stage transition, either carrying the audience along in an even flow or emphasizing a break between scenes. The timing of these sound cues—when they begin and how long they last—sets a pace for the production as a whole. In David Ives's (b. 1950) *All in the*

Timing (1993), multiple scenes replay attempts at a pickup in a café. Every time one of the characters says the wrong thing, a buzzer goes off. The frequency of the sound accelerates the more the characters fumble, adding to the rising comic action.

> **More and more playwrights are aware of how sound can help their work and write suggestions for sound into the script.**

Today, as more and more playwrights write plays with short scenes or plays that are collections of unrelated short sketches, sound becomes even more important for its ability to provide a unifying element. Producers have discovered that changing scenes through sounds can be easier and less costly than doing so with sets.

Reinforcing the Central Image or Theme of the Text

Sometimes sound can sum up the action of the drama in a way that gives the audience a visceral, intuitive understanding of its meaning. At the end of Chekhov's *The Cherry Orchard*, the script indicates that the audience hears the sound of a breaking string dying away followed by the thud of an ax hitting a tree. The sound of the ax reveals that the destruction of the cherry orchard has begun, but together these sounds poignantly convey the end of an era and the dissolution of the world of the aristocracy, the central theme of the play.

THINK

How should a designer balance audience comfort against the need to use light or sound for a shocking effect?

The Sound Designer's Process

WHAT steps does a sound designer's process involve?

Because comprehensive sound design is a relatively recent development, the work of sound designers varies from production to production and differs according to designers' specific skills. Some may work on amplification only, whereas others create an overall *sound score*. Some use original music and effects, whereas others draw from existing material to meet the needs of a production.

Discussion, Collaboration, and Research

A sound designer's work usually begins with reading and analyzing a text for sound requirements and meeting with the director to discuss how sound can help realize the director's vision. Before this meeting, some sound designers ask themselves what the rhythm, impulse, or energy of the play is to locate a feeling for the sound. Sound designers conceive of their work as an art in time. Because audiences experience sound through change, sound designers consider the structure of the story and how rhythm and tempo can support that dramatic structure. They think about a field

of possibilities without making specific choices. The director usually has some very specific ideas in mind that further limit the range of effects. The director discusses the style and setting of the play and how its time and place, concept, and mood can be evoked by sound. When a director already has very specific ideas, the sound designer becomes a researcher to hone the director's choices. Some directors describe a feeling they want and set the sound designer free to create that feeling in an individual way.

Sound designers work with the other members of the design team to determine the placement of sound equipment and microphones on stage. They may need to hide a microphone in a costume. Attending rehearsals can give a clear idea of the required timing and duration for sound cues and may provide new ideas about how sound might support the production.

Sound designers, like others on the creative team, do research to find material appropriate to particular settings and times: A setting in the Middle East may require a call to prayer and chanted passages from holy texts; Latin America

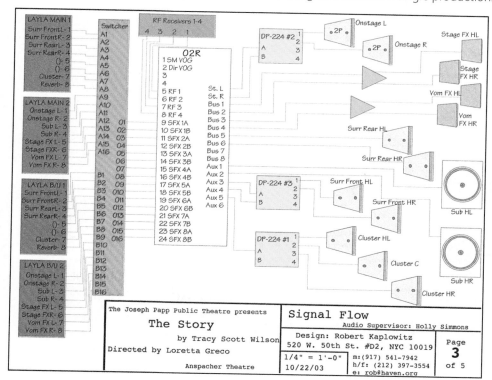

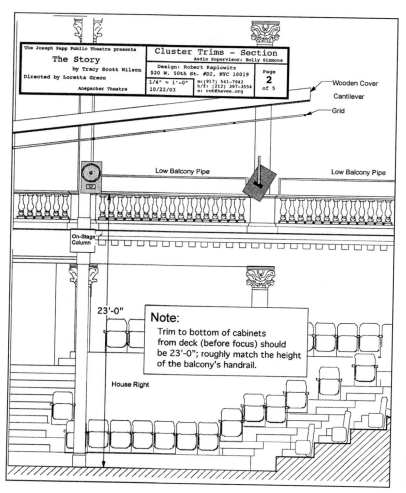

◀ **Figure 13-2a: SIGNAL FLOW-CHART** Sound designer Robert Kaplowitz's signal flowchart for Tracy Scott Williams's *The Story* at the Joseph Papp Public Theatre, directed by Loretta Greco shows what sound devices are being used for the show, where they are placed, which switches operate them, and the flow of sound from microphones and players to speakers.

◀ **Figure 13-2b: SOUND PLOT** Robert Kaplowitz's sound design for Tracy Scott Williams's *The Story* at the Joseph Papp Public Theatre, directed by Loretta Greco shows the placement of speakers in the theatre. It guides the crew in the placement of equipment and helps the designer keep track of places of sound emanation.

Reprinted with permission from Robert Kaplowitz, composer/sound designer, and Matthew Gratz (for section of Anspacher Theatre).

Cue	Cue Name	Placement	Description	O2R Scene	Type	VO?
167	Fade out	p 096 Transition complete	Fade out	O2R Scene 03	SFX	☐Y ☒N
168	Theme	p 098 J: You're lying. I know you are.	marimba from theme	O2R Scene 03	SFX	☐Y ☒N
169	Fade out theme	p 099 Yvonne in place	Fade out	O2R Scene 03	RF	☐Y ☒N
172	Radio Transition	p 103 P: You're under the arrest for the obstruction of justice.	News radio hit (redman) into voice over text plus low traffic rumble and hi traffic add	O2R Scene 03	SFX/RF	☒Y ☐N
173	Pulldown to Radio	p 104 With butts in seats	Pull down level to "Radio Like"	O2R Scene 03	SFX	☐Y ☒N
174	Fade Traffic	p 104 With reporter text complete in VO "48 hours to reveal her sources"	Traffic add out plus hit of garbage truck	O2R Scene 03	SFX	☐Y ☒N
175	Traffic Out	p 105 Y: Went into an apartment	Pull main traffic out of surrounds to subs only	O2R Scene 03	SFX	☐Y ☒N
178	Cop and Girl, RF 1&3	p 107 J: Two days, Yvonne. Two days.	Tension rhythm (hip hop) plus RF 1, 3 Up O2R SCENE 45	O2R Scene 45	SFX	☒Y ☐N
178.5	Music Fade	p 107 As girls exit/Yvonne moves A to chair	Music fade	O2R Scene 45	RF	☒Y ☐N
179	RF OUT	p 107 Girl: I ain't do nothin' A	RF 1, 3 out - O2R Scene 3	O2R Scene 03	SFX	☐Y ☒N
180	Trans to 12C	p 111 P: And one for people who think she'll get caught.	Single bass note, distant.	O2R Scene 03	SFX	☐Y ☒N
180.5	Trans to 13 - Prayer	p 112 P: ... you're not taking A Outlook with you.	Walking Bass version of theme	O2R Scene 03	SFX	☐Y ☒N
181	Fade Music	p 112 Yvonne in place Up Center B	Fade out with Yvonne in place	O2R Scene 03	SFX	☐Y ☒N
182	RF 4 UP	p 112 Y: What am I going to... B	RF 4 UP - O2R SCENE 58 RF into surrounds, ambient reverb.	O2R Scene 58	RF	☐Y ☒N
184	RF Out	p 112 Latisha Exits D	RF 4 Out -O2R SCENE 3 UP.	O2R Scene 03	RF	☐Y ☒N

◀ **Figure 13-2c: SOUND CUE SYNOPSIS** Sound designer Robert Kaplowitz's sound cue synopsis for Tracy Scott Williams's *The Story* at the Joseph Papp Public Theatre, directed by Loretta Greco is shown here. Each sound cue has a number and a name; the chart records a description of the sound and the line of the play that cues the sound.

Reprinted with permission from Robert Kaplowitz, composer/sound designer.

might require particular music and rhythms. Many sound designers own libraries of recorded sound. Today many effects can be downloaded from the Internet. In addition to sounds created specifically for a director's concept, researched sounds may become part of a design or may be adapted to fit the needs of a production. Discoveries and creations are shared with the director as part of the evolution of the design.

Creating the Sound Design

When sound choices are finalized, the designer edits the sound samples onto separate discs or tapes (depending on theatre equipment) or onto one disc or tape, in the order in which the cues are to be played during the course of the show. The sound operator can layer and mix multiple sound sources with a *mixer*, a device that merges the sound sources into one or more streams of sound.

Sound designers may use sound systems already in place in the theatre, or they may be responsible for acquiring and setting up the necessary sound equipment. A **sound plot** shows all the equipment the show will use and how the different pieces (microphones, amplifiers, etc.) connect to one another (see Figures 13-2a and b on page 319). Before technical rehearsals, the sound designer makes sure all the equipment is working properly. During technical rehearsals, the sound designer, in consultation with the director, helps set sound levels and timing for sound cues, often coordinating sound effects with lights, set changes, and the actors' physical actions (see Figure 13-2c). Designers adjust equipment and balance the sounds coming from the loudspeakers so they reach all areas of the auditorium evenly. They also adjust the sound so that amplified and recorded sounds reach the audience at the same time as live sound from the stage. The sound designer's job, like that of other designers, ends when the show opens. Technicians continue to test, run, and maintain the equipment during the run of the production.

Think TECHNOLOGY

Stage microphones detect the sounds on stage and amplify them through loudspeakers. *Area mikes* pick up sounds in a wide area, whereas *shotgun mikes* focus on a specific direction. Today many actors wear wireless *body mikes*, attached either to their clothes or to their heads.

New technologies for creating and playing sound cues in the theatre continue to give designers greater control of sound quality. Although a few theatres may still use reel-to-reel tapes, digital sound technology is now the norm, with sound designs stored on compact discs, minidiscs, stand-alone digital workstations, or a computer's hard drive.

Both lighting and sound design have evolved in the past 100 years through advances in technology unthinkable in past eras. The number of possible cues and the complexity of effects, the accuracy and timing of the execution of designs, and the range of artistic vocabulary far surpass those of even a generation ago. Technical progress will surely continue to offer innovations, and light and sound design will be limited only by the power of the imagination.

ROBERT KAPLOWITZ

ARTISTS IN THEIR OWN WORDS

Robert Kaplowitz was awarded the 2010 Tony Award for Sound Design for the musical Fela. *He has participated in the development of hundreds of new plays. and spent five years as the resident sound designer at the Eugene O'Neill Playwrights Conference. In addition to his many New York and regional theatre credits, he is also the producing artistic director of the Relentless Theatre Company.*

What drew you to this profession?

I studied jazz saxophone as a child and was enamored of the notion of composition through improvisation. In high school, while I was never interested in being a performer, I did think all those actresses were cute, and so I became a stagehand. That, coupled with an amazing electronic music lab, led me to explore the idea of creating soundscapes and music for plays.

I attended NYU's undergraduate design program, which did not teach sound design; however, the conceptual training I received—learning to understand my visceral response to a text and translate it into a concrete landscape—was invaluable to my growth as a designer.

My first year in New York, I saw Mark Bennet's sound design for Caryl Churchill's *Mad Forest*. The play featured an amazing score, and in the middle of it was a two- or three-minute scene that took place without any words—just a deep silence accentuated by a very subtle set of environmental sounds and actor movement. In that instant, I became fully committed to my choice to become a sound designer.

Can you outline the steps in your creative process?

I begin, always, with the text. I read a play all the way through in a single go to grasp the flow, the rhythms, the linguistic evolution of the world. I do this without a pencil or any music in the background. I then read it again and write down anything at all that comes to my mind—words, phrases that stand out, responses to moments, scenes that excite me, questions. I am also looking for the moments when the text must stand on its own, without any other sounds. The third reading is for what is essential, sonically, to the text—I make a list of everything from "doorbell, p. 15, rich house" to "playwright says to score sc. 4, think about how." The fourth reading prepares me for my first conversations with my director. I make a list of every possible cue I might throw in, including the above "essentials" list. I take that list, plus all of my other thoughts, into conversation with the director, and this leads us to a complete list of possibilities, which eventually gets honed down into the actual cue synopsis.

The other major leaping off point for my work is time in the theatre. I try to arrange for 10 or 15 minutes alone in the space, just to listen. Not for any advanced acoustical research; I just like to hear the room and get a sense of the environment in which the play is going to happen. The theatre is my palette, and I like to get to know it before I begin. I also double-check all of the technical drawings—measuring out the room, adding information about the house. My main concern is the propagation of sound into the ears of the audience, and I need to have accurate spatial information about the room. How does the stage relate, physically, to the house? How far is the closest point between actors and audience? How far is the farthest? How deep is the balcony overhang? What's the distance between potential speaker positions and various audience locations? Are the walls parallel, or slightly angled, or broken up with architecture? Where can I put surround speakers and subwoofers? A million more questions

(continued)

(*continued from page 319*)

like these must be answered before I can design the physical sound system.

The next step is my favorite—I get to sit in the rehearsal room and play with my collaborators. The symbiosis between performers and the music or sound around them is probably the single most thrilling part of sound design for me. Modern technology enables me to sit in the room with a laptop and alter whatever work I've done in the studio. I've actually written entire scores while in rehearsals, gleaning an understanding of rhythm, pace, counterpoint, support, and dynamics as the actors and director are making similar discoveries for themselves.

What skills must a sound designer possess?

The ability to make writers and directors comfortable and confident. To be able to read for dramaturgical analysis. To be able to talk with everyone on the team, accepting their notions and offering your own. Sometimes, you need a lot of restraint—tongue-biting is a good skill to have. Every

collaborator is an artist, and it's sometimes important to let the others make choices without throwing your own two cents in.

You really need to know how to listen—to what the characters are saying, to what the room is doing, to the real world around you, and to every piece and style of music that comes your way. To understand that in theatre, everything is heightened. So you need to understand how the ordinary becomes extraordinary in theatre, and to stay specific with every choice you make.

What we do is a marriage of the artistic to the technical, so there are also a slew of technical skills to be developed. You must learn an array of sound system details—terms like *phase coupling*, *feedback loops*, *precedence effect*, *equalization*, *delay*, and *microphone field patterns*. We have to understand how the sound moves through the room, the best way to get it there, and how the room itself is going to behave in the process. How I deliver a sound cue is as important as its content.

And how I deliver an actor's voice is probably even more important.

Do you have any advice for aspiring sound designers?

Aspiring designers should pursue all knowledge—read, listen to music, go to museums and galleries, follow politics, learn about genetics, study a language . . . the more influences a designer has, the more open he or she can be to the world that we, as a profession, comment on. Avoid bogging down in any sort of "personal aesthetic"—a designer, at his or her core, is meant to be responding to the world of the play rather than letting personal taste steer the soundscape. The key, for me, is to become a blank slate. I have a lot of information rattling around in my brain, but I never have any answers until I've spent time with the words, and with my collaborators. Only then can I create a sound design that is an accurate reflection of the play.

Source: Used with permission from Robert Kaplowitz.

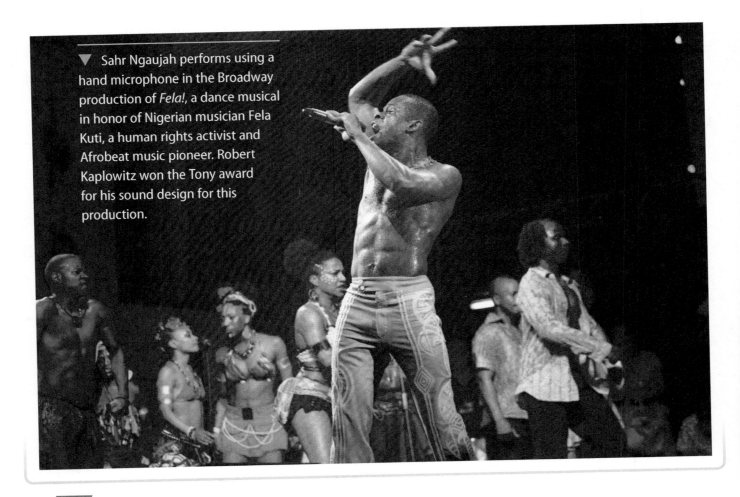

▼ Sahr Ngaujah performs using a hand microphone in the Broadway production of *Fela!*, a dance musical in honor of Nigerian musician Fela Kuti, a human rights activist and Afrobeat music pioneer. Robert Kaplowitz won the Tony award for his sound design for this production.

Summary

WHAT are the goals of stage lighting design? p. 302

▶ Lighting designers translate their understanding of how natural and artificial light connect us to the world into lighting effects for the stage.

▶ Lighting creates the emotional atmosphere for a theatrical event and plays a crucial role in unifying the visual elements on stage.

▶ The development of lighting design is closely tied to technological advances such as safe, efficient electricity and new lighting instruments.

▶ The goals of stage lighting include creating mood, providing visibility, defining style, establishing time and place, focusing attention on stage, telling the story, reinforcing a central image or theme, and establishing rhythm.

WHAT steps does a lighting designer's process involve? p. 307

▶ Lighting designers develop a design through careful reading of a text, discussion with the director and creative team, and research. A significant part of their work is accomplished during technical rehearsals.

▶ Lighting designers manipulate the four basic qualities of light—intensity, distribution, color, and movement.

WHAT are the visual elements of light design? p. 311

▶ The visual elements of design—line, mass, texture, color, and scale—are revealed through the composition of light.

▶ Lighting designers accommodate a range of lighting options within an overall design.

WHAT are the goals of sound design? p. 315

▶ Sound design has only recently emerged as a theatrical art. Advances in digital technology now afford a greater ability to create, control, and amplify every kind of sound.

▶ The goals of sound design include audibility, establishing the environment, telling the story, defining mood and style, aiding the flow of the action and providing rhythm, and reinforcing a central image or theme.

WHAT steps does a sound designer's process involve? p. 318

▶ Sound designers develop a design through careful reading of a text, discussion with the director and creative team, and research.

▶ Today's theatrical soundscapes include the traditional and nontraditional use of actors' voices, live music, recorded music, synthetic sound and stage effects, and specifically composed sound scores.

▶ Some sound designers use original music and effects, whereas others draw from existing material to meet the needs of a production

MySearchLab®

▼ In 2002, after the end of Taliban rule which forbade theatrical performance, actors in the ruins of the Kabul theatre staged a play about Afghanistan's destruction. The actress dressed as a bride symbolizes the return of peace.

Making Theatre Happen

The Necessity of Theatre

Around the world, despite obstacles and difficulties, people are committed to making theatre. In Sarajevo and Bagdad, Cape Town, and Ground Zero, artists use the theatre to express their strivings, hopes, and fears. Some overcome political barriers, some leap financial hurdles, some combat social and religious custom, and some even risk their lives to express their human yearnings through theatre. Fortunate theatre artists are celebrated for their activities by the state, their communities, or an adoring public. While some find fame and fortune, many do not, and most create at great personal sacrifice. There is no single model for creating the theatrical event. In each case artistic vision, talent, and passion confront a set of social, political, and economic realities.

How one enters a life in the theatre can vary from society to society. Some are driven by personal talent and ambition, some by cultural heritage and community values. In some places national traditions and institutions provide a conduit for artists. In China, elementary school children are auditioned for theatre training and begin years of rigorous training at government-funded conservatories to receive positions in government-funded theatres; those not displaying precocious talent are excluded from entering the national schools. *Kabuki* theatre roles are passed within families from generation to generation. In Australia, the Americas, and Europe, theatre is usually the place for individual expression and self-realization. This reflects the premium placed on individual freedom in these cultures where actors and directors peddle their talents. In the West, even in the noncommercial world, creating theatre may depend on an artist having the ability to personally assemble and inspire a collaborative team.

In some repressive cultures, individual freedom is feared, and theatre artists may be labeled as political dissidents. Theatrical activity can land artists in prison, as in the cases of Czech President Vaclav Havel (b. 1936) and Nigerian Wole Soyinka (b. 1934), or even get them killed, like Indian director Safdar Hashmi (1954–1989). Nevertheless, the need to make a statement in theatrical form about political conditions inspires some performers to risk all, performing in clandestine underground venues with minimal technical equipment.

1. How do social, political, and economic realities affect making theatre?

2. How do different cultures support and train theatre artists?

3. What risks do theatre artists take to create performances around the world?

Where **Theatre** Happens

How and where a theatrical performance is created is inextricably tied to who is doing it and why. Theatre happens in many different venues around the world. In this section we discuss some of these places and the types of theatre they produce and host.

State-Subsidized Theatres

Many countries around the world have state-subsidized professional theatres. In Europe, the tradition of state funding goes back to the royal theatres chartered by the ruling monarchs of the Renaissance. In the era before electronic media, theatre was the only way to reach mass public audiences, and state licensing was often used as a means of censorship. The central authority funded only those theatres with approved messages, a tradition that continued in many dictatorships. In contrast, today's subsidized European theatres are frequently places of artistic exploration and experimentation. Municipalities and provincial governments fund local theatres and cultural centers that often provide convenient schedules and child care to facilitate theatre-going.

The Japanese National Theatre and the French Comédie Française preserve classical theatrical forms but also present modern works.

In Africa and Asia, colonial powers used the subsidized theatre to stamp their cultural imprint on local populations. With the growth of democracy in many developing nations, subsidized national theatres now belong to the people and celebrate popular indigenous culture. Across Africa and Asia, countries such as Nigeria, Namibia, and Thailand all provide government subsidies for national theatres to preserve excellence or local traditions.

The United States is actually an exception among most prosperous nations in having no nationally funded theatre. In contrast, even many developing countries consider government support essential for the theatre and its artists. Plans to privatize the National Arts Theatre of Nigeria led to massive protests that forced the government to restore funding. Sadly, national and local support for the arts in the United States is limited to competitive grants and subject to budget cuts and political pressure. In 1990, the National Endowment for the Arts (NEA) withdrew its support for individual artists who had been recommended by a peer review panel, claiming that their work was too sexually explicit. This engendered a protracted court battle over freedom of speech and First Amendment protection for applicants for government grants, in a suit brought by artists Karen Finley (b. 1956), Tim Miller (b. 1958), John Fleck (b. 1951), and Holly Hughes (b. 1955), now referred to as the NEA Four. The legal battle centered on the amendment to the 1990 congressional reauthorization of the NEA that required consideration of standards of decency in awarding grants.

> THINK
>
> Should the government fund individual artists whose work offends certain communities but is deemed excellent by a peer committee?

During the Great Depression of the 1930s, the U.S. government briefly flirted with state-supported theatres in the form of the Federal Theatre Project, founded to provide a buffer against massive unemployment in the arts. Wonderful artists emerged from that era, including Orson Welles (1915–1985) and John Houseman (1902–1988). The foundations for the Black Theatre movement, the innovative work done under government auspices, and the thousands of theatre artists provided with a decent wage demonstrate that government subsidy can produce significant theatre in the United States.

In countries with state-subsidized theatres, the luxury of strong public support is evidenced in the stable working lives it provides to actors, designers, and directors. State funding allows companies to develop ensembles, to have long rehearsal periods that facilitate complex projects, and to enjoy the freedom of creating without concern for ticket sales and profit margins.

Government subsidy is not without drawbacks and controversy, however. There is always a threat of censorship, as was evidenced in Eastern Europe during the Soviet era. Groups in Canada and England have argued that the government gives too much support to large national theatres and not enough to smaller local troupes, choosing to support tourism over culture. Some theatre practitioners are concerned that subsidized artists grow complacent.

Censorship and Government Support

Mark Blitzsteins's musical *The Cradle Will Rock* was originally produced during the depression as part of the Federal Theatre Project in 1937. It was directed by Orson Wells. The play deals with a greedy businessman who oppresses workers and tries to deny them the right to unionize. Under political pressure from business groups that feared its leftist content, the production was shut down by the WPA. Financial cutbacks were blamed for the closing. Props and scenery were seized by the government.

Incensed, Wells and John Houseman rented a larger theatre and performed the piece to a sold-out house. This event led them to create the Mercury Theatre, so they could work unfettered by government control. Today *The Cradle Will Rock* has become topical once again as workers rights are threatened around the world. This photo is from a 2010 London production at the Arcola Theatre.

State-supported theatre can also become embroiled in culture wars, such as when the South African government withdrew its support for theatres that produced European and American forms, preferring to allocate resources to indigenous culture. This decision put actors out of work and forced artists to abandon the theatre of their choice, or to work at great personal cost. Despite these assorted problems, state-subsidized theatre is an important cultural investment and most American theatre artists would relish the idea of working with dependable economic support for their efforts like their counterparts around the globe.

THINK

Should governments provide funding for theatre institutions or artists?

International Theatre Festivals

Begun as havens for experimental work, international theatre festivals now are organized around many different themes. A festival can earn cultural recognition for a particular city or country. An invitation to perform at a prestigious festival can, in turn, give a theatre company the artistic legitimacy that facilitates grants and other funding.

International theatre festivals have been growing in numbers since the 1960s.

One of the best ways to get a sampling of theatre from around the world is to attend one of the many international theatre festivals held each year. They offer a broad spectrum of theatrical activity; in a week's time, you may be able to attend a dozen productions. Both emerging trends

Jane Alexander's (b. 1939) life demonstrates the marriage of artistic excellence and distinguished public service. Her acting career includes a Tony, an Obie, a Drama Desk Award for The Great White Hope, *four Oscar nominations, and an Emmy. In 1993, President Clinton nominated her to serve as chairperson of the National Endowment for the Arts (NEA), and during her tenure in that position from 1993 until 1997, she defended the arts in a charged political climate.*

Can art that really expresses diverse and particular points of view avoid offending someone?

Art has the ability to excite and stimulate people who think differently and also to outrage them. I think that comes with the territory. The way you enhance the experience for everybody is through education. If you are doing a difficult piece of work or one where you might anticipate a negative reaction, it is important to prepare the audience through news coverage, and through the schools.

What if a work intends to provoke?

We live in a free society and some people will choose to provoke, and those people should be free to do that. There is in my mind a difference between propaganda and provocative art. Propaganda is always provocative, and not all art should be. I would estimate that only about 10 percent of art is provocative, and that 90 percent is created for beauty or comfort. It comforts by reinforcing feelings and beliefs.

Can you think of a specific example in which theatre was used to heal?

After the 1995 Oklahoma City bombings, we used theatre to heal through storytelling. Healing also happens a lot with preventative theatre that takes an issue or subject such as teen pregnancy and deals with it in the schools or in prescribed community situations.

Should the NEA use government money to fund arts that might offend particular communities?

I think it is the business of the government to honor and fund works of art that are deemed excellent by a peer panel, which is what the NEA tries to do. And I think those peer panels are first-rate. They are a diverse body pulled together from different states, backgrounds, races, and ethnicities, so as a whole they represent a community standard of excellence. Some of their choices will be provocative, and some will offend certain groups.

How do you react to the NEA giving all its support to institutions at the expense of individual funding?

Congress has put an end to individual funding except for literature fellowships, and honorifics for jazz, folk, and traditional artists. One-person shows like those of the NEA Four could not be funded any more through the NEA. I think that it is very important for the government to support and nurture the individual artist. I love that Mexico gives a stipend to the artists they consider national treasures. We don't have anything like that. Of course there is private giving, but I do think the federal government should be in the business of honoring our individual artists, both those that are coming up in the world and those that are at the end of their lives.

What is the most salient lesson you took from your experience as head of the NEA?

That our rights as a people in the United States are inviolable. That First Amendment rights with regard to the artist and free expression should be inviolable, and that this is a battle one has to fight again and again because there are legislators who seek to reinterpret the Constitution in a manner that treads on the sacred ground of basic human rights.

If you could create an ideal NEA, what would it do?

It would support individual artists, nurture new and promising talents, and recognize older talents. It would promote arts education. It would shore up our institutions nationally.

When you look at how Europe funds its theatres, how do you compare the situation for theatre artists there to the United States?

I thought for a long time that European state-subsidized theatre was the most wonderful thing. But after working in Germany in 2004, I saw that there was

▲ As chairperson of the National Endowment for the Arts, actress Jane Alexander speaks at the White House. President and Mrs. Clinton watch in the background.

little hunger, figurative hunger, to create something wonderful. Many people have grown complacent. The state-subsidized system creates glorious design elements, but not necessarily inspired art. And it often blocks getting things done. The state-subsidized system is not a panacea. You can't buy and sell creativity.

I love the spirit here in the United States where there is no complacency.

There is something to be said for struggling with a creative idea and trying to bring in others to make it viable. I do, however, wish there were more money for people to draw on.

Should the government be involved in the arts?
It is the business of the federal government to fund art in our society because the government is of the people and should be interested in developing inquiring minds, creative thought, imagination, and critical thinking, and the arts are the area of human endeavor that most readily promotes that for society. We must be secure in that opinion.

Source: Used with permission from Jane Alexander.

HIDDEN HISTORY

Juliano Mer-Khamis: The Price of Political Performance

Juliano Mer-Khamis (**1958–2011**) was both Israeli and Palestinian, born to an Israeli Jewish mother and an Arab Christian father in the town of Nazareth. He devoted his life to the performing arts, to peace, and to empowering people through theatre.

Mer-Khamis produced and directed his first documentary film, *Arna's Children*, in 2003. The film traces his mother's efforts to enrich the lives of children in the Jenin refugee camp through her theatre group Care and Learning. She used theatre to heal young Palestinians traumatized by the Israeli occupation. Following the first *intifada* (Palestinian uprising), in 2000, Mer-Khamis went to Jenin to follow the paths of several of the children who had acted in his mother's troupe in the 1990s for the film. He found that all but one of his mother's young actors had died. Many had become hardened terrorists and renounced his mother's optimism.

Never losing hope for peace, Mer-Khamis founded the Freedom Theatre (www.thefreedomtheatre.org) in Jenin in 2006 to keep his mother's dream alive. The theatre offers Palestinian children a rare opportunity to express their feelings through art and to develop a healthy sense of their place in the world. The theatre's goal is to create social change, and its website reminds us that

▲ Palestinians mourn Arab-Israeli actor and director Juliano Mer-Khamis during a rally outside the Freedom Theatre following his assassination. The poster reads: "The martyr of freedom and culture, the talented Palestinian ideologist, Juliano Khamis."

"the creative process consists of imagining alternatives, rearranging reality and accepting new ways of life."

Mer-Khamis was assassinated outside his theatre on April 4, 2011, by a masked Palestinian gunman, raising the question of whether art and idealism can triumph over political extremism. This extraordinary man received an extraordinary farewell. His coffin was brought from Israel through a checkpoint into the West Bank, so that his Palestinian friends, unable to cross into Israel, could say a final good-bye. An Israeli singer, Miri Aloni, sang "Song for Peace" in both Hebrew and Arabic before Mer-Khamis was returned to Israel for burial next to his mother.

THINK

What advantages does theatre offer as a forum for controversial political issues?

and cultural difference are clearly in evidence at the better festivals. Almost every country in Europe sponsors at least one theatre festival, as do many cities around the United States, Canada, New Zealand, and Australia. African companies have now organized several pan-African festivals (in Benin, Burkina Faso, Côte d'Ivoire, Ghana, Cameroon, and the Democratic Republic of the Congo, to name a few) that promote African artistic freedom from the European tradition and encourage talented African actors to work locally. New York, of course, hosts several events each year.

Some festivals are juried, and others are open to all who wish to perform.

Some festivals celebrate local theatre. Many are open to all kinds of theatre; others have a specific focus. Some are devoted to the avant-garde and others to more traditional forms. The director of the Festival TransAmériques, held in Montréal, travels the globe looking for interesting performances and a wide range of theatrical activity. The Next Wave at BAM and the Lincoln Center Festival in New York is devoted to the more established avant-garde. Many well-known international theatre festivals have spawned satellite festivals more open to unknown theatre performers and groups such as the Edinburgh Fringe Festival in Scotland, which is open to almost all who wish to appear and accommodates even minor companies and solo artists. The New York Fringe Festival has followed the Edinburgh festival's lead. The Avignon Theatre Festival in France is focused on the recent avant-garde, but the city now has a "Festival Off," which offers a wider variety of entertainment. UNIMA (Union Nationale de la Marionette) unites puppeteers from around the globe and sponsors international puppet theatre festivals every four years in different venues around the world. The Asia-Pacific Festival of Children's Theatre in Toyama, Japan, focuses on theatre for young audiences. The festival international de la francophonie held in Limoges offers the opportunity for French and postcolonial French theatre to appear side by side. The Internet offers guides to festivals, performances, and ticket information.

The growing number of international festivals is subject to positive and negative effects, like so much else in our global world. Although these festivals are a source of cross-fertilization, as artists from various cultures exchange ideas, some fear that such exchange can lead to homogeneity and cultural appropriation or, worse, domination of indigenous traditions by the Western theatre establishment.

▲ Since 1947, the Avignon Theatre Festival has attracted summer crowds. Today its events play to audiences of 100,000, who come to see first showings of contemporary theatre and dance from around the world in this magnificent old city. Featured here is an outdoor performance near the Papal Palace.

Colleges and Universities

Universities around the world have traditionally been hubs for theatrical activity. In Africa in particular, many universities have resident theatre companies and groups promoting classical and indigenous art forms on campus that transform the university into a cultural center for the general population. In some developing nations, universities also provide training in both European and traditional forms. In the United States, colleges and universities are the center for professional theatre training and have forged new partnerships with the professional theatre. As part of their training, students participate in productions that serve not only the campus, but the larger community as well. Free from financial concerns, educational theatre can do interesting and innovative work. Most college repertories range from musical theatre to the European avant-garde and multicultural presentations. Because faculty often have significant professional theatre credentials, the quality of educational theatre can be quite high. Many universities have resident professional theatres in which students are given the opportunity to perform or work backstage alongside professionals in the field. College productions are an important opportunity for students to be exposed to live performance and to learn how theatre is made.

Summer Theatres and Shakespeare Festivals

Summer theatres and Shakespeare festivals in the United States do more than provide entertainment for vacationers. They offer the opportunity for student interns and young professionals to exercise their craft under the guidance of professional directors. The quality of these theatres varies widely. Some, such as the Williamstown or Berkshire Theatre Festivals, employ well-known actors and directors and also train students. They produce tried-and-true plays and experimental work in the same season. Shakespeare festivals often draw their directors and staff from the professionals teaching at local universities, who bring students along for a summer of learning, building yet another bridge between the educational and professional theatre communities. Others recruit actors and directors from regional theatres or New York professionals. Often these festivals are at outdoor theatres where the festive atmosphere makes theatre-going a jubilant event. The New York Shakespeare Festival, founded by Joseph Papp (1921–1991), takes the festival to its populist limits, offering free Shakespeare in Central Park with high-quality star actors such as Anne Hathaway (b. 1982), Meryl Streep (b. 1949), and Kevin Kline (b. 1947) performing for a general audience.

▲ Around the United States, summer Shakespeare theatres attract crowds of theatre-goers, who enjoy these performances in an informal environment. The Utah Shakespeare Festival, honored with a Tony Award for Outstanding Regional Theatre, offers free Elizabethan music and dance on its park-like grounds, as well as seminars, classes, and Shakespearean and contemporary productions.

Community Theatres

Around the world and throughout history, community theatre has played and continues to play an important role in many cultures. Native American storytelling and dance performances, African festivals, Mexican Corpus Christi plays, and medieval cycle plays are community theatre examples that reinforce shared cultural values. *The Oberammergau Passion Play* is an event that involves an entire city and has been performed every 10 years as a civic event since 1634. Even the iconic ancient Athenian theatre began as a state-subsidized community theatre.

Many small towns around the world that cannot attract professional resident companies rely on community theatres. And many large cities have community groups as well. Some are run on a totally volunteer basis; others employ basic staff and sometimes a professional director to lead a troupe of dedicated volunteer actors. Some community theatre companies produce high-quality work, whereas others are distinctly amateur. They contribute to the cultural life of a locality and provide a place for shared experiences that reinforce the social fabric. Many young people would have no exposure to the live theatre were it not for such groups.

Community theatre companies may work in well-equipped small theatres or commandeer the town hall, a church, or the village square.

Another form of community theatre, sometimes called *community-based theatre*, draws on the concerns and experiences of marginalized groups to create theatre that promotes social change. Community-based theatre has been done with prisoners, youth at risk, and minority and economically disenfranchised groups. In the United States, Living Stage (now disbanded), an outreach of Washington, D.C.'s Arena Stage, helped spread this approach. It is now practiced by many organizations and individuals, such as The Cornerstone Theatre in Los Angeles, which creates theatre for the community about issues of importance to that community. The Philippines Educational Theatre Association (PETA) has conducted workshops throughout Asia. Community-based theatres also exist elsewhere around the globe, in places such

▲ Members of the larger community are included in every step of the The Cornerstone Theater Company's creative process. They gather stories from community members, ask for audience feedback, and may even turn helpers into actors. Seen here is *3 Truths* (2010), which explores the inequities of the criminal justice system and its impact on minority communities in Los *Angeles.*

The Oberammergau Passion Play: Tradition in Changed Times

In an effort to ward off the bubonic plague in 1633, the residents of Oberammergau, Germany, made a vow to God to perform a play depicting the life and death of Jesus every 10 years. The *Oberammergau Passion Play* has been the ultimate demonstration of community theatre ever since. This seven-hour extravaganza is a living link to medieval religious drama. It employs spoken text, choral and musical components, and *tableaux vivants* in which actors pose in frozen biblical scenes accompanied by narration and music. Once performed to knit the fabric of the community around core beliefs, the play now attracts tourists from around the globe.

The production is performed in public spaces, and approximately half the townspeople help make up the cast of 2,200 performers. All participants must be at least 20-year residents of the town. The play holds such a place in the psyche of the town's inhabitants that in the intervening years between performances, people are referred to by the names of the characters they played in the most recent performance. The death rate even drops in the year before the production as people cling to life for one more chance to participate.[1]

Performers were limited to Catholics in good standing until 2000, when non-Christians were allowed to play pagan roles for the first time. Despite the fame, longevity, and popularity of the play, charges of anti-Semitism have been leveled at the play, because it portrays the Jewish community as the killers of Christ. European passion plays were often the source of anti-Semitic sentiment that gave rise to violence against Jews and have long been cited as part of the cultural backdrop for the Holocaust. Indeed, Adolph Hitler attended and praised the 1934 Oberammergau production for its anti-Semitic message, and passages were even rewritten that year to reaffirm the Nazi agenda.

In recent times, protests from organizations around the world have led to changes in the centuries-old text. Jesus is now referred to as Rabbi and speaks a Hebrew prayer. The Roman role in the crucifixion has been acknowledged, and lines that incite revenge against Jews along with other elements that demonized the Jews have been expurgated from the text. Many believe that the historic text should not be altered to meet the demands of outside groups but also acknowledge that there was no protest when the text was doctored to meet the needs of Nazi propaganda. Although the event fills the coffers of the small Bavarian town and is a source of local pride, both Christian and Jewish organizations have questioned continuing these performances in a post-Holocaust world.

[1] James Shapiro, *Oberammergau* (New York: Pantheon Books, 2000), 4.

◀ This *tableau vivant* from the 2000 performance of the *Oberammergau Passion Play* enacts a scene from the passion of Christ.

as Costa Rica, the Middle East, Bosnia, Australia, and Kenya. Facilitators help community members dramatize their own stories, histories, or social concerns. Performances done for the community can take a variety of forms, including agitprop, comedy, musical, and melodrama, and may use masks, puppets, dance, and music. In Kenya, the Kawuonda Women's Collective, which also runs a bakery and a child-care center, uses storytelling and performance to depict women's changing roles in a changing society. Theatre work is integrated with the women's daily chores, as they often work together raising crops and making meals to meet personal needs while creating public performance. Community-based theatre empowers local groups by giving them a voice through theatre.

Today, many community theatres have carved out an important role reinforcing identity and providing cultural education. The Sen'Klip Native Theatre Company in Canada and the Red Eagle Soaring and Thunderbird Theatres in the United States are examples of groups that provide a sense of community identity and purpose to Native Americans. Small towns in Africa often receive funding for their community theatres to preserve traditional cultural forms of entertainment. In Zimbabwe, local cultural centers in townships are charged with the preservation of folklore theatre. Across Africa, local groups, aware of the possible loss of traditional forms, use community theatre to provide cultural memory.

Commercial and Not-for-Profit Theatre in the United States

HOW do commercial and not-for-profit theatre in the United States differ?

In the United States, productions may be amateur (done out of love) or professional (done for money) and may fall into either the **commercial theatre** or the **not-for-profit theatre** category. In the commercial theatre, investors back a single production and take a capital return if a show is a success. A commercial production will run as long as it is making money. In not-for-profit theatre, the profit is channeled back into the producing organization to defray costs for the institution and to fund new projects.

> **Although all amateur productions are not-for-profit, not all not-for-profit theatre is amateur.**

Commercial Theatre

When we think of the commercial theatre, we usually think of **Broadway** and the great concentration of commercial houses around Times Square in New York and London's **West End**, but there are commercial theatres all around the country and around the world in almost every major cosmopolitan city. Because the financial risks are high, commercial theatre is rarely the home of experimentation or performances with limited appeal. Many bemoan the dearth of serious and interesting drama on Broadway compared to the days when costs were low and investors could take greater chances with material. Nevertheless, the Broadway theatre maintains its cachet and remains a symbol of "making it" in the professional theatre. Despite the burgeoning theatre activity in cities such as Seattle and Chicago, New York remains the theatrical center of the United States, with at least 30 commercial productions and well over 100 other professional and semiprofessional performances available on any given night. Touring companies will take a successful Broadway show on the road and set up in touring houses for limited runs in cities around the country and Canada. Tours can generate millions of dollars for Broadway investors. In New York, some smaller theatres in and out of the theatre district are designated **Off-Broadway** because they have fewer than 500 seats. Often, a well-received Off-Broadway production will be moved to a larger theatre on Broadway if investors are convinced they can fill the house and turn a profit.

Professional Not-for-Profit Companies

Many important theatres in New York and **resident theatres** around the country are professional not-for-profit companies.

▲ *Urinetown*, which debuted at the New York International Fringe Festival, moved from off-off-Broadway to Off-Broadway. When word-of-mouth made it a hot ticket and producers were certain they could turn a profit, it moved again and enjoyed a two and a half year run on Broadway. Seen here are members of the Broadway cast which featured Jeff McCarthy, Jennifer Laura Thompson, John Cullum, and Nancy Opel.

Originally conceived as **regional theatres** to combat the centralization of theatre activity in New York, resident theatres have grown over the past 50 years and now provide a permanent theatre presence in almost every major city in America, including New York. They typically present a season of plays for runs of predetermined length. Some focus on particular kinds of performance—the classics, new plays, or multicultural performances—while others offer an eclectic repertory. Resident theatres have played the important role of expanding theatrical activity around the country, providing a source of employment for both local and New York theatre professionals, and enlarging theatre audiences.

To qualify for tax-exempt not-for-profit status, a theatre must develop goals and a mission statement and file for not-for-profit status with the Internal Revenue Service. A not-for-profit theatre must have a board of directors responsible for fund-raising and finance and the hiring and firing of the managing and artistic directors. These theatres depend on subscriptions, grants, private donations, and foundation and corporate support for their survival. To limit their costs, they negotiate salary waivers with theatrical unions.

In recent years, many resident theatres have noticed that the majority of their subscribers are over age 50. This disturbing situation indicates that young people in their areas are not getting into the habit of going to the theatre and that the theatres are not building their future audiences. To keep their older subscribers coming back, companies frequently present traditional and less experimental pieces. They are caught in the bind of trying to hold onto their audience base while simultaneously attracting a new population to the theatre with innovative work. Theatres have also found that the majority of their audience members are white. Although when they produce a play by an African American or Asian American playwright, they are able to lure in new audiences, unfortunately, audiences rarely cross over to see plays that they don't feel are intended for them.

◀ The Children's Theater Company in Minneapolis caters to a community of interest. Shown here is a scene from *The Wonderful Wizard Of Oz*.

Many resident theatres are searching for ways to bring their various audiences together around new work through special events, lectures, and talks with artists.

THINK

> Does producing works with broad audience appeal limit creativity and innovation?

Common **Interest** Theatres

Common interest theatres are created when groups of artists come together with particular goals or visions—be they political, artistic, or educational. Such theatres may be created by professionals or amateurs. **Off-Off-Broadway** theatres were founded by amateurs and professionals who sought an alternative to the artistic constraints imposed in the commercial theatre. Such artists seek freedom to make radical political statements, to experiment artistically with less financial risk, and to showcase their talents. Such theatres are often driven by a dominant artistic vision, such as Mabou Mines or the Wooster Group, or by a community of interest, such as the Puerto Rican Traveling Theatre, the Pan-Asian Repertory Company, the Mixed Blood Theatre, or the Children's Theatre Company in Minneapolis. Sometimes groups are formed around political issues and share a combined political and artistic point of view; examples are the Tectonic Theatre and Teatro Campesino.

Producing Theatre

The scale and finances of theatrical endeavors may vary, but the process always begins with an idea that someone believes in and for which support is recruited. Who that someone is and how the support is raised depends on the nature of the venture. The originator of the idea can be a director, a playwright, an actor, a composer, an artistic director, a government agency, or a professional producer who must sell a group of collaborators on the validity of a project.

At some point early in the process, every production requires a producer. A producer needs a clear perception of the project and then needs to bring together a creative team with the necessary resources to get the work done before the right audience, in the right place. We associate producers with the commercial theatre, but for every production, someone must serve in this role, with or without the title. In university theatres, the department chairperson may set the budget, assign the space, and determine the designers and directors. In regional theatres, it may be the managing and artistic directors. In small experimental companies, it may be the director. But no production will ever be realized unless someone is doing the job of producing the event.

The producer is the artistic, financial, and administrative coordinator of a theatrical production, and the list of producer responsibilities is dizzying. A producer's first job is to find a worthwhile project and to secure the performance rights, which means negotiating with publishers, agents, playwrights, directors, or actors—whoever holds the rights to the piece. Once the right to perform is guaranteed, the producer assembles a creative team, starting with the director. Then, with the director's collaboration, the producer engages actors, designers, stage managers, and running crews. This may require negotiating with agents and unions. Crews also need to be assembled to carry out the work of the designers. If a scenic production studio is hired to build the set, the producer hires the technical liaison with the studio.

A rehearsal and performance space must be procured that suits the nature of the project in size, layout, and location, and a rental agreement needs to be negotiated. Running crews to staff the theatre are necessary at every performance. The producer must supervise the management of the theatre, making sure that box office staff, ushers, and house managers are doing their jobs properly. The producer is also responsible for advertising and programs. When things are not going well, the producer may have to fire the director or an actor.

Making sure the entire endeavor is on time and within budget is ultimately also the responsibility of the producer.

Commercial Producers

The goal of commercial producers is to make money. That means they must have an unerring sense of what the public will pay to see. They search for a *property*—a play, a story, or an idea for which they can purchase the rights for a professional production. They find properties by developing relationships with playwrights and directors who bring them their new work and ideas. Sometimes producers commission new work. High-end producers may employ *play readers* to read through hundreds of submitted plays in search of a vehicle for success. They also may send out scouts to look at new plays that may hold commercial promise in the not-for-profit theatres. Today, very few new works begin their lives on Broadway because the costs and financial risks are too high. Instead, commercial producers often work with regional theatres, whose productions serve as out-of-town tryouts for new plays. Commercial producers raise money to fund production costs. They find backers who invest in productions in the hope of realizing a financial return. Some commercial producers own several theatres, which enables them to control rental expenses.

Many **playwrights** prefer having the first airing of new work outside **New York,** where the effects of negative reviews are less **damaging.**

Not-for-Profit Producers

Many not-for-profit companies have both managing and artistic directors who share the responsibilities of producing with a board of directors. The board is responsible for overseeing fund-raising and planning. The artistic director may decide what plays to produce and whom to hire for the artistic staff and may also work as a director. The managing director is responsible for budgets and staff hiring for specific productions, publicity, and all other aspects of administration and theatre management. If a company owns a theatre, the managing director is also responsible for maintaining the facilities.

Readings and Staged Readings

Even before a play has an out-of-town tryout, it often goes through a process of readings. Producers use this occasion to judge its commercial viability. It is not unusual to have several readings while a play is in development. For the first reading, actors sit in chairs with scripts in hand. The playwright is present. There are no props, and the stage manager reads the stage directions. An invited audience is present, and actors often volunteer their time or work for a small stipend to help the playwright, in the hope of being cast in the final production. This is the opportunity for the playwright to hear the characters' voices and gauge audience response, so the audience is also a collaborator in a play's development. The writer then rewrites the script to address problems clarified by the reading.

Sometimes a play goes through a transitional step called a **staged reading**. Actors are on their feet, scripts in hand, and there are minimal set pieces. This is a chance to discover practical staging problems and other needs of the script. In the commercial theatre, working on a play in this manner saves time and money and leads to a greater likelihood of success. This model is often followed for not-for-profit theatre as well.

▲ Tim Abrams and J. Stephen Brantley perform in a play reading for Hunter Playwrights.

Dramaturgs

Some theatre companies employ a dramaturg to serve as an in-house critic. They use their skills in critical analysis and knowledge about stage practice to help producers, playwrights, directors, designers, and actors create thoughtful and meaningful productions. Dramaturgs have been called intellectual attachés to the theatre.

Dramaturgs have long been an established part of the theatre in European countries but have risen to prominence in the American theatre only in recent years. Dramaturgs today take on many tasks. *Production dramaturgy* is done before and during the rehearsal process for a particular show. A dramaturg might help prepare a text for performance by updating a classical play, translating a text, or assisting a playwright who is developing a new script. To help the director and the actors understand the world of the play, a dramaturg often does research on the playwright; the setting of the story; and terms, ideas, or conventions of the text that are not readily understood. If a director is altering the time and place, the dramaturg can help recontextualize the story in its new setting. Directors draw on a dramaturgs understanding of a play to develop and articulate a vision for a production.

Dramaturgs today are often called on to bring the audience to an appreciation of the production. They may write notes or essays for the program, for a lobby display, or for the show's publicity. They might moderate talk-back sessions after the show between the actors and the director and the audience or create study guides for schoolchildren. This kind of work is usually called *audience outreach*.

Many dramaturgs in the United States hold positions as **literary managers**. Literary managers often do the tasks listed earlier, and they are also responsible for reading and evaluating plays submitted to the theatre, recommending plays to the artistic director, and helping in other forms of play development, such as hosting workshops or play readings.

Alternative Theatre Producers

Both commercial and not-for-profit producers function in relative luxury compared with producers in many small theatres around the world who have no staff, no facilities, and no money. Often directors with specific projects in alternative theatres play the role of producer, procuring funds, renting theatres, sometimes even building the sets, buying props, and costuming out of their own closets. Often the responsibilities for production in alternative venues are shared with the actors and designers, who volunteer time to work on other aspects of the production. Such community-spirited theatrical endeavors provide an alternative model.

Behind the Scenes: The Unsung Heroes of the Theatre

WHO works behind the scenes at the theatre?

When we attend the theatre, we are aware of the actors, and we may think about the work of the designers and dramatist, but we often forget the many highly skilled professionals on whose efforts every successful production relies. Readying a theatrical event requires the work of technicians, managers, and crews. Each performance depends on the teamwork of diverse personnel to run the show. In fact, a large commercial production may have as many as 100 salaried employees working on any given performance.

The following sections introduce the set of characters who create a theatrical production. It is important to keep in mind that someone must do these jobs on every production. Sometimes money is available to hire individual personnel for each position, but if a theatre cannot hire separate individuals for every function, people will take on two or three jobs to get the show up and running, no matter how tiring and difficult that may be. Theatre professionals are a dedicated group who will do whatever it takes to "go on with the show."

Stage Managers

The figure who holds a show together emotionally, practically, and technically is the stage manager. This is the person with whom the director works most closely in preparing the production. The director depends on the stage manager to take care of all pragmatic concerns by functioning as a liaison between the director and all other members of the theatrical team, including the actors. All information about the developing production flows through the stage manager, and complicated shows may require the work of several assistant stage managers. Stage managers must be able to multitask and function effectively under stress. They must be organized to a fault and have strong interpersonal skills to balance all the artistic temperaments involved in production. Staying calm under fire and being able to think on their feet and solve problems quickly when things go wrong in performance are necessary skill sets. Stage managers must also have enough ego to be strong leaders and enough selflessness to be the facilitators for everyone else's artistic needs.

Coordinating a Production

Stage managers must be present at all rehearsals in a managerial role, organizing and maintaining discipline. They call rehearsals to order and are responsible for keeping a precise and orderly prompt book (see Figure 14.1 on page 340), a copy of the performance text in which all rehearsal work—blocking, lighting and sound cues, and changes to the script—is noted (Figure 14.1). Actors rely on the stage manager's accurate recording of movement, cuts, and additions to jog their memories, and stage managers may prompt actors during rehearsals.

A good stage manager immediately recognizes when an artistic discovery in rehearsal necessitates a change in props, set, lights, or costumes—sometimes even before the director. Once the director approves such a change, the stage manager is in charge of communicating the information to actors, designers, and technical and house staff—everyone the change affects—through written memos called *rehearsal reports*. Stage managers facilitate the rehearsal process by readying the space, taping the ground plan on the floor to outline where set pieces will be, setting up rehearsal furniture, and getting props or costume pieces for the actors.

Stage managers attend production meetings to keep abreast of any new developments and make sure everyone has all the necessary information and changes. They ensure that the efforts of all the people involved in the show are coordinated so work will be harmonious and efficient.

Stage managers provide the information bridge between those who are present at production meetings and those who are present at rehearsals.

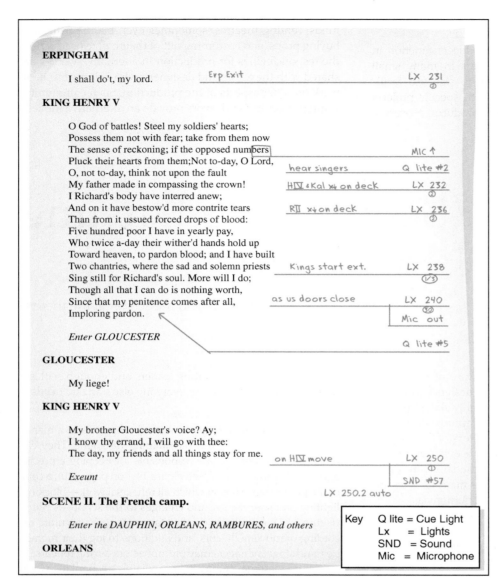

◀ Figure 14-1: A SAMPLE STAGE MANAGER'S PROMPT BOOK includes notes on the actors' blocking and cues for calling light and sound effects during a performance. The key on the lower right provides a guide for reading the stage manager's notes.

Managing the Actors

Stage managers relay information from the director to the actors. They call actors to rehearsal, let them know of changes in the schedule, and deal with actors who show up late or are absent. In union productions, stage managers must report infractions of the rules. A stage manager may help with a personal problem or act as a go-between when personality conflicts arise. Stage managers look out for the actors. They alert the director when the actors need a break and make sure the theatre space is clean and safe for rehearsal and performance. They maintain a first aid kit and always have aspirin and antacids on hand for those stressful moments.

Running the Show

During technical rehearsals, stage managers make sure that all of the director's cues are properly entered in the prompt book and executed. Once the show opens, the stage manager is in charge of keeping the rhythm and pace of the show by *calling cues*, which means telling the lighting and sound operators and the stage crew the precise moment

of all changes in light, sound, and set. Communicating on headsets, they alert other members of the crew that a lighting, sound, or set change is coming up and then give them the "go" to make the change. Stage managers keep time for the entire production by making sure the actors know when to arrive at the theatre and by giving time warnings until the show begins. They communicate with house managers about the state of readiness backstage and alert them to any problems requiring a delay of the **curtain**, or starting time. When everything is set, they call "places" to get the actors and crew ready to start the performance.

Preserving the Director's Vision

After opening night, when the director completes an active role in the production process, the stage manager takes over the show and makes sure all the elements of production stay as close as possible to the way the director envisioned them. If a new actor is called in to substitute in a role, the stage manager teaches the part as the director expects it to be played. Attending all rehearsals and production meetings, recording all decisions made about the production,

Ruth Sternberg is in her seventh season as Director of Production and Facility Management at the New York Public Theatre. She previously served for 10 seasons as director of production at Trinity Rep under the artistic direction of Oskar Eustis. Ruth has been the production manager for the Newport Music Festival and the McCarter Theatre, as well as several international tours for Philip Glass. She was also the production stage manager for Philip Glass and Robert Wilson's 1992 world tour of Einstein on the Beach. *She was stage manager for ESPN's 1996 X Games, as well as for directors Ann Bogart, Emily Mann, Amanda Dehnert, David Rabe, David Wheeler, Scott Ellis, Richard Foreman, Mark Lamos, and Ken Bryant at theatres such as Hartford Stage Company, Dallas Theatre Center, American Repertory Theatre, and McCarter Theatre. Sternberg is dedicated to training future stage managers and theatre professionals and has served as a stage management instructor at Rhode Island College.*

What drew you to stage management, and what personal qualities do you think are essential for someone in that position?

I was drawn to stage management because I love theatre and I wasn't a very good actor. I believe that the essential personal qualities are patience, lack of ego, communication, and organizational skills. You must be comfortable with the idea that your role is to facilitate others doing their art (which is in itself an art).

How has new technology affected the job of the stage manager in the last two decades?

I think that the technological advancement of the last two decades has made some things easier and some things harder. The biggest plus has been voicemail systems and cell phones. You can always leave a message for someone and know that they'll get it. That wasn't necessarily true 20 years ago. Personal comput-

ers have made it easier to organize and distribute information.

The advancement in sound technology has made it much easier to run shows. More theatres employ sound operators (as opposed to expecting stage managers to run sound), and the technology is more user friendly. The equipment that theatres can afford is of a higher quality because it has become relatively less expensive. On the other hand, the advancement of computer lighting systems has made it easier for lighting designers to write more complicated cues. There are robotic lights that can be programmed to do a multitude of things. These advancements have made cues much easier to run during a performance, but it generally takes more time to program in a technical rehearsal. It is very important for a stage manager to understand what the cues are in order to maintain the show and to know what needs to happen to be able make adjustments as a show evolves.

How does the job call on your creativity?

A stage manager's creativity is called upon often. It starts with how to set up a room for rehearsal that will be the most efficient and that will make people feel the most comfortable in their new working environment. The stage manager is the center of the information gathering and information distribution. This makes you the logical point to solve all things logistical for everyone involved. You need to know whose conflicts and problems take priority without ever letting anyone feel that their request is not very important. The larger the production and theatre, the greater the number of conflicts that may arise. It is up to you to schedule and coordinate the needs of the various departments. This can mean setting up meetings with the director for the designers, making sure that people see new articles as they are brought into the room, scheduling costume fittings,

recording sessions, video tapings, photo calls, fight rehearsals, dialect sessions, wig fittings.

Calling a show can be a performance, and should be, to a point. A stage manager needs to understand what every cue does and how it should look on the stage and also how the actors interact with what that cue is. Every part of a performance is interdependent.

Why did you move to production management, and can you talk about the related skills?

I moved into production management primarily because it is a steadier job, at least in a regional theatre. A lot of the skills are the same. I think that people come to production management via different paths. Because my path was stage management, that is the approach that I take to my job. The biggest difference between production management and stage management is that a production manager is simultaneously working on several productions at any given time, and a stage manager is generally working on one at a time.

What is the biggest challenge of a production manager, and are there particular challenges working with creative artists?

I think that the biggest challenge of a production manager is to realize that your resources, both money and workforce, will ebb and flow with the economy and the political climate.

The biggest challenge with creative artists is to make sure that all involved in a conversation are using the same vocabulary when trying to solve a problem. Getting artists to explain what a specific solution represents to them within the piece makes it easier to understand what a workable option might be, and that is only possible when you share a common language.

Source: Used with permission from Ruth Sternberg.

and acting as an assistant to the director enables the stage manager to reliably retain and communicate the director's intentions.

Production Managers

A theatre may employ a production manager who is in charge of schedules, staffing, and making sure that the information relayed by the stage manager is carried out in a timely manner. The production manager decides the order in which things will be done—for example, when certain set pieces will be moved into the theatre, when lights will be hung, and who will have the performance space at times when there are multiple claims. When the producer does not make up production budgets and oversee changes in allocations and spending, the production manager may do so. In theatre companies with large theatres and multiple spaces, the production manager coordinates the scheduling of various productions. To do these things effectively, the production manager must have knowledge of all aspects of production and their technical and financial requirements. When there is no production manager, someone still must do this job, or nothing would ever get done on time. It may be the producer or the managing director. In a small theatre company, it may fall to the director. In college theatre, it may be the job of the department chairperson or a member of the faculty. Sometimes it is the job of the technical director.

Technical Directors

The **technical director**, or TD, is responsible for readying and maintaining the theatre space, ensuring that the theatre is safe, and keeping all equipment and stage machinery in tip-top working order. No one knows more about a theatre and how it works than the technical director. The technical director's other major responsibility is executing the set designer's plans. The TD writes technical specifications from the design drawings, costs out and orders the materials needed to build the set, and keeps running inventories of stock supplies. The TD is part of the design process and may provide reality checks to the set designer's ambitions by suggesting alternative or cheaper construction strategies or noting structural flaws or practical problems in design plans. These are ironed out between the set designer and the TD, with the approval of the director. During the construction of the set, the designer may visit the **scene shop**, where the set is constructed, to check on progress or make changes. Sometimes even the director will visit if there is a question about a particular set piece. In small theatres the TD runs the scene shop and supervises the construction of scenery, making sure everything is done to the designer's specifications. Large theatres may have a shop foreman who oversees the construction crew.

The TD supervises technical rehearsals and fixes any technical problems that arise.

The technical director supervises the load-in of scenery—placing scenic elements according to the designer's plan in the theatre. When there is no master electrician to oversee the hanging and focusing of lights, this job may fall to the TD, as may the job of the sound engineer. In college theatres, the TD may be working with inexperienced crews and may also be teaching while organizing and coordinating the technical and scenic elements. Often, TDs without staff find themselves building the sets as well. When a production is over, the technical director oversees the **strike**, the taking down of the set and lights that follows a show's closing. They create a system for the efficient dismantling of all the scenic elements and then clean and ready the theatre for the next production.

Large commercial productions with complex sets often hire the services of a scenic studio to execute the designs. The designer and technical director hired by the producer will be assigned a project manager who works through the designs with the chief engineer. The chief engineer, along with draftsman engineers, determines the best construction method and materials. On the production floor, various department heads—wood, steel, machine shop, automation, and electrical—take charge of their parts of the construction. The producer's technical supervisor is constantly in touch with the scenic studio during the construction process, making sure everything is done to the designer's specifications. Most large commercial productions are built at such studios, where the latest technology and computerized systems for changing sets are integrated into the designs.

Master Electricians and Sound Engineers

The **master electrician** helps execute the lighting designer's plan, supervising the lighting crew as it hangs, focuses, and filters lights according to the lighting plot. Master electricians set up electrical circuitry that links the instruments to the lighting console, getting the lighting board ready for the adjustment of the lights by the designer and director during technical rehearsals.

The **sound engineer** is responsible for implementing the sound designer's effects. The job includes choosing appropriate microphones and speakers and placing them properly in the theatre or on the actors. The sound engineer hooks up equipment to amplifiers and speakers so the sound designer and the director can adjust the sound from a sound console.

Costume Shop Managers

Once costumes have been designed, they are created in a **costume shop**, under the oversight of a **costume shop manager**. Every costume shop keeps an inventory of fabric, sewing notions, and, most importantly, old costumes. The manager's job is to know what is available for immediate use and to order supplies, equipment, and repairs. When a shop owns a costume that can be used to fulfill a specific design, the manager tells the designer

Today computers help the backstage staff run the show. They facilitate the execution of traditional theatre tasks through automation. Computerized light and sound boards are now standard equipment, even in small community theatres and school playhouses. They can store and run a large number of complicated light and sound cues. Large theatres use computerized motion-controlled systems to effect and regulate set changes. Producers like using computers because they are more predictable than equipment that requires manual labor and are thus more cost-efficient for large productions. They are also able to produce more sensational and cinematic effects. Computers give directors greater control of their work by bringing reliability and precision to lighting cues and set placement, but they may take away some of the spontaneity and excitement of live theatre.

When a show relies heavily on technological elements for its success, a breakdown in performance can lead to disaster. Early versions of Disney's *Aida* (2000) experimented with a robotic pyramid that changed shape for different scenes. Frequent problems caused the device to be cut from the show before it moved to Broadway. A rare computer failure at *The Producers* in the summer of 2003 prevented curtains from rising and scenery from moving, temporarily

▲ Hudson Scenic Studios, a full-service production and scenic fabrication company located in Yonkers, New York, regularly sends an entire bank of high-tech equipment, such as computers, monitors, and operating boards, to theatres to operate and monitor the technological design elements constructed in Hudson's shops. This entire group at the loading dock is waiting to be shipped to a Broadway theatre to operate a single production.

stopping the show. During the months of previews of *Spiderman: Turn Off the Dark* in 2010–2011, performances were often stopped multiple times for technical glitches that often left actors in flying sequences suspended above the audience. Breakdowns during performances are rare, but they can create havoc. On the other hand, they may also create opportunities for actors and crew to save the day by improvising on the spot, returning the theatre to its fundamental nature as a live and ephemeral art.

that a costume can be *pulled* from stock and altered in the shop to fit a particular actor. This is a cost-cutting aid, as building a costume from scratch requires fabric shopping, pattern making, cutting, and sewing that is expensive and time-consuming—and can be difficult for financially strapped theatres. Large cities have rental companies where designers can shop for appropriate costumes for a particular production. The Costume Collection in New York receives contributions of used costumes from productions that have closed, which are borrowed by designers

from around the country. They are brought to the costume shop where the manager and the designer work to make the costume achieve the effect of the original designs. The manager assigns tasks such as cutting, stitching, and dyeing to the costume shop crew, and the manager is present at the costume parade and technical dress rehearsal to take notes from the costume designer. Theatres without costume shops may engage the services of a professional costume shop, which may assign individual project managers for various productions.

Props Managers

In addition to costumes, the director, stage manager, and designers put together a list of **props**, or **properties**. These are objects that will be used by the actors on stage or that are part of *dressing the set* and complete the scenic design. The props manager is responsible for either procuring or constructing these objects, which are subject to the approval of the director and designers, who may have very specific notions of how a prop will be used and what it should look like.

Running Crews

When we are in the audience watching a performance, we are often unaware of the different crews of people making the performance happen night after night in unseen roles. As the stage manager runs the show from the control booth, his or her work is supported by many people carrying out various jobs. These people are collectively referred to as the *running crews*.

The stage manager calls the cues in the prompt book to the *lighting board operator*, who must execute lighting effects with split-second accuracy. In the days before computer-operated boards, the operator was also responsible for setting up lighting cue changes and controlling the exact timing of fades and blackouts. Even today, in theatres without computerized equipment, lighting board operators must have a sense of the subtleties of the lighting designer's intentions and have exquisite timing. Imagine what would happen if at the height of a dramatic finale, actors had to hold their positions because a blackout was late. Even two seconds can be an eternity on stage and ruin a dramatic moment.

The *sound operator* executes the sound designer's effects and follows the cues given by the stage manager. For sound as well as lights, timing is everything. That telephone must

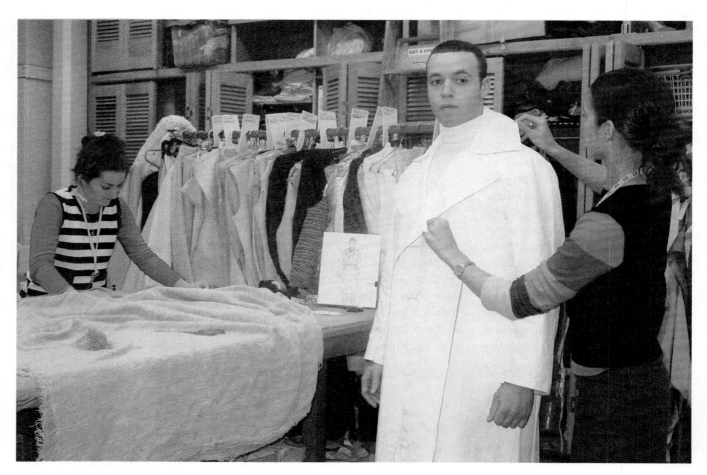

▲ Designer Louisa Thompson fits an actor for a costume. The sketch from which the costume was fabricated sits on the cutting table. The rack contains the costumes in progress for the rest of the cast. Each white tab has the actor's name and the role he or she will play marked. Every costume worn by that character in the performance is hung in its place. Costume shops are busy places, filled with supplies, fabric, notions, and trimmings.

ring at exactly the right moment and stop when the phone is answered. Musicals and special effects often require a *follow spot operator*, who moves a spotlight as it follows an actor on stage. The *stagehands* in the *stage crew* also must be ready to change the set on precise cues. The number of stagehands depends on the complexity of the sets and the changes.

After every performance, a *costume crew* collects all the costumes and launders, presses, and repairs any damage that occurred in performance. Costumes are readied and set out in an orderly manner for the actors' next performance. Emergency repairs to tears, replacement of lost buttons, and the like are performed backstage by the costume crew while the show is running. Difficult costumes and rapid costume changes may require the services of a *dresser* to assist the actor. The *prop crew* maintains and repairs props and sets them out on stage. **Personal props**, those carried on stage by actors, are placed on a prop table backstage. No greater panic can ensue for an actor than finding that a prop is missing in performance. Imagine an actor looking for a gun that the prop crew forgot to place in a drawer and trying to figure out how to commit a murder without a weapon, a mishap that actually occurs. *Assistant stage managers* usually oversee all these backstage functions and make sure that all the crews are working effectively. They check to make sure the set and props are ready for performance before the house is opened to the public.

House **Managers**

Every theatre has a **house manager** who makes sure the theatre is clean and safe and ready to receive the public. House managers organize and instruct the ticket takers and ushers, resolve any disputes about seats, and clear the theatre and notify the authorities in case of an emergency. They work closely with the **box office manager**, who oversees ticket sales and staff to make sure the audience has a positive experience in the theatre. The stage manager relays information to the house manager at the start of a performance and at intermission about backstage readiness and when the actors are in their places so the house manager can signal the audience that the performance is about to begin and secure the house.

Methods of Collaboration

WHAT methods of collaboration are common in theatrical production?

Methods of collaboration are a reflection of cultural values and of the kind of theatre people want to create. In the United States, theatre typically consists of a producer and director at the top of a hierarchical structure. Within that structure is a chain of command, and all communication follows that chain. A problem in set construction is typically relayed by the crew to the shop foreman, from there to the technical director, then to the set designer, who might alert the stage manager that it is important to discuss solutions with the director. If costs are involved, any changes must be approved by the producer. Following this line of communication helps avoid misunderstandings.

Although this is the common structure in the professional theatre in Europe and North America, and in theatres modeled on this tradition, many theatre artists prefer a method of collaboration that challenges the top-down structure. It is possible to work communally, dividing responsibilities among members of a creative team. Designers may write, build, or act. Actors may assemble props or make costumes. The director may be the house manager or lighting board operator. Sometimes this group effort is fostered by financial necessity, but just as often, it stems from a shared commitment to the theatrical process. Even this kind of organization, however, requires that someone be in the position of making final decisions, or nothing would ever be ready. A theatre troupe that stays together over time may choose to rotate positions, so that no one person is always in a position of absolute authority. Much amateur theatre is put together in this way, and many small professional groups work communally out of conviction or necessity.

In some community-based theatres around the world, the audience is also involved in the preparations, readying the playing space, sewing the costumes, making masks, and then taking their places as spectators. South African Township Theatre is created for the people and about the people. Stories are often culled from the community and developed into a script based on the conditions of local life by a *playmaker*, who combines the roles of playwright and director. Performances take place in found spaces adapted by adding a few meager props or set pieces. In many traditional Asian performance styles, because every detail of a performance is passed down from generation to generation, and the set and costumes are iconic, long rehearsal periods are unnecessary. As a result, the importance of the roles of the director and stage manager are greatly reduced. Theatres in these traditions often organize around the talents of a great actor.

People create methods of theatrical collaboration based on tradition, political, religious, and cultural beliefs, artistic goals, and financial necessity. No one model serves all, and how we create is as diverse as what we create in the theatre.

Closing the Show

At the end of every theatrical creation is the moment when the efforts of so many people end. We have ritualized the moment: *Striking the set* marks the end of the creation. The closing-night party turns the theatrical event into shared memory. No other art form is so like our common journey through life: launched in hope; realized through hard work, relationships, and travail; struck down; and then immortalized in memory. The collective memory of theatrical productions forms the traditions that guide us in our work, yet all theatre artists dream of yet-unimagined possibilities.

▲ Cast and crew strike the set after the last performance of the *Merry Widow*, performed by the Amato Opera.

Review

Summary

WHERE does theatre happen? p. 326

▶ People around the world create theatre under a wide variety of conditions and often at great personal risk.

▶ In many countries, theatre is subsidized by the government, often in an effort to preserve traditional forms.

▶ Theatre festivals offer the opportunity to sample a variety of theatrical experiences in a short period of time.

▶ Community theatres and community-based theatre can contribute to the culture of a locality and provide a place for shared experiences.

HOW do commercial and not-for-profit theatre in the United States differ from each other? p. 334

▶ Theatre in the United States falls broadly into commercial and not-for-profit categories.

▶ Because the financial risks are high, commercial theatre is rarely the home of experimentation or performances with limited appeal.

▶ Common interest theatres are created when groups of artists come together with particular goals or visions—be they political, artistic, or educational.

WHAT is the producer's role? p. 337

▶ The producer is the artistic, financial, and administrative coordinator of a theatrical production.

▶ Every production requires someone to function as a producer, who unites a creative team and procures resources for the production.

WHO works behind the scenes at the theatre? p. 339

▶ All theatrical activity results from a team of people working together, many behind the scenes. The audience is often unaware that the performance cannot proceed without the efforts of these people.

▶ The director depends on the stage manager to take care of all pragmatic concerns.

▶ The stage manager manages rehearsals and communication among the creative team and runs the show from the control booth. Many people carrying out various jobs support the stage manager's work.

WHAT methods of collaboration are common in theatrical production? p. 345

▶ There are many models of collaboration, based on tradition and goals.

▶ In the United States, theatre typically consists of a producer and director at the top of a hierarchical structure.

▶ Many theatre artists prefer a method of collaboration that challenges the top-down structure; it is possible to work communally, dividing responsibilities among members of a creative team.

MySearchLab®

Glossary

actor-manager.   In the seventeenth through the nineteenth centuries in Europe and America, the head of an acting company who organized the production.

adaptations.   Adjustments actors make in response to the changing circumstances of their character.

aesthetic distance.   The ability to observe a work of art with a degree of detachment and objectivity.

affective memory.   *See* emotional memory.

agitprop.   From *agitation* and *propaganda*, a form of political theatre first used by Marxists during the 1920s in Russia that conveys information in a simple and entertaining way to persuade an audience to its point of view.

Alba Emoting.   A set vocabulary of emotional expression using breath, facial attitude, and physical position to elicit six primary emotions; developed by Chilean neurophysiologist Susana Bloch.

alienation effect.   The emotional distancing of the audience from the dramatic action.

alliteration.   The repetition of consonant sounds used to provoke an emotional response in the audience.

antagonist.   A character who directly thwarts the desires of the protagonist.

apron.   An extension of the proscenium stage protruding past the proscenium arch.

aragoto.   The rough style of performance used for superhuman figures in *kabuki* developed by the actor Ichikawa Danjuro (1660–1704). These characters, found in history plays, wear bold makeup called *kumadori* and wild, colorful costumes.

archetypal characters.   Characters who embody the essence of particular human traits that enable them to speak across cultures and centuries.

Aristotelian plot.   *See* climactic structure.

asides.   Short comments that reveal a character's inner thoughts to the audience, often to comic effect.

assonance.   The repetition of vowel sounds for emotional effect.

audition.   A tryout for a role in a performance at which actors either perform prepared material or read from a play for the director.

auteur.   A French term meaning author and originator of a concept; applied to stage directors who conceive a total performance rather than beginning with a play.

autos sacramentales.   Christian religious drama developed in Spain circa the sixteenth century.

avant-garde.   A French term for the soldiers who march ahead of a military formation; applied to artistic works and artists who rebel against tradition and experiment with new forms.

backlighting.   Lights coming from behind the actor that create silhouettes on stage.

balconies.   Seating areas that overhang a third to a half of the orchestra or form horseshoe-shaped tiers around the periphery of the auditorium in proscenium theatres.

beat.   A unit of dramatic action reflecting a single emotional desire or character objective.

biomechanics.   A physical training system for efficient and expressive movement developed in Russia by Vsevolod Meyerhold (1874–1942).

black box theatre. A performance space, usually painted black, that permits the rearrangement of seating and playing areas for every production in a variety of traditional and nontraditional arrangements.

blackface. The derogatory comic black stereotype expressed in makeup consisting of a blackened face with white circles around the eyes and mouth; originated in minstrel shows.

blackout. A rapid and complete dimming of the lights on stage.

blocking. The pattern of actors' movement on stage.

book. The written text of a musical.

book musical. A musical in which the story is told through spoken text, song, and dance.

booth stage. A portable thrust stage used by actors during the Middle Ages.

boxes. Private seating areas in proscenium theatres set in the balcony above the orchestra that once separated the nobility and the wealthy classes from the rest of the theatre-going public.

box office. A booth where theatre tickets are sold.

box office manager. The person who oversees theatre ticket sales and box office staff.

box set. A stage design in which flats form the back and side walls and sometimes even the ceiling of a room.

breeches roles. During the seventeenth to nineteenth centuries, roles in which actresses played young men or characters disguised as men and dressed in short pants, or "breeches," revealing their legs.

Broadway. The great concentration of commercial theatres around Times Square in New York City.

bunraku. A Japanese tradition of puppetry that combines the arts of puppet manipulation, ballad singing, and playing the three-stringed *shamisen*. The puppets are three to four feet tall and are operated through direct manipulation by three puppeteers who work together to create a seamless unity of action.

burlesque. A variety entertainment of the early twentieth century that included musical numbers, acrobatic bits, and comedy duos, but was especially known for its bawdy humor and striptease acts.

CAD (computer-assisted drafting). Computer programs that allow theatre designers to draft precise and uniform drawings and to visualize design options.

callback. A second audition for a role that only a few actors are invited to attend.

catharsis. The purging of our aggressive desires through art and enactment; the term was first used by Aristotle in the fourth century B.C.E.

centering. A process of focused relaxation through which an actor integrates breath, movement, feeling, and thought to harness the body's physical, emotional, and intellectual energy for performance.

chariot-and-pole system. A device for accomplishing instantaneous set changes invented by Giacomo Torelli (1608–1678) and consisting of a series of ropes and pulleys attached to a succession of painted flat wings set in grooved tracks on the stage.

cheat out. To turn on an angle on a proscenium stage to allow the audience to see one's face.

cliffhanger. A complicating incident usually placed at the end of an act so the audience is sent off at intermission impatient to find out how this last twist of fate will be resolved.

climactic structure. A tight-knit plot form in which the action builds causally to a moment of high emotional intensity followed by a final resolution.

climax. The point of highest emotional intensity in a drama.

commedia all'improviso. *See commedia dell'arte.*

commedia dell'arte. A theatre form that emerged in Italy during the sixteenth century, in which masked actors playing stock characters improvised on a scenario using broad physical humor.

commercial theatre. Theatre done for profit in which investors back a production and take a capital return if a show is a success.

complication. Circumstances of a drama building on each other through cause and effect.

concentration of attention. A technique developed by Constantin Stanislavski to keep actors' focus within the stage reality and not on the audience.

concert parties. A form of variety entertainment that developed in Anglophone Africa in the 1920s combining African culture and American and European entertainments.

conflict. Tension between two forces working against each other, creating struggles and obstacles for the characters to overcome.

control board. A computerized system that regulates the execution of light cues.

conventions. *See* theatrical conventions.

costume plot. A chart recording the costume pieces worn by each character in each scene of a play.

costume shop. The workshop where stage costumes are built and assembled.

costume shop manager. The person who oversees costume shop personnel and the process of building and assembling stage costumes.

crisis. The place in the dramatic action where the conflict comes to a head.

cross-dressing. When a man or woman on stage wears clothing traditionally associated with the opposite gender.

cross-fading. Slowly diminishing one lighting cue while adding another to gradually transition from one cue to the next.

curtain. The starting time of a show or the end of a show.

cycle plays. Medieval religious drama taken from events in the Old and New Testaments of the Bible.

Dada. An artistic movement that reached its height from 1916–1922 as a response to the violence of World War I. It reflected the meaninglessness of the world, and replaced bourgeois conventions with spontaneity and freedom.

dance play. A danced theatre piece without dialogue in which characterization, narrative, and dramatic conflict are expressed in choreography, not words.

deconstruction. The movement in literary criticism that questions the idea of fixed meanings, truths, or assumptions about texts. It is the hallmark of the postmodern aesthetic and has given license to directors to search for new meanings and forms in plays once thought to be confined to particular interpretations and styles.

denouement. A translation of Aristotle's "unknotting," the act of bringing all the parts of the play to a final conclusion.

deus ex machina. Any dramatic device, outside of the main action, used to bring the play to a final resolution. Developed in ancient Greek drama, the "god from a machine" arrived at the end of a play to finalize the fates of the mortal characters on stage.

dimmer board. A board that controls the intensity of stage lights.

dimmers. Instruments that permit the gradual adjustment of the intensity of light.

discovery space.   A curtained space at the back of the Elizabethan stage where characters or items could be concealed or revealed.

distancing effect, or distanciation.   *See* alienation effect.

dithyrambs.   Ancient Greek hymns sung and danced in praise of Dionysus, the god of wine and fertility.

docudrama.   A performance in which primary sources serve as the play text; often addressing pressing issues with theatrical immediacy.

documentary theatre.   *See* docudrama.

downstage.   The area of the stage closest to the audience.

dramatic structure.   The scaffolding on which a playwright plots a tale to frame or shape the action.

dramaturg.   A preproduction aide who works with a director to help explain the text or with a playwright to help define it.

drapes.   Fabric panels hung on stage as part of a design, or to outline the playing area, mask lighting or scenic elements, and conceal actors before they make their entrances.

dress parade.   A procession of actors in costume that offers the director and designer an opportunity to see all the actors together, in costume, under stage lights.

dress rehearsal.   A rehearsal at which actors run through the show dressed in their costumes; usually occurs just before opening night.

dressing the set.   Adding final touches to a stage set, which might include upholstery ornaments, small objects for tables and shelves, and pillows and curtains.

drops.   Large pieces of painted canvas hung at the back of the stage to set a particular locale or atmosphere.

ekkyklema.   A platform on wheels that rolls on stage; first used in the ancient Greek theatre.

ellipsoidal reflector spotlight.   A stage lighting instrument that projects a light with a sharp, clearly defined edge.

emotional memory.   The recalling of the sensory details around a significant event in an actor's life to evoke an emotional response.

empathy.   The capacity of the audience to identify emotionally with the character on stage.

emotional recall.   *See* emotional memory.

epic theatre.   A proletarian theatre trying to create social change by pioneering new approaches to the stage and stage technology.

existentialism.   A philosophic movement after World War II that depicts a senseless, godless world where human beings live in a meaningless void.

exposition.   The revelation of events that occurred before the start of the play through dialogue, often employing a device such as a confidant or a soliloquy to enable a character to speak all the necessary information to set up the plot.

expressionism.   A style of theatre that projects characters' inner emotional reality onto objects in the external world.

fade.   A gradual dimming of the stage lights.

flats.   Single units of canvas or other material stretched over a wooden frame that can be painted and connected to each other to create walls or other elements of a stage set.

fly spaces.   Very high ceilings behind the proscenium arch of a theatre used to house painted scenery that is literally "flown" up and down on a system of pulleys to change the sets.

follow spots.   Stage lights with clearly defined beams that follow an actor in movement across the stage.

footlights.   Stage lights placed at the front of the stage.

foreshadowing.   Hints about events to come in the dramatic action that can be used to create or break expectations.

fourth wall.   The theatrical convention of an invisible wall separating the stage from the audience.

fresnel.   Also known as a spherical reflector spotlight, a stage lighting instrument that produces a beam of light with a soft edge.

futurism.   An artistic movement in the early twentieth century that questioned old authority systems and structures and emphasized the energy, dynamism, and movement of time in modern existence.

gels.   Thin, colored films inserted in slots in front of lighting instruments to color stage lights.

genres.   Categories of drama.

gesamtkunstwerk.   Literally "total art work." The union of all the theatrical elements to create a thematically unified stage work, a concept developed by Richard Wagner (1813–1883).

given circumstances.   The physical and emotional conditions that determine the actions of a character.

gobos.   Small metal plates with cutout, stencil-like patterns that slide in front of a light source to project shapes and patterns or effects on the stage.

green room.   A space where actors and audience members can socialize after a performance; first developed during the late seventeenth century in England.

groundlings.   The name for lower-class spectators in Shakespeare's time who could not afford seats and stood for the duration of the performance in the open pit area in front of the stage.

ground plan.   A view of the dimensions of the stage and the placement of set pieces as seen from above.

guerrilla theatre.   Political action theatre in the street, so called because it sneaks up on the audience where they least expect it and aggressively exhorts them to engage politically.

half-mask.   A mask that covers only the top half of the face, keeping the mouth uncovered so the actor can speak and be heard.

hanamichi.   Literally "flower path." A runway in the Japanese *kabuki* theatre that cuts through the audience and leads to the stage on which actors make entrances and exits and perform important poses and speeches.

high-concept productions.   Innovative interpretations of plays that express a unique directorial vision and provide illuminating new readings of well-known works.

house.   The audience or the area of the theatre allocated to the audience.

house manager.   The person who makes sure the theatre is clean and safe and ready to receive the public.

inciting incident.   An event that sets the dramatic action into motion.

instrument schedule.   A chart that lists each lighting instrument by its number, specific location, purpose, wattage, the color of the gel, and other important information.

interculturalism.   Valuing and promoting an exchange and interaction among various cultures that may ignite interest or friction.

kabuki. A popular Japanese performance tradition begun during the early seventeenth century.

kathakali. A classical Indian dance theatre using highly stylized movement and elaborate make-up and costumes.

kyogen. A Japanese performance tradition that is the comic counterpart to the *noh.*

lazzi. Set bits of comic stage business all guaranteed to get a laugh, used by actors of the *commedia dell'arte.*

light plot. A blueprint of the stage and auditorium, with the lighting grid and the location of each light to be used for a production specifically marked.

lighting grid. The metal pipe structure from which the lights are hung.

lines of business. Roles in an acting company that particular actors played designated by types such as young lover, fop, ingénue, or old crone.

literary managers. Dramaturgs attached to theatre companies who are responsible for reading and evaluating plays for the artistic director and helping in other forms of play development such as hosting workshops or play readings.

liturgical drama. Theatrical performance that emerged from the Catholic liturgy during the Middle Ages.

loft. *See* fly spaces.

magic *if*. The ability to act as *if* the imaginary circumstances of a character were real.

master electrician. The person who oversees the hanging, focusing, and filtering of lights.

mēchanē. The large hand-powered crane that hoisted actors above the *skene,* or back wall of the stage in ancient Greece, usually to portray a god.

meter. The patterns of stressed and unstressed syllables that can draw attention to significant meanings in the text.

mie. Dramatic physical poses executed by *kabuki* actors at climactic moments, underscored by the beats of wooden clappers.

mime. A popular unscripted theatrical performance form in ancient Greece and Rome with stock characters, short improvised comic sketches, broad physical and acrobatic humor, juggling, music, and bawdy jokes. Today the term refers to silent or nearly silent performances and the actors who create them.

minimalism. A style of modern art that uses the fewest elements necessary to convey meaning.

minstrel show. A nineteenth-century racist performance style in which whites both appropriated African American culture and music and simultaneously created the denigrating blackface, white-lipped racial stereotype.

miracle plays. Medieval dramas depicting events from the lives of saints.

mobile stages. *See* pageant wagons.

model. A three-dimensional mock-up of the set design that gives the production team and the actors specific information about how the design will actually look and work in the space.

monologues. Passages from a play for a solo actor.

morality plays. Late medieval plays using allegorical characters to depict a moral lesson.

motivated light. Light changes specifically indicated in the play text, such as a lamp turning on.

motivated sounds. Sounds with an identifiable source within the context of the play, such as the ring of a telephone.

mudras. Hand gestures used in Indian theatrical traditions.

multiculturalism. A philosophy calling for respect for neighboring cultures living under the same political system.

multifocus theatre. Simultaneous performance in several playing areas during the same event that gives the audience a choice of focus and may require them to move about.

mystery plays. *See* cycle plays.

naturalism. A nineteenth-century movement that sought to paint a scientifically accurate stage picture of life as it is lived.

Natyasastra. A text on Sanskrit drama written sometime between 200 B.C.E. and 200 C.E. containing an encyclopedia of information about theatre from the classical Sanskrit tradition.

naumachiae. Spectacular Roman theatrical events in which flooded arenas permitted naval battles, often resulting in real casualties.

new stagecraft. The expression of highly theatrical trends of European modernism in American stage design.

noh. A highly stylized classical Japanese performance tradition begun during the fourteenth century.

not-for-profit theatre. A theatrical institution in which the profit is channeled back into the producing organization to defray costs and to fund new projects.

objective. In acting technique, what a character wants at any given moment that drives the action.

Off-Broadway. Smaller New York theatres in and out of the commercial theatre district that are so designated because they have fewer than 500 seats.

Off-Off Broadway. New York theatres that seek an alternative to the artistic constraints imposed in the commercial theatre.

onnagata. The female role type in *kabuki*; an idealized woman played by male actors in white makeup, black styled wigs, and women's kimono.

onomatopoeia. The use of words that express the feeling of their meaning through sound.

opening night. The show's first full-price public performance.

opera. A dramatic musical form born in the Renaissance in emulation of the heightened emotions of Greek tragedy and written in the tradition of great European art music.

operetta. A mid-nineteenth-century bourgeois entertainment that borrows many features from opera and incorporates dance, farce, and clowning to tell a simple story that always culminates in romance fulfilled.

orchestra. The circular playing space on the ground in front of the *skene* in ancient Greek theatres. Today, the floor-level seating area in front of a proscenium stage.

orchestra pit. The space below the apron of a proscenium stage that houses musicians and often can be elevated to form an extended apron when an orchestra is not required.

Orientalism. A romanticization of Asia that led to the appropriation of Asian arts. Today the term connotes derisive stereotyping.

pageant masters. In the Middle Ages, those responsible for organizing theatrical events.

pageant wagons. Mobile platform stages on wheels used in the Middle Ages to carry scenery through the town to the location of the performance.

pantomime. In Roman times, a silent storytelling dance. In the eighteenth and nineteenth centuries, the term applied to certain popular entertainments in England and France that used *commedia*-type characters. In the twentieth century, a silent storytelling.

paper tech.   A walk-through of the technical aspects of the production with the designers and staff and without actors present.

PAR (parabolic aluminized reflector) lamps.   Small, inexpensive, portable lights that can generate different types of beams.

parallel plot.   *See* subplot.

parody.   The exaggerated imitation of individuals or artistic styles to make them appear ludicrous.

passion plays.   Plays depicting events from the passion of Christ.

performance art.   An avant-garde form that saw performance as an extension of visual art in time, with more significance accorded to the visual image than the spoken text.

performance studies.   An academic field that looks at theatre as one kind of performance on a continuum with other kinds of performance such as ritual and sports events that helps us understand and discuss today's varied theatrical forms.

performance text.   A record of all that will happen on stage.

performance traditions.   Theatrical forms whose staging, music, dance, characterization, masks, and acting are passed from generation to generation as a totality, preserving the form.

personal props.   Objects carried on stage by actors.

picture frame stage.   *See* proscenium stage.

pit.   In the Elizabethan theatre, the area around the raised stage in which spectators could stand to watch the performance.

plastiques.   Difficult physical exercises for actors that were developed by Jerzy Grotowski.

platforms.   Raised wooden constructions that can provide playing spaces on different levels.

platform stages.   During the Middle Ages, playing areas placed in front of background sets.

play text.   A written script containing dialogue spoken by characters that can be interpreted by actors and directors as the basis for action on stage.

plot.   The ordering or structuring of the events that actually take place on stage.

point of attack.   The point in the story at which the action begins.

postmodernism.   A late-twentieth-century concept that replaces absolute values with relativism, opening up the possibility of many new and equally valid forms of artistic expression.

practical.   An onstage light such as a lamp or a fire in a fireplace that needs to appear to be controlled from the stage.

presentational.   A theatrical style that openly acknowledges the artificiality of a stage performance.

preview.   A performance before a production has officially opened that gives the director an opportunity to hone the show in front of a live audience.

processional stage.   Moving stages that require the audience to move from place to place to follow the action or to wait for the next wagon stage to appear.

producer.   The person who brings together a creative team with the necessary resources to complete a production.

production manager.   The person in charge of schedules, staffing, and making sure that the information relayed by the stage manager is carried out in a timely manner.

prompt book.   The stage manager's copy of the script on which is recorded blocking and cues.

props, or **properties.**   Objects that will be used by actors in performance that may be carried on stage by the actor or that are part of the set.

proscenium arch.   A frame constructed over the front of the stage separating the audience from the performance space and forming a frame for the set.

proscenium stage.   A configuration of a theatre space in which the audience faces the actors on only one side.

protagonist.   The lead role in a drama; from the Greek word *agonistes*, which means both "actor" and "combatant."

psychological characters.   Character portraits so rich in detail and interest that spectators feel they can comprehend motivations and desires, and even fabricate a life for them that preexists their appearance in the play.

psychophysical action.   Constantin Stanislavski's term for physical behavior that reveals the character and the objective.

Rabinal Achí.   A pre-Hispanic Mayan masked dance drama that may represent the oldest surviving theatrical text from the Americas uncontaminated by European influence.

raked seating.   Seating areas on an incline providing solutions to sight line problems for the audience.

rasa.   Literally "tastes" or "flavors." A term from Indian theatre that refers to the different moods or feelings expressed in plays and by actors on stage.

realism.   The presentation of a stage world as a believable alternate reality where things happen much as they would in life and people behave in seemingly natural ways.

regional theatres.   *See* resident theatres.

representational.   A theatrical style in which the stage reality attempts to represent real life and the actor seems to be living the part.

resident theatres.   Professional not-for-profit theatres around the United States that now provide a permanent theatre presence in almost every major city.

revenge plays.   Bloody dramas from the Roman era that influenced Elizabethan theatre.

review.   The brief, immediate response to a theatrical event that appears in a newspaper, magazine, or television or radio segment.

revue.   A musical form that does not tell a continuous story and moves from number to number.

run-through.   Performance of a play from beginning to end without stopping during a rehearsal.

saint plays.   *See* miracle plays.

satyr plays.   A burlesque of mythic legends that provided comic relief after performances of tragedies in ancient Greece.

scenario.   A general plot outline used as the basis for improvisation.

scene house.   A curtained area at the back of a platform stage for concealment and costume changes.

scene shop.   The workshop where the set is constructed.

scrim.   A translucent cloth or gauze that can appear opaque when light shines on it from the front, or transparent when light shines on it from the back, used to create special effects and magical transformations through changes in lighting.

serial structure.   A series of scenes that do not follow a continuous story or even include the same characters.

shamans.   Priests or priestesses charged with communicating with the spirit world on behalf of the community to bring peace and prosperity to the populace or healing to the sick.

sidelighting.   Light coming from the side of the stage that provides accents and highlights that is used often in dance and musical theatre to highlight the dancers' legs.

sides.   Actors' individual lines and cues, once copied by a stage manager.

sight lines.   Clear vision of the stage action by the audience.

silhouette.   The overall shape of a costume.

skene.   In the ancient Greek theatre, the stage house behind the area where the main characters performed.

soliloquy.   A lengthy solo speech through which a character reveals an interior state of mind.

sound engineer.   The person responsible for the functioning of acoustical equipment in a theatre.

sound plot.   A chart of all the connections and sound equipment used for a production.

special.   A light with a specific and unique dramatic function.

spherical reflector spotlight.   *See* fresnel.

spine.   A central line of dramatic action that can guide directors in their creative choices.

stage curtain.   A curtain contained just inside the proscenium frame that can be raised and lowered to conceal set changes and to reveal the stage action.

stage left.   The area to the actor's left when standing center stage facing the audience on a proscenium or thrust stage.

stage manager.   The person who works closely with the director in preparing the production and who functions as a liaison between the director and all other members of the creative team, including the actors. The stage manager oversees the accurate execution of the show in performance.

stage right.   The area to the actor's right when standing center stage facing the audience on a proscenium or thrust stage.

staged reading.   A reading of a play with actors on their feet, scripts in hand, with minimal set pieces.

stock characters.   Representatives of a type that are defined by externals such as class, occupation, and marital status, rather than by their individual characteristics.

story.   All the events that happen or are mentioned in the text.

storyboard.   A series of sketches that show how the sets or costumes change to tell the story through time.

street theatre.   Compelling theatre that uses music, spectacle, masks, costumes, dancing, drumming, or direct audience confrontation to engage with the public in co-opted public spaces.

strike.   The orderly dismantling of a production that follows a show's closing; includes taking down the set and lights, readying costumes for storage, and cleaning and preparing the theatre for the next production.

style.   The manner in which a performance depicts the world.

subplot.   A secondary dramatic action that echoes the main plot of a play through common subjects and themes that reinforce or comment on the central meaning of the drama.

subtext.   The meaning of dialogue to the character, which may be different from what is actually said. Literally, the thoughts that lie under the text.

superobjective.   The main goal of a play or character that drives the dramatic action.

surrealism.   A twentieth-century artistic style inspired by Freudian psychology that mined the unconscious for images that expressed the truth of our hidden desires and the free association of thought.

symbolism.   A late-nineteenth-century artistic style that opposed the naturalists' search for meaning in the concrete objects of the world, and felt truth lay in a metaphysical realm.

t'alch'um.   An ancient Korean masked danced theatre suppressed after the Japanese invasion in 1910 and now enjoying renewed interest.

technical director.   The individual responsible for executing the set designer's plans and maintaining the theatre space, including its safety and equipment.

technical dress rehearsal.   A rehearsal in which all the elements of the production—costume, sets, lights, sound, and acting—are coordinated to make any final changes before opening night.

technical rehearsal.   The first opportunity for the director to work with all the design elements and designers simultaneously in rehearsal.

theatre of the absurd.   A term coined by critic Martin Esslin to describe plays that reflected the sense of alienation and meaninglessness of the generation that had lived through the horrific events of World War II.

theatre of cruelty.   A name used by Antonin Artaud for a visceral theatre of sounds, movements, and images that assaulted the senses of the audience, opening up new levels of awareness.

theatrical conventions.   Rules of conduct and understood communication codes used in the theatre.

upstage.   The area of the stage farthest from the audience in proscenium or thrust staging.

upstaged.   The claiming of audience attention when one actor walks directly behind another, obliging the downstage actor to turn away from the audience to address lines to the actor upstage.

vaudeville.   A popular American variety show form toward the end of the nineteenth and the early twentieth centuries that relied heavily on stand-up comedy routines and musical numbers.

verisimilitude.   The concept that the theatre should present an idealized reality.

Viewpoints.   A system of physical actor training that develops awareness of the basic components of movement—line, rhythm, shape, tempo, and duration.

voms.   Aisles for actors' entrances named for the *vomitoria*, or entryways, of the ancient Roman amphitheatres that often run through the audience in an arena theatre.

wagon.   A moving platform on wheels that serves as a mobile stage.

warm-up.   A series of physical and vocal exercises that prepare the body to act.

wayang kulit.   Indonesian leather shadow puppet tradition.

well-made play.   A form developed during the nineteenth century that uses a tightly woven plot filled with complications that keep the audience deeply involved in the dramatic action.

West End.   London's commercial theatre district.

wings.   Areas on the periphery of the playing area that can be masked to hide actors, technicians, props, and scenery.

xiqu.   A generic term for traditional Chinese performance forms developed from the thirteenth to the early twentieth century (from *xi* for "play" and *qu* for "melody" or "song").

yellowface.   The use of make-up and prosthetics by white actors to portray Asian characters. It is now felt to create racist stereotypes.

yūgen.   An aesthetic term from the *noh* tradition usually translated as "grace," "suggestive beauty," or "mystery."

Photo Credits

Alamy; 200: The Builders Association; 202: Jack Vartoogian/FrontRowPhotos; 204: Photostage; 205: Louise Leblanc/Ex Machina; 206: Carol Rosegg.

Text Credits

CHAPTER 2 PAGE 35: In Their Own Words: Interview with Bill Talen, aka Reverend Billy. Used with permission of Bill Talen, aka "Reverend Billy"; **43–44:** In Their Own Words: Interview with Stanley Kauffman, "Criticism: An Art about Art." Copyright © 2006 by Stanley Kauffman. Used with permission of Stanley Kauffman; **44:** In Their Own Words: Interview with Alisa Solomon. Used with permission of Alisa Solomon.

CHAPTER 3 PAGE 51: In Their Own Words: Interview with Tina Howe. Used with permission of Tina Howe; **64:** Golden Child, 1st Edition, by Henry David Hwang. Copyright © 1998 by Theatre Communications Group. Reprinted with permission of Henry David Hwang; **Page 65:** Excerpt from The Homecoming by Harold Pinter copyright © 1965, 1966, 1967 by H. Pinter Ltd. Used by permission of Grove/Atlantic, Inc. **65:** Extract taken from The Homecoming © 1965 the Estate of Harold Pinter and reprinted by permission of Faber and Faber Ltd; **68:** From The American Play and Other Works by Suzan-Lori Parks. Copyright © 1995 by Suzan-Lori Parks. Published by Theatre Communications Group. Used by permission of Theatre Communications Group.

CHAPTER 4 PAGE 79: Felner, Mira; Orenstein, Claudia, The World of Theatre: Tradition and Innovation, 1st Edition, © 2006. Reprinted by permission of Pearson Education, Inc., Upper Saddle River, NJ; **87:** Approximately 65 words from The Rope and Other Plays by Plautus, translated by E.F. Watling (Penguin Classics, 1964). Copyright © E.F. Watling, 1964. Reproduced by permission of Penguin Books, Ltd.

CHAPTER 5 PAGES 106, 109: Felner, Mira; Orenstein, Claudia, The World of Theatre: Tradition and Innovation, 1st Edition, © 2006. Reprinted by permission of Pearson Education, Inc., Upper Saddle River, NJ.

CHAPTER 6 PAGE 129: Scenarios of the Commedia Dell'Arte: Flaminio Scala's Il Teatro Delle Favole Rappresentative, translated by Henry F. Salerno. Copyright © 1967 by New York University Press. Used with permission of Michelle Korri and David Salerno; **131:** Joseph Chaikin and Susan Yankowitz with the Open Theater Collective; **137:** Giacomo Balla, "To Understand Weeping," in Futurist Performance, Michael Kirby and Victoria Nes Kirby. Copyright © 1971, 1986 by Michael Kirby and Victoria Nes Kirby. Copyright © 1986 by PAJ Publications. Reprinted by permission of PAJ Publications; **149:** Reprinted by permission of International Creative Management, Inc. Copyright © 1977 by Robert Fosse; **151:** Copyright © Robert Wilson. Courtesy of Paula Cooper Gallery, New York.

CHAPTER 7 PAGE 166: Felner, Mira; Orenstein, Claudia, The World of Theatre: Tradition and Innovation, 1st Edition, © 2006. Reprinted by permission of Pearson Education, Inc., Upper Saddle River, NJ; **181–182:** In Their Own Words: interview with Matsui Akira. Translated and transcribed by Richard Emmert. Used with permission of Richard Emmert.

CHAPTER 8 PAGE 199: In Their Own Words: Interview with Elizabeth LeCompte. Used with permission of Elizabeth LeCompte, Director, The Wooster Group.

CHAPTER 9 PAGES 213, 217, 220, 223, 224, 225, 226: Felner, Mira; Orenstein, Claudia, The World of Theatre: Tradition and Innovation, 1st Edition, © 2006. Reprinted by permission of Pearson Education, Inc., Upper Saddle River, NJ; **228:** Reprinted by permission from Louisa Thompson.

CHAPTER 10 PAGE 246: Interview with Stanley Allan Sherman. Copyright © by Stanley Allan Sherman. Reprinted with permission. www.maskarts.com.

CHAPTER 11 PAGES 266–267: In Their Own Words: Interview with Louisa Thompson. Used with permission of Louisa Thompson.

CHAPTER 12 PAGES 288–289: In Their Own Words: Interview with Linda Cho. Used with permission of Linda Cho; **292–293:** In Their Own Words: Interview with Judith Dolan. Used with permission of Judith Dolan.

CHAPTER 13 PAGE 308: Light plot and instrument schedule for Kalidasa's Sakuntala at Pomona College Theatre, California by James P. Taylor. Reprinted with permission of James P. Taylor; **319–320:** Signal Flow Chart, Sound Design and Sound Cue Synopsis for Tracy Scott William's The Story at the Joseph Papp Public Theatre, director Loretta Greco, by Robert Kaplowitz. Reprinted with permission of Robert Kaplowitz, Composer/Sound Designer;

319 (bottom): Drafting of Anspacher Theatre in Robert Kaplowitz's Sound Design for Tracy Scott William's The Story at the Joseph Papp Public Theatre, director Loretta Greco, by Matthew Gratz. Reprinted with permission of Matthew Gratz; 321–322: In Their Own Words: Interview with Robert Kaplowitz. Used with permission of Robert Kaplowitz.

CHAPTER 14 PAGES 328–329: In Their Own Words: Interview with Jane Alexander. Used with permission of Jane Alexander; 340: Felner, Mira; Orenstein, Claudia, The World of Theatre: Tradition and Innovation, 1ˢᵗ Edition, © 2006. Reprinted by permission of Pearson Education, Inc., Upper Saddle River, NJ; 341: In Their Own Words: Interview with Ruth Sternberg. Used with permission of Ruth Sternberg.

Index

(Note: pages with photographs and illustrations are designated.)